UFOS AND THE NATION OF ISLAM

UFOs And The Nation Of Islam:
The Source, Proof, And Reality Of The Wheels

ILIA RASHAD MUHAMMAD

Copyright © 2013 Ilia Rashad Muhammad
ISBN 978-0-9899774-2-5
All Rights Reserved.

Revised Edition

For details and inquiries contact the following:

Nation Brothers
nationbrothers@nationbrothers.com
www.nationbrothers.com
Memphis, TN

Cover designed by Ilia Rashad Muhammad using images of the Most Honorable Elijah Muhammad, the Honorable Minister Louis Farrakhan, and luminous wheel-like planes (two photographed by Carlos Diaz)

DEDICATION

This book is dedicated to the Nation of Islam, the followers of the Honorable Elijah Muhammad who have struggled and sacrificed with the Honorable Louis Farrakhan to establish truth in a world governed by lies and deceit.

To my wife Angela and our children: Terrika, Kurteous, Autezia, Barak, Kushmir, and our progeny. This is dedicated to you.

This research is also dedicated to my parents, James and Mary Cross, who have always been there for me and my siblings: Andre, Mubaarak, Jacques, Ivan, and Jamique. This is dedicated to you as well.

This message is dedicated to our ancestors who lived and died for us and to the future of our people, which has already been foretold.

Last, but certainly not least, this book is dedicated to people of righteousness and good will across the globe who are bold enough to investigate this intriguing topic with objectivity during an age when thinkers have been shunned for exploring matters outside of mainstream thought. This is for you.

TABLE OF CONTENTS

DEDICATION V
LIST OF FIGURES VIII
FOREWORD IX
ACKNOWLEDGEMENTS XII

INTRODUCTION 1

1. THE CHALLENGE: SCIENCE, THEOLOGY, AND THE WORLD 3
   THE NATION OF ISLAM AND UFOS 3
   A RELIGIOUS ANOMALY 6
   A SUPERIOR EDUCATION 7
   A THREAT TO WORLD POWERS 9
   THE CLOSEST ENCOUNTER OF ANY KIND 11
   AN UNPOPULAR TRUTH 14

2. UFOS IDENTIFIED BEFORE THEY BECAME A CONCERN 20
   NOT JUST ANOTHER PLANE 20
   THE PURPOSE: DESTRUCTION AND SALVATION 25
   EXTRATERRESTRIAL OR EXTRAORDINARY? 27
   THE TIME AND WHAT WAS DONE 32
   1929 TAKE OFF 34
   A MASTERPIECE OF MECHANICS 35
   THE BABY PLANES 38
   THOSE BABIES CARRY BOMBS! 40

3. NOT JUST ORDINARY PEOPLE 44
   UFOS AND THE NATION OF ISLAM AFFILIATION 44
   UFO PILOTS 46
   BE CAREFUL WHO YOU'RE ENTERTAINING, IT MIGHT BE A UFO PILOT 49
   NO GREYS, MAYBE GREY SUITS 51
   TUNING-IN AND THE 'RADIO IN THE HEAD' 56

4. THE PROPHECIES: THY WHEELS BE DONE 61
   ELIJAH MUHAMMAD GIVEN THE KEYS 61
   HISTORY VS PROPHECY 63
   EZEKIEL'S WHEEL 65
   GOD RIDES AROUND ON SOMETHING IN THE CLOUDS! 68
   GOD'S THRONE UPON THE MOTHER WHEEL 73
   GOD'S THRONE IN THE OLD TESTAMENT 74
   THE THRONE AND THE GOSPEL 76

5. UFOS AND THE HOLY QUR'AN 79
   ISLAMIC SCHOLARS' CONTROVERSY 79
   THE THRONE OF ALLAH 80
   ALLAH'S EXALTED ASSEMBLY 86
   TRADITIONAL ISLAM'S UFO DILEMMA 90

6. THE DWELLING PLACE OF GOD 93
- THE CHARIOTS OF GOD – TOO DANGEROUS FOR JEWS 93
- GOD HAS FLYING CHARIOTS OF FIRE 97
- THE AIRCRAFT OF ANGELS 100
- THE NEW JERUSALEM 103

7. HISTORY AND THE NEW ERA 108
- WHERE WERE UFOS BEFORE ELIJAH MUHAMMAD? 108
- ANCIENT ALIENS OR THE ORIGINAL MAN? 116
- WHO IS THE ORIGINAL MAN? 121

8. THE ENCOUNTER, THE ARREST, AND THE AFTERMATH 128
- A NEW AUTHORITY 128
- THE BATTLE OF LOS ANGELES – FEBRUARY 25, 1942 132
- THE ARREST OF THE MESSENGER 135
- THE COVER-UP BEGINS 143
- THE HOLLYWOOD ACCOMPLICE 145

9. THE MESSENGER, THE PROOF, AND THE DENIALS 151
- THE CRITICS' ROUTINE: OMIT FACTS, OFFER OPINIONS 151
- A MAN LIKE MOSES, A TYRANT LIKE PHARAOH 155
- ROSWELL: THE KNOWN, THE UNKNOWN, AND THE POSSIBILITY 158
- TOO MUCH EVIDENCE TO IGNORE 166
- THE WASHINGTON D.C. UFO INCIDENT 169

10. THE TRUTH IS OUT THERE 174
- TIME REVEALS THE TRUTH 174
- ENCOUNTERS CONFIRM MUHAMMAD'S AUTHORITY 180
- BROTHERS FROM ANOTHER 187

11. THE WHEELS AND DIVINE JUDGMENT 192
- THE CHANGING OF WORLDS 192
- THE BATTLE IN THE SKY 196
- IT'S ABOVE THEIR HEADS 201
- ELIJAH'S GOD MUST BE GOD! 202

12. UFOS AND THE MESSIANIC CONNECTION 206
- HE COMES IN THE VOLUME OF THE BOOK 206
- THE MESSENGER PREDICTS HIS DEPARTURE UPON THE WHEEL 210
- ELIJAH TAKEN ON A CLOUD 213
- MADE TO 'APPEAR' DEAD 216
- THE MESSENGER OUT OF SIGHT, THE WHEELS OUT OF MIND 218
- THEY PLAN AND ALLAH PLANS 224

13. THE VISION-LIKE EXPERIENCE 228
- THE NIGHT JOURNEY 228
- A PRESIDENTIAL PROBLEM 233
- FARRAKHAN'S DARING PROOF 237
- THE WHEELS GUIDE FARRAKHAN 240
- HE KNOWS WHAT THEY DON'T WANT KNOWN 243
- REMEMBER THE 17TH OF SEPTEMBER 246
- BIG MONEY SPENT ON UFO INVESTIGATIONS 251

14. THE CLEAR EVIDENCE, THE SURE TRUTH	**254**
ELIJAH'S BOOK	254
THE 33ʳᵈ PARALLEL	256
HE CALLS FOR ELIJAH	260
HE LIVES, MORE THAN A POSSIBILITY	261
NO ROOM FOR DOUBT!	265
BIBLIOGRAPHY	**271**
INDEX	**283**
ABOUT THE AUTHOR	286

LIST OF FIGURES

Figure 1: WHERE IT ALL STARTED	32
Figure 2: WHEELS OF TIME	45
Figure 3: FULFILLMENT	78
Figure 4: WONDERS OF THE ORIGINAL MAN	127
Figure 5: THE ENCOUNTER & THE ARREST	142
Figure 6: STATISTICAL DATA	144
Figure 7: THE SURE TRUTH & AUTHORITY	172
Figure 8: THE DEPARTURE & RESCUE	223
Figure 9: THE CLEAR EVIDENCE	231

FOREWORD

I am very excited about the release of this long-anticipated volume researched and written by Ilia Rashad Muhammad on a subject near and dear to the hearts of all followers of the teachings of the Most Honorable Elijah Muhammad. Allah (God) guided, strengthened and ordained the rebuilding of the Nation of Islam in America by the Honorable Minister Louis Farrakhan. And as a result a new generation has been exposed to the rich transformational contents of the teachings of the Most Honorable Elijah Muhammad. Ilia Rashad Muhammad is a part of that new generation.

Minister Farrakhan's expression of "the Teachings," has always been marked by a beautiful and articulate delivery; strong and powerful preaching; courageous and bold truth telling; and research-laden empiricism. Minister Farrakhan gives his listeners access to the depth and substance of what the Honorable Elijah Muhammad initially introduced in "the Teachings." In fact, by his own admission, Minister Farrakhan made promoting the proper understanding of "the Teachings" his top priority in his rebuilding work.

This prioritization in the Minister's methodology grew out of his analysis and study of the events that took place in what we consider to be "the fall of the Nation of Islam" in 1975. During this tumultuous time there was the complete dismantling of all Nation of Islam institutions so that the existing body of followers of the Honorable Elijah Muhammad might be used to make up an entirely new organization under the leadership of the late Imam Warithudeen Mohammed.

The famed 80 million dollar empire of mosques, schools, farms, businesses and properties could not be dismantled unless the fundamental ideas that gave birth to them were first discredited and destroyed in the minds of the followers. Those fundamental ideas that were successfully attacked by Imam Mohammed are what make up the Nation of Islam's controversial theology. Minister Farrakhan understood that in order to rebuild the Nation of Islam, he had to rebuild in the minds of the followers the rightness and truthfulness of the teachings of the Most Honorable Elijah Muhammad.

Therefore the Minister's approach in the rebuilding was necessarily apologetic in nature. The term apologetic derives from the Greek word "apologia," which means to make a defense. It has come to mean a defense of the faith. It is also described as a systematic argumentative discourse in defense of a doctrine or teaching; also a branch of theology devoted to the defense of the divine origin and authority of one's religion.

With this approach, Minister Farrakhan attracted many of the so-called "learned" of the people. Minister Farrakhan delivered many lectures to students on college campuses and even made outreach to students one of the main priorities of the Nation of Islam. As a result, the Nation of Islam's teachings gained a new audience of listeners and a new generation of members began to populate the rebuilt Nation of Islam under Minister Farrakhan's leadership.

All of these facts help to provide the very important context of what the author of this book has been blessed and guided by Allah (God) to publish in this newly released volume. He, under the inspiration of Minister Farrakhan's ministry, has addressed one of the most controversial aspects of the teachings of the Most Honorable Elijah Muhammad.

Theology, eschatology, theodicy, theophany, exegesis are just a few words that make up the language of Religious Studies. And most of what is written about the Nation of Islam fails to honestly examine its teachings through the lens of the scholarship of Religious Studies. The Nation of Islam is widely viewed as a racial movement, of the many, who emerged as a response to the institutionalized racism visited upon Black people in America. Thusly, the Honorable Elijah Muhammad is lauded for his economic emphasis, moral reforms and dignifying impact on the lives of his followers. This is of course a great minimization of the Honorable Elijah Muhammad. Because none of what the Nation of Islam accomplished in other areas (business, politics, etc.) could have been accomplished without the foundation provided by its religious teachings and the conquering spirit it produced in all who believed.

What Ilia Rashad Muhammad has produced honors the teachings of the Most Honorable Elijah Muhammad by first of all examining it through the appropriate academic and religious lenses. He has taken up, with passion, the area of "the Teachings" that contains the Nation of Islam's so-called belief in U.F.O.s.

Rashad's research makes one of the most compelling cases for the rightness and truthfulness of "the Teachings" on what the Honorable Elijah Muhammad calls "The Wheel." Every objective reader will be caused to do a reassessment of this critical area of Muhammad's teaching that many have dismissed as being borne of his own design. Those who believe in "the Teachings" will be fortified and strengthened in their belief. This quality of what Rashad has written makes this an important work for the general public as well as the Nation of Islam membership.

With this work, Rashad makes a strong contribution to the growing field of Nation of Islam Apologetics, of which the Honorable Minister Louis Farrakhan is the father. The increasing activity among Minister Farrakhan's followers to scripturally, academically and historically vindicate "the Teachings" constitutes an intellectual thrust that is at the heart of a revival of the Nation of Islam's impact on the American religious and political landscape. As the "learned" and "well educated" are exposed to the proofs that back up and support "the Teachings" they are able to have a proper assessment and arrive at the proper conclusion with respect to the Nation of Islam and what it represents.

It is my hope that what is written within the pages of this book moves the reader closer to that which is the ultimate satisfaction for the soul of all who seek the truth. It is my hope that Rashad's ambitious effort to vindicate one of the most foreign and less spoken of areas of the "the Teachings" will cause the reader to acknowledge the rightness and truthfulness of every area of "the Teachings."

So please enjoy what follows of a groundbreaking labor of love offered by one of Minister Farrakhan's many students.

Best and Warmest Regards,
Brother Demetric Muhammad
NOI Research Group

ACKNOWLEDGEMENTS

All praise belongs to Allah (God), the Originator of heaven and earth on whom all things depend. It is Allah, the Supreme Being, whose wisdom, force, and power appeared in the Person of Master Fard Muhammad, the Great Mahdi. To Allah I am forever indebted for his intervention in our affairs.

I thank Allah for raising the Most Honorable Elijah Muhammad whom I recognize as that messianic one who has been expected to liberate the people of God and lay the foundation for a new world.

I thank the Honorable Minister Louis Farrakhan for being the divine instrument of God's voice and the official representative of that destined Messiah. I thank our Queen-Mother Khadijah Farrakhan and the Farrakhan family for their continued sacrifices.

My beautiful wife, Angela L. Muhammad, for making me the luckiest man I know. She has given me five blessed children whom I am most grateful for: Terrika, Autezia, Kurteous, Barak, and Kushmir.

I'm so grateful for my parents James Cross Jr. and Mary Cross (artist name Wendy Rene) who provided me with a solid spiritual base and some common sense that eventually came around in my adult years.

I thank Allah for my siblings whom I love dearly: Bishop Andre Cross, Mubaarak Muhammad, Jacques Cross, Ivan Cross, and our one and only sister Jamique Cross.

I'm so grateful for Student Minister Anthony Muhammad and his lovely wife Jill for their support and guidance throughout the years.

Much thanks to Brother Demetric Muhammad, my brother and friend, who has continuously served as my colleague and fellow *bean soup scientist*. Of course I'm thankful for my friends and colleagues of the NOI Research Group for all their assistance to defend the program and position of the Nation of Islam.

As a proud student and citizen of the Nation of Islam, I thank every Registered Believer for being bold and wise enough to accept this truth despite its unpopularity in this insane world. Special emphasis is given to the Believers of

Muhammad Mosque 55 who have watched me grow and continue to encourage me to reach new heights.

I thank our known and unknown Ancestors and Pioneers on whose shoulders we stand. This includes the spiritual and intellectual powerhouses of the NOI whose knowledge I have greatly benefited from—living legends such as Mother Tynnetta Muhammad, Jabril Muhammad, Abdul Allah Muhammad, Abdul Akbar Muhammad, and other NOI Pioneers that are far too many to name in this short space.

Thanks to the various UFO researchers who have compiled tons of useful references that have made truth attainable for the public, particularly those few who have been bold enough to acknowledge the NOI's contributions to this topic: Jaime Maussan, Ademar Gevaerd, Antonio Urzi, Dr. Roger Leir, Donald R. Schmitt, Fernando Correa, Steve Colbern, Michael Lieb, and others.

Thank you Sister Shahida Sade Muhammad for your meticulous care in helping me edit and revise this work. Of course Brother Jesse Muhammad, Sister Ebony S. Muhammad, Sister Landra Muhammad and the Twitter Army, you all have my love and thanks for sharing the truth through social media.

A special thanks to all the readers of this book, whether critics, pundits, believers, or otherwise. It is because of you that hearts and minds are opened which will create meaningful dialogues that can allow people to discover truth—a truth that will ultimately lead to the establishment of freedom, justice, and equality throughout our planet.

INTRODUCTION

All truth passes through three stages. First, it is ridiculed, second, it is violently opposed, and third, it is accepted as self-evident. – Arthur Schopenhauer

The most baffling aspect surrounding the entire dialogue and debate over the reality of UFOs (Unidentified Flying Objects) is why no one ever mentions the Honorable Elijah Muhammad and the Nation of Islam. When viewing UFO documentaries and special television programs on this subject, he's never mentioned. Why? When witnesses are called upon to share their experiences, members of the NOI are never called. Why? When disclosure hearings and panel discussions are held, no one invites any officials from the NOI. Why? One may ask why would they invite such a man or group to the table of discussion on this serious subject? The simple fact is that the Honorable Elijah Muhammad and the NOI have been teaching in great detail and description about these objects for over 80 years starting in the 1930s.

As a matter of fact, it is a core aspect of the teaching and theology of the Honorable Elijah Muhammad. What one would find more interesting is that Elijah Muhammad only attended school up to the 3rd or 4th grade in rural Georgia. Elijah Muhammad was the son of a Baptist minister and a sharecropper. Surely they did not teach such subjects as UFOs to blacks in the south. Come to think of it, it would not be a course of study in any school system at that time, nor present. It is a subject that is "above top secret".

This should leave one to ponder, where did he get such intricate detailed knowledge on this subject? How did he know where they were manufactured and what materials were used? How did he know who helped engineer this craft and when it first took flight? How did he know how fast they travel? How did he know who and what each one of these baby planes (UFOs) carries? How did he know what kind of propulsion system these crafts use? How was he able to point them out in the sky and tell the times when it (Mother Wheel/Plane) comes in and out of our atmosphere and for what purpose? He even held the secrets as to what the purpose of such superior crafts are used for in the divine judgment of the current world and the establishment of a whole new world of peace. Who taught him this superior knowledge ... a 3rd grader from Georgia? We can no longer ignore him in the discovery of the real truth about UFOs.

Many have mocked and ridiculed the Honorable Elijah Muhammad as they do his student, the Honorable Minister Louis Farrakhan, who has never shied away from what his teacher taught on the Wheel (Mother Plane), but has continued to boldly teach and point out their reality and purpose. Minister Farrakhan in his "Announcement" speech (Oct. 24, 1989) boldly detailed his vision-like experience that took place on September 17, 1985 when he was in a small town in Mexico. He shared his personal experience being taken aboard the Mother Wheel. This would be the most defining moment and experience in his life. The world events following his experience would confirm, indeed that all he learned on the Wheel (that was later recounted) actually came to pass. He even held a special panel discussion during the 2011 Saviours' Day convention which gathered some of the world's foremost scholars on this subject to finally put before the world what we know to be the truth about UFOs.

People often make mockery of him as some did his teacher, but the more people make mockery, the more these UFOs manifest themselves in the skies over major U.S. cities and across the world. While mockery is made in the public, in private, the government knows that what Elijah Muhammad taught is the truth. Now it's time for all to know, not only that they indeed exist, but the deeper spiritual and social implications.

In his epic book entitled *The Fall of America*, the Honorable Elijah Muhammad writes, "Space here in this book is limited, but what Allah (God) taught me concerning the Mother Plane could be put into book form". Fortunately, members of the Nation of Islam Research Group (NOIRG) have assumed the arduous task of making this controversial topic known to the world. This book can be considered a part of that series of work aimed to demystify this frequently misunderstood topic and to expose the truth behind this reality.

When people learn the complete truth, based on undeniable facts, they will learn the stunning truth that they are connected to a man that walks among us and a people who have been chosen from among all people. Soon, after reading this book, it will become self-evident that these wheels that pose as "a cloud by day and a pillar of fire by night" are indeed with the Nation of Islam, Minister Farrakhan, and something beyond your greatest imagination.

Brother Jason Karriem
NOI Ministry of Education

1. THE CHALLENGE: SCIENCE, THEOLOGY, AND THE WORLD

THE NATION OF ISLAM AND UFOS

Elijah Muhammad only went to the 4th grade of school, but he taught us what no college professor could teach us. And it was Elijah Muhammad 55 years ago [from January 1987] who started teaching us about a plane in the sky that was made like a wheel. He said his teacher, a man— Master Fard Muhammad pointed out to him a dreadful looking plane in the sky, a half a mile by half a mile, built like the universe itself. It's circular and it holds within it 1500 little wheel-like planes! When we heard Elijah say these things, many of us believed and some of us disbelieved.[1] – The Honorable Minister Louis Farrakhan

The Honorable Elijah Muhammad challenged the world of education, religion, and science to contend with his position that he was taught by the Supreme Being who appeared in the form of a human being by the name of Master Fard Muhammad. This "God in person" as he is described, transformed Elijah Muhammad from a welfare-dependent migrant into one of the most impactful leaders of the 20th Century. Elijah Muhammad credits his unparalleled success to the omnipotent God whose spirit, force, power, and wisdom appeared 'in person.' It was during the early 1930s when Master Fard Muhammad taught Elijah Muhammad for nearly three and one half years and revealed to him the knowledge of matters that were unknown to the world at that time.

As evidence that he encountered a divinely supreme power, the Honorable Elijah Muhammad (who never proceeded past the fourth grade of elementary school) confounded the scholarship of the world with his actions and his teachings. Empowered by the wisdom of his God, this relatively small man put forth arguments containing strange information that continues to confound world scholars today. This unique pedagogy included knowledge

---

[1] Louis Farrakhan, "The Reality Of The Mother Plane" (Chicago, IL: The Final Call Inc., January 4, 1987).

about the earth, the planets, the origin of people, the splitting of atoms, and much more. Muhammad claimed that he received his knowledge directly from the Supreme Being who appeared in the person of Master Fard Muhammad. This strange knowledge was easily accepted by the poor, the convicts, and the social outcasts during the early stages of Muhammad's ministry, but the masses of the people, especially the learned of society, often approached Muhammad's teachings with skepticism, mockery, and ridicule.

Aside from the notion of having met God, one of the most controversial aspects of the Honorable Elijah Muhammad's teachings involves the existence of a gigantic wheel-like plane known as the Mother Plane (also called *the Mother Wheel* or *the Wheel*), along with its host of 1500 smaller planes. Like the belief in God appearing in human form, this aspect of the Nation of Islam's theology is one that clearly distinguishes it from practically all mainstream religious traditions and educational schools of thought. During Master Fard Muhammad's nearly three and one half years of teaching his messenger, he pointed out to Elijah Muhammad the reality of that huge Mother Plane in the sky. This included direct knowledge of its capabilities and its divine purpose. As Elijah Muhammad was shown the firsthand reality of this supreme power, he was commissioned and equipped by Master Fard Muhammad to spread this truth to his people and ultimately the world. Elijah Muhammad recognized that he was taught directly by Allah (God) in the person of Master Fard Muhammad.

This bold and shocking claim has been mocked by some, ignored by many, and studied by few. Perhaps even more shocking is that despite the popularity of the Nation of Islam (NOI) in modern society, the theology and position of this group have been seldom understood by the public. Despite blatant attempts to propagate and proselytize this teaching, there remains an element of blatant ignorance about this intriguing community of Muslims. There remains an ignorance surrounding the theology, program, and position of the NOI despite efforts to reason and dialogue with those of different beliefs and customs. Unfortunately, this level of ignorance seems to be a shared attitude when many approach the subject of UFOs. Naturally, the position of the NOI is seldom, if ever, heard in most public forums, and discussions surrounding UFOs. When engaging this controversial topic, mainstream media, researchers, educators, and scientists have failed to include the group that first brought this phenomenon to the modern world. It is no accident that the Muslims' position has been deliberately left out of such discussions. Even more perplexing is that the Nation of Islam, who has so blatantly warned about these crafts, are frequently avoided in most public forums that attempt to address the UFO topic.

As an integral part of the NOI's theology, the Muslims who follow the Honorable Elijah Muhammad with the guidance of the Honorable Louis Farrakhan have been the most persistent proponents of these flying objects.

THE CHALLENGE: SCIENCE, THEOLOGY, AND THE WORLD

The Muslims belonging to the NOI do not approach this subject as mere speculators or enthusiasts; instead this group deems themselves as authorities on this subject matter with practical reasons. Considering that Elijah Muhammad was given the integral details about the purpose of these planes, it should behoove those who study the topic of UFOs to at least recognize the primary entity responsible for propagating the existence of these circular crafts. As the original proponents of a mother ship and other wheel-like crafts of supreme intelligence, the Nation of Islam can easily argue that it was the first community in the modern era that has known and propagated the existence of what the world later referred to as flying saucers and disc-shaped UFOs. It is for this reason that many followers of Muhammad's teachings don't refer to such crafts as "Unidentified Flying Objects" (UFOs); instead, these crafts have been clearly *identified* by this peculiar community of Muslims. Although the NOI has identified the power and intelligence behind those crafts, the term *UFO* will still be used throughout this text so that diverse readers may understand this reality in common terms.

Since insurmountable evidence already proves beyond doubt that such wheel-shaped crafts exist, this study does not spend an inordinate amount of time or space attempting to prove the existence of UFOs. More importantly, this book emphasizes the most indispensable knowledge concerning UFOs that virtually all leading researchers, enthusiasts, and skeptics have failed to acknowledge. Hence, this writing puts forth incontestable arguments that demonstrate *who* and *what* is responsible for the intelligence and power of these phenomenal objects. Since the wheel-shaped planes that Muhammad described do not account for all UFO activity, this research also offers rational analyses that debunk and demystify many assumed concepts about UFOs, their origins, and their purpose. While the bulk of this research provides lucid data about these objects, a few logical suppositions are mentioned to allow readers to draw their own conclusions when inconclusive data has been expressed.

To the surprise of some, a thorough research about the modern UFO phenomenon does not lead to extraterrestrials from other galaxies. Instead, the evidence leads to a 'mild-mannered' Black man as the cardinal representative of these modern wonders. The Honorable Elijah Muhammad, his National Representative Louis Farrakhan, and the NOI have been the primary proponents of the wheel-like planes that have been sighted as UFOs. This fact has gone virtually unchallenged by UFO researchers and pundits. Fortunately this book unleashes those undeniable truths about so-called UFOs that even UFO researchers, scholars, and skeptics haven't dared to deal with before the public.

A RELIGIOUS ANOMALY

While some may not see the relevance that the subject of UFOs may have in their personal lives, there are a few concepts that should be considered. In a world where a vast majority of people follow religious beliefs and traditions, none of the major world religions have a solidified doctrine concerning UFOs. If UFOs exist as contemporary data shows, then most religious ideologies would be seriously questioned if not debunked altogether. Billions of religious adherents would be left with unanswered questions.

History has shown that when certain scientific discoveries conflicted with the dominant religious beliefs, those who brought such discoveries were often ridiculed, deemed heretic, and even killed. When Galileo Galilei's findings concluded that the earth revolved around the sun, his greatest opposition came from the church leaders under Pope Urban VIII. Although Galileo was much more accurate than the church during a time when they believed the sun revolved around a flat earth, he was vilified, threatened, and charged with heresy because his findings conflicted with the Roman Church of that time.[2] Like the days of Galileo in the 1600s, a similar mindset exists somewhat dominantly in modern religion. This is demonstrated in the reluctance of many theologians to even acknowledge the reality of UFOs, much less reconcile this reality with conventional religious thought. Imagine the responses toward traditional religious beliefs if the people realized that these crafts and *higher beings* exist when their religion cannot explain them. How would preachers reconcile this concept with conflicting religious traditions?

Consider the possible apostasy[3] that could take place if the people realize they have been deceived all this time. Perhaps this may explain why so many religious scholars have deliberately turned a deaf ear to the Nation of Islam when it comes to the topic of UFOs and theology. **If theologians acknowledge UFOs as a reality, they would have to acknowledge the entity that introduced these crafts to the modern world.** To do so would force religions to accept the fact that a mild-mannered Black man from Georgia may have actually met the Supreme Being. It would be almost unheard of for religious denominations to openly admit that a child of slaves was taught by God. This may also explain why few religious sects that believe in UFOs fail to credit Elijah Muhammad for bringing such a message to the world. Interestingly, all modern religious sects that believe in UFOs as an inherent part of their theology started believing after the Honorable Elijah Muhammad's public ministry. Some of those groups include *The Church of Scientology* founded in the early 1950s, *The Aetherius Society* founded in the

---

[2] Rachel Hilliam, *Galileo: Father Of Modern Science (Rulers, Scholars, and Artists of Renaissance Europe)* (Rosen Pub Group, 2004).

[3] **apostasy:** n. an abandonment from a religious ideology or religious order.

United Kingdom in 1955, *The Industrial Church of the New World Comforter* founded in 1973, *The Raëlian Church* founded in 1974, and *The Church of the SubGenius* founded in 1979. Is it a coincidence that these groups and their beliefs all formed several years, even decades after the Nation of Islam brought the initial message?

J. Gordon Melton claims that the *Ascended Master Teachings* was the first group to accept a belief in UFOs.[4] Such an argument is easily invalidated. The Ascended Master Teachings, also known as "I AM" Activity, was founded in the 1930s by Guy Ballard. Ballard's religious publications never mentioned anything regarding flying vessels or spacecraft that can be equated to what are now referred to as UFOs. In fact, the attribution of UFOs to the Ascended Master Teachings did not come about until decades later by other UFO enthusiasts outside of their sect. **Not only is it evident that Muhammad's Nation of Islam was the first to offer a solidified knowledge of these crafts as an integral part of their theology, but Muhammad remains unparalleled in answering the specific details about these planes that modern religion, education, and science have yet to answer!**

A SUPERIOR EDUCATION

For Elijah Muhammad to make such bold claims in the early 1930s then have his claims substantiated decades later through millions of sightings and reports, one must ask, **"Where did he get his information from?"** How is it that a man who never graduated from elementary school could know so much about truths that the most brilliant scientists of this world are just now realizing? **How does one explain the fact that Elijah Muhammad knew so much about these spacecrafts before the world ever witnessed or reported them?** Since Elijah Muhammad claims he received this information from the Supreme Being, should not his claims be approached with careful research and study? Instead of even scrutinizing his claims, many educators and scholars have dismissed Muhammad's teachings altogether.

When approaching the NOI's affiliation with the UFO phenomenon, Ney Rieber, a staunch evangelical critic of the NOI writes, "How does one deal with the followers of the Nation of Islam? Many of their doctrines and positions are difficult to answer because they have little to do with reality. It is impossible to deal with these arguments."[5] Contrary to Rieber's assumptions,

---

[4] Christopher Partridge, *UFO Religions* (Routledge, 2003).
[5] Ney Rieber, "The Nation of Islam - Islam: Truth or Myth?," *Bible.Ca* (Bible.ca, September 2002).

only those who are devoid of facts find it impossible to deal with these arguments. The NOI's doctrine provides substantial evidence to support its claims, particularly concerning the so-called UFO phenomenon. Furthermore, the evidence of this truth is not relegated to religious terms because science, history, statistics, logic, and eyewitness reports validate the NOI's position. Many critics attempt to use similar diversionary tactics to prevent others from objectively investigating the NOI's theology. Hence, the UFO topic causes problems for educators and theologians alike because their schools of thought have not provided plausible answers to this reality. Contrastingly, the Honorable Elijah Muhammad and the Honorable Minister Louis Farrakhan offer answers to this subject that religious and educational philosophies are not equipped to deal with.

To contend with Muhammad's claim that he received such information from the Supreme Being requires that one must approach his claims in a scholarly and scientific manner. If Muhammad's claims about these spacecrafts are true, then the scholarship and scientists of this world would have to admit that Elijah Muhammad was taught by an entity far superior to any conventional wisdom of this world. How is it that even some of his critics admit that he was the first to provide data on this subject, yet they deny that he received it from the Supreme Being? Since his critics do not accept that he received this information from God, wouldn't those critics have to conclude that Elijah Muhammad must have been the most visionary thinker of the last few centuries? How else could one explain his exclusively detailed knowledge about these crafts before any widespread sightings or reports ever took place? Denying that he acquired this knowledge from a superior source might require educators to explain how an uneducated child of slaves from rural Georgia could come up with such realities decades before they became evident. Maybe this is why Elijah Muhammad, Louis Farrakhan (his National Representative), and the Nation of Islam have been excluded from virtually all educational forums that attempt to study or discuss UFOs.

What credible researcher would study a topic and leave out the primary sources related to that topic? Any research, book, or documentary that is regarded as an authority on a subject, yet deliberately excludes the most credible sources, can never be considered a truly reliable work. This research, however, offers that primary data that has been purposely disregarded by so-called *experts*. This research synthesizes what all other UFO researchers have failed to do—recognize the insight from the source that started this phenomenon. Moreover, this work is to serve as a vanguard on the UFO topic by including the most authentic primary data from the source that introduced this reality to the modern world.

If carefully studied, the topic of UFOs provides learning across content areas as it engages practically every subject matter: research, science, math, sociology, history, philosophy and theology. However, the subject matter of

UFOs is one that has been treated as taboo by educational systems, institutions, and curricula. Like in religion, very few desire to delve into such a phenomenal subject that challenges the intelligence of this world. If the power associated with those UFOs exist as described and recorded by millions of people, it would prove beyond doubt that there is an intelligence far superior to all the scholarship of this world combined. Such intelligence would blatantly demonstrate the inferiority of this world's education, which many academics would agree is on a decline anyway. If the masses of the people continue to witness, record, or become intrigued with UFOs, there is a huge possibility that many would be directed to the teachings that started it all. This would mean that the most scholarly minds of the world would have to concede that the Honorable Elijah Muhammad, the Honorable Louis Farrakhan, and the Nation of Islam represent a *supreme* power. Of course, it is highly unlikely that this world's scholarship is ready to admit such a reality. Nonetheless, it becomes increasingly clear that Elijah Muhammad's teacher was far more advanced than any educational system of this world.

A THREAT TO WORLD POWERS

In a world filled with wars and rumors of wars between countries, there seems to be a level of competition by those who rule the nations to become the world's superpower. Heads of state often boast of their country's power and flex their military prowess upon weaker nations. But where do UFOs fit in this picture? The knowledge of such crafts and its supreme intelligence could openly demonstrate the incompetence of global powers and their military strengths. Consider how many international conflicts have arisen because of airspace violations. Imagine UFOs flying over strict military airspace at will and how countries can do nothing to stop them. How do the world's military powers react knowing there are crafts that can fly through their "restricted airspace" with impunity? How would the masses react if they knew how the intelligence guiding these crafts intimidates the tyrannical powers of the world? This type of knowledge would pose national threats to those governments that continue to conceal this information from the people.

The United States has more reported UFO sightings and abductions than any country in the world[6], yet the U.S. Government refuses to answer critical questions concerning its knowledge of UFOs. If the American people

---

[6] People's Daily Online. (2012, May 18). Ten Countries Most Often Visited by Extraterrestrials. *People's Daily Online* . People's Daily Online. The U.S. tops the list with the most reported UFO sightings and abductions.

discover how their government has deceived them, rebellious protests may emerge as never witnessed before. Perhaps this is why a few other governments have opened their UFO files to their constituents. America, however, refuses to follow suit. Have America's military and its Intelligence agencies invested decades, billions of dollars, and resources to investigate something that does not exist? Their efforts presuppose that they would not imbue such energy into something unless it is a tangible reality. UFO researcher Jenny Randle makes the following observation:

> UFOs have also been investigated by every major government on earth, and are still being studied at an official level in China, France, Spain, the USSR, the USA, and the United Kingdom – to name but six leading nations. If UFOs were 'bunk', or of no great importance, do you really think every leading power and super power would make the same crass error and submit to this absurdity?[7]

In essence, the reality of UFOs would prove that the entity that revealed this reality to Elijah Muhammad is supreme above worldly powers, which has been the primary reason for the denials, the propaganda, and the cover-ups of UFOs. This writing intends to illustrate beyond doubt, that what Elijah Muhammad and his Nation of Islam (NOI) brought to the world is in fact a reality that deserves to be objectively studied, scrutinized, critiqued, and evaluated. To do so requires that those approaching this subject must engage it with objectivity, not being driven by emotions, but by sound judgment.

If the world powers, world religions, and educational schools of thought CANNOT adequately explain the UFO phenomenon, the people should seriously reappraise what they have been led to believe! Any person remotely curious about this topic should also reappraise those persons, institutions, and entities that claim any form of expertise on this subject matter. Since the most intelligent powers in this world CANNOT explain it, why have they deliberately excluded the entity that introduced this reality to the world? A subject matter of this magnitude demands a synthesizing of information from various disciplines because the concept of UFOs branches off to nearly every imaginable field of study. One should not exclude the authority of Messenger Elijah Muhammad on this subject simply because of their personal dislikes of him. To do so would be asinine. Fortunately, the Honorable Elijah Muhammad shared the most important, firsthand information about these crafts that can be examined, vetted, and shared with the world. Since the world cannot answer the truth about this phenomenon, this book offers the most important perspective on this subject because it encompasses those firsthand primary sources that brought this knowledge to

---

[7] Jenny Randles, *The UFO Conspiracy* (New York, NY: Barnes & Noble Inc, 1987).

the modern world. It is this perspective that has been purposely ignored in most UFO research. Simply put, this book offers the information and the understanding that religion, education, and the power structure are incapable of providing concerning the subject of UFOs.

THE CLOSEST ENCOUNTER OF ANY KIND

Perhaps few subjects have sparked more inquiry in the last century than UFOs—a subject that to this day still remains unresolved to the public. Questions still arise ranging from *whether or not they exist* and *exactly what are they? What do they want* and *what relationship do they have to earthly human affairs?* Before such questions had ever arisen in modern culture, the Honorable Elijah Muhammad had already been shown the specific answers concerning these crafts, their purpose, their capabilities, and most importantly, who was responsible for its creation. As questions are asked about these crafts, hardly any inquiring minds seem willing to seek the source of this phenomenon. Those questions have been answered since the early 1930s by a child of former slaves. A man who did not reach beyond the fourth grade of elementary school was given the intricate details about UFOs before there was ever a mass sighting or widespread concern. A mild-mannered Black man from rural Georgia was given the firsthand knowledge of UFOs and he taught about these crafts for over forty years. That man who was shown the power of these things was the Honorable Elijah Muhammad.

Interestingly, Muhammad's firsthand knowledge of UFOs came directly from his teacher, Master Fard Muhammad, whom Elijah Muhammad boldly claimed was Allah (God) in person. This claim has distinguished the Nation of Islam (NOI) from practically all schools of thought. Unlike any of his predecessors, Elijah Muhammad and his Nation of Islam are distinguished for their unique theology that encompasses the reality of a human built planet, known as **The Mother Plane**, along with 1500 accompanying smaller wheel-like planes. None of Muhammad's predecessors including Noble Drew Ali and Marcus Garvey ever spoke of such. They certainly never claimed to have been taught directly by Allah (God) in person. While Muhammad respected the struggle of those before him, he consistently held that he was taught by the all-wise, true and living God who appeared in the person of Master Fard Muhammad. Of course, this claim did not come without opposition from traditional religion. Despite his bold claims, Elijah Muhammad literally dared the scholarship of the world to disprove his teachings and his position:

> *This is why they don't attack me and put in their paper to make me prove what I teach. ... Therefore, he doesn't want to challenge me out here before you. I would love to have him [scholars] stand here and challenge me. I would give him 20,000 dollars every hour if he would come here and try to contend with me.*[8]

Although his Nation of Islam (NOI) has been considered a religious organization, Muhammad doesn't challenge the world based solely on religious terms; instead, he allows even his detractors to scrutinize his teachings as they would all bodies of knowledge. Put it under the microscope of scientific scrutiny. Apply reasoning and logic as one would other scientific disciplines. Muhammad, like his National Representative Louis Farrakhan, still challenges the world to bring their best minds to objectively discuss this teaching.

Before getting deeply involved into a study of UFOs, it should be clearly understood that all UFOs don't refer to the planes that Elijah Muhammad introduced to the world. Even though the planes he represented account for many of the authentic wheel-like UFO related cases, it should be known that a UFO can refer to any *unidentified flying object*; whether the object is a natural weather occurrence, a balloon, a fire lantern, a golf ball, or a deliberate hoax. As long as an aerial object has not been definitively identified, it can be categorized as a UFO. Therefore, it becomes necessary to distinguish between any UFO and the realistic crafts that were brought to the world's attention by Elijah Muhammad. These planes constitute many of the circular planes that have been sighted, witnessed, reported, and encountered by several millions of people around the globe. These are the crafts that have caused governmental concerns because of their seemingly inhuman capabilities. These are the planes that were first detailed by Elijah Muhammad before any major UFO concerns ever arose.

Before any public concerns arose about flying saucers or UFOs, the Nation of Islam had already baffled the authorities during the 1930s with a special kind of teaching that was unknown to the modern world. The most peculiar part about this teaching is that the Honorable Elijah Muhammad claimed he got it directly from God in person who taught him for nearly three and one half years. Elijah Muhammad didn't make such bold claims without substantiation. As proof of his claims, Elijah Muhammad was given the knowledge of things that had yet to become evident in the known world. Muhammad was taught about the life on other planets, the origin of the moon, and the origin of human races. He was given the keys of wisdom regarding the ancient mysteries, the understanding of prophecies and of course, the reality of these planes that are now referred to as UFOs. What was shown to

---

[8] Elijah Muhammad, "The Theology of Time (Lecture Series)," Vols. June 4, 1972 (Chicago, IL: MUHAMMAD Mosque No. 2, 1972).

Muhammad did not become evident to the public until decades after it was revealed to him.

Since the 1930s Elijah Muhammad claimed that his God taught that the moon was once a part of the earth. Due to a cataclysmic explosion that took place on earth some 66 trillion years ago, that part of the earth was formed into what is now known as the moon, the earth's satellite.[9] It took the National Aeronautical and Space Administration (NASA) over forty years after Muhammad's claim before they even hypothesized on a theory regarding the moons origin.[10] It wasn't until 1975 that scientific research papers were published suggesting that the moon was formed due to a cataclysmic explosion with the earth. Although these early hypotheses leaned toward the belief that an external object collided with the earth, their theories became closer to what Master Fard Muhammad revealed to Elijah Muhammad in the early 1930s. Even more perplexing is that nearly 36 years after that 1975 hypothesis, scientists reappraised their previous theories in 2012 only to conclude that the moon's material came EXCLUSIVELY from the earth.[11] This conclusion comes even closer to the Nation of Islam's teachings that had been mocked for decades for what seemed to be religious mysticism. **How is it that Elijah Muhammad with barely a fourth-grade education knew more about the origin of the moon than the astrophysicists who had more education, resources, equipment, money, and technology at their disposal? How does one explain Muhammad's knowledge of such advanced astronomical sciences?** Why didn't the scientists, universities, and NASA engineers reference Elijah Muhammad as a proponent of their scientific findings? Could it have something to do with Muhammad's claim that he received his data from Allah (God) who appeared to him in the person of Master Fard Muhammad? To admit that Elijah Muhammad was accurate would be to admit that his teacher must be the Supreme Being!

The NOI's teaching about a God who appeared in person and taught Elijah Muhammad for nearly three and one half years deserves a careful study, not just because of its fascinating nature, but due to the substantial merit of the claims. **If Elijah Muhammad made astonishing scientific claims in the 1930s and those claims became evident many decades later, then it makes sense to**

---

[9] Elijah Muhammad, *MESSAGE TO THE BLACKMAN In America*, Original Published by MUHAMMAD'S Temple No. 2 in Chicago 1965 (Chicago, IL: The Final Call Inc., 1965). 31.
[10] Jeffrey G Taylor, *Origin of the Earth and Moon*, Article, Hawaii Institute of Geophysics and Planetology, NASA (Hawaii Institute of Geophysics and Planetology, 09/20/2012).
[11] Ray Villard, *Celestial Paternity Test: Moon is Earth's Child*, News, Discovery (Discovery Channel, 04/11/2012).

examine and evaluate the validity and source of such information! This is what the scientific approach is for. The credibility of the Honorable Elijah Muhammad warrants a professional examination of his teachings, his works, and his prize pupil, the Honorable Minister Louis Farrakhan. These components provide substance and evidence for his claims regarding UFOs.

AN UNPOPULAR TRUTH

For several decades the NOI has endured tremendous mockery, ridicule, and attacks for teaching an unpopular doctrine. While hardly any of these attacks have come from scientific entities, most have stemmed from religious and ideological conflicts. Just as Galileo's discoveries put him at odds with the religious order of his day, the Muslims who follow the Honorable Elijah Muhammad have taken plenty of unnecessary abuse from religious traditionalists. The NOI has been accused of heresy for their teaching about the existence and capabilities of a Mother Wheel and baby planes that were built on earth at the behest of God himself. Strangely, much of the ridicule against the NOI has come from religious clergy. The absurdity in this scenario is that most of the world's faith traditions believe in scriptures that describe people floating into clouds, traveling through whirlwinds, and even having cities stationed in the heavens. Yet some of those who accept such fanciful beliefs in religion have mocked the NOI for believing in man-made planes that can travel in the sky.

During a public television show, Christian ministers Larry Wessels and Wilford Darden went on air to lambaste the NOI and its leadership about their belief in these wheel-like planes.[12] Darden claimed that Louis Farrakhan wants to exalt himself above other leaders and the "spaceship thing" is what he uses to try to get that done. Wessels relegated that the NOI "seems to be more of a sensual emotional-type experience, not really based on doctrine or teaching, but more of a sensual reaction to the presence of this man [Louis Farrakhan]."[13] He also added, "It's not the message that matters, it's the experienced emotions" that causes people to gravitate toward the Nation of Islam's teachings. To relegate Minister Farrakhan and the teachings of the Honorable Elijah Muhammad as 'emotionally-based' is merely a ploy to prohibit other Christians from probing into the validity of the NOI's teachings. If Christians were to discover that such planes exist as described by the NOI, this may cause Christians to seriously question why their own theology does not address this issue, which could expose the gross incompetence of Christian

---

[12] Larry Wessels, *Nation of Islam Revisited #2A: Farrakhan Says UFOs Follow Him Wherever He Goes*, YouTube, Christian Answers, 09/21/2010.
[13] Ibid.

theologians to stand against scientific scrutiny. Such would also show the validity and superiority of the Nation of Islam's teachings that provide answers to this worldwide phenomenon. As a precautionary measure, many Christian Ministers have mocked and debased the NOI's teachings in hopes that their parishioners will never investigate this subject with an objective mind. Although the aforementioned evangelists do not represent the view of all Christian clergy, they do, however, exemplify some of the pervasive attitudes and attacks that have come from many leaders in the Christian community against the Nation of Islam.

If not mocking the subject matter, it seems that most Christian evangelists avoid and ignore the topic of UFOs altogether. In his article entitled, *UFOs and the Christian Worldview*, Jefferson Scott gives his report regarding the Christian attitude toward UFOs:

> Most Christians don't think about UFOs. Except for catching the occasional episode of X-Files or maybe watching the latest Independence Day wannabe, the topic of extraterrestrial life simply never comes up.[14]

How is it that there have been more reported UFO sightings and abductions in a Judeo-Christian based America than anywhere in the world,[15] yet the topic of UFOs doesn't come up in most churches? Could it be that this is a subject matter that the church is unable to address? Furthermore, wouldn't the existence of such planes prove that Elijah Muhammad was right all along? It becomes more obvious why many evangelists avoid this subject.

Many influential Jews and Jewish organizations have lampooned the NOI for its uncompromising position on various topics. However, most Jewish critics, who are perhaps the staunchest detractors of the NOI, don't openly mock the Muslims for their position concerning UFOs. One would think that the vilest Jewish propagandists would use the NOI's belief in UFOs to make this group appear insane before the world. Ironically most Jews don't attack the NOI in this regard. Maybe it has to do with prophecies that associate the chosen people of God with strange heavenly vessels throughout the Hebrew Scriptures. The prophetic scriptures of the Jewish Torah depict God's chosen people as having a mysterious object described as a *cloud by day* and a *pillar of fire by night* that will guide and protect them from their seemingly powerful

---

[14] Jefferson Scott, "UFOs and the Christian Worldview," *Jefferson Scott Intelligent Christian Thrillers* (Jefferson Scott, 2007).

[15] People's Daily Online, "Ten Countries Most Often Visited by Extraterrestrials," *People's Daily Online* (People's Daily Online, May 18, 2012).

oppressors. These heavenly vessels are characterized in other parts of Jewish scriptures as chariots of fire, cherubim[16], and even wheels.

Although most Jews today don't subscribe to a belief in UFOs as an inherent part of their theology, many of them are aware that the prophecies they study will include heavenly wheel-like vessels that will be used to protect the real *chosen people of God*. It stands to reason that this is probably the primary reason most Jews who ridicule Minister Farrakhan and the Nation of Islam, do not ridicule on the topic of UFOs. To do so would invalidate those Jews as being God's chosen. As a people who have gained world sympathy and influence for their claim as God's chosen people, it is ironic that part of the criterion for being the "chosen people" involves an inherent belief in strange flying wheels. It is no wonder why influential Jews continue to debase Minister Farrakhan and the Nation of Islam; it is because the Muslims' belief in these wheel-like planes proves who fits the messianic descriptions of the *chosen people* of God.

Many Muslims in the mainstream Islamic world have severely criticized the Nation of Islam's teachings on UFOs as heretical and inherently un-Islamic. While the NOI is clearly distinguished in this regard, the Muslims who attempt to challenge the NOI on this point do so from a strictly traditional perspective. Like some Christian evangelists, those Muslims who charge the NOI with *shirk*[17] have not offered any proof to substantiate their charges. Interestingly, most of those who have criticized the NOI followers for their belief in UFOs don't acknowledge the Holy Qur'an's many references to Allah's *Throne of Power* that is stationed in the heavens. Like the Bible, the Holy Qur'an too depicts God in a tangibly celestial position along with his host of angelic beings.[18] Even more perplexing is that traditional Islamic worldviews include the belief that the Prophet Muhammad (PBUH)[19] was taken on a Night Journey from Mecca to Jerusalem on a legendary winged creature called *Al-Buraq*.[20] Apparently, the traditional Muslims' charge against the Nation of Islam's position on UFOs is based solely on an argument that would easily invalidate their own traditional beliefs.

When comparing attitudes between religion and science, it becomes evident that the level of mockery and ridicule about UFOs starts to diminish when approached from a scientific perspective. In fact, the more educated people are about UFOs, the less they appear to mock this subject. However,

---

[16] **cherubim** (the plural of cherub) a type of spiritual or angelic being mentioned in the Hebrew Bible. (Isaiah 37:16).
[17] **shirk** (sharik) idolatry and polytheism, which are regarded as heretical in Islam.
[18] The Holy Qur'an 39:75, 2:255.
[19] **PBUH:** an abbreviation for Peace Be Upon Him. It is a prayer-like expression for the Prophets of Allah (God).
[20] Ṣaḥīḥ al-Bukhārī. (n.d.). Al-Hadith. *Al-Hadith*. 5:58:227.

this has not stopped academics from deliberately ignoring the NOI perspective altogether when they discuss related topics. A simple observation will show how very few scholars recognize the NOI as the earliest proponent of UFOs in modern culture. Furthermore one may observe that many publications and so-called UFO experts do not even recognize the NOI as proponents of the UFO phenomenon at all! Certainly all of the wise researchers who collect data throughout the universe could not have overlooked one of the most outspoken and influential groups from right under their noses. This deliberate omission of information suggests that even the scholars and scientists of the world have something to hide about UFOs! Scientists, who are perhaps the most qualified to research this phenomena, have been primarily guilty because they have knowingly omitted Muhammad's data from their public research and reports.

Despite having been accused of heresy by traditional religious clergy, ignored by scientists, and painted as insane by the media, the Muslim followers of the Honorable Elijah Muhammad with the guidance of the Honorable Minister Farrakhan continue to baffle even their most relentless pundits. The little man with hardly any formal education produced some of the world's most impactful thinkers. It was Elijah Muhammad who taught, mentored, and buttressed Malcolm X into the man and spokesperson he grew to become. That little man from Georgia who claimed to have met God in person was the one responsible for transforming Malcolm X from a drug-addicted criminal into a respected thinker and leader. It was Elijah Muhammad who gave Imam Warith D. Mohammed the platform that enabled him to become a globally recognized leader and thinker. Elijah Muhammad turned Cassius Clay into Muhammad Ali whose name became synonymous with the most famous Black man on earth in the 1970s and one of the most famous faces in the world during that time.[21] Elijah Muhammad's influence prompted Reader's Digest to identify him as the "most powerful Black man in America."[22] Even today Messenger Elijah Muhammad is recognized by his staunchest critics as being the source of influence behind Black consciousness and enlightenment.[23] Despite the fact

---

[21] William Andrews, Francis Smith Foster and Trudier Harris, *The Oxford Companion to African American Literature*, ed. William Andrews, Francis Smith Foster and Trudier Harris (New York, New York: Oxford University Press, 03/27/1997). The authors remark: "...in the early and middle 1970s, Muhammad Ali was, without question, the most famous African American in history and among the five most recognized faces on the planet."

[22] The Final Call Newspaper, *The Nation of Islam: What has been said..*, Special 70 Year Commemorative Edition, Vol. February (Chicago, IL: Final Call Newspaper, 2000).

[23] Daniel Pipes, "How Elijah Muhammad Won," *Daniel Pipes Middle East Forum* (Daniel Pipes, June 2000).

that cynics have downplayed him and hailed many of his students, little Elijah Muhammad proved to be a big man through his unparalleled profundity. His impact, his wisdom, and his teaching have been best exemplified through his prize pupil, Minister Louis Farrakhan. Since the departure of Elijah Muhammad, it has been Louis Farrakhan whom the pundits and detractors have now targeted their attacks. Louis Farrakhan has consistently upheld Elijah's teachings and has been the primary proponent of the wheel-like planes that his teacher introduced to the world.

For an inarticulate man with virtually no education to become the most powerful Black man in America (with no carnal weapons), and produce the most influential students, and introduce the world to the reality of UFOs is a phenomenon itself. Even more impactful is that he was able to accomplish these unparalleled works with the world's greatest superpower against him, yet he never backed away from his position that he was shown these wheel-like crafts by God in person. Should not this man be studied, examined, and regarded as a primary source for such a study? As the reality of UFOs become more evident in society, most critics have become very skillful on how they criticize the NOI on this subject because of the credibility it could give to the NOI above other philosophies, ideologies, and schools of thought. Therefore, they find it more suitable to use "bait and switch" tactics to divert people into believing that aliens control these planes or to ignore the Muslims' claims altogether.

Amazingly Muhammad challenged the world's powers, the world's ideologies, religious traditions, and even conventional scientific thinkers to disprove his teachings. He dared these schools of thought with his money, possessions, and even his life if they could disprove what his God showed him. Muhammad easily distinguished himself from any leader or spokesperson to ever walk the earth in modern history by challenging world powers to defeat the revelation he received. He distinguished himself as a man who is backed by the power and intelligence associated with those wheel-like planes, not as a mere theorist or speculator. Muhammad seemed exceedingly confident about the wisdom that supported him. He distinguished himself from all other scientists and theorists in these words:

> We must have a man today to teach us, who knows and doesn't guess. We no more are going to rely on guessing and theories. Theory is not truth until you prove it true. Many of us can have theories, but not all those can bring our theories true. I hope you have patience with me a little longer.[24]

---

[24] Elijah Muhammad, "The Theology of Time (Lecture Series)," Vols. June 4, 1972 (Chicago, IL: MUHAMMAD Mosque No. 2, 1972).

THE CHALLENGE: SCIENCE, THEOLOGY, AND THE WORLD

By encouraging his listeners to 'have patience' with him, did he know that much of his teachings would not become evident until years later? Apparently he realized that scientific and technological capabilities were not advanced enough to grasp the fullness of what he brought to the world. It would take decades after his preaching before the average person possessed the type of technology, mobile devices, and recording systems to share the proof of what he taught concerning UFOs, planetary life, and other truths he brought to the world. Coincidentally, the advent of such technology has allowed millions of people around the globe to photograph, record, and share UFO activity on a daily basis. Despite personal or emotional dislikes of this man, his credibility and unparalleled track record warrant that his teachings be rightfully scrutinized, evaluated, and studied. Muhammad never capitulated from his position that he was taught by God in person. The proof of his claim would be determined on whether or not these God-based crafts actually exist. **If these planes DO NOT exist as he taught, then the world would be justified in dismissing Elijah Muhammad, Louis Farrakhan, and the Nation altogether. However, if such planes DO exist as the Nation of Islam teaches, then the world would have to bear witness that the God who taught Elijah Muhammad is the true Supreme Being!**

2. UFOS IDENTIFIED BEFORE THEY BECAME A CONCERN

NOT JUST ANOTHER PLANE

The modern context of the UFO phenomenon started when Master Fard Muhammad pointed out to Elijah Muhammad that huge wheel-like object in the sky, which he called the Mother Plane (also called the Mother Wheel and Mother Ship). This monumental event took place in the early 1930s before there was such a thing as a "UFO" in modern vernacular. The Honorable Elijah Muhammad shared part of that experience in these words, "He pointed out a destructive dreadful-looking plane that is made like a wheel in the sky today. It is a half mile by a half mile square; it is a human built planet." [25] Aside from the knowledge and supreme wisdom that Master Fard Muhammad gave his messenger, one of the tangible evidences he provided was the power of that enormous craft in the sky—the likes of which had never been witnessed before. Pointing this object out to Elijah indicated that Master Fard Muhammad had full control and authority of such a plane. Obviously he knew of its whereabouts and its capabilities, which is why he gave his messenger the keys of knowledge about this huge plane and the myriad smaller planes associated with it.

Leaving Elijah Muhammad with this supreme knowledge would be a determining factor on whether or not Master Fard Muhammad is what Elijah represented him as. If the knowledge that Master Fard Muhammad left Elijah Muhammad becomes true, then it stands to reason that the man who brought the knowledge is truly the manifestation of a supreme being. Totally convinced that he met God, Elijah Muhammad recognized himself as Allah's divine Messenger. As the divinely appointed Messenger of Allah (God), Elijah Muhammad remained steadfast in his preaching that the all-wise, true, and living God visited America and gave him the supreme wisdom and knowledge of the ancient mysteries, prophecies, and scientific realities that had yet to be discovered. The Holy Qur'an confirms that Allah (God) would disclose his secrets to his specially chosen messenger:

---

[25] Elijah Muhammad, *MESSAGE TO THE BLACKMAN In America*, Original Published by MUHAMMAD'S Temple No. 2 in Chicago 1965 (Chicago, IL: The Final Call Inc., 1965). 17-18.

UFOS IDENTIFIED BEFORE THEY BECAME A CONCERN

The Knower of the unseen, so He makes His secrets known to none Except a messenger whom He chooses. For surely He makes a guard to go before him and after him (Al-Jinn 72:26-27).

The concept of God revealing his secrets to his designated messenger clearly distinguishes and authenticates the divinity of this recipient from others. Elijah Muhammad proved that he was granted the divine secrets of the all-wise true and living God and brought tangible proof of the divine secrets revealed to him. This included the firsthand knowledge about the Mother Plane and its host of 1500 smaller crafts. **If these planes exist as Elijah Muhammad argued, then the world should consider the man who first brought this truth to the world.** As remarkable as Messenger Muhammad's authentication about these planes have proven to become, his evidence about these crafts cannot be isolated from the source that disclosed this craft to him because all of his teachings are predicated upon his meeting Allah (God) in person. It is this central reality that both UFO critics and enthusiasts deliberately fail to acknowledge.

Since so much has been said, hypothesized, postulated, accused, and believed about UFOs from outside sources, it would be fitting to focus research around the most credible data. Since the Honorable Elijah Muhammad is the foremost authority on this subject matter, then his data, claims, and hypothesis should deservingly be examined and tested. Consider the following information, which gives only a general synopsis of the Nation of Islam's authoritative teachings concerning what has now become the UFO phenomenon:

> The present wheel-shaped plane known as the Mother of Planes, is one-half mile of a half mile and is the largest mechanical man-made object in the sky. It is a small human planet made for the purpose of destroying the present world of the enemies of Allah. The cost to build such a plane is staggering! The finest brains were used to build it. It is capable of staying in outer space six to twelve months at a time without coming into the earth's gravity. It carried fifteen hundred bombing planes with most deadliest explosives -- the type used in bringing up mountains on the earth. The very same method is to be used in the destruction of this world.[26]

The aforementioned quote gives a synoptic glimpse into the vast body of knowledge that Messenger Muhammad put forth about UFOs. Muhammad

---

[26] Elijah Muhammad, *MESSAGE TO THE BLACKMAN In America*, Original Published by MUHAMMAD'S Temple No. 2 in Chicago 1965 (Chicago, IL: The Final Call Inc., 1965). 291.

described this plane as a human built planet constructed at the behest of God. Along with its 1500 baby (bomber) planes, these vessels will be used to enact judgment against the wicked world superpowers, and it will be used to establish the divine kingdom of peace on earth. These planes are what have now been sighted as *Unidentified Flying Objects (UFOs)*. They have been sighted and filmed moving with unparalleled maneuverability and acceleration. They have been described as luminous metallic objects that shine lights, change colors, and move unconventionally. They have been responsible for abductions, radar interference, and destabilizing military installation programs. All of these characteristics bear witness to the descriptions shared by Messenger Muhammad before the UFO craze ever began.

A UFO by any other name still bears witness to Muhammad's teachings. Although the term UFO is perhaps the most common name used to describe these mysterious crafts, there are actually several names that apply to these objects. Of course the huge gigantic craft is distinctly known as the Mother Plane, the Mother Wheel, the Wheel, the Mother Ship, Mother Craft, New Jerusalem, and several other names. Some of the names stem from the sacred prophecies while others are directly from Muhammad's nomenclatures that coincide with the prophecies. He used several terms for these crafts throughout his forty-plus years of public ministry: wheels, baby planes, and bomber planes to name a few. Even though the NOI and the prophecies refer to these crafts under various terms and symbols, Muhammad clarifies why the term 'wheel' is often used:

> *The Great Wheel which many of us see in the sky today is not so much a wheel as one may think in such terms, but rather a place made like a wheel.*[27]

Describing these planes as wheels give a major indication of the spherical, circular, disc-like characteristics that delineate them. In many other instances they have been described as oblong spheres and as orbs. It is no coincidence that the UFO craze has centered around sightings that describe circular crafts, which explains why they were latter dubbed "flying saucers" by witnesses. How is it that hundreds of millions of witnesses use wheel-like qualities when describing UFOs? Is it a lucky coincidence that millions of witness accounts link directly to Messenger Muhammad's initial descriptions? Why aren't flying boxes or rectangles witnessed by millions? If most of the reports indicated something other than Muhammad's description, researchers would be justified in dismissing his body of work, but since practically all

---

[27] Elijah Muhammad, *MESSAGE TO THE BLACKMAN In America*, Original Published by MUHAMMAD'S Temple No. 2 in Chicago 1965 (Chicago, IL: The Final Call Inc., 1965). 290.

UFOS IDENTIFIED BEFORE THEY BECAME A CONCERN

'legitimate' reports meet Muhammad's criteria, his data should be the recognized authority on UFOs.

The dimensions of the Mother Plane are one half mile by one half mile. The mere sight of such an object would likely appear larger than that since the likeness of its kind has never been witnessed before. The size of this craft matches several credible reports and sightings from witnesses around the globe. It is circular like a wheel as a human built planet or as Muhammad notes, "it is made up of revolving spheres."[28] Depending on the vantage point of onlookers, it may appear as oblong, orbital, or cigar shaped. The smaller baby (bomber) planes are like miniature versions of the Mother Wheel. They are capable of traveling at comparable speeds of several thousand miles per hour and can "dart out of the sky" instantaneously in any direction.[29] The lights emitted from these planes have been reported to change colors and the planes themselves have been reported to change colors.

The Honorable Elijah Muhammad taught that the finest and toughest steel was used to build these crafts. The composition of the steel used for these planes have yet to be emulated by any engineers of this world. This peculiar type of steel, along with the intelligence working with it, can form force shields that make these crafts practically impenetrable. These characteristics have proven themselves to be true as military confrontations with these crafts have shown.

The U.S. Military encountered a large round dome-shaped object in the sky with several smaller crafts in February of 1942 off the coast of Los Angeles, California. The Military fired several hundred rounds of heavy artillery at these crafts as the large round craft remained unmoved by some of America's most powerful weaponry.[30] During this ordeal that lasted several hours, the large unmoved object remained stationed in the sky while the smaller baby planes dodged all of the artillery. This confrontation demonstrated the speed, maneuverability, and power that Muhammad described nearly a decade earlier.

Messenger Muhammad explained, "A Plane that is wheel-shaped can turn in any direction, at any time."[31] The orbital shape of such planes along with the intelligence that governs them illustrates the scientific majesty of their

---

[28] Ibid.
[29] Elijah Muhammad, "The Theology of Time (Lecture Series)," Vols. July 2, 1972 (Chicago, IL: MUHAMMAD Mosque No. 2, 1972).
[30] Richard M. Dolan, *UFOs and the National Security State: Chronology of a Coverup, 1941-1973*, Kindel Edition (Charlottesville, VA: Keyhole Publishing Company, 2000).
[31] Elijah Muhammad, *The Fall Of America* (Chicago, IL: Elijah Muhammad, 1973). 238.

maneuverability. Such precision allows them to move at lightning speeds in any direction at the blink of an eye. They can move as slow as a worm and can remain motionless in a fixed position for long periods of time. While in their affixed position, these planes can easily disguise themselves as clouds during the sunlit parts of the day and they may appear as distant stars in the darker hours. In his book *The Fall of America*, the Honorable Elijah Muhammad gives a brief description of the supreme stealth that can make the Wheel impossible to detect if it does not desire to be noticed:

> The Mother Plane can hide behind other stars and make herself invisible to the eye because she does not have to wait on a power from the earth. She can produce her own power to go wherever she desires to go in space.[32]

While human flight has advanced significantly in the last century, modern engineering has yet to master aerodynamics that allow them to produce flight with comparable speed or maneuverability. Although modern science has been tremendously inspired by the technology of UFOs, their attempts to emulate them have only taken them so far because the wheels are produced from a wisdom that has not been revealed to this world. The Messenger explained, "It can dart out of your eyesight so fast, until it looks like nothing was there."[33] Reports from all around the world bear witness to the speed that Muhammad spoke of. Military and governmental intelligence agencies know that those planes cannot be the product of conventional powers because present aerodynamic engineering has barely allowed human flight to successfully reach 4000 mph. Even with those speeds, conventional aircraft cannot compare to the maneuverability of the wheels that can dart, move, and stop instantaneously. Minister Farrakhan describes some of the flight capabilities of the wheels in these words:

> Those planes are deadly. They move at speeds this world has never seen before. They have motion that this world has not seen. They take off going straight up and they can move going right and left, forward and back, stop on a dime, move back, go forward.[34]

The movement associated with most of the UFO sightings proves that they must be controlled by a supreme intelligence. Having dodged and withstood some of the most powerful military weaponry, world governments have admitted that a superior intelligence and power are upon those crafts.

---

[32] Ibid. 242
[33] Elijah Muhammad, "The Theology of Time (Lecture Series)," Vols. July 2, 1972 (Chicago, IL: MUHAMMAD Mosque No. 2, 1972).
[34] Louis Farrakhan, "The Shock of The Hour" (Chicago, IL: The Final Call, April 26, 1992).

UFOS IDENTIFIED BEFORE THEY BECAME A CONCERN

While many try to attribute this power to otherworldly beings, the Honorable Elijah Muhammad filled the voids that most UFO researchers still baffle over. He said that the Mother Plane has the ability to create a **protective shield** around it, which allows it to produce an impenetrable force field. He likened the Wheel's capabilities to the earth's atmosphere that serves as "a protected coat of arms" against any external forces.[35]

THE PURPOSE: DESTRUCTION AND SALVATION

The purpose of this advanced spacecraft is manifold for it involves history, prophecy, science, mathematics, life, death, war, and peace. Simply put, it is proof of the majestic work of Allah (God). The creation of the Mother Plane did not come about from some rash decision. In fact the plans and intentions to build such a plan had been in development for thousands of years. According to the Honorable Elijah Muhammad, "Ezekiel saw it a long time ago; it was built for the purpose of destroying the present world."[36] It was made to destroy the current world of wickedness and to usher in a new world of righteousness. Since the scriptural prophecies depict that God's people would not be able to defend themselves against their powerful oppressors, God would use his heavenly powers to execute judgment and destruction against the oppressors that hold his people in bondage. This is part of the divine purpose of this plane.

The God who revealed this plane to Elijah Muhammad loves his people so much that he visited them himself as it is written that the *Son of Man* would seek and save what was lost.[37] The Nation of Islam contends that no people fit the description as this lost people more than the Black people of America. No other people have endured the traumatic experiences as the people who suffered through the Trans-Atlantic Slavery. No other people have lost their names, their culture, their land, their religion, their God, and their right to exist as humans the way Black people have. A people who have inherited centuries of traumatic aberrations from the world's sociopathic superpower are

---

[35] Elijah Muhammad, *MESSAGE TO THE BLACKMAN In America*, Original Published by MUHAMMAD'S Temple No. 2 in Chicago 1965 (Chicago, IL: The Final Call Inc., 1965). 290.
[36] Elijah Muhammad, *MESSAGE TO THE BLACKMAN In America*, Original Published by MUHAMMAD'S Temple No. 2 in Chicago 1965 (Chicago, IL: The Final Call Inc., 1965). 18.
[37] Matthew 18:11, Luke 19:10.

the most deserving people to receive divine protection and intervention. Conversely, a superpower that oppresses such a people are befitting of a divine destruction. If any of the prophecies render themselves true, then it would take a masterpiece of mechanics to protect the oppressed people from the overly armed superpower called The United States of America. This is just one aspect of the purpose of these so-called UFOs.

Essentially the Mother Plane is the fulfillment of divine prophecies. The Messenger stated, "In the Bible, you have a prophecy of a wheel in a wheel, in the book Ezekiel. This represents Ezekiel's wheel. You've read about it in the Bible."[38] Messenger Muhammad explained that the Mother Wheel represents the fulfillment of that prophetic wheel that was shown to the Prophet Ezekiel. Muhammad also distinguishes that "Ezekiel's vision has become a reality."[39] The divine plans and intentions spoken of thousands of years ago have finally materialized in this Mother Wheel that the Black Muslims have so adamantly spoken of.

The Mother Wheel and its baby planes are rooted in an eschatological[40] purpose. The Honorable Elijah Muhammad recognized himself as the divine Messenger of Allah (God) and he recognized his mission as the fulfillment of the prophecies that depict God's people enslaved by an oppressor so powerful that only God himself could save his people from their grip. Therefore these prophecies show that a condition would be so unique that it would warrant the direct intervention of God in person. The Bible predicts that before the coming of that great and dreadful day of the Lord, God would send one under the definitive name *Elijah*.[41]

The Mother Wheel has two natures. "The Mother Plane was made to destroy this world of evil and to show the wisdom and mighty power of the God Who came to destroy an old world and set up a new world."[42] The prophetic nature of this craft plays a dual role: destruction of the present world of wickedness and to establish the kingdom of God's everlasting peace on earth. It is great for the righteous and dreadful for the wicked. The *great* and *dreadful* day of the Lord wherein he prophesied to send Elijah will include a *great* and *dreadful* craft to carry out this prophecy. The Honorable Elijah

---

[38] Elijah Muhammad, "The Theology of Time (Lecture Series)," Vols. June 2, 1972 (Chicago, IL: MUHAMMAD Mosque No. 2, 1972).

[39] Elijah Muhammad, *MESSAGE TO THE BLACKMAN In America*, Original Published by MUHAMMAD'S Temple No. 2 in Chicago 1965 (Chicago, IL: The Final Call Inc., 1965). 290.

[40] **eschatological** (adjective) of or relating to Eschatology. **Eschatology** is the field of theology that deals with end time prophecies and the final judgment of mankind.

[41] Malachi 4:5.

[42] Elijah Muhammad, *The Fall Of America* (Chicago, IL: Elijah Muhammad, 1973). 236.

UFOS IDENTIFIED BEFORE THEY BECAME A CONCERN

Muhammad fulfills this role with great details. The ancient wisdom of the original fathers of civilization is gradually being brought back to the present day children. With Muhammad's guidance the children of God will be returned back to that forgotten wisdom. The reality of these wheels is one of the clearest signs of such wisdom.

EXTRATERRESTRIAL OR EXTRAORDINARY?

To the surprise of some, the manufacturing and development of this highly advanced spacecraft did not come from outer space. The components, manufacturers, pilots, and intelligence associated with those UFOs come from the best minds and materials from this planet earth. No little green or grey men asking, "take me to your leader" were involved in this process. This position may not make for a blockbuster Hollywood film, but this position does demystify the notions that many people have become accustomed to about UFOs. After all, nations build huge contraptions from earth that are sent to orbit the heavens: satellites, the *International Space Station (ISS)*, space shuttles, and rockets. With this in mind, there should be no doubt that an earthly intelligence can produce crafts that can surpass the earth's atmosphere. Fortunately, Muhammad takes away the fictional mysticism from the UFO phenomenon by providing sobering answers that are not designed to tickle the fancies of the public.

So where did these UFOs come from? According to Muhammad the construction of these planes took place on the islands of Nippon (Japan) and launched in 1929. Interestingly, this location would prove to be the most befitting place to construct highly advanced machinery while the world remained totally oblivious. Crafts of this magnitude did not appear in a 'hocus pocus' fashion. Instead, it took years of manpower and some of the most methodical vocation to complete such an arduous undertaking.

The Nipponese Islands of Japan have a strange geography and oceanography that baffle even contemporary scientists. Information concerning Japan's vast hills and underground caves are still being discovered as Takanori Ogawa points out these findings:

> At present, 95 caves are known which are over 30 meters in length, and two or three more are discovered every year. The longest is Mitsuike Ana, which is

2,139.75 meters long. Eight caves are more than 500 meters long. The caves formed on level ground and have a complicated plan and profile.[43]

These locations would aptly serve as suitable sites to set about such a covert project. The specific histories of the Japanese islands and their bordering waters are somewhat obscure too. This region produced some of the most bizarre activity on earth, which may explain why it became dubbed *The Dragon's Triangle*. It is often compared to the Bermuda Triangle, but is said to be more of a danger zone because of the mysterious cases of missing planes, ships, and lives that have been lost there.

Nearly thirty years after the Mother Plane launched from that region in 1929, anomalous occurrences began to take place there. Since the early 1950s several ships, planes, and military vessels mysteriously vanished, never to be seen or heard from again.[44] Several accounts of missing ships and planes made this general area a "danger zone" for pilots and navigators. There have been several hypotheses and postulations put forth by theorists to explain these incomprehensible events, but regardless to their theories, it has proven to be an area that yields apprehensions and concerns from even experienced navigators. The geography of Japan represents an archipelago of four major islands and over 4,000 smaller islands, most of which consist of mountainous regions with only about 15% considered cultivatable. Many of these islands were said to look identical, thus serving as somewhat of a camouflage. An area with such topography would have been extremely problematic for the average navigator during that time period. This is consistent with Elijah Muhammad's description of Master Fard Muhammad's work: "He would do this work in a Day that they least expected. Therefore the Bible says he Came without observation as a thief in the night."[45] These words describe part of the covert work of God that would take place without the enemy forces being aware of his activity. In other words, he outwitted the intelligence of the world's powers by choosing a sequestered location to conduct a most magnificent task.

This region off the coast of Japan has been labeled, the *Dragon's Triangle*, the *Devil's Sea* and the *Bermuda Triangle of the Pacific*. This part of the world is said to hold one of the world's few existing vile vortices, which are those areas where the pull of the planet's electromagnetic waves is supposed to

---

[43] Takanori Ogawa, *ON LAVA CAVES IN JAPAN AND VICINITY*, Speleological Society of Japan: Association of Japanese Cavers, The Commission On Volcanic Caves (Vulcanospeleology, 2012), 73.
[44] Charles Berlitz, *The Dragon's Triangle*, 03/02/1991 (Fawcett,1991).
[45] Elijah Muhammad, *Our Saviour Has Arrived* (Chicago, IL: MUHAMMAD'S TEMPLE No. 2, 1974). Chapter 34 Days of the Son of Man: Confusion of Nations.

be stronger than anywhere else in the world.[46] [47] Some suggest that this may account for the number of missing vessels that have been mysteriously lost over the years. Others opine that erratic volcanic activity associated within Japan's archipelago could account for such occurrences. One writer suggests, "Ancient legends, some dating back to 1000 B.C.E. tell of dragons that lived off the coast of Japan."[48] The mythological fire-breathing dragon likely stems from the fiery volcanic activity witnessed there throughout centuries, hence the term *Dragon's Triangle*.

The enigmatic geography of this region proved to be a fitting place in the development of the Mother Plane. The huge wheel-like plane was covertly manufactured in a location that would not alert the attention of any world powers during its construction. The strange activity of missing ships and planes did not occur in this area until almost 30 years after the Wheel had already taken off, which makes a strong case for Elijah Muhammad's position. Is it a coincidence that Elijah's wheels were constructed in a location that later became identified as a zone of inexplicable activity? Either Muhammad's source of information was eons ahead of the modern world or he was just an EXTREMELY lucky guesser.

Unlike most of the public who are unaware of Elijah Muhammad's majestic teachings about so-called UFOs, scientists approach his teachings with a much different mindset. While they are unlikely to publicly admit that his teachings are true, they frequently center many of their studies and experiments around his teachings. This has become more evident in some of their recent studies. According to writer Jim Kane, "Information is now being revealed indicating there are secret UFO bases deep beneath the mountainous regions of Japan."[49] One must critically ask, "What would even prompt researchers to involve themselves in a study like this unless they had some valid clues to lead them in that direction?" Kane continued, "Paranormal observers have opined that the rugged terrains of the Japanese countryside contain secret UFO bases."[50]

---

[46] Dan Shaw, "12 Devil's Triangles-10 Vile Vortices Around the World," *12 Devil's Triangles-10 Vile Vortices Around the World* (Vortex Maps, April 27, 2008).
[47] Sharda, "Unexplained Mystery: The Devil's Sea (The Dragon's Triangle)" (Marine Insight, November 30, 2011).
[48] Ada Dimmick, "The Dragon's Triangle" (Mystery Mag-Earth Energies , April 18, 2005).
[49] Jim Kane, "UFO Bases Concealed Under Japanese Mountains? ," *Gather* (Gather.com, October 9, 2012).
[50] Ibid.

The location of an important endeavor determines much about the quality of the product or service it renders. Just as business operations rely on location as a pivotal factor for their success, so did the construction of the Wheel. As otherworldly as these planes may appear, they were made by human beings on this earth. More specifically, they were made in that region called Japan. This is not to suggest that Earth is the only planet with intelligent life because Master Fard Muhammad taught Elijah Muhammad about the life on other planets; however, he also taught that human life on earth is the most advanced in this solar system.[51] The Honorable Minister Farrakhan recalls what his teacher said in this regard:

> Now, the Honorable Elijah Muhammad said to me, "You can tell that the most intelligent life is on the earth because of the degree of experimentation. And you measure experimentation by mountains. So the mountains that were brought up on the earth are experiments that prove the high level of intelligence.[52]

Elijah Muhammad's representation of a realistic God with an earthly and heavenly workspace is consistent with the prophetic descriptions of God in the Bible and Holy Qur'an. The sacred scriptures speak of God's authority encompassing all that is within the heavens and the earth. Yet, the earth is depicted as being the natural dwelling place of a God whose power reaches throughout the universe. He is described as walking, talking, sitting, breathing, and acting in a naturally human capacity while conducting his business on earth, but he seems to conduct his heavenly activity through vessels labeled as his throne, chariot, wheels, and clouds. God, according to the Hebrew and Christian Bible states, "Thus says the LORD, The heaven is my throne, and the earth is my footstool: where is the house that you build unto me? and where is the place of my rest?"[53]

The term 'footstool' is most frequently used to suggest the dwelling place of someone, which is why the terms 'foot' and 'stool' are used. A foot is used by humans to walk or tread while a stool is an object used to sit or stand upon. So as his 'foot-stool', the earth is God's primary place of dwelling, but he expands his workspace to a more celestial position called his throne that is commonly stationed in the heavens. This Biblical description of God's operational activity is congruent with the Honorable Elijah Muhammad's teachings concerning God, his Mother Craft, and the baby planes that the world misinterprets as UFOs.

---

[51] Elijah Muhammad, "The Theology of Time (Lecture Series)," Vols. July 2, 1972 (Chicago, IL: MUHAMMAD Mosque No. 2, 1972).
[52] Louis Farrakhan, *5th Annual Educational Challenge Conference* (Chicago/Bloomingdale, IL: The Final Call, August 2, 2012).
[53] Isaiah 66:1, Acts 7:49 KJV.

UFOS IDENTIFIED BEFORE THEY BECAME A CONCERN

The Honorable Minister Farrakhan continues Muhammad's teachings concerning God's earthly dwelling:

> Before Galileo, people thought that the earth was the center of the universe. They're not wrong. It just depends on how you look at it. Now it's true that the sun is the center of the universe, but the earth is the home of God. So if the earth is the third planet from the sun, yet it is the home of God, then the most intelligent life in the universe is where God is![54]

Unsurprisingly, Astronomical Science agrees with Muhammad's teachings concerning life on earth as it relates to other planets. Scientists conclude that earth is best suited for human life due to several factors including its distance from the sun, its atmospheric surface, and of course its water.[55] [56] The Holy Qur'an offers a description of Allah (God) that is consistent with the Nation of Islam's teaching of an anthropomorphic God who operates from both an earthly and heavenly vehicle. Maulana Muhammad Ali's English translation of The Holy Qur'an reads as such:

> *And He it is Who created the heavens and the earth in six periods; and His Throne of Power is ever on water that He might manifest (the good qualities in) you whoever of you is best in deeds. And if thou sayest, You shall surely be raised up after death, those who disbelieve say: This is nothing but clear deceit. – Hud 11:7*[57]

Other English translations of this verse use the past tense, stating that Allah's throne **'was'** over the waters. If the Holy Qur'an depicts Allah's throne as over the waters, it stands to reason that his throne has an earthly base. Moreover, **over the waters** could also signify the specific part of the earth upon which his throne (the Mother Plane) was built, which was constructed in the Nipponese Islands of Japan—a geographic location that sits upon many waters. While the Islamic scholars have no clear explanation for this verse, the Honorable Elijah

---

[54] Louis Farrakhan, *5th Annual Educational Challenge Conference* (Chicago/Bloomingdale, IL: The Final Call, August 2, 2012).
[55] Clara Moskowitz, "What Makes Earth Special Compared to Other Planets," *Space.com* (Space, July 8, 2008).
[56] Brad Meltzer's Decoded, "UFO," *Brad Meltzer's Decoded*, Vol. Season 2 (History Channel, 11 30, 2011). In a public conversation with famed astronaut Story Musgrave, researcher Christine McKinley noted, "What' so interesting about earth is the atmospheric pressure, the amount of water, and how close it is to the sun. I mean all the dials are set perfectly for life…"
[57] The Holy Qur'an, Hud 11:7 English translation by Maulana Muhammad Ali.

Muhammad clearly synthesizes the wisdom of the Holy Qur'an with the practical reality that was shown to him, thereby demonstrating that his mission represents the fulfillment of prophecy.

Figure 1: WHERE IT ALL STARTED

Clockwise from top left: Japanese coast circa 1920s, Master Fard Muhammad, Detroit's Black Bottom circa 1920s, Aerial view of Japan. Center: Elijah Muhammad.

THE TIME AND WHAT WAS DONE

The time used to construct this plane took several years leading up to 1929.[58] This decades-long process began during a time when Japan was becoming the dominant power in the Far East. After successful wars against China and Russia, Japan's military and political attention was focused heavily on potential tensions with foreign powers, which served as a strategic time for

---

[58] True Islam, "The Wheel And The War Of God," in *The Book of God: An Encyclopedia of Proof that the Black Man is God* (Atlanta, GA: A-Team Publishing, 1999).

UFOS IDENTIFIED BEFORE THEY BECAME A CONCERN

Master Fard Muhammad to conduct a covert construction. This may have also proven to be a protective time and place against Western world interference as Japan became cautiously watchful of its territories against foreign invasions.

The Mother Wheel's construction was not comprehensible by all those involved in it. Only a select few, headed by Master Fard Muhammad, knew the ultimate purpose of the construction plans. Most of the builders were relegated to their respective assignments and were unaware of what the final project would yield. A project of this magnitude involved nearly two decades of specific assignments that required thousands of people working their particular tasks.

Still recognized as a technological hub of the modern world, Japan has been a pioneer for industry and technology. Several factors are believed to have contributed to Japan's growth during a time of its military and industrial prowess in the world. Arguments could be made that the intelligence involved in the Mother Ship's construction may have influenced some of the innovative thinking associated with Japan's technological progression.

Japan's advanced capabilities during WWII were enough to spark concerns from Western powers. However, their capabilities didn't just pop up; instead, it has been noted that Japan's technological growth "was built on a solid foundation of industrial technology erected during the Meiji era (1868-1912)."[59] This early part of the 20th Century was the time of Master Fard Muhammad's interactions with Japan before and during the construction of The Mother Plane. His influence in that part of the world may be heavily responsible for its awakening against Western (Caucasian) hegemony just as his presence in North America has been heavily responsible for the awakening of the darker people against White supremacy. This may very well explain why certain Japanese became intrigued with the program and position of the Honorable Elijah Muhammad in the following decades.[60]

Japan would later foreshadow an interesting role as U.S. authorities became increasingly concerned about Elijah Muhammad's teachings in the early 1940s. While he was teaching an unorthodox style of Islam that included these never-before-seen planes, America was in an intense conflict with Japan after the 1941 bombing of Pearl Harbor. Muhammad's bold and controversial

---

[59] National Museum of Nature and Science, "Center of the History of Japanese Industrial Technology" (2008).

[60] **The Japanese Interview**: A recording of The Honorable Elijah Muhammad being interviewed by the Japanese press covering a variety of topics during the 1960s or 1970s. The Japanese press demonstrated tremendous interest and curiosity in the program, position, and theology of The Honorable Elijah Muhammad and the Nation of Islam. This famous interview can be widely viewed from various online and media sources.

teaching about the supreme power that backs him ultimately prompted the U.S. Government to step in and arrest him. As a son of former slaves encouraging Black people not to fight for their former slave masters (the White-based U.S. Government) against their own Asian brothers and sisters, his teachings and growing influence were not the only things that alerted authorities. The Messenger's Asian-like physical features drew even more suspicion about his alliances and support. While Messenger Muhammad always held that he was backed by the power of Allah who came in the person of Master Fard Muhammad, the U.S. Government obviously took him seriously enough to know that he was backed by an unexplained intelligent power. Whether that power was Master Fard Muhammad or whether it was from Japan, the American Government did not take any chances. During a heated conflict with Japan and just after a momentous encounter with UFOs, the U.S. Government arrested Elijah Muhammad without a trial or formal charge in May of 1942.

1929 TAKE OFF

The year that the Wheel actually launched from the earth's atmosphere was in 1929. America and the world were heavily affected by a global economic Depression that occupied most of the attention of the industrialized world. Japan, however, was minimally impacted by this condition as the tiny island-based nation was heavily involved with exports.[61] It is uncertain what factors allowed Japan not to be as affected by the Depression as other nations, but the timing could not have been better for a massive plane (with its smaller ships) to lift off virtually unnoticed by the world.

Interestingly, there were no massive reports of UFOs of this measure or characteristics until after 1929. This is not to say that there were no strange occurrences of unexplained activities in the sky before then, but the type of wheel-like crafts that have constituted the bulk of UFO sightings did not occur until after the 1929 launching. The photographs, widespread sightings, widespread reports, and common characteristics attributed to the modern UFO phenomenon all began to happen afterwards. **Outside of Master Fard Muhammad and his host of workers, Elijah Muhammad was virtually the only person on earth with this foreknowledge and is on record for having taught this reality before they were commonly witnessed by the world.** Having accurate foreknowledge of these unfathomable realities cannot be a

---

[61] Mother Earth Travel, "History of Japan Between the Wars, 1920-36," *From Area Handbook of the US Library of Congress* (Mother Earth Travel © 2000-2011, 2000).

UFOS IDENTIFIED BEFORE THEY BECAME A CONCERN

mere coincidence; Elijah Muhammad must have been the recipient of divine revelation.

The Honorable Minister Louis Farrakhan notes, "This human-built planet went up in 1929, the same year of the Stock Market crash."[62] It has been suggested that the launching of this plane had a direct correlation with the stock market crash that led into the Great Depression—an economic downfall that affected most of the Western industrialized nations. Peter Goldman gives his account of the Black Muslims' theology in his biography on Malcolm X: "The stock-market crash in 1929 was caused by some rich men who saw a UFO rising out of the Pacific—the Mother Plane."[63] Economists and historians often differ concerning the exact reasons for the stock market crash, although many theories center around the fact that several key investors abruptly sold their stock and got out of the market. The suggestion that certain wealthy men witnessed an apocalyptic craft and frantically abandoned the market may very well be a valid cause since records show that several investors suddenly extricated themselves from the market during the October 1929 crash.

Imagine how absurd it must have seemed to teach about these highly advanced spacecraft in the 1930s before UFO sightings began to emerge. Consider the limited technological discoveries of that era and how difficult it would have been for people to grasp the concept of mobile phones or rockets being sent to the moon. This was a time when most people did not own a black and white television in their homes. An era recovering from an economic Depression where major manufacturers had closed their doors may have been a difficult time to believe that super-advanced spacecraft had just been created. For a former sharecropper from Georgia to boast that he was taught by Allah (God) and given this data before any mass sightings occurred proves that Elijah Muhammad had access to the most privy knowledge that no other power in the world had. This proves he was taught by an out-of-this-world power!

A MASTERPIECE OF MECHANICS

Elijah Muhammad gave straightforward information about the wisdom, power, and authority behind the work of the objects that have now become termed UFOs:

---

[62] Louis Farrakhan, "The Wheel," *The Time And What Must Be Done Lecture Series* (Chicago, IL: Mosque Maryam, March 7, 2010).
[63] Peter Goldman, *The Death and Life of Malcolm X* (IL: Univ. of Illinois Press, 10/01/1972).

The Mother Plane and her work is a display of the power of the mightiest God, Master Fard Muhammad, to Whom praises are due forever. Master Fard Muhammad, to Whom praises are due forever, is the Wisest and Best Knower; He is the Mightiest of Them All.[64]

Master Fard Muhammad was at the helm of a project unlike any ever seen since the creation of the planets. According to Messenger Muhammad, Allah (God) used 25,000 of the best minds from around the globe in the development of this massive project. Muhammad also explained that a project of this magnitude was done in somewhat isolated capacities. The majority of those working on this project had no idea they were constructing what would later become labeled UFOs.

Messenger Muhammad writes, "The cost to build such a plane is staggering!"[65] The amount used to finance this feat involved 150 million dollars in gold at the time. Much of this heavy financing came from certain people in Mecca.[66] The fact that gold was used as opposed to fiat money may have been a factor why Japan was not as affected by the *Depression* that affected much of the industrialized world. Having a price tag associated with the construction of this plane also demystifies the 'otherworldly' element that has commonly been attributed to UFOs. This dollar amount would be considered overwhelmingly astronomical even by contemporary standards. The gold-based funding of this clandestine project may further indicate how it was effectively arranged during the eve of a worldwide economic Depression.

How did Master Fard Muhammad acquire all those people and all that gold? It stands to reason that any man who can successfully develop such interstellar spacecraft (as witnessed by millions) can summon the resources to construct it. Those crafts didn't just pop up by happenstance. Instead, the development of those crafts required precise mathematics and science beyond the intelligence of this world. If Master Fard Muhammad could take a non-educated drunkard and make him become the most powerful Black Man in America despite opposition from world powers, it stands to reason that he can cultivate the best qualities from the people of the earth. If Elijah Muhammad's God can equip him with knowledge that has left the most intelligent scholars dumbfounded, then certainly he is wise enough to acquire the resources to accomplish a major engineering project.

---

[64] Elijah Muhammad, *The Fall Of America* (Chicago, IL: Elijah Muhammad, 1973). 241.
[65] Elijah Muhammad, *MESSAGE TO THE BLACKMAN In America*, Original Published by MUHAMMAD'S Temple No. 2 in Chicago 1965 (Chicago, IL: The Final Call Inc., 1965). 291.
[66] Jabril Muhammad, "The Wheel" (Los Angeles, CA, September 18, 1985).

UFOS IDENTIFIED BEFORE THEY BECAME A CONCERN

Master Fard Muhammad left his Messenger, the Honorable Elijah Muhammad, with certain lessons that expressed these words: "The Righteous Nation is now, Living in every part of the planet Earth."[67] This small sentence is indicative that people of tremendous capabilities and untold resources can be found throughout the earth and only someone with a supreme knowledge can utilize humans and resources to such a high degree. The daunting task of assembling 25,000 of the best minds could only be done by someone possessing the most comprehensive knowledge of the earth, its resources, and its talents. A person capable of this could be considered the *best knower*.

The Messenger publicly wrote about some of the advanced science exuded on the Wheel in these words, "The Mother Plane is capable of staying out of the earth's gravity for a whole year. She is capable of producing her own sphere of oxygen and hydrogen, as any other planet is able to do."[68] The mechanics of this man-made planet permit it to create its own atmosphere much like the earth, providing an entirely new civilization on it that is unaffected by the troubles of this world—a utopian society that houses the personage of God. Muhammad stated, "You will see this plane one day, because it has a civilization on it. They stay up there a year and sometimes a year and a half in that plane. It's a wonderful thing. Dreadful looking plane."[69] This civilization encompasses people, food, vegetation, water, animals, and other life forms. Whatever is on earth is up there with the exception of the corruption, diseases, madness and frivolity that consumes this present world. The answers and solutions for all the earth's problems exist on this Mother Wheel.

It is a small living planet and as such, it creates its own atmosphere much like the earth that travels in its sphere at a rate of 1037 and 1/3 miles per hour.[70] Yet the life on this planet is not disarrayed by the force of its speed, nor is human life even mildly agitated by the planet traveling through space at such speeds. This is because of the atmospheric force field protecting it. Similarly, the God of the Wheel created a living entity permitting a smooth ride for the life that occupies it—this is technology that continues to baffle scientists who study this reality. The God of Elijah Muhammad made manifest that vehicle

---

[67] The Supreme Wisdom, "Instructions Given To The Laborers By Master Fard Muhammad," *THE SUPREME WISDOM* (Detroit, MI: The Nation Of Islam, 1930-1934).

[68] Elijah Muhammad, *The Fall Of America* (Chicago, IL: Elijah Muhammad, 1973). 240.

[69] Elijah Muhammad, "The Theology of Time (Lecture Series)," Vols. July 2, 1972 (Chicago, IL: MUHAMMAD Mosque No. 2, 1972).

[70] The Supreme Wisdom, "Actual Facts," *THE SUPREME WISDOM* (Detroit, MI: The Nation Of Islam, 1930-1934).

prophesied in the Book of Ezekiel. "Ezekiel saw wheels in the middle of a wheel. This is true (the universe in the universe; it is made up of revolving spheres). There are wheels in the wheel"[71] he said.

Knowing the superior technology of the wheels, some scientists give their own hypothesis based on what the Messenger already gave the world, although they give no reference to the man who presented this truth. One observer gives his characterization about the supreme mechanical capabilities of the wheels using these familiar terms, "part of the propulsion system of the spacecraft he went on involved a "wheel within a wheel," the principal process by which they derived their motive power."[72]

THE BABY PLANES

Messenger Muhammad spoke of the numerous smaller planes that often accompany the larger Mother Plane. These smaller wheel-like crafts make up the bulk of the circular-shaped UFO sightings that take place all over the world. Muhammad observed, "The small circular made planes called flying saucers, which are so much talked of being seen, could be from this Mother Plane."[73] The baby planes, as they are often called, have many of the same characteristics of the Mother Craft. They move at terrific speeds unknown to this world. They maneuver in unfathomable ways. They can exhibit enormous power, intelligence, and capabilities resulting from the intelligence that controls each plane.

Since the Honorable Elijah Muhammad had a direct relationship with the intelligence on those crafts, one cannot disassociate these crafts from their divine and prophetic purpose. Muhammad taught that these planes are tools of Allah (God) that will be used to execute his judgment as the prophecies indicate. The Bible reads that God would be seen upon his heavenly throne with his hosting army beside him. One verse reads, "And he said, Hear thou therefore the word of the Lord: I saw the Lord sitting on his throne, and all the host of heaven standing by him on his right hand and on his left."[74]

The prophecies continuously predict that God would use his many instruments to destroy the wicked powers of the world, especially those powers

---

[71] Elijah Muhammad, *MESSAGE TO THE BLACKMAN In America*, Original Published by MUHAMMAD'S Temple No 2 in Chicago 1965 (Chicago, IL: The Final Call Inc., 1965). 290.
[72] Timothy Good, *Earth: An Alien Enterprise: The Shocking Truth Behind the Greatest Cover-Up in Human History* (Pegasus, 2013). 89.
[73] Elijah Muhammad, *MESSAGE TO THE BLACKMAN In America*, Original Published by MUHAMMAD'S Temple No. 2 in Chicago 1965 (Chicago, IL: The Final Call Inc., 1965). 291.
[74] 1 Kings 22:19.

that oppress his chosen people. Messenger Muhammad audaciously preached that this is the same power that supports him:

> It's there in your Bible in Revelation. God was angry. The Lamb was angry. Everybody was angry, because the war of the devils were against God and His Messenger. God and His Messenger were both angry. I'm angry now and ready to fight. This is why I'm here. I come out alone. I don't have any armies with me. My few followers are very weak, they have no arms. If they follow me to my God, they have perfect arms. Arms that don't miss.[75]

The Nation of Islam teaches that these smaller planes serve as divine tools of a real God. Minister Farrakhan reiterates Muhammad's teachings concerning the power of God's Wheel:

> The Wheel is there to destroy the United States of America at the command of God. Why is God angry with America? It's because of you [Black people]. Why did God destroy Pharaoh? He was angry with Pharaoh over Pharaoh's mistreatment of the Children of Israel. Allah is angry over America's mistreatment of the Black man and woman of America who are His people![76]

Although *benevolence* and *peaceful* are the most evangelized aspect of God's character, the scriptures of the Bible more frequently depict God in a lovingly **warlike** mode. He is the author of love, yet his deep love for his people would bring his divine wrath against those who oppress his people. The God of the Bible is frequently shown to have armies that accompany him upon his heavenly throne in the sky. There are nearly 300 occurrences where God is called *Jehovah Tsaba'* (the Lord of Hosts) in the Bible. The representation of the word *host* in these passages refers to masses of persons, especially organized for war.[77] Thus, he is literally the Lord of Armies. Any Bible believer and critical thinker must ask, "Why does God need armies if he is already the all-powerful God?" The Honorable Elijah Muhammad answered this question through his teachings. Muhammad demystified the traditional concepts of God as a formless, shapeless, spirit; instead, his real-life God demonstrates a practical deity who can address the real issues of a real world and real people.

---

[75] Elijah Muhammad, "The Theology of Time (Lecture Series)," Vols. July 9, 1972 (Chicago, IL: MUHAMMAD Mosque No. 2, 1972).

[76] Louis Farrakhan, "The Time And What Must Be Done: The Great War," *Part 2 of the 2010 Saviours' Day Lecture delivered by The Honorable Louis Farrakhan* (Chicago, IL: The Final Call, March 14, 2010).

[77] **Lord of Hosts** (Jehovah Tsaba'/Sabaoth) from the Hebrew (צְבָאוֹת) meaning army, war, warfare, i.e. The Lord of Armies.

Elijah Muhammad acquainted the modern world with a God who would use realistic means, methods, and resources to address real issues. Such a pragmatic ideology distinguishes his Nation of Islam from virtually all religious traditions and it allows his teachings to be approached in a scientific and scholarly manner.

The plight of the Black man and woman's sojourn through chattel slavery is a realistic trauma that cannot be solved by fictitious means. The horrendous wars that take place throughout the world killing millions cannot be expected to go away by a pipe dream. Real problems in a real world require realistic solutions that only a realistic God can address. The God of the Honorable Elijah Muhammad, the Honorable Minister Louis Farrakhan, and the Nation of Islam proves to be such a deity! It is this God in person who fulfills the prophetic depictions of a corporeal God who would use tangible weaponry to protect his chosen people from their wicked captors.

If the God of traditional religions has been depicted as using strange celestial vessels to accomplish his will, then the fulfillment should come to no surprise to anyone who really believes these prophecies. As the Nation of Islam propagates, these wheel-like planes will be used to execute God's inevitable destruction against a wicked world. As the Lord of Host today, Master Fard Muhammad's baby planes that accompany his Mother Wheel represent a major part of this divinely prophesied army.

THOSE BABIES CARRY BOMBS!

According to the NOI, the baby planes from that Mother Wheel carry the most powerful weaponry that will be used to bring down the powers of this present world. At a certain point in time, the wheels will release bombs into strategic parts of the earth that will demolish everything within a certain radius. Minister Farrakhan states, "That Wheel has been up there since 1929 and it has bothered nobody!"[78] The destructive potential of these wheels has yet to be demonstrated because of the grace period alloted for warning to be heard and for the people to adhere to either good or evil. The Satanic forces and powers of the world, particularly America, are expected to receive the deathblow of this fate. This is why the Bible speaks of a lake of fire, not the entire earth. The lake of fire refers to a particular geographic location that will receive the brunt of God's chastisement:

---

[78] Louis Farrakhan, "The Time And What Must Be Done," *Saviours' Day 2010 Keynote Address by The Honorable Minister Louis Farrakhan* (Chicago, IL: The Final Call, February 28, 2010).

UFOS IDENTIFIED BEFORE THEY BECAME A CONCERN

God has taught me, so thorough, about the knowledge of the devil that I'm not afraid to tell him to go jump in the lake. A very fiery lake is being built for him, not a lake of water, but a lake of fire. According to the teaching of Allah to me, North America is that lake of fire. Not lake Michigan, but the lake is on the Earth of North America. The atoms will be exploded and set a fire.[79]

Since the American powers dealt the most horrendous *deathblow* to God's people, America will be the utmost recipient of these bombs, especially since American powers have been relentlessly unwilling to atone for their inherent wrongs. Minister Farrakhan makes this position poignantly clear:

> The Wheel is there to destroy the United States of America at the command of God. Why is God angry with America? It's because of you [Black people]. Why did God destroy Pharaoh? He was angry with Pharaoh over Pharaoh's mistreatment of the Children of Israel. Allah is angry over America's mistreatment over the Black man and woman of America who are His people![80]

The 1500 baby planes are bombing planes. Messenger Muhammad was given vivid descriptions about the bombs contained on each plane and how they will be used. The following excerpts contain some of the information regarding the bombing capabilities of these wheels:

> When it flies over the place where it's going to drop bombs out of it, he sends one of the small planes. Then it drops a bomb out of that plane onto the earth. That bomb that he drops has a bomb inside of it. He has in that bomb a thing made like an earth drill, like you see people drilling out here in the streets. He has that type, but it's so much more powerful. It comes down from this plane, drops it on the earth and when it strikes the Earth, a motor goes off in it which takes this bomb into the earth a mile before she explodes. That bomb has a steel drill that batters and won't stop until it drills a mile. At that depth, the explosion goes off. One hundred percent dynamite is used in it.[81]

> The Plane is to drop bombs which would automatically be timed to burrow quickly to a position of one mile below the surface of the earth where they are

---

[79] Elijah Muhammad, "The Theology of Time (Lecture Series)," Vols. August 20, 1972 (Chicago, IL: MUHAMMAD Mosque No. 2, 1972).
[80] Louis Farrakhan, "The Time And What Must Be Done: The Great War," *Part 2 of the 2010 Saviours' Day Lecture delivered by The Honorable Louis Farrakhan* (Chicago, IL: The Final Call, March 14, 2010).
[81] Elijah Muhammad, "The Theology of Time (Lecture Series)," Vols. July 2, 1972 (Chicago, IL: MUHAMMAD Mosque No. 2, 1972).

> timed to explode. Allah (God) taught me that these bombs are not to be dropped into water. They are to be dropped only on the cities.[82]

The bombs, like the planes themselves, are comprised of the toughest steel, the likes of which are unknown to the scientists and engineers of the present world. Minister Farrakhan comments on the material of the plane, the bombs, and the drills thereof:

> The steel [on the drill] is not known to this world. It's the same steel that's in those wheels. It is not known to this world and if you read anything that the white man writes on Unidentified Flying Objects, they talk about a *steel* that they've never seen anything like it before.[83]

The knowledge of how to develop such weaponry and explosions has been deliberately sequestered from this world. The Honorable Elijah Muhammad noted that the original Black man used similar capabilities millions of years ago throughout the earth:

> Allah taught me that that the same type of bomb that God used to make mountains on the earth; it's the same thing. It goes into the earth with a very powerful steel motor like an air hammer. The bomb digs out nothing, it just sucks itself right into the earth like an air hammer. It chisels down into the earth. Yet, its' timed not to explode until it gets a mile into the earth.[84]

In related lectures, Muhammad added more details regarding the present wheels' roles in the divine destruction of America:

> This plane carries 1,500 of these small bombing planes. Each one of the bombing planes carries three bombs, and will take these bombs over a designated area, dropping them for covering and destroying 150 miles where they're dropped.[85]

Although America is expected to receive the brunt of this chastisement, her cohorts are said to share some of this fate, especially England. The following week after the aforementioned statement, the Messenger shared more details regarding this predicted ordeal:

---

[82] Elijah Muhammad, *The Fall Of America* (Chicago, IL: Elijah Muhammad, 1973). 239.
[83] Louis Farrakhan, "The Shock of The Hour" (Chicago, IL: The Final Call, April 26, 1992).
[84] Elijah Muhammad, "The Theology of Time (Lecture Series)," Vols. July 2, 1972 (Chicago, IL: MUHAMMAD Mosque No. 2, 1972).
[85] Ibid.

UFOS IDENTIFIED BEFORE THEY BECAME A CONCERN

They will go a height over North America and will drop off these bombs. They will save three of these bombs to drop on England. It will only take just three of them to rip England apart. I'm not trying to frighten you to believe, that's immaterial to me. I'm only telling you what was told to me by God to tell you, before these things take place. The plane will make one trip across America and drop her bombs and when she drops one, she knows the distance of which the explosion will take affect, then three of these planes will be sent to the British Island to take care of England. Believe in what I'm saying or wait around a few days.[86]

Muhammad's firsthand relationship with these flying objects is largely responsible for the surety he exudes. His connection to such a powerful force is responsible for making him the most powerful Black man in America. Conventional wisdom cannot explain how the unarmed and seemingly inarticulate Muhammad could rise to such stature in light of his overwhelming opposition. With nothing more than a truth from his mouth, the Honorable Elijah Muhammad reached incomparable success that could not have been attained through explainable means. Knowing the truth behind Elijah Muhammad's connection to the UFO phenomenon, the American Government and its cohorts are very aware of the divine warnings that have been voiced by the Nation of Islam. It is for this reason that the powers of this world have taken extremely calculated precautions on how they deal with Elijah Muhammad, Louis Farrakhan, and the Nation of Islam.

---

[86] Elijah Muhammad, "The Theology of Time (Lecture Series)," Vols. July 9, 1972 (Chicago, IL: MUHAMMAD Mosque No. 2, 1972).

3. NOT JUST ORDINARY PEOPLE

UFOS AND THE NATION OF ISLAM AFFILIATION

The Messenger gave specific details regarding the common characteristics of the wheels such as their bombs, maneuvering capabilities, their intelligence and purposes, but he did not suggest that the baby planes looked exactly alike nor did he mention that they were all the same size. Hence, it could be that some of the wheels may have slightly different qualities. As far as size goes, it can be deduced from the Messenger's teachings that the baby planes are smaller than the Mother Wheel and that they have circular shapes. With that as a criterion, these planes may possibly be of varying styles. This may explain why thousands of yearly reported sightings describe slightly varying sizes of disc-shaped UFOs. Depending on the position of the observer, these planes may appear to be flat disc-like planes, round globe-like orbs, oblong cigar-like spheres, and dome-shaped crafts. The common factor among these objects is that they all reflect wheel-like shapes. This does not include other aircraft and aerial objects that have been confused with the wheels.

    Just as different automobile manufacturers produce different styles of the same automobile, they all still have some basic commonalities: wheels, steering devices, gears, etc. Likewise, the baby planes could possibly have varying styles and sizes, but they all reflect the work of the divine Supreme Being. Moreover, the Messenger spoke of the Wheel as a living entity. In fact, he stated, "This wheel corresponds in a way with the sphere of spheres called the universe."[87] He added that like the universe, "it is made up of revolving spheres."[88] Since the universe is ever-moving and constantly producing, this comparison gives a strong indication that the supremely advanced technology of those wheel is a living entity itself. As indicated, many of the photographs and videos of these wheels have shown characteristics of living vessels. They have been seen pulsating, communicating, and moving intelligently as living organisms. This masterpiece of mechanics reflects that majestic attributes of the God who created it.

---

[87] Elijah Muhammad, *MESSAGE TO THE BLACKMAN In America*, Original Published by MUHAMMAD'S Temple No. 2 in Chicago 1965 (Chicago, IL: The Final Call Inc., 1965). 290.
[88] Ibid.

NOT JUST ORDINARY PEOPLE

Figure 2: WHEELS OF TIME

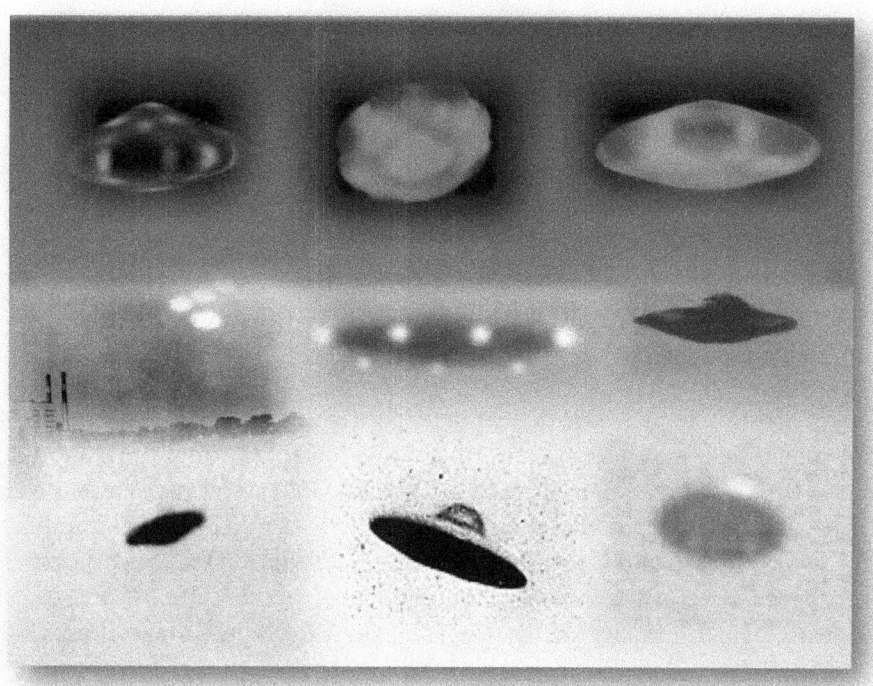

Top row: Luminous UFO wheels photographed by Carlos Diaz
Middle row: Luminous UFOs in Salem, MA 1952 by the U.S. Coast Guard, UFO filmed in China August 8, 2006, & UFO photographed in Russia, 1965.
Bottom row: UFO pictured from 1940s, an amateur photo of a UFO in Passoria, NJ July 31, 1952, & UFO photographed circa 1950-1960s.

While the planes represented by the Nation of Islam account for much of the UFO activities throughout the world, many other alleged UFO beliefs don't constitute the plane brought into the world by Master Fard Muhammad. There is no doubt that much of the claimed UFO activities are pranks, media manipulation, commercial and military aircraft, and other unexplained items. As far as those other unexplained occurrences and objects that have been reported, the NOI does not speak for them. The numerous hoaxes, computer generated images (CGI), and strange flight craft produced by other entities are not what the Messenger and his followers refer to when they speak of the Mother Wheel and its smaller planes.

Just as rockets, space shuttles, and space programs have certain affiliations with organizations and states, so do the so-called UFOs. The wheel-like crafts, as represented by the Honorable Elijah Muhammad, have a special affiliation. They are not the products of NASA's space programs (although NASA frequently records the activities of these planes). They are not a part of any government's military of this world (although defense initiatives have attempted to imitate the likeness of these planes). The so-called UFOs that Muhammad's described are affiliated with the Nation of Islam (NOI) and the righteous people of the earth. This is not to suggest that every plane is relegated to the daily activities of the NOI; it does however, suggest that the NOI is guided and protected by the wisdom upon those planes. After all, there is a vast Universe that has to be tended to. There is life on other planets that requires Allah's maintenance as well. In the Holy Qur'an Allah (God) is called the Lord of all the worlds (Rabbi l-ʿāl-Amīn).[89] As such, his divine wisdom is not limited to any particular country nor is he limited to the earth, but it should be noted that these planes have an intrinsic connection to the Nation of Islam and its leadership.

Most ufologists have deliberately ignored the source of the modern UFO phenomenon. There are many others who blatantly omit the Nation of Islam's direct connection to this reality. Several UFO researchers have turned a deaf ear to the firsthand knowledge of these crafts shared by the Honorable Elijah Muhammad and his servant, Minister Farrakhan. This is a common propaganda strategy that attempts to *separate the message from the messenger*. No reasonable thinker would disassociate Moses from the Torah or Jesus from the Gospel. It would be irrational to do so. To separate the NOI's connection with the UFO phenomenon would be as fallacious as disassociating the Prophet Muhammad from the Holy Qur'an.

UFO PILOTS

The baby planes are piloted by wise scientists who have been taught and trained since very young ages under the tutelage of Allah (God). Those scientists who control the planes act at the behest of Master Fard Muhammad to execute his will. According to the Honorable Elijah Muhammad's teachings, these scientists are what the scriptures describe as angels. He exclaimed in regard to the piloting angels aboard the wheels, **"These are not spooks. They are men!"**[90] Unlike common notions of angelic beings, Muhammad's representation of angels offer a more pragmatic concept of something that religion has mystified. Angels are not spirits or figments with wings emerging from their backs as has often been depicted. The angels are real people who have access to special wisdom, resources, and capabilities that are unbeknown

---

[89] Al-Fatihah 1:2.
[90] Elijah Muhammad, "The Theology of Time (Lecture Series)," Vols. July 9, 1972 (Chicago, IL: MUHAMMAD Mosque No. 2, 1972).

to the present world. In his insightful book *The Fall of America*, Elijah Muhammad clarified the meaning of the *four living creatures* who inhabit Ezekiel's wheel:

> Ezekiel saw great work going on in the wheel and four living creatures "and their work was as it were a wheel in the middle of a wheel." (Ez. 1:16). And when the living creatures went, the wheels went with them: and when the living creatures were lifted up from the earth, the wheels, were lifted up Ez. 1:19. The power of the lifting up of the four creatures was in the wheel. The four creatures represents the four colors of the original people of the earth.[91]

The people who occupy and maneuver the wheels are comprised of the darker original people of the earth, which does not seem to include Caucasians. This is not to suggest that the darker inhabitants may not have light-skin. After all, the creator of the Wheel himself is a white-skinned Black man—Master Fard Muhammad. It was he who illustrated the meaning of these *four creatures* to the Honorable Elijah Muhammad. They are the human occupants of the wheels. Many of them have a personal relationship with the Honorable Elijah Muhammad. During his famous Theology of Time Lecture series, the Messenger shared some of the prophetic roles that these angels have regarding his mission:

> There was two of that type of people visiting my home. They both look like brothers. Whenever there is a God-raised man or prophet to do a big job, these type of scientist visits him to assure him of their friendship—that whenever the right time comes, they will be with him. "We will take care of you". These are the type of Scientists that you read of in the Bible who wanted to go forth and do this and another one do that. These are the ones I'm telling you about, who visited me at my home ... These are the type of men I'm speaking of. I know them and they know me.[92]

Throughout his teachings, Muhammad often uses the term *scientist* interchangeably with *angel*. In other cases, he has used related terms like '*wise scientist*' to refer to the personage of Allah (God). His categorization of the angels as scientists indicates the practicality of their work. This offers a sobering contrast to the popular winged creatures that many people have

---

[91] Elijah Muhammad, *The Fall Of America* (Chicago, IL: Elijah Muhammad, 1973). 238.
[92] Elijah Muhammad, "The Theology of Time (Lecture Series)," Vols. July 9, 1972 (Chicago, IL: MUHAMMAD Mosque No. 2, 1972).

associated with angels. He explained that they are people like us. "**Those in this plane you may see look like us here**"[93] explained the Messenger.

Moreover, the *scientists/angels* that maneuver the baby planes have unique characteristics that make them a force that no power in this present world can contend with. The pilots of the wheels are advantageously powerful and intelligent because of their access to information that is intentionally unavailable to this world. Master Fard Muhammad revealed to Elijah Muhammad that only one out of sixty-thousand books of higher wisdom was allotted for the operation of this present world.[94] There are another 59,999 books of higher wisdom and mathematics that would not be offered to the people until after the destruction of this wicked world. The Messenger reiterates this point in *The Fall Of America*:

> The knowledge and power of this world's life (white race) is limited. The world of the white man was made from what he found and what he has seen and learned from the work of the original Black man. The white race is far from being able to equal the power and wisdom of the original Black man.[95]

The wheel-like spacecrafts did not appear out of nowhere; nor did the pilots who maneuver them. Instead, they are real human beings from this earth. Although they are human beings, they possess knowledge and capabilities far beyond the norm of this world. The pilots of the wheels were taught since very young ages to perform their divine roles. Although their physical appearances are basically like other humans, they do not think or feel as regular people because they operate from a totally different paradigm. They have different experiences, training, and diet that make their countenance unlike the average person. They are not titillated or stimulated by the appetites and urges that normal people in this world are affected by. The feelings they convey reflect their reverence for the Supreme Being[96] and their anticipation to execute destruction upon America's evil influence throughout the world. These are the people, not aliens or extraterrestrials, who operate these divine crafts.

---

[93] Elijah Muhammad, "The Theology of Time (Lecture Series)," Vols. July 2, 1972 (Chicago, IL: MUHAMMAD Mosque No. 2, 1972).

[94] The Supreme Wisdom, "Instructions Given To The Laborers By Master Fard Muhammad," *THE SUPREME WISDOM* (Detroit, MI: The Nation Of Islam, 1930-1934). Problem #25.

[95] Elijah Muhammad, *The Fall Of America* (Chicago, IL: Elijah Muhammad, 1973). 239.

[96] See *The Holy Qur'an*. There are several verses that depict the angels showing reverence and praise to their Lord: Ar-Ra`d 13:13, Az-Zumar 39:75, and Ash-Shura 42:5 to name a few.

NOT JUST ORDINARY PEOPLE

BE CAREFUL WHO YOU'RE ENTERTAINING, IT MIGHT BE A UFO PILOT

The sacred scriptures depict angels in a humanly, yet superbly advanced manner. They walk, talk and eat, yet they have the power to summon the elements of nature. Consider the angels who accompanied the Lord God in the plains of Mamre when meeting with Abraham (Genesis Chapter 18). Both the angels and God are clearly **anthropomorphic**[97] in this passage, yet these same human angels were responsible for the destruction that brought down Sodom and Gomorrah (Genesis 19). Though human, they seem to have capabilities that allow them to do magnificent things such as manipulate different elements of nature: wind, rain, earth, and fire. Other characterizations of these angels show them to have telepathic insight, whereas they can read and foresee the thoughts of other men without physical communication. The Honorable Minister Farrakhan has frequently discussed some of the intrinsic powers of the angels in these words, "Those people are the angels. They are up there. They know what you think and before you can execute, they know it. These are the people from God!"[98]

Perhaps one of the most common characterizations of angels depicts them possessing the ability of flight. Both the Bible and the Holy Qur'an illustrate the angels in a heavenly position, often as attendants to God's heavenly throne. The scriptures give beautifully symbolic descriptions of God's flight, but it doesn't give clarity on the specific means by which God and the angels travel throughout the sky. Thus, a whole world of religion has been left confused about God, the angels, and their means of flight. This confusion has led many religious believers to accept some of the most asinine beliefs about angelic beings as in the winged cupid-like images. Fortunately, the Honorable Elijah Muhammad and the Nation of Islam have been shown the meaning behind these prophetic symbols. Even for those who don't subscribe to the Nation of Islam's theology, those who study scriptures would have to agree that **GOD AND THE ANGELS RIDE SOMETHING IN THE SKY!**

Aside from their activities from above, the angels play a significant role on the earth and throughout America. Being that they are scientists who look like any other person, there is virtually no way of knowing who they are. There are many of these persons inconspicuously functioning throughout America and the world. Messenger Muhammad pointed out that they all have a certain

---

[97] **anthropomorphic:** *adj.* having human form or characteristics.
[98] Louis Farrakhan, "The Time And What Must Be Done," *Saviours' Day 2010 Keynote Address by The Honorable Minister Louis Farrakhan* (Chicago, IL: The Final Call, February 28, 2010).

job to do. Just as honeybees perform different roles at different times for the ultimate good of their colony, so do the scientists/angels. Whether they work directly from the wheels or as functioning people in society, they all work for the divine good of Allah (God) who came in the person of Master Fard Muhammad. Having personal relationships with many of them, the Honorable Elijah Muhammad spoke about these people and their ubiquitous presence throughout the world. "There is nothing strange about a few scientists—one or two maybe in here, but you'd never know it"[99] he said.

Like the wheels, the scientists may have their unique qualities. Some may be short and others tall. They may have dark features, while some may be very light-skinned. Like Master Fard Muhammad, some may appear white-looking. These qualities can allow them to be inconspicuously present within various social systems of the world. Master Fard Muhammad's appearance served as a fitting disguise for him to fulfill his own mission. He was said to have resided and conducted much of his business among whites who had absolutely no idea who he was. Similarly, some of the angels may very well utilize these stealth-type qualities. According to Mother Tynnetta Muhammad (wife of the Honorable Elijah Muhammad), Master Fard Muhammad informed his Messenger that there were even some of the scientists planted within the movie industry.[100]

There is no aspect of the modern world that Allah (God) and his angels are not aware of. The most declassified covert thoughts cannot remain hidden from this type of intelligence. With this in mind, people are urged to take certain precautions when dealing with people unless they are willing to make the dangerous mistake of mistreating an *angel of death*. Some of the angels, especially those who maneuver the wheels, have been prepared for the primary purpose of destroying America's powers. They can be considered some of the *death angels* the scriptures speak of (like the ones who destroyed Sodom and Gomorrah). Perhaps this is why the Bible gives warnings that many people have unknowingly entertained angels.[101]

The people aboard the so-called UFOs are the people whom Messenger Muhammad identified as the angels. Knowing the superior power behind Elijah Muhammad, Louis Farrakhan, and the Nation of Islam, governments and militaries have reasons to be concerned. Knowing the evil treatment that America has consistently done to Master Fard Muhammad's chosen people is just one of many reasons why the authorities of this world view UFO activity in an antagonistic light. Even though these planes have not enacted any of their deadly capabilities yet, the American Government is well aware that those

---

[99] Elijah Muhammad, "The Theology of Time (Lecture Series)," Vols. July 2, 1972 (Chicago, IL: MUHAMMAD Mosque No. 2, 1972).
[100] Tynnetta Muhammad, "Minister Farrakhan's Vision-like Experience on the Wheel is Real," *The Final Call* (July 11, 2011).
[101] Hebrews 13:2.

planes are from a power far beyond the reach of any power of the conventional world. Fully aware of his divine support, the Messenger boldly writes, "The white man has learned that this is not a plane to be played with. Planes come out of the Mother Plane."[102]

NO GREYS, MAYBE GREY SUITS

Since the UFO Phenomenon became more popularized, the media portrayals of the beings associated with UFOs have often been portrayed as little greenish-grey men with small slender frames, large heads, and huge dark eyes that would reflect something other than human. These features have become heavily engrained in the minds of the American public as it relates to UFO occupants. These inhuman portrayals are frequently conveyed by the mainstream media for numerous reasons. Since UFO related information is considered 'above top secret' by the U.S. Intelligence Agencies, it behooves them to deter the public from information that proves there is a power much greater than all their military forces combined. Therefore, the media, acting as an arm of U.S. Intelligence, frequently spins and twists information about UFOs, its pilots, and its reality in order to sway the public. This is one of the primary reasons for the frequent portrayals of little greenish-grey aliens that have now become dubbed the ***greys***[103] among ufologists.

While practically all of the credible UFO witnesses and abductees have described the inhabitants of these crafts as human beings, there are some that reported humanoid characteristics that resemble the qualities of the commonly depicted greys. This research does not speak for those claimants who try to relegate UFO technology to aliens, greys, or other concoctions that cannot be proven.

If there is credibility to what appears to be alien features of UFO pilots, there is a possibility that those features are actually the result of certain outfits or uniforms. Since the Wheel is capable of creating its own atmosphere, this man-made planet can practically travel anywhere in space it wants. It stands to reason that the humans aboard these crafts where clothing as other civilized persons do. There is a vague possibility that the outfits worn by these people could be purposely mistaken for so-called greys. After all, many abduction cases and researchers have described the UFO occupants as humans with

---

[102] Elijah Muhammad, *The Fall Of America* (Chicago, IL: Elijah Muhammad, 1973). 237.

[103] The term ***greys*** refers to the portrayed extraterrestrial beings that have become associated with UFOs in popular culture.

grayish uniforms and outfits. Moreover, it is documented that the U.S. Government has embarked on a disinformation campaign against both the Nation of Islam and the UFO reality. Could it be that the sudden push of so-called greys is part of this campaign to deter the public from the truth?

Among few credible *close encounter* cases, some of them have described the inhabitants of UFOs as wearing form-fitting outfits. Take for example the abduction case of Antonio Villas Boas. This case is considered one of the first credible UFO abduction cases to reach widespread attention. During his alleged October 16, 1957 encounter, Villa Boas recalled,

> All...of them wore a very tight-fitting siren-suit, made of soft, thick, unevenly striped **gray** material. This garment reached right up to their necks where it was joined to a kind of helmet made of a grey material that looked stiffer and was strengthened back at nose level ... There was no visible hem between the trousers and shoes, which were actually a continuation of the former, being part of the self-same garment.[104]

The tight-fitting grayish outfits that covered their entire body have an uncanny resemblance to the extraterrestrial imagery that has permeated the media. Most of the accepted UFO abduction cases follow a strikingly similar description of the crafts' occupants. This reality has been deliberately twisted in the mainstream media to fit their purposes of disinformation. Furthermore, Antonio Villas Boas mentioned that the uniform covered part of their body except for the two *round lenses* that covered their eyes—lenses that made seeing their eyes almost indeterminable.

As for those huge elongated heads that have become popularly identified with aliens, Boas further gave more details of his vivid experience:

> Above their eyes, those helmets looked so tall that they corresponded to what the double of the size of a normal head should be. Probably there was something else hidden under those helmets, placed on top of their heads, but nothing could be seen from the outside.[105]

Big heads or big helmets? It is far more reasonable to accept humans in uniforms than to believe in make-believe monsters with big heads. It is no wonder that cases like Boas' describe people in body forming suits with seemingly large headgear. When the occupants' attire along with America's disinformation campaign is factored in, it becomes understandable why the media has portrayed the human pilots as extraterrestrial aliens to the public.

---

[104] Terry Melanson, "Antonio Villas Boas: Abduction Episode Ground Zero," *Conspiracy Archive* (2001).
[105] Ibid.

NOT JUST ORDINARY PEOPLE

Besides, make-believe aliens cannot hold America and world governments accountable for their evils, especially against Black people.

The Honorable Elijah Muhammad taught that many of the pilots of the baby planes have been taught and trained for their assignments since very young ages. Additionally he spoke of the wisdom aboard these wheels that can inhibit, and in some cases, reverse the aging process. During one of his major addresses at the NOI's flagship mosque, Minister Farrakhan conveyed the Messengers teachings about this process: "There's a new vegetation on the Wheel. There are new feed on the Wheel. There is new life on the Wheel. You don't age on the Wheel."[106] Taking this into consideration, the scientists/angels piloting the wheels are likely to maintain certain childlike qualities. This knowledge provides plausible explanations for the varying heights of reported UFO occupants. The life altering capabilities upon the wheels may likely constitute for the childlike size of some of the occupants. Boas' reported various sizes, but stated that many of them were about 1.64 meters tall (nearly 5 feet 4 inches tall). Besides, the Honorable Elijah Muhammad only stood about that size himself—this is nothing strange for a human being.

Several other cases of UFO encounters follow similar descriptions. Consider the Betty and Barney Hill abduction case from September of 1961. Like Boas' case, the Hills were subjects of unusual bodily examinations (including reproductive organs), lapses in time, round crafts, and of course human occupants who were relatively short. After their abduction, the Hills drew sketches of the round UFO and their abductors. Their sketch of the people resembled the description of Boas' and others.

Other notable abductees such as Sid Padrick, Travis Walton, and President Kirsan Iliyumzhinov clearly described *people*, NOT *extraterrestrial aliens*. The famous Travis Walton abduction case of 1975 illustrated that human beings were in control of these planes. Walton writes, "I whirled around and looked at the door. There, standing in the open doorway, was a human being!"[107]

The case of Sidney Padrick, a forty-five year old private pilot who once served in the U.S. Air Force, was taken aboard one of the wheels on January 30, 1965. During this encounter, Padrick reportedly approached the ship where he was met by **human beings**. Timothy Good in his book *Need to Know: UFOs, The Military And Intelligence* provides an excerpt of Padrick's encounter reported to The United States Air Force Personnel:

---

[106] "The Shock of The Hour" (Chicago, IL: The Final Call, April 26, 1992).
[107] Travis Walton, "Human?," *Fire In The Sky* (1997 August). Condensed Version.

By our own standards I would say they all looked between 20 and 25 years old; very young, pert, energetic and intelligent looking. Their features were similar to ours. There was only one feature I noticed that would differ from us greatly, and that was that their faces came to a point, much more than ours. They had sharp chins and noses. Their skin was somewhat of an 'Armenian' colour. Their eyes were all very dark... there was nothing unusual about them – their brightness, depth or luminescence... All of them were wearing two-piece suits – slip-on type – light bluish-white in colour [and] no buttons or zippers that I could see.[108]

In a video recorded interview, Kirsan Ilyumzhinov, President of the southern Russian region of Kalmykia, shared details about his famous UFO abduction from his Moscow apartment on September 17, 1985. Here, he described a circular UFO whose occupants abducted him. "They are people like us. They have the same mind, the same vision. I talked with them."[109] Even though he was able to communicate clearly with the people aboard this wheel, he stated that they were able to communicate with him telepathically—another capability that Elijah Muhammad shared about these angels. During his interview with *The Guardian*, Ilyumzhinov stated, "They put a spacesuit on me, told me many things and showed me around. They wanted to demonstrate that UFOs do exist." Again, practically all of the credible UFO abductions and encounters fit the description given by the Honorable Elijah Muhammad before such activity ever became witnessed or reported in the public.[110] This is not to say that it is impossible for nonhuman entities from other planets to accompany the human scientists aboard those planes. After all, the Messenger was given divine knowledge about life on other planets; some of those life forms include humanoids. He described most of the planets in this solar system as being 'inhabited'; however, it can be argued whether or not 'inhabited' connotes humanoid life forms or any type of life, be it microbial or otherwise. Therefore it is possible that other life forms may accompany the earthly 'people' who govern these wheels. Even though Muhammad mentioned that there is new life on the Wheel, he made it clear that the Wheel and its smaller planes are under the intelligence of humans.

Despite the clearly stated firsthand accounts of people like Walton, Ilumzhinov, Padrick, and others who encountered humans from those crafts, the media continues to categorize their experiences as *alien* or *extraterrestrial* abductions. Such misleading reinterpretations are intended to sway the public

---

[108] Timothy Good, *Need to Know: UFOs, the Military, and Intelligence*, First Pegasus Edition (New York, NY: Pegasus Books, 2007).
[109] Kirsan Ilyumzhinov, interview by British TV, "Meet The President Kirsan Ilyumzhinov," *Meet The President Kirsan Ilyumzhinov*, YouTube, UFO Database, 2007.
[110] Tom Parfitt, "King of Kalmykia," *The Guardian*, September 20, 2006.

from the teachings of the Nation of Islam. Nonetheless, the aforementioned encounters bear witness to the wisdom and power of the Honorable Elijah Muhammad's divine role. There is no plausible explanation that justifies how the Honorable Elijah Muhammad could have obtained so much information about these crafts and the intelligence that guides them, except that he was shown these things by a supremely higher power. It is this particular reason that scientists, academics, and ufologists fail to acknowledge this little Black man from Georgia who claimed he was shown these realities by God in person.

Different from the firsthand reports given by those who experienced UFO encounters, Hollywood and the media have done their part to sensationalize UFOs and the people who pilot them. Many of the characteristics attributed to aliens and UFOs seen in the movies can be traced back to fictional characters described in earlier literature. In 1893, the fiction writer H. G. Wells wrote an article entitled "Man of the Year Million" where he describes humanity being transformed into a race of grey-skinned beings who became stunted with big heads. He writes the following:

> Great hands they have, enormous brains, soft, liquid, soulful eyes. Their whole muscular system, their legs, their abdomens, are shriveled to nothing, a dangling degraded pendant to their minds.[111]

Sound familiar? Nearly eight years later in his 1901 book *The First Men in the Moon*, Wells described people from the moon as having grey skin, big heads, and large black eyes.[112] These fictitious characteristics have an uncanny resemblance to what Hollywood and the media have continuously promoted as grey aliens from UFOs. Even though this image has a known origin in make-believe, those who deliberately mislead the people use it to deter the public from the human reality associated with the wheels. This explains why the controlled media attributes UFO activity to the fictitious greys. The same entertainment industry that has swayed people to believe in fictitious werewolves, ghosts, and monsters under the bed, have swayed people to believe that little grey aliens control man-made planes.

Is it possible that there have been strange humanoids from the Wheel? When speaking about Allah's Judgment, Minister Farrakhan noted these warnings, "I heard the Honorable Elijah Muhammad say that Allah may make new creatures—terrible looking creatures with human heads and wings… to

---

[111] *The Time Machine - Phoenix Science Fiction Classics* (Phoenix Pick, 2009).
[112] *The First Men in the Moon*, Dover Thrift Editions (Dover Publications, 2000).

terrify the hell out of the people."¹¹³ Fellow NOI Minister Jabril Muhammad recalled similar words spoken to him by the Messenger regarding some of the new creatures that Allah would create for his divine purposes. Some of these purposes include the chastisement of the wicked:

> Imagine an insect body about 3, 4, 5 feet tall, 8, 9 feet tall and a human face on it looking at you, trying to get in your house...
> He [Elijah Muhammad] also said nearly 70 years ago that "Allah will produce monster-like creatures that will terrorize the wicked." At a certain point when the chastisement comes down in full, that will be one of the factors producing the chastisement. And he talked about these big 4, 5, or 6 foot insect-bodies... 3, 4, 5 feet tall with a human face on them.¹¹⁴ (Jabril Muhammad, lecture series entitled "Motives" Phoenix, AZ 2000)

Although it is clear that Hollywood and the U.S. Government have used fictitious aliens as part of their misinformation campaigns against UFOs and the NOI, there is a vague possibility that few of the reported humanoids beings could be of these new creatures. If there is any credibility in such reports, it could possibly represent some of the new life and new creatures that Master Fard Muhammad would produce on the Wheel. Even if these humanoid beings accompany the scientists on the wheel, it is clear that the central power behind these crafts are exactly who and what the Honorable Elijah Muhammad revealed as '**people like us**'.

TUNING-IN AND THE 'RADIO IN THE HEAD'

Another major characteristic displayed by the people aboard those planes involves their ability to communicate nonverbally (telepathy) and their ability to manipulate things without the use of direct physical contact (telekinesis). Many of the abductees have reported these common characteristics in their encounters. Unsurprisingly, these descriptions bear witness to the characteristics given by the Honorable Elijah Muhammad.

The Honorable Elijah Muhammad stated that these scientists have the ability to *tune-in* to the thinking of other people. Messenger Muhammad described this ability in other instances as *tuning-up* or using the *radio in the head*. These telepathic capabilities have been observed in many of the credible abduction cases. The abduction cases of Betty and Barney Hill, Sidney Padrick, President Kirsan Ilyumzhinov, and others further confirm the mentally communicative powers possessed by those on the wheels. As a firsthand

---

[113] Louis Farrakhan, "God's Judgment on America" (Los Angeles, CA: The Final Call, 09 09, 1981).
[114] Jabril Muhammad, "Motives" (Phoenix, AZ, 2000).

witness of the telepathic capabilities of these angels, Minister Farrakhan adds, "Those people are the angels. They are up there. They know what you think and before you can execute, they know it. These are the people from God!"[115] Minister Farrakhan does not speak from the perspective of one who inquires about these things; instead, he has had direct experiences with the intelligence on those planes.

The ability to tune-in is not strictly reserved for the scientists aboard the wheels. In fact, this is a rather lost capability that lies dormant among the original people today. These skills were once commonplace among the original people before a drastic fall that rendered this people almost totally lost from their original capabilities. Some of the prophets and messengers of old were granted these telepathic-like abilities. Elijah Muhammad explained that the prophet Jesus used these skills and that the scientists who pilot the wheels use this technology today:

> They are like Jesus was when he was here. He had the knowledge of tuning-in; hearing what you're thinking about. If the Jews started in on him on one side of town, he would go on the other side, because he heard them in his ears, when they were planning to come near him.[116]

There are several congruent passages in the New Testament that refer to Jesus' ability to tune-in. These scriptures often speak of Jesus "knowing their thoughts..."[117] In the Old Testament, there are verses that demonstrate God's ability to tune-in on the thinking of people. After God (in a physical form) told Abraham that his wife, Sarah, would conceive a child, she overheard their conversation and began to laugh within herself (mind). Even though she was in the tent alone and did not physically express laughter, God knew that she laughed and asked why she did so. Sarah was quite shocked at this ability and denied that she ever laughed (probably because she did not physically laugh). Yet, God assured her that he knew what was in her mind (Genesis 18:10-15).

This type of science has always been commonplace for God and his angels. It used to be the norm for the original people before an exponential fall from a once godly state. Yet this science is not totally lost from the people today. During his *Theology of Time* lecture series, Messenger Muhammad

---

[115] "The Time And What Must Be Done," *Saviours' Day 2010 Keynote Address by The Honorable Minister Louis Farrakhan* (Chicago, IL: The Final Call, February 28, 2010).

[116] "The Theology of Time (Lecture Series)," Vols. July 9, 1972 (Chicago, IL: MUHAMMAD Mosque No. 2, 1972).

[117] Matthew 9:4, 12:25; Luke 9:47.

explained that one out of every one hundred (or one hundred-eighty) of the truly righteous people are able to tune-in on the thinking of people from across the globe. The evidence of this ability lies in the fact that many average people demonstrate similar mental powers unwillingly. Most people have had experiences, dreams, déjà vu, and premonitions that have rendered themselves true (without the use of drugs or substances). This is an amazing phenomenon that gives clues to the true potential of the human being. Even though these type of experiences are not consciously done, it shows how the human mind often makes automatic calculations when the conscious mind is unaware.

Unlike the angels who are capable of performing these techniques at will, the average person has these occurrences by happenstance. Nonetheless, these type of mental experiences demonstrate that there remains a latent ability within the human being that has yet to be untapped. Unfortunately, the present world order makes it almost impossible to cultivate certain powers of the human mind by depriving the people of the right knowledge. Additionally the people have not been exposed to the right teaching and environment that can further nurture such skills because much of that knowledge has been deliberately withheld from this current world.

The Honorable Elijah Muhammad expressed that with certain efforts, those who follow his guidance can attain the ability to tune-in today:

> You could do it yourself if you would take time, clear your mind and then go get into someplace where no one is around you, concentrate on nothing but that wheel or that brother, after a while, you'll hear what that brother is saying yourself, and maybe you'll hear the motors going in the wheel. It is not that we're such people that we have to wait to see everything happen before we know what's going to happen. We would not be Gods if we did not know what was going on around us...[118]

Along with the ability to tune-in, the scientists who operate from the wheels have the technology of manipulating materials from afar, much like what is described as telekinesis. This technology is partially what will be used to destabilize the military weaponry of America and other world powers as Messenger Muhammad stated. He gave chilling accounts of the wheels' capabilities that attest to the power that guides them. They have the ability to stop the technology of this world's military powers from a distance. He stated that the wheels would make it so that the airplanes and jets would not even be able to leave the ground in these words, "…you won't have no planes up there. No. They won't fly up there with your jets. They're going to get rid of your jets on the ground first."[119]

---

[118] Op. cit. Vols. July 9, 1972.
[119] "The Theology of Time (Lecture Series)," Vols. July 2, 1972 (Chicago, IL: MUHAMMAD Mosque No. 2, 1972).

NOT JUST ORDINARY PEOPLE

As a glimpse of this technology, the angels' telekinetic abilities have allowed them to easily destabilize and manipulate the most advanced military installations weaponry of this world. Military Airmen from The United States Air Force (USAF) and Great Britain have come forth claiming that UFOs have deactivated and destabilized many nuclear missiles and installations projects from around the world.[120] They have boldly claimed that since 1948, Military bases and weapons projects around the world have been infiltrated, deactivated and thwarted by these UFOs from afar. These official witnesses of military and aviation backgrounds have put their lives and legacy on the line to make such admissions. They have charged that the U.S. Government has been deliberately covering up the truth about UFOs from the public.

Dr. Steven Greer, Founder of The Disclosure Project, The Center for the Study of Extraterrestrial Intelligence (CSETI) and The Orion Project, stated that the ETs (as he calls them) can 'remotely pick up on thoughts and disarm missiles' as in the case of the Iranian missile disarmament in 1976.[121]

In September of 2010, UFO researcher Robert Hastings gathered numerous former top military personnel who came forward to testify that unknown flying objects have interfered with the most advanced military programs throughout the world. Hastings made it clear:

> Declassified U.S. Government documents and witness testimony from former or retired military personnel confirm beyond any doubt, the reality of ongoing UFO incursions at nuclear weapons sights. When I say UFO, the witnesses have described these crafts as **disc-shaped**, or **cylindrical-shaped**, or **spherical**. These objects are capable of both hovering at high-velocity flight, usually completely silently. [122]

Hastings has interviewed over 130 military personnel who all have seen and witnessed UFO encounters over their nuclear missile sights, nuclear storage areas, and military test-sites. They have explained that their weaponry and testing programs were deactivated as a result of these discs that were spotted around their military bases and sites. Practically all of the witness accounts of UFO activity match the clear descriptions given by the Most Honorable Elijah

---

[120] Andy Bloxham, "Aliens have deactivated British and US nuclear missiles, say US military pilots," *The Telegraph* (Telegraph Media Group Limited, September 27, 2010).
[121] Steven Greer, "Steven Greer - Sirius Film, Free Energy, ET's and Freeing Humanity from the NWO" (Red Ice Radio, June 13, 2013).
[122] Robert Hastings, et al., "UFO Press Conference from The National Press Club," *Robert Hastings Presents* (Washington, DC: CNN, September 27, 2010).

Muhammad and the Nation of Islam. Months before Hastings and former military personnel arranged their press conference to disclose this UFO activity before the world, Minister Farrakhan spoke of the same truth before a crowd of 20,000:

> Those planes know everything about your military installations. You've caught them over all the military installations not only here, but in England, in France, in Germany, in Russia, in China, in India...[123]

It is no coincidence that the UFO encounters with this world's military programs have performed as accurately as Muhammad said they could.

The angelic scientists who pilot the wheels also have proven capabilities of temporarily suspending the consciousness and memory of those whom they abduct. The Betty and Barney Hill case of 1961 showed that they did not have any recollection of their abduction experiences until they returned home. Minister Farrakhan's 1985 experience was all but forgotten until an earthquake hit Mexico two days later, which brought it back to his consciousness. The Antonio Villas Boas case showed similar characteristics. The deep telepathic capabilities of these angels are also common practices with God. The Holy Qur'an says that God often takes the souls of people during their sleep. (Az-Zumar 39:42). This emphasizes a type of ability that has not been made available to this world yet. Nonetheless, those angelic scientists who have been taught and trained at the behest of Master Fard Muhammad have a record of performing similar activities. While researchers, scientists, and theologians still ponder over these mysterious concepts, the Nation of Islam has already pointed out these practical truths of God, angels, and their flight capabilities.

Angels are real—not the concepts that have been deeply engrained into the people's minds, and not those cute winged images resembling cupid that are shown in religious art and portrayed throughout the world. Elijah Muhammad spoke on this issue with authority because of his firsthand relationship with these people-angels (whom he called scientists) and the so-called UFOs that they operate. They are human beings with extraordinary intelligence and capabilities because they have been groomed under the direction of Allah (God).

---

[123] "The Time And What Must Be Done," *Saviours' Day 2010 Keynote Address by The Honorable Minister Louis Farrakhan* (Chicago, IL: The Final Call, February 28, 2010).

4. THE PROPHECIES: THY WHEELS BE DONE

ELIJAH MUHAMMAD GIVEN THE KEYS

The Honorable Elijah Muhammad's untraditional theology makes his teachings worthily unique because he proved the existence of a God in the most plausible, scientific, and tangible terms. To be practical, Muhammad provided clear evidence of the highest intelligent power ever recorded in the modern world. He illustrated that the Supreme Being intervened in the affairs of humanity by fulfilling the prophecies that have been gravely misunderstood and misinterpreted in religion. He demystified the fanciful *spookism*[124] that permeates religion. He made the scriptures pragmatically relevant to the condition of his people by distinguishing symbolic ***prophecy*** from its realistic ***fulfillment***.

Unlike any other scholar or theologian, the Honorable Elijah Muhammad demonstrated a special ability to decipher the scriptures and make them practically relevant. Both the Bible and the Holy Qur'an acknowledge that someone would appear in the latter days who would make the deeper wisdom of the scriptures more manifest to the people. A passage is given in the Bible that illustrates how the deeper wisdom of the Bible's words would be kept secret until the end times.

> *But you, O Daniel, shut up the words, and seal the book, even to the time of the end: many shall run to and fro, and knowledge shall be increased.*[125]

Other versions and translations of this passage read similar:

> *But you, Daniel, keep this prophecy a secret; seal up the book until the time of the end, when many will rush here and there, and knowledge will increase.*[126]

---

[124] **spookism:** (noun) a term commonly used by members of the Nation of Islam to describe an intensely emotional commitment to that which does not exist.
[125] Daniel 12:4 from the *American King James Version* (AKJV).
[126] Ibid. from the *New Living Translation* (NLV) 2007.

This passage gives a clear indication that the true meaning of scriptures and prophecies would not be accessible until a certain time—a time when people would have the ability to travel *to and fro* (all over the globe). A time period characterized by an exponential increase in knowledge is used to describe how long before these prophecies would be revealed. If this criterion is used to measure how long this wisdom would be kept secret, then it would be frivolous to deny that this day and time fits that script.

Modern history bears witness that much of the technological advances started to rise exponentially during the Twentieth Century, especially after 1930. The growth of the automobile industry, accelerated commercial travel, transcontinental flights, and space travels reflect an era characterized by people *rushing here and there*. This proves to be a huge contrast to the *horse and buggy* days that characterized the Pre-20th Century era. In fact, a significant growth of technology and information increased after Elijah Muhammad was shown these mysterious planes.

This dispensation of time fulfills that time when *knowledge shall be increased*. Now dubbed the Information Age, the 21st Century is represented by technological advances that were unfathomable before 1930. Warfare has evolved from horseback and rifles to nuclear and atomic weaponry. The ability to communicate information across the world has advanced from taking several months to milliseconds. There is no doubt that knowledge has increased more in the last few decades than it has over the last few thousand years. Since the wisdom of the prophetic scriptures would be sealed until the end time, then this modern era qualifies as the time when people should expect someone to manifest this wisdom to the world.

Just as the *Book of Daniel* makes a distinct prophecy concerning the concealment of prophetic meaning, other Biblical scriptures point to the time when this messianic figure will make such mysteries known. The apocalyptic *Book of Revelation* gives a more cryptic description of this time:

> *But in the days of the voice of the seventh angel, when he shall begin to sound, the mystery of God should be finished, as he hath declared to his servants the prophets.*[127]

This forecasted time period would include a powerful figure who, with the backing of God, would have the unique ability to open the seals of the book that had been locked since the days of the prophet Daniel. This messianic figure has been described as the *Lamb* and the *Lion of Judah* in the *Book of Revelation*. Among theologians, this person is understood to be synonymous with the Christ figure of the New Testament Gospels. Revelation 5:5 of the Bible gives a cryptic picture of this individual's role:

---

[127] Revelation 10:17 *King James Bible* (Cambridge Ed.).

THE PROPHECIES: THY WHEELS BE DONE

And one of the elders said to me, Weep not: behold, the Lion of the tribe of Juda, the Root of David, has prevailed to open the book, and to loose the seven seals thereof.[128]

Like the Bible, the Holy Qur'an tells of the messiah who would be taught by Allah (God). This messiah would be taught the hidden wisdom of the Torah, the Gospel, and the Book (Holy Qur'an):

And He will teach him the Book and the Wisdom and the Torah and the Gospel:[129]

The Honorable Elijah Muhammad recognized himself as the one who was given those keys to unlock the seals of the sacred prophecies. On several occasions he stated quite explicitly that he fulfills the role of that Lamb in Revelation and aspects of the messiah of the Holy Qur'an. The knowledge he obtained from his God clearly distinguishes him from all other theologians and theologies for he was shown the ancient mysteries and the keys of prophecies. He recognized himself as that Messenger of Allah who was taught by Allah (God) in the messianic mission.

HISTORY VS PROPHECY

Although the belief in mysterious objects in the sky has been a part of the sacred scriptures for thousands of years, the Nation of Islam's teachings distinguishes between the prophetic references and the actual fulfillment. The NOI debunks common religious beliefs that suggest that all of the events written in the scriptures (Bible or Holy Qur'an) were actual occurrences. **History** is not necessarily Prophecy! History can be described as the study of past events, especially as it relates to human affairs. **Prophecy** relates to the predictions of future events. If the scriptures were revealed to prophets, then it presupposes that they were given foresight to speak of things to come.

The Nation of Islam clearly makes the distinction that the Holy Qur'an and Bible are NOT history books. If the books were solely history, then they can be put in the same category of other history books. Instead, these are books of prophecy and guidance that happen to contain some historical elements. Likewise, prophets are not historians. The prophets were given the

---

[128] *American King James Version.*
[129] Al-Imran 3:48 translated by Maulana Muhammad Ali.

responsibilities of foretelling future events using the terminology and symbols of their day and time.

For example, the *Book of Isaiah* offers a cautionary prophecy using these words:

> *Woe to the land shadowing with wings, which is beyond the rivers of Ethiopia;*[130]

If the prophet Isaiah was shown a future place that would be abundant with airplanes throughout its skies, how would this prophet describe his account? Would not he use items from his era to symbolize what he saw? There is no way he could have used terms like *airplane* and *jets* because such planes were not even thought of yet. Furthermore, the English language was not even developed at that time so there is no way he could have foretold what he was shown unless he used symbols and terms from his day.

This process was required of all the prophets. Imagine if a prophet was shown the type of automobiles and traffic of today's time. How would a prophet recall such a prophecy? Well, the prophet Nahum gives a vivid utterance of what he saw:

> *The chariots shall rage in the streets, they shall justle one against another in the broad ways: they shall seem like torches, they shall run like the lightnings.*[131]

Nahum's account offers a striking resemblance to any modern metropolitan city during rush hour. There were no Chevrolets or Toyotas during that time. Naturally Nahum used the language of his time to describe events of today. This is the gist of prophecy. Most religious adherents often make the mistake of interpreting scriptures in ways that do not allow them to fully grasp the relevance of the scriptures. It would be imprudent to take all the scriptures as literal historical events. This grave misinterpretation of scriptures has caused people's understanding to remain stuck in the ancient days of scripture. This is primarily why the religious world has not been able to justify the UFO phenomenon in the light of scriptures. Minister Farrakhan admonished this out-dated attitude that pervades religion:

> The thing is, when the Bible becomes real and somebody jumps off the pages of the Bible and start living it, that's when you get frightened! You don't mind reading the Bible in your bathroom or under the bed somewhere![132]

---

[130] Isaiah 18:1.
[131] Nahum 2:4 *King James Bible* (Cambridge Ed.).
[132] "The Reality Of The Mother Plane" (Chicago, IL: The Final Call Inc., January 4, 1987).

THE PROPHECIES: THY WHEELS BE DONE

EZEKIEL'S WHEEL

If the prophet Isaiah described modern airplanes using the symbols of his day and the prophet Nahum described automotive traffic in symbols, then how would a prophet describe this man-made planet and the 1500 baby planes that God introduced to Elijah Muhammad? Did the prophets foresee what would become the UFO phenomenon of today? If so, how would they have described their visions? The prophet Ezekiel's vision fits this description. The Biblical story about Ezekiel's wheel is one that theologians and scholars still baffle over. In short, the event gives an account of the prophet Ezekiel's visions while exiled in Babylon. During this time Ezekiel is approached by a strange vehicle described as a wheel within a wheel (Ezekiel 1:16). This wheel is commonly associated with God's throne chariot (*Merkabah*).

The name Ezekiel literally means *God will strengthen*.[133] The Actual meaning of this name gives clues to the power of God. The God represented by the Honorable Elijah Muhammad and the Honorable Minister Louis Farrakhan is that God who strengthens them and the Nation of Islam to stand strong on this truth. Not only has the NOI evangelized the strength of God, but they have proven that their God has the strength and power beyond the powers of this world. The existence of these planes and their proven capabilities throughout the world offer clear evidence of the all-powerful God.

While exiled, the Biblical Ezekiel had visions of God who has the likeness of a man and appears in a dazzling manner (Ezekiel Chapters 1 and 10). Different from practically all contemporary theologians or religious leaders, Elijah Muhammad makes the distinct claim that he was taught by God who appeared in the personage of a living man. Moreover, Elijah Muhammad claims that this man-God pointed out the physical fulfillment of Ezekiel's wheel. Just as the scriptures suggest, this wheel serves as the primary vehicle of God. Like Ezekiel, Elijah Muhammad made it clear that the true and living God is not a spook; instead, his God is seen as a man who uses a circular vehicle to travel. If the vision of Ezekiel's man-God upon a throne chariot is true, then there has been no other person to fit this prophecy like the Honorable Elijah Muhammad's God. To this day, there have been no significant leaders to introduce such bold claims to the world.

During his visions, Ezekiel's God was seen accompanied by strange creatures upon dazzling crafts. The first and tenth chapters the Book of Ezekiel

---

[133] Holman Bible Dictionary, "Ezekiel," *Holman Bible Dictionary*, ed. Trent C. Butler (Study Light, 1991).

give various descriptions of these objects. Perhaps the most notable is that it seemed to be a wheel within a wheel. The Honorable Elijah Muhammad gave meaning behind these passages:

> Ezekiel said that he saw in a vision of a wheel in a wheel. Now you see, not only the outer part of the great wheel did he say he saw, but he said he saw a wheel in a wheel. Where is the other wheel Ezekiel? If Ezekiel saw any vision, he wasn't seeing visions of lies. Whenever they have a vision, it's the truth.[134]

The Messenger gave several clarifications about the meanings behind the symbolism pertaining to Ezekiel's vision. The first Chapter of Ezekiel gives descriptions of God as the likeness of a man as he is seen in the most dazzling manner. Part of his *being* appears adorned with gems and beautiful colors of the rainbow, while another part of his *being* is as fiery amber. Muhammad writes:

> As Ezekiel says, with the appearance of a man with all of this science on him and the dividing of him-an upper and a lower part of him, he said, "It was as it were the appearance of fire..." from the first description of the Wheel. It teaches the reader that the Wheel is designed for war purposes.[135]

The imagery in Ezekiel's vision of a man-like God whose being is part fire and part rainbow is indicative of the dual nature of the Wheel. The dazzling color signifies the beauty of God's healing power and the new world of peace that will be ushered in through the Mother Plane. The fiery aspect refers to the destructive nature of the Wheel that will be used in the total destruction of the present world's corrupt order. There is much symbolism pertaining to the angelic creatures that have been clarified by Muhammad, yet the religious world still wonders in amazement about its meaning.

The God in prophet Ezekiel's vision is directly associated with this wheel within a wheel. No other leader of influence in modern history even claims of being taught by a God who is responsible for these wheels! Elijah Muhammad was the FIRST and virtually the ONLY one to do so! This is a clear distinction of the Honorable Elijah Muhammad's position in prophecy. Although there are other theorists who link Ezekiel's wheel to the modern UFO phenomenon, these theorists have rendered their theories and hypotheses long after Master Fard Muhammad summoned the Wheel for Elijah Muhammad in the early 1930s.

---

[134] Elijah Muhammad, "The Theology of Time (Lecture Series)," Vols. July 9, 1972 (Chicago, IL: MUHAMMAD Mosque No. 2, 1972).

[135] Elijah Muhammad, "From Muhammad Speaks Newspaper article dated September 21, 1973," *The Mother Plane*, comp. Nasir Makr Hakim (Secretarius MEMPS, 1992).

THE PROPHECIES: THY WHEELS BE DONE

Both ufologists and nonreligious researchers tend to mistake prophecy for history when examining the scriptures. The story of the prophet Ezekiel's sighting of a huge wheel within a wheel is a scripture that has puzzled even nonreligious researchers. Many take this Biblical story as a historical craft that existed several millennia ago. Some authors such as Erich von Daniken and Zecharia Sitchin[136] have theorized that Ezekiel's vision was the occurrence of ancient alien astronauts visiting earth. Even though some of their works tie a belief in UFOs with Ezekiel's wheels, they don't mention anything about the Nation of Islam who already solved the puzzle and made these connections. To his credit, author Michael Lieb[137] has been one of the few researchers to acknowledge the contributions of Elijah Muhammad, Louis Farrakhan, and the NOI on this subject. While many theories and postulations are continually put forth, the Honorable Elijah Muhammad made it clear exactly what this Biblical scenario represents:

> He [Prophet Ezekiel] said he saw a wheel in a wheel and that this wheel rose up from the Earth. He didn't say nothing about where it was made at on the earth, but he said a wheel rose up from the earth and that it got so high that it looked dreadful.[138]

This assessment debunks the notion that Ezekiel's wheels were from an extraterrestrial source from outer space. Even though the objects were seen in the wind and in the sky, there is nothing that indicates these crafts came from outside of the earth's atmosphere. Instead, Ezekiel's vision coincides with Elijah Muhammad's teaching that such planes originate from the earth as illustrated in this scripture:

> ...and when those were lifted up from the earth, the wheels were lifted up together with them, for the spirit of the living creatures was in the wheels."[139]

The varying creatures mentioned throughout Ezekiel's visions are another anomaly that has stifled theologians. While theologians and scientists

---

[136] **Erich von Daniken** is the author of *Chariots of The Gods?*, which theorizes the notion that ancient aliens visited earth and have contacted humans. Similarly **Zecharia Sitchin** was another proponent of the *ancient alien hypothesis*.
[137] **Michael Lieb** is the author of *Children of Ezekiel: Aliens, UFOs, the Crisis of Race, and the Advent of End Time*, a book that attempts to connect the modern UFO phenomenon with the Biblical story of Ezekiel's wheel.
[138] Muhammad, op.cit.
[139] Ezekiel 1:21, *New King James Version*.

are still attempting to decipher the symbolic meaning behind these *creatures*, the Messenger gave the most reasonable explanation of these symbols. Bible scholars agree that these creatures represent the angels of God, however, they cannot explain exactly what angels are. Are they spirits, men, aliens, solids, liquids, or gases? Muhammad states:

> Ezekiel saw great work going on in the wheel and four living creatures "and their work was as it were a wheel in the middle of a wheel." (Ez. 1:16). And when the living creatures went, the wheels went with them: and when the living creatures were lifted up from the earth, the wheels, were lifted up Ez. 1:19. The power of the lifting up of the four creatures was in the wheel. The four creatures represent the four colors of the original people of the earth.[140]

Here, Elijah Muhammad pointed out the practical evidence concerning angels. He said they are men (humans). This truth is written amidst the symbolism of the scriptures that speak of these creatures having the likenesses of men (Ezekiel chapters 1 and 10).

The Nation of Islam does not have to speculate about the meaning of Ezekiel's wheel because this reality was already identified before the public began to witness its fulfillment. There have been many who have attempted to discard the NOI's position about these planes by suggesting that Muhammad's teachings were mythical, metaphoric, or strictly spiritual. The Honorable Elijah Muhammad and the Honorable Minister Farrakhan have made it clear what this plane is and what it represents. Although the Mother Wheel and the baby planes have deeply spiritual connotations, this is not to discard the tangible reality that has become evident since the mid-Twentieth Century.

GOD RIDES AROUND ON SOMETHING IN THE CLOUDS!

> *Sing unto God, sing praises to his name: extol him that rides upon the heavens by his name, the LORD, and rejoice before him.* – Psalm 68:4 (KJV)

Although Ezekiel's visions are probably the most repeated scripture related to UFO Biblical research, there are several other prophecies that are congruous to the Nation of Islam's authentic position on UFOs. In fact, the overall mission of the NOI is rooted in the prophetic scriptures of the Bible and the Holy Qur'an. These wheels are symbolized in scriptures under several different names, terms, symbols, and stories.

---

[140] Elijah Muhammad, *The Fall Of America* (Chicago, IL: Elijah Muhammad, 1973). 238.

THE PROPHECIES: THY WHEELS BE DONE

Why is it that the prophets and messengers described God in humanly terms, yet they described him as stationed up in the skies? On many occasions he walks, talks, eats, and moves like most humans. On other occasions he is said to sit upon his high throne, yet he stoops down to deal with earth's human affairs. He travels in manners that seem unconventional by operating from a heavenly position in the skies. The scriptures are filled with references where God speaks and acts from clouds. As the theologies that stem from these scriptures are examined, it becomes clear that **God uses some kind of flying vehicle**. Consider this scripture:

> *There is none like unto the God of Jeshurun, who rideth upon the heaven in thy help, and in his excellency on the sky.* – Deuteronomy 33:26 (KJV)

Cedric Muhammad, a researcher in the NOI makes keen observations concerning the use of Clouds in the scriptures to symbolize vehicles of God. He notes that these objects that God and his angels use are characterized under various terms:

> The scriptures of both Bible and Holy Qur'an contain several references to entities, in today's lexicon, that could be described as unidentified flying objects (UFOs). In particular, three books in the Bible - Exodus, Ezekiel and Revelations contain detailed descriptions that directly connect flying objects with the Supreme Being, His Chief Representative(s) to the people, and the plan of salvation and judgment which includes the saving of some people and the wholesale destruction of others.[141]

The term clouds not only imply the heavenly position often held by these crafts, but it also represents a type of camouflage used. In many literary analysis, the use of clouds often symbolize that which is lofty, celestial, dreamy, unclear, and sometimes ambiguous. One could easily argue the point that the concept of God operating from a cloud is extremely ambiguous. Unless practical explanations are given to decipher these symbols, it would be highly illogical to simply accept that people just magically float on clouds without the use of proper equipment. What good would it do to accept such a belief if it has no practical bearing for today? The Honorable Elijah Muhammad and the Honorable Louis Farrakhan have made these scriptures pragmatically relevant by presenting a realization of scriptural symbols.

---

[141] Cedric Muhammad, "Scripture, The Mother Plane, And Minister Farrakhan's Vision From Tepoztlan, Mexico," *Black Electorate* (BlackElectorate.com, July 23, 2002).

The Old Testament Book of Exodus gives prophetic descriptions of God using a cloud to guide and protect his people out of bondage away from their oppressors. The God-driven intelligence from this cloud serves as a guide and as a protective mechanism for his chosen people. It appeared as a cloud during the daytime and emerged into a pillar of fire during the night hours (Exodus 13:21, Numbers 9:16-17). The following Old Testament passages from the Book of Exodus give insight into God's airborne crafts that he would use for his people:

- *And Moses went up into the mount, and a cloud covered the mount. (Exodus 24:15).*
- *And the glory of the LORD abode upon mount Sinai, and the cloud covered it six days: and the seventh day he called unto Moses out of the midst of the cloud. (Exodus 24:16).*
- *And Moses went into the midst of the cloud, and gat him up into the mount: and Moses was in the mount forty days and forty nights. (Exodus 24:18)*
- *And the LORD descended in the cloud, and stood with him there, and proclaimed the name of the LORD. (Exodus 34:5)*
- *Then a cloud covered the tent of the congregation, and the glory of the LORD filled the tabernacle. (Exodus 40:34).*
- *And Moses was not able to enter into the tent of the congregation, because the cloud abode thereon, and the glory of the LORD filled the tabernacle. (Exodus 40:35).*
- *And when the cloud was taken up from over the tabernacle, the children of Israel went onward in all their journeys: (Exodus 40:36).*
- *But if the cloud were not taken up, then they journeyed not till the day that it was taken up. (Exodus 40:37).*
- *For the cloud of the LORD was upon the tabernacle by day, and fire was on it by night, in the sight of all the house of Israel, throughout all their journeys. (Exodus 40:38).*

Cedric Muhammad cites Minister Jabril Muhammad's annotation about the *cloud* references from the Bible's Book of Exodus. Jabril Muhammad is a theologian in the Nation of Islam, student of the Honorable Elijah Muhammad, and close companion to the Honorable Minister Louis Farrakhan. With his keen insight on the subject of these wheel-like planes, Jabril Muhammad notes the following:

> So, in plain language, the God Who first came to where Moses was, down on the ground, right here on this earth, according to the book of Exodus, and commissioned him to represent Him, later went up above the people and the country into "the pillar of fire and of the cloud". Whatever one may think that

THE PROPHECIES: THY WHEELS BE DONE

object was, which the text clearly says God was in, and regardless to what interpretation one may (or that the scholars have) put on these words, the book clearly says that God was in something, out of which He looked down and interfered with, disturbed and defeated those who were trying to kill His people.

...What does all of this mean? First, God meets Moses on earth. Later He guides Moses and his people and deals with Pharaoh from within some kind of object in the sky. This object is called "pillar of cloud by day and a pillar of fire by night." Just what is a "pillar of cloud/pillar of fire"? Why was this "thing" described, in the text, in such a cloudy, or unclear manner? Try and identify a "pillar of cloud by day" and a "pillar of fire" by night. Tell us what this was. If such existed back then where can we find one, or one like it today? Identify it. What would such an object mean to us today? How would we identify it? Let's ask it: Was God in a "UFO"?[142]

Several New Testament passages give further acknowledgment of God upon clouds. Some include God taking his servants up into clouds. In the case of Jesus, he is said to leave on a cloud and he is expected to return in a like manner (Acts 1:9-11). Luke 21:27 predicts that the Son of Man will be seen coming on a cloud with great power and glory. In the 14th Chapter of Revelation, this man is seen sitting on a cloud. If scriptures predict that people can do all of these things upon clouds, there would have to be some type of aerodynamic vessel that will allow them to operate from such a position. Basic science illustrates that clouds alone are not capable of holding and transporting bare humans in such a manner. Therefore, mechanical objects are necessary if these scriptures are to make any sense. Did these things actually happen back then or are they prophetic pictures for today's time? If these things did happen, what good would it do for people today?

These are just a few of the many passages that refer to God's clouds in the Bible. Too, the Holy Qur'an describes Allah (God) in a heavenly establishment under similar terms. The Holy Qur'an makes references to a relationship between Allah and his clouds:

Will they wait until Allah comes to them in canopies of clouds, with angels (in His train) and the question is (thus) settled? but to Allah do all questions go back (for decision). (Al-Baqarah 2:210)[143]

Another English translation of this same Qur'anic verse reads as follows:

---

[142] Ibid. Cedric Muhammad cites from an unpublished book by Jabril Muhammad.
[143] Yusuf Ali Translation of The Holy Qur'an.

> They wait for naught but that Allah should come to them in the shadows of the clouds with angels, and the matter has (already) been decided. And to Allah are (all) matters returned.[144]

This ayat (verse) from the Holy Qur'an suggests that by the time the people see Allah and the angels in the clouds, all questions would be settled—all matters would have already been decided. It has become apparent that this is that day and time when Allah, his angels, and their crafts are being witnessed all over the world. Both the Honorable Elijah Muhammad and Minister Farrakhan have warned that a day is coming when these wheels will become even more evident. This will be a time when the wheels are prepared to execute their destructive capabilities against America and her oppressive cohorts. By the time the people witness the wheels on this level, the matter will have already been decided. Still, Elijah Muhammad's position on these planes has caused tremendous confusion in the Islamic world because these planes conflict with the traditional understanding of the Muslim world.

Regardless of one's interpretation of scriptures, one cannot argue with the fact that these planes have been witnessed throughout the world as unidentified flying objects (UFOs). These planes have been witnessed within clouds, beyond clouds, and even as clouds. UFOs have been recorded forming clouds and disappearing into clouds. The Honorable Elijah Muhammad spoke of the stealthy capabilities of these planes:

> The Mother Plane is capable of staying out of the earth's gravity for a whole year. She is capable of producing her own sphere of oxygen and hydrogen, as any other planet is able to do.[145]

Based on Muhammad's teachings, these planes are capable of producing different affects through the use of the elements. They can appear as clouds during the day and they can appear to be fiery stars at night. Again, Muhammad explains this ability:

> The Mother Plane can hide behind other stars and make herself invisible to the eye because she does not have to wait on a power from the earth. She can produce her own power to go wherever she desires to go in space.[146]

With these kind of capabilities, the Mother Plane and the baby planes can easily appear undetectable by appearing as clouds by day and as fiery stars by

---

[144] Maulana Muhammad Ali Translation of The Holy Qur'an.
[145] Elijah Muhammad, *The Fall Of America* (Chicago, IL: Elijah Muhammad, 1973). 240.
[146] Ibid. 242.

THE PROPHECIES: THY WHEELS BE DONE

night. This is consistent with the prophetic pictures given in the scriptures. Unsurprisingly this is also consistent with thousands of reports and sightings throughout the world.

GOD'S THRONE UPON THE MOTHER WHEEL

The Religious world should not be too surprised about the UFO phenomenon since hundreds of their scriptures promise that God would use something to operate from the skies. Yet, the Nation of Islam's inherent UFO theology has been mocked and ridiculed by Jews, Christians, and Muslims alike. Ironically all of the world's major faith traditions give references to God's heavenly throne. The Hebrew Torah, the Christian Bible, and the Holy Qur'an give clear depictions of God being stationed upon his throne where he is often seen accompanied by his angels.

It is utterly negligent to dismiss the many scriptural passages that give credence to God's physical location, especially since they all virtually seem to point to the same thing. Many prophets were said to witness a type of room location that houses God's throne. Moses and the elders saw Gods feet on the crystal sea (Exodus 24:9-11). Isaiah saw God's throne up high (Isaiah 6). Micaiah saw God sitting on his throne in heaven with a host of angels standing by his sides (1 Kings 22:20). Jeremiah witnessed God's high throne (Jeremiah 17:12). The list goes on and on.

Still confusing to the religious world, the many references to God's throne have left scholars unable to explain the meaning of this mystery. The Bible and Holy Qur'an give numerous passages expressing God's establishment upon his throne. Many attribute it to a strictly metaphorical throne that represents God's supreme status above all things, i.e. his sovereignty. Even though God's power and wisdom is not limited to any particular space, it is obvious that he has designated places where he performs certain activities. Hence, it can be understood that this throne represents the central hub of God's dwelling.

It cannot be denied that the God of scriptures is said to perform certain jobs on earth, in mountains, upon clouds, and in the heavens. The scriptures are filled with passages that verify this. While some of these verses have symbolic meanings, it cannot be denied that there are clear examples that validate God's physical existence and his physical motion on earth and within the skies. If God is said to operate from the skies, it would be wise to ask how does he operate when acting within the sky? What type of vessel does he use? How is it that angels are seen upon and around God's heavenly throne, yet religious scholars deny the existence of vessels that can explain how this is possible? Though the scriptures clearly depict God's angelic attendants around his throne, there are many religious scholars in denial of the tangible truth offered by the Nation of Islam.

GOD'S THRONE IN THE OLD TESTAMENT

> *And above the firmament that was over their heads was the likeness of a throne, as the appearance of a sapphire stone: and on the likeness of the throne was the likeness as the appearance of a man above on it.* – Ezekiel 1:26

The throne mentioned in Ezekiel's vision was seen "over their heads" and contained the "likeness of a man." The Honorable Elijah Muhammad clarified the meaning of this prophetic verse:

> In Ezekiel's Vision, 'the Voice that he heard coming from the firmament that was over their heads,' this really is referring to the future of the work of the Plane's Master. The Voice is the Voice of the Master of the Plane.

The Throne is both metaphorical and practical. It is metaphorical in the sense that it gives seemingly vague prophetic imagery associated with God's presence. These are images that represent the high wisdom, power, and loftiness of God. Yet, many descriptions of the throne of God point to a material place and a physical positioning that cannot be negated. The prophet Isaiah cried, "I saw the Lord sitting on a throne, high and lifted up"[147] The prophet Daniel foresaw this throne of God in his visions of one referred to as the **Ancient of Days**:

> *I watched till thrones were put in place,*
> *And the Ancient of Days was seated;*
> *His garment was white as snow,*
> *And the hair of His head was like pure wool.*
> *His throne was a fiery flame,*
> *Its wheels a burning fire;*[148]

Since Daniel was a prophet and he had a vision of prophecy, it should be clearly understood that these events were not actual occurrences of yesterday. Instead it can be deduced that these visions are predictions of things to come. The language used by Daniel makes it easy to deduce that his visions

---

[147] Isaiah 6:1, New *King James Version (NKJV)*.
[148] Daniel 7:9 New *King James Version (NKJV)*.

match the evidence brought by the Honorable Elijah Muhammad. Interestingly, the thrones witnessed by Daniel are directly associated with strange fiery wheels. What do heavenly thrones, fiery wheels, and God have to do with one another? Religious scholars have not been able to make sense of these apocalyptic texts. These scriptures cannot make any practical sense unless one accepts the evidence that Elijah Muhammad pointed out to the world.

It is not a coincidence that so many visions of the prophets involve a human God with human angels upon vessels that travel throughout the earth and the skies. It is not happenstance that so many prophets describe virtually the same visions of God and his flying vessels. The interesting point in this is that no scientist or theologians made the connection of these texts with the modern UFO phenomenon before Elijah Muhammad.

The aforementioned passage of Daniel's vision gives his account of one called the *Ancient of Days* being seated upon his heavenly throne. Who exactly does this Ancient of Days refer to? The Holman Bible Dictionary gives this description of this majestic figure:

> Ancient of Days is a phrase used in Daniel 7:1 to describe the everlasting God. Ancient of days literally means "one advanced in (of) days" and may possibly mean "one who forwards time or rules over it."[149]

The Ancient of Days refers to a human God whose throne sits upon a wheel—a God who can demonstrate that his wisdom and power is highly advanced in time. The existence of the Mother Plane and its wheels are mechanical proofs that Master Fard Muhammad's wisdom is far beyond this world's grasp. When asked about the engineering technology of UFOs, aviation expert John Lear stated "it's a million years ahead of us."[150] The human God of the Nation of Islam has clearly demonstrated that his wisdom and power extends far beyond time. His wheel-like planes are tangible proofs that his wisdom, power, and throne exist.

Elsewhere in the Old Testament, God is seen upon his holy throne in the heavens (Psalm 47:8, 103:19; Isaiah 6:1). This throne is the location from whence he rules over all. One could argue that this throne serves as an office headquarters for God's sovereignty. Although the Bible and Holy Qur'an acknowledge that God rules over all things, both scriptures make it clear that

---

[149] Holman Bible Dictionary, "Ancient of Days" *Holman Bible Dictionary*, ed. Trent C. Butler (Study Light, 1991).
[150] Brad Meltzer's Decoded, "UFO," *Brad Meltzer's Decoded*, Vol. Season 2 (History Channel, 11 30, 2011).

he has a particular place of establishment from whence he rules. The scriptures agree that he rules from some strange object from above.

The throne of God is frequently accompanied by angels. It is written that prophets saw God on his throne with his hosts by his sides (1 Kings 22. 19). As previously mentioned, the term *hosts* in the Bible often refer to armies of persons engaged for war. The New Testament continues this concept with a glimpse of what takes place upon this throne.

THE THRONE AND THE GOSPEL

Heaven is my throne, and earth is my footstool: what house will you build me? said the Lord: or what is the place of my rest? – Acts 7:49 American King James Version

Jesus echoes the sentiments of the Old Testament scriptures as he also spoke of God's position on a heavenly throne (Matthew 5:34-35). Like the prophets of old, Jesus recognized a human God that commissioned him for his divine mission (John 8:16-18). The anthropomorphic God of the Honorable Elijah Muhammad may appear to be a new concept by today's religious standards, but in truth, Muhammad's concept of God is the most ancient and scripturally congruent description of God. This may as a surprise to religious preachers, not because Muhammad is in error. Instead, the confusion stems from the traditional religious teachings that are not congruent with the scriptures. How is it that the bulk of the Biblical scriptures speak of God in humanly terms, yet practically all religions find it difficult to believe that God is a man?

The Apostle Paul spoke of God on a heavenly throne. Not only did Paul speak of God on this throne, but asserted that the Christ would be seated at the right hand of God after his ascension. The Holy Qur'an verifies this prophecy whereas the messiah is said to escape from what appeared to be his death. Rather, he would be exalted to the presence of God (An-Nisa 4:157-158). Unsurprisingly, the Holy Qur'an refers to God's heavenly throne of power as well. Both the Bible and the Qur'an connect God's exalted position with the messiah who is destined to save the people of God and destroy the enemies of God.

The Book of Revelation gives cryptic insight into the inner court of God's heavenly throne. The Book of Revelation was given to a rather obscure person mentioned as John of Patmos. It was on this island that John received apocalyptic revelations of the end times. This book contains some of the most cryptic passages of all the sacred texts. Many evangelists have purposely averted preaching any in-depth sermons from this book because of its seemingly inexplicable content. Of course these cryptic passages would not be

THE PROPHECIES: THY WHEELS BE DONE

difficult to unravel for a man who was taught by the Supreme Being. Such a man is the Honorable Elijah Muhammad.

John of Patmos (also called John the Revelator) was shown things that had not been seen on the earth, but of things that would be seen in the latter days. The 4th Chapter of Revelation describes the *One* who sat on the throne in similar terms as the prophet Ezekiel. This *One* on the throne is bedazzled with stone gems and rainbows. However, this picture shows him surrounded by twenty-four enthroned elders along with seven others called the seven Spirits of God. Also like Ezekiel, this book envisions four creatures that accompany God's throne.

Each of the elders, spirits, and creatures represent different types of angels-scientists that the Honorable Elijah Muhammad spoke of. As previously stated, each of the angelic scientists has different and specific functions. The twenty-four elders who surround the *One* represent the twelve major and twelve minor scientists who have acted as the inner-circle of God for millions of years. This circle has served as a heavenly court of God's affairs. Messenger Elijah Muhammad shared some of their responsibilities from what he was taught by God in person:

> We make such history once every 25,000 years. When such history is written, it is done by twenty-four of our scientists. One acts as Judge or God for the others and twenty-three actually do the work of getting up the future of the nation, and all is put into one book and at intervals where such and such part or portion will come to pass, that people will be given that part of the book through one among that people from one of the Twelve (twelve major scientists) as it is then called a Scripture which actually means script of writing from something original or book.[151]

This godly circle of scientists and other angel-scientists compose part of the body of God that represents the *Elohim*, or the plural body of God. This is synonymous with the plural pronouns *We* and *Us* that represent Allah (God) in the Holy Qur'an. Revelation describes the *Seven Spirits* (angels) of God who surround the throne. These seven angels have some of the most powerful responsibilities according to the Honorable Elijah Muhammad. He publically spoke of his relationship with some of these most powerful scientists:

> Each one is to do a certain job. Like you read of it in the Bible, that one Scientist went out, and his job was to send a plague of wind or send a plague

---

[151] *MESSAGE TO THE BLACKMAN In America*, Original Published by MUHAMMAD'S Temple No. 2 in Chicago 1965 (Chicago, IL: The Final Call Inc., 1965). 108.

of storms or send a plague of fire or something like that. These are the type of men I'm speaking of. I know them and they know me, and every one of them has a job to do.

It's seven of them. Allah says that the job is not enough for one, but seven of them will be ordered to do it. And think over it. These are not spooks. They are men![152]

There have been no significant leaders in the world who have come close to even making these type of claims besides the Honorable Elijah Muhammad. No person of notable influence has made such claims as having direct relationships with the physical manifestation of God or his angels in this manner. Not only does he make such bold claims, but his claims give rational meaning to the symbolism that still has the world of religion dumbfounded.

Figure 3: FULFILLMENT

Clockwise from top: Isaiah scroll from Dead Sea Scroll of Qumran, Ayat Al-Kursi (Verse of the Throne) from the Holy Qur'an Al-Baqarah 2:255, Article from the Seattle Post-Intelligencer, July 29, 1952, Phoenix Lights March 1997, Holy Bible. Center: Messenger Elijah Muhammad

---

[152] "The Theology of Time (Lecture Series)," Vols. July 9, 1972 (Chicago, IL: MUHAMMAD Mosque No. 2, 1972).

5. UFOS AND THE HOLY QUR'AN

ISLAMIC SCHOLARS' CONTROVERSY

Just as Jewish and Christian scholars often mistake prophecy for history, the Islamic scholars (*ulema*) often make the same costly misinterpretations. This is one of the primary reasons why religious scholarship cannot reconcile the UFO phenomenon with their traditional doctrines. Even more appalling is that many religious theologians have rejected the clear fulfillment of the scriptures that they claim to study. This blatant oversight has left the Muslim world without any clear explanation to justify these crafts that have been witnessed by millions across the world.

Does the Holy Qur'an address the UFO phenomenon? The answer is clearly Yes! However, the ulema have not been able to explain this reality with their traditional understanding of Islam and the Holy Qur'an. In this revered book, Allah (God) revealed his divine words of guidance and prophecy to the Prophet Muhammad (PBUH). Since this book contains certain prophecies, it was already understood that the full meaning behind all its verses would not become fully evident until latter times. This is why the Holy Qur'an mentions that its verses continually make manifest:

> *Ha-Mim. By the Book that makes manifest! Surely We have made it an Arabic Qur'an that you may understand. And it is in the Original of the Book with Us, truly elevated, full of wisdom.* – Surah 43:1-4, Az-Zukhruf

This term for manifest stems from the Arabic word *mubeen*, which suggests that the verses of the Holy Qur'an would become clearer, and more evident in every age. While its verses may have one meaning during a certain time, that same verse may take on other layers of meaning during future times and places. This is because the truth of the Holy Qur'an is a truth that becomes more manifest and evident as time progresses.

Even Prophet Muhammad (PBUH) recognized that the wisdom behind the scriptures would be taught to Allah's messiah in the latter days. This is verified in both the Holy Qur'an and the Hadiths of the Prophet. It is written that Allah would teach the messiah the Torah, the Gospel, the Book (Qur'an) and the wisdom thereof (Al-Imran 3:49). The Prophet promised that this messianic figure would appear in the latter days to fulfill his divine role. Since the Muslim world has no explicit knowledge of UFOs, it can be understood that the promised messiah would know something about them. With that in mind, does the Holy Qur'an speak of these wheel-like planes that Elijah Muhammad introduced to the world? Could this be why they have not even addressed this issue?

One such concept that Islamic scholars baffle over involves Allah's throne. The Holy Qur'an makes several references to Allah's throne in both a spiritual and physical context. The clarity behind Allah's throne becomes clearer over time. Since the Mother Plane was not completed until 1929, Allah's throne has been his spiritual sovereignty and power over his creation. However, it should be noted that the Qur'an is also a book of *prophecy*. Otherwise, there would be no clear reason to reveal it to a *prophet* if he could not *prophesy* about things to come.

THE THRONE OF ALLAH

He it is Who created the heavens and the earth in six periods, and He is established on the Throne of Power. He knows that which goes down into the earth and that which comes forth out of it, and that which comes down from heaven and that which goes up to it. And He is with you wherever you are. And Allah is Seer of what you do.[153] – Al-Hadid 57:4

In the Book of Revelation, the throne of God surrounded by other enthroned elders represents a divine assembly under the direction of God himself. That vision shown to John the Revelator has now been realized by Elijah Muhammad's teaching. The same concepts of God and his host of accompanying angels that are found in the Bible are cross-referenced throughout the Holy Qur'an. Although most of the Islamic world does not view God or his angels in a physical capacity, the Holy Qur'an gives clear evidence of God's spiritual and physical throne as well as the angels who accompany it.

All Muslims believe in the revelation of the Holy Qur'an and all Muslims believe that there is *no doubt* in this holy script. While all Muslims recognize the authenticity of the book, there remains grave confusion concerning exactly what Allah's throne is, which is mentioned throughout the book. The common belief among Muslims is that Allah has no physical shape or form (although the Qur'an does not explicitly state such). Yet the Qur'an gives several descriptions of Allah being established upon his throne of power. Like the Bible, this throne of God is witnessed in a highly exalted position above the earth. Consider the context of this *ayat* (verse):

---

[153] Maulana Muhammad Ali translation of The Holy Qur'an.

UFOS AND THE HOLY QUR'AN

Surely your Lord is Allah, Who created the heavens and the earth in six periods, and He is established on the Throne of Power. – Al-A'raf 7:54

The Holy Qur'an describes Allah's establishment upon His **Throne of Power (al-istiwa 'ala al-'Arsh),** which is normally stationed in the heavens. While some of the references of Allah's throne of power can have spiritual meaning, there are too many references that make it evident that Allah's throne has a corporeality associated with it. The expression of Allah being *established on* the throne is also written in various English translations as *he mounted, he settled himself,* and *positioned himself.* These English expressions are translated from the Arabic verb *is'tawā* (اِسْتَوَى), which means *he established, he ascended upon,* or *he turned.* All these expressions have both mental and physical attributes.

If these Qur'anic expressions are solely spiritual, then why would Allah (God) have to establish himself in a position he already holds? If Allah (God) is a formless, shapeless being (as most traditionalist Muslims believe), why would he require a throne or any position at all unless he also has an anthropomorphic quality? When these simple questions are considered, it becomes easier to accept the teachings of Elijah Muhammad who makes the bold and unique assertion that he met Allah (God) in a physical person. It was this wise person who established himself upon the heavenly throne called the Mother Plane that has shocked the world into a UFO craze.

The term for throne used in the Holy Qur'an comes primarily from two different Arabic terms. The lesser of the terms used for throne is from the Arabic word **kursi.** The literal meaning of this word means a *chair* or *seat.* This term is used most notably in Surah Al-Baqarah 2:255, which some Muslims believe is the greatest ayat in the Qur'an according to a Hadith saying of Prophet Muhammad (PBUH).[154] This verse has become known as the *Verse of The Throne,* which reads as follows:

Allah! There is no god but He,-the Living, the Self-subsisting, Eternal. No slumber can seize Him nor sleep. His are all things in the heavens and on earth. Who is there can intercede in His presence except as He permitteth? He knoweth what (appeareth to His creatures as) before or

---

[154] Muhammad reportedly said in Hadith: When you lie down in your bed, recite ayat al-Kursi, Allah! La ilaha illa Huwa (none has the right to be worshipped but He), the Ever Living, the One Who sustains and protects all that exists… [al-Baraqah 2:255] until the end of the ayah, then you will have a protector from Allah and no shaytan (devil) will come near you until morning comes. [Sahih al-Bukhari 6.530, 4.495, & 3.505.1].

after or behind them. Nor shall they compass aught of His knowledge except as He willeth. His Throne doth extend over the heavens and the earth, and He feeleth no fatigue in guarding and preserving them for He is the Most High, the Supreme (in glory).

Here, it could be recognized that Allah's throne (kursi) signifies Allah's sovereignty over the heavens and the earth. The throne in this verse may connote Allah's spiritual status over his creation (which happens to be physical). If Allah's kursi encompasses all within the heavens and the earth, then this still suggests that Allah has physical attributes since he resides in a material world. The Holy Qur'an further makes it clear that a kursi also refers to a material seat made for a physical body:

And certainly we tried Solomon, and We put on his throne a (mere) body, so he turned (to Allah). – Sad 38:34.

Here again the term *kursi* is used to represent a material throne for a material body. Although it is understood that Allah's throne represents his spiritual sovereignty over all things, it is also just as clear that his throne is a material position as well.

The term more frequently used to describe Allah's throne in the Holy Qur'an comes from the Arabic word **'arsh**, which literally is *a throne*. Allah (God) asks a question in the Qur'an concerning his throne:

Say: Who is the Lord of the seven heavens and the Lord of the mighty Throne of power? – Al-Mu'minun 23:86

While this throne may indicate a spiritual quality, the Holy Qur'an gives several other verses that signify the tangibility aspect of his throne. Most verses suggest that this throne is in the heavens, but there are others that give earthly descriptions of its location:

He it is Who created the heavens and the earth in six Days - and His Throne was over the waters - that He might try you, which of you is best in conduct... – Hud 11:7

Where is Allah's throne? According to the aforementioned ayat, it was over the waters. Does this mean that Allah's throne was once established on a boat or island of sorts? If his throne was over the waters, then it should not even be an argument that his throne has a tangible quality. Water (H_2O) is a physical property that constitutes most of the earth. Could it be that Allah's primary residence has been on the earth until the making of his Mother Plane? Could it be that Allah (God) has a physical earthly form although his mind and power encompasses all things? This is reminiscent of the Biblical passage that refers to the earth as God's footstool while heaven is his throne (Isaiah 66:1, Acts 7:49). Similarly, the Qur'an depicts Allah's throne as once being over the waters (earthly) even though he directed himself toward the heavens (41:11). The person of Allah (God) is earthly, while his mind, spirit, and power encompasses all within his universe.

Variations of the Arabic verb *istawa* are used throughout the Qur'an to describe Allah's *position* on his throne. When translating this Arabic term into English, some translators use expressions such as *to sit, to ride, to mount, to establish Himself on,* and *to rise over*. Most so-called orthodox Muslims believe Allah's position can never refer to a physical location; therefore, Allah's position on his throne only refers to his spiritual sovereignty over all things. While the NOI does not dispute that Allah's throne has spiritual connotations, his position on the throne also has undeniable physical denotations. It would be extremely negligent to assert that Allah's position is strictly spiritual in nature when the same verb *istawa* is used to denote the physical position of persons seated on Allah's creatures (as in horses and camels) as illustrated in this verse:

> *That you may sit firm (**istawaytum**) on their backs, then remember the favour of your Lord, when you are firmly seated thereon, and say: Glory be to Him Who made this subservient to us and we were not able to do it.* – Az-Zukhruf 43:13

This is just one of many examples that demonstrate how many Muslim scholars have missed the fulfillment of Allah's prophecies. They have continuously held on to traditions that are not truly rooted in Islamic principles, nor are they rooted in a proper understanding of prophecy.

The concept of God appearing in person as taught by Elijah Muhammad does NOT conflict with the wisdom of the Holy Qur'an! In fact, his description of Allah's characteristics is much more in sync with the Qur'an than traditional understandings. While traditional schools of Islamic thought suggest that Allah (God) could never be a human, this belief contradicts the Holy Qur'an. It is written that Allah has appeared in the form of a well-made man:

> *So she screened herself from them. Then We sent to her Our spirit and it appeared to her as a well-made man.* – Maryam 19:17

There is no doubt that Allah (God) has anthropomorphic qualities according to the Holy Qur'an. So why has the Islamic scholarship denied the truth that was revealed to Elijah Muhammad who proved that Allah appeared in the person of a man who manifested his throne of power called The Mother Plane? This denial may explain why they have not been able make sense out of UFOs and the reality of Allah's throne.

The Holy Qur'an provides other characteristics of Allah's throne ('arsh) that affirm its material properties because it will be seen. Consider the following ayat that speaks of a time when the physical manifestation of Allah's throne will be witnessed:

> *And you shall see the angels going round about the throne glorifying the praise of their Lord; and judgment shall be given between them with justice, and it shall be said: All praise is due to Allah, the Lord of the worlds.*[155] – Az-Zumar 39:75

If angels will be seen going around Allah's throne, this proves that both angels and the throne can be seen. If they will be seen surrounding the throne, then the throne has to be a material manifestation. If the throne can be seen, then Allah (God) who establishes himself on this throne can be seen. These descriptions make it plain that the Nation of Islam's teachings about these crafts are truly manifest. The Holy Qur'an has made its words clearly manifest (*mubeen*). The evidence lies in the reality of the wheels as taught by the Nation of Islam and as seen by hundreds of millions of witnesses today.

The evidence of this verse is also found in thousands of witness reports of UFOs being sighted surrounding or accompanying a much larger circular UFO (the Mother Wheel). The famous case of JAL Flight 1628 bears witness to this prophecy. While flying a Boeing 747 over Alaska, Captain Kenju Terauchi witnessed a huge walnut shaped UFO accompanied by two smaller UFOs. These planes performed spectacular movements before flying off at terrific speeds.[156] This is just one of numerous official reports that convey similar experiences.

The Honorable Elijah Muhammad taught that these planes are controlled by wise scientists (angels) who far exceed the intelligence and powers of this world. These scientists work at the behest of Allah (God) in the person of Master Fard Muhammad. Many of them have been taught since young tender ages to perform special tasks. They have a degree of reverence for the Supreme Being whom they work for. Both the Bible and Holy Qur'an confirm this notion. The Qur'an says that they sing praises to Allah while tending to his throne:

---

[155] Muhammad Habib Shakir translation of the Holy Qur'an.
[156] Timothy Good, *Above Top Secret: The Worldwide U.F.O. Cover-Up* (New York, NY: Quill William Morrow, 1988). 432.

UFOS AND THE HOLY QUR'AN

Those who sustain the Throne (of Allah) and those around it Sing Glory and Praise to their Lord; believe in Him; and implore Forgiveness for those who believe: "Our Lord! Thy Reach is over all things, in Mercy and Knowledge. Forgive, then, those who turn in Repentance, and follow Thy Path; and preserve them from the Penalty of the Blazing Fire![157] – Ghafir 40:7

The Holy Qur'an paraphrases Elijah Muhammad's teaching that the angels sustain the Mother Plane. Not only do these scientists occupy and sustain this divine craft, but their whole objective is to execute Allah's will. These Qur'anic prophecies verify the Biblical prophecies that virtually predict the same thing. The *Book of Revelation* puts it like this:

And all the angels stood round about the throne, and about the elders and the four beasts, and fell before the throne on their faces, and worshipped God. – Revelation 7:11 (AKJV)

The angels, the elders, and the four beasts all symbolize types of people, which is why it states they fell on *their faces* and worshipped God who is on the throne. This demonstration of reverence for Allah (God) is further validated in the official UFO abduction case of Sid Padrick. During his report to the USAF, Padrick gave a riveting account of his experience:

Padrick was taken to a 'consultation room' whereas for the first time in his life, he 'felt the presence of the Supreme Being'. It's obvious that they are on a very high scientific level,' he reported, 'but their relationship with the Supreme Being means a lot more to them than their technical and scientific ability and knowledge. I would say that their religion and their science are all in one.'[158]

How is it that Elijah Muhammad knew so much about these things, which the world still ponders over? Elijah Muhammad is credited for having exclusively detailed knowledge of the inner-workings of what are now called UFOs. This truth presented by the Nation of Islam has upset traditional religious thought. The Honorable Elijah Muhammad and his representative, Minister Louis Farrakhan, have posed challenging material to the religious and scientific world concerning UFOs that have yet to be truly challenged. The NOI's explanation of a human God accompanied by human angels with

---

[157] Yusuf Ali translation of the Holy Qur'an.
[158] Timothy Good, *Need to Know: UFOs, the Military, and Intelligence*, First Pegasus Edition (New York, NY: Pegasus Books, 2007). 250.

material vessels (so-called UFOs) is verifiable through the texts of the Holy Qur'an and the Bible. Nonetheless, these truths have yet to be accepted by the religious world. Instead, mainstream religion continues to ignore the subject of UFOs altogether.

ALLAH'S EXALTED ASSEMBLY

The Holy Qur'an proves that Allah's throne has physical properties from whence Allah officiates. Just as the Bible describes Allah being seen with his hosts (army of Angels), the Holy Qur'an refers to Allah's office of his chief angels as his "Exalted Assembly" (37:8), a group that often resides in the heavens with Allah (God). This is the same assembly mentioned in the Hebrew Bible as **Elohim**, which is a pluralized name of the one God, i.e. a body of Gods. The Bible depicts visions of God being seen upon his exalted throne with others close surrounding. The Holy Qur'an verifies the truth of these Biblical references. According to the Holy Qur'an, Allah (God) has an *Exalted Assembly* (al-Malā al-ā 'lā). This is believed to represent Allah's holy council, which involves an assembly of his highest angels. Other English translations of this assembly use terms such as *Highest Chiefs, lofty Council,* and *Supreme Council.* This body of beings is clearly amongst the highest order with Allah for they are privileged to be in his presence. This assembly is so lofty and exalted that even the holy Prophet Muhammad (PBUH) had limited knowledge pertaining to them and their interactions.

The Honorable Elijah Muhammad enlightened his followers to some of the inner-workings of Allah's lofty council as Master Fard Muhammad revealed it to him. This heavenly body represents Allah and some of his highest-ranking scientists/angels who operate from the Mother Plane. Elijah Muhammad often made it plain that the technology and scientists of this world cannot even get close enough to the Mother Plane to find out the inner-workings upon this huge craft. This has not stopped this world's powers from trying though. Muḥammad gives a description of America's military attempts toward the Wheel:

> It's up there now, and the devil knows it's up there. This is why he is continuing to go up there and make planes that can fly so swift, that if he could discover it in the skies, he would be able to shoot a rocket at it before they would know. He's making planes to search the space with the highest speed known to scientists.[159]

---

[159] "The Theology of Time (Lecture Series)," Vols. July 2, 1972 (Chicago, IL: MUHAMMAD Mosque No. 2, 1972).

UFOS AND THE HOLY QUR'AN

On a separate occasion, Elijah Muhammad reaffirms that the powers of this world would like to reach and destroy Allah's assembly upon the Mother Wheel, and he warned of the consequences thereof:

> The Mother Plane, according to what has been described of it by the devil scientists, is capable of not only staying up for long periods of time; but it is also capable of eluding the scientists. They want to attack and destroy it; but if a plane did get close enough to attempt to carry out this purpose, it would be destroyed instead. The white man has learned that this is not a place to be played with. Planes come out of the Mother Plane.[160]

One of the reasons it is called an *exalted assembly* is due to the heavenly position from whence this council confers. The Mother Plane, which houses the throne of Allah and his assembly of human angels has been the target of intrigue by UFO enthusiasts and military powers alike. The scholars of this world have realized that there is a superior intelligence upon these crafts, which they often call *aliens* or *extraterrestrials*. They continue their attempts to surveillance and possibly capture the power behind these planes although Elijah Muhammad already cautioned them of the consequences. The Holy Qur'an verifies Elijah Muhammad's realization:

> *Surely We have adorned the lower heaven with an adornment, the stars, And (there is) a safeguard against every rebellious devil.*
> *They cannot listen to the exalted assembly and they are reproached from every side* – As-Saffat 37:6-8

Here the Holy Qur'an foretells and warns that the devils will attempt to surveillance what comes from this exalted assembly. This is one reason why the Honorable Elijah Muhammad referred to those Caucasian powers as *the universal snooper*—which implies that they will reach far lengths to spy around on what is taking place in the universe. There is no doubt that the Holy Qur'an and Elijah Muhammad's words have been manifested in modern activity. Numerous reports have shown where the United States Air Force and other world militaries have attempted to chase and strike these UFOs (to no avail). **Space Fence** is a U.S. Air Force Space Surveillance System set up to track *spinning* and *orbital* objects entering Earth's orbit to protect satellites and astronauts before a disaster strikes.[161] Is this part of America's elaborate plan to

---

[160] *The Fall Of America* (Chicago, IL: Elijah Muhammad, 1973). 237.
[161] Patty Welsh, "Space Fence program moves forward," *The Official Web site of the United States Air Force* (United States Air Force, December 21, 2012).

surveillance UFO activity? After all, Muhammad did assert that the Wheel could be seen quite regularly (even though it can become undetectable at will).

Reality shows that millions of people around the world, including governments, are fascinated with UFOs. The scientists of this world are mesmerized because they know that only a supremely advanced and exalted wisdom can guide those crafts. Those planes are actual proofs of an exalted body of persons whose wisdom reaches far beyond the scope of this world. This is part of Allah's exalted assembly mentioned throughout the Holy Qur'an that Islamic scholars still have no real clue about.

Both the Bible and Holy Qur'an share the concept of God with an assembly of angels stationed in the heavens. While these type of prophecies were uttered by prophets, many of them did not know the meaning behind their visions. This is because there is a difference between *revelation* and *actual teaching*. God often revealed visions to his servants, but that does not mean they were taught the full meaning behind their prophecies. The prophet Daniel received prophetic revelations, but did not understand its meanings (Daniel 12:8). John the Revelator was given visions of the high court of God's enthroned assembly but he did not know the full meaning of his visions. Similarly, the holy Prophet Muhammad (PBUH) was revealed the majesty of the Holy Qur'an, but the full meaning of its verses were not taught to him, which is why he prophesied that the messiah would come in the last days—the one whom Allah would teach the meaning of the scriptures to (Al-Imran 3:48).

The ayats (verses) pertaining to Allah's exalted assembly were *revealed* to Prophet Muhammad (PBUH), but even he realized that he was not given the full meaning of these verses. Allah instructed the Prophet to deliver this prophetic message plainly even though he did not know the details pertaining to Allah's exalted chiefs. This is reflected in the following ayats from the Holy Qur'an:

> *I have no knowledge of the exalted chiefs when they contend. Only this is revealed to me that I am a plain warner.* – Sad 38:69

Prophet Muhammad (PBUH) had no knowledge of this exalted body of God because one would later come into the world who would realize the wisdom behind those verses. Here again Elijah Muhammad fulfills this divine role for he has provided the confirmation of the Prophet's prophecies. Strangely, many traditionalists have rejected Elijah Muhammad's evidence even though his mission fulfills what the holy Prophet Muhammad (PBUH) promised.

Throughout the Holy Qur'an Allah (God) uses the term *We* and *Us* in regard to himself. How is it that the one God can have a plural pronoun to refer to himself? This is another question that has dumbfounded the Islamic scholarship. The whole creed of Islam is predicated on the oneness of Allah

UFOS AND THE HOLY QUR'AN

(God), known as *Tawhid*. How can Allah be *one* without any partners when he is part of an assembly of others? The Nation of Islam answers this critical question with practicality. Elijah Muhammad frequently taught about the 'well-trained crew' of scientists who accompany Allah aboard the Mother Plane. Among this assembly of Godly beings, one is the wisest and the best knower who is the Supreme Being. Muhammad states this in plain language:

> When we say Allah, many times we are referring to the Supreme One among us, Allah. His name is Allah, the Supreme Being. We call Him Supreme, because no other being is His equal. We don't mean that He's a spook.[162]

Muhammad clarifies the concept that Allah frequently has persons near him who are exceedingly lofty in wisdom, but Allah is the wisest among them, the most powerful, for there is none like him. Having been taught by this Supreme Being, Elijah Muhammad was very careful how he presented this truth to the broader world of Islam and religion because he was well aware of their lack of understanding. He was aware that even his followers had limited accessibility to the wisdom he possessed:

> I can't talk to you like I want to, because you have not studied what I have studied and have not been told what I have been told of the Supreme being; therefore, I try taking you along as mildly and pleasantly as I possibly can, because I know that you don't know what I know.[163]

This man was given firsthand knowledge about the inner-workings of Allah (God), his assembly of angels/scientists, and the wheel-like vessels they occupy that the world has now labeled UFOs. **Elijah Muhammad gave the truth about UFOs before they ever became a mystery.** He has consistently held that God showed him this vessel (with its numerous smaller planes) and gave him the details about them. It is from this plane that God would back him in his divine mission. He was taught the meaning of the prophecies that religious scholars still do not understand. While theologians can only believe in the scriptures, Elijah Muhammad was given the evidence of its meaning. The Mother Wheel and the baby planes, which are the mechanical works of God in person, are exactly what many of the prophets foresaw in their visions. Otherwise, it would be utterly naïve to take the meaning of those scriptures as literal events in history. This is the mistake that has crippled the world of

---

[162] "The Theology of Time (Lecture Series)," Vols. August, 1972 (Chicago, IL: MUHAMMAD Mosque No. 2, 1972).
[163] "The Theology of Time (Lecture Series)," Vols. October 8, 1972 (Chicago, IL: MUHAMMAD Mosque No. 2, 1972).

religion. In spite of all the evidence, the mainstream religious world has found it difficult to accept the rational proof of God represented by Elijah Muhammad, Louis Farrakhan, and the Nation of Islam.

TRADITIONAL ISLAM'S UFO DILEMMA

For most people, it would sound strange to discuss UFOs in a religious context, especially when dealing with the cultural traditions associated with the Islamic world community (*ummah*). The Islamic world presents somewhat of a peculiar study. Having been the recipients of divine revelation, the Arabs transformed themselves from an intense state of savagery into world leaders in culture, mathematics and various sciences. This was primarily due to the fact that Allah (God) strongly encourages Muslims to read, study, and reflect upon the majesty of his creation. Since the Qur'an contains tons of highly scientific truths (most of which were not discovered until almost a thousand years later), the Muslims who followed its guidance found themselves advancing civilization like never before. The scientific exploration of the Qur'an led to what has become known as *The Golden Age of Islam*. During this time Muslims became the leading proponents of science, mathematics, and civilization who led Europe and the world out of its Dark Ages. However, this reign came to an abrupt halt.

After a while, many Muslims began to re-shift their focus from the scientific exploration of the Qur'an and instead, relied on the Islamic scholars for interpretations of the book—a term known among some Islamic scholars as *taqlid*.[164] The Holy Qur'an contains the most astonishing scientific truths that have yet to be exhausted, but the old understanding has rendered Islamic thought from its *Golden Age* to the *Stone Age*. This ritualistic focus on the *Salafiyyah*[165] and tradition has led much of the Islamic world back in time, which has blinded them from being able to realize the fulfillment of Prophet Muhammad's utterances.

It is evident in the Holy Qur'an that Allah (God) has anthropomorphic qualities and that his throne of power has material qualities associated with it. These verses have caused problems for the *ulema* (Islamic scholars) because such verses imply that Allah has an angelic council who surround him, which makes it difficult to reconcile their notion that Allah has no partners as

---

[164] **Taqlid:** a term used in some schools of Islamic thought that involves following the decisions of religious scholars without necessarily examining the scriptural basis or reasoning of that interpretation.

[165] **Salafiyyah:** a strictly conservative Islamic school of thought that seeks to emulate the generation of Muslims during the time of Prophet Muhammad (PBUH). It is believed that this generation represents a sense of purity in Islam.

mentioned elsewhere in the Holy Qur'an (59:23). Some Muslims believe that "Allah has no partner in anything whatsoever."[166] How can Allah be one, yet have a plural council with him? How can Allah not have a physical presence yet others accompany and surround him? Even still, mainstream Muslims have yet to accept either of these realities. What is more absurd is that the holy Prophet Muhammad (PBUH) gave descriptive prophecies that someone would come in the latter days to make sense of the wisdom contained in the books. The Prophet predicted that there will be a place near Allah's throne which will be a dwelling place for some of his closest and beloved servants:

> "...Paradise has one-hundred grades which Allah has reserved for the Mujahidin who fight in His Cause, and the distance between each of two grades is like the distance between the Heaven and the Earth. So, when you ask Allah (for something), ask for *Al-firdaus* which is the best and highest part of Paradise." (i.e. The sub-narrator added, "I think the Prophet also said, 'Above it (i.e. Al-Firdaus) is the Throne of Beneficent (i.e. Allah), and from it originate the rivers of Paradise.")[167]

The term *Al-firdaus* is said to be the highest part of heaven, which includes the throne ('arsh) of Allah. The Prophet spoke of a time and a place where people would actually be with Allah (God) in the hereafter. It was even suggested that rivers would originate from this paradise, which proves that Allah's heavenly position involves a physical location. The attachment to traditions has to be pretty strong if it won't allow Muslims to accept the prophecies of the holy Prophet.

There is no wonder why the broader Muslim world has not been able to grasp the clear proof that Elijah Muhammad presented to the world. There is no wonder why the Islamic scholars have not been able to realize how the UFO phenomenon fits into the context of Islamic eschatology. Perhaps the worst part of this scenario is that many of the so-called scholars refuse to even reason with the data provided by the Nation of Islam, particularly concerning Allah's relationship to so-called UFOs.

After the departure of the Honorable Elijah Muhammad in 1975, many of the followers of the NOI were led to believe that his teachings concerning the Mother Plane was inherently un-Islamic, heretical, and even mythical. As a result, thousands abandoned Muhammad's teachings and began to follow the old traditional customs of the Muslim world that to this day have no solidified explanation for UFOs. Of course, the UFO phenomenon was not as prevalent

---

[166] Ibn Kathir, "Allah Has No Partner In Anything Whatsoever," *The Holy Book* (theholybook.org, 2006).
[167] Sahih Bukhari 4.48.

in the public back then because the average person did not have the technology that allowed them to see or hear about the many sightings. Furthermore, the media did not convey UFO sightings on the airwaves as much when mass sightings took place (allegedly to prevent any hysteria). As a result, the teachings of the Honorable Elijah Muhammad were mocked by many of his former followers. Little did those Muslims know, Elijah Muhammad's teachings would become more manifest after his departure.

Many Muslims have slowly begun to reconsider the vast body of wisdom within the NOI that was gravely overlooked. Thanks to the Honorable Minister Louis Farrakhan who has worked tirelessly to reestablish the teachings of the Honorable Elijah Muhammad, the world can now examine what was overlooked when the Messenger was among the people. Farrakhan has made the commission of the Honorable Elijah Muhammad known in a world that tried to dismiss him and his unorthodox message of truth. Farrakhan's presence has made it difficult for the religious world to negate the truth of Elijah Muhammad and the wheel-like planes he introduced to the world.

Minister Farrakhan has clarified Elijah Muhammad's role in the messianic prophecies, which is directly connected to the UFO phenomenon. Since Muslims believe that the messiah will teach the deeper wisdom of the scriptures as promised, then it stands to reason that this messianic figure will teach concepts that would seem strange to the traditions that have occupied the religious world. Islam has many prophecies of what is to take place in the latter days, but very few have been willing to reason with the evidence once it is presented. To make things worse, Muslim scholars do not even have a rational *tafsir* (Qur'anic explanation) to reconcile the modern UFO reality with their traditional religious concepts.

6. THE DWELLING PLACE OF GOD

THE CHARIOTS OF GOD – TOO DANGEROUS FOR JEWS

The chariots of God are myriads, thousands upon thousands; The Lord is among them as at Sinai, in holiness. – Psalm 68:17 King James Bible (Cambridge Ed.)

The mysterious objects that God and his angels use to maneuver through the skies are listed under several different terms: wheels, clouds, thrones, whirlwinds, etc. Another common symbol seen in the scriptures involve God's throne chariot. Images of God's chariot have been envisioned by the Major Prophets: Isaiah, Jeremiah, Daniel, and Ezekiel. The term chariot is often mentioned in the Bible as a vehicle of travel. While most of its uses refer to land vehicles, some of the chariots clearly refer to a heavenly mode of transportation.

The ambiguities surrounding God's heavenly travel has been a concept that even Jewish scholars have grappled over. For thousands of years, the scriptures have spoken of God's celestial vessels, but there had not been any evidence of this mystery in the real world. For this reason, many orthodox Jewish scholars have dismissed any literal interpretation of a physical God upon a physical vehicle in the sky. Instead, they have accepted only the spiritual and metaphoric meaning behind those related scriptures. This is because most of the scriptural passages give prophetic glimpses of things that are to come, not actual events that took place yesteryear. In the last few thousand years, there has been no physical evidence of God's heavenly throne-chariot wheels before 1929, so the scholars had no choice but to accept the metaphoric aspects of these prophecies. But now that one has come to make these realities known to the world, these scriptures are no longer a mystery. They have become a reality. **The God who operates from a vehicle in the sky has made himself known by raising the Honorable Elijah Muhammad with clear evidence of his coming.**

Since the Hebrew Bible is filled with prophecies surrounding God's heavenly travels, the throne chariot of God has become the center of certain mystical Jewish sects known as *Merkabah* mysticism. **Merkabah** refers to the throne chariot of God that has been prophesied about throughout the Hebrew Bible. Since Jews have been confounded over the concept of God's sky travel, schools of thought have been formed that attempt to explain this phenomena. One reason behind the fascination is because this Merkabah concept is directly associated with the long-awaited messiah and the chosen people of God. In Hebrew, Merkabah signifies God's throne-chariot as described in the prophetic visions. It is often referenced to Ezekiel's vision (although the term is not explicitly stated there).

Jewish rabbinical scholars have studied and anticipated the coming of the messiah who is expected to have a direct relationship with these wheel-like crafts. The anomaly lies in the fact that the more they study this concept, the more problems arise with the Jewish theology. The more these scriptures are studied, it debunks the whole foundation of Jewish claims of being the Chosen people of God. Jeffrey J. Harrison writes the following:

> According to the rabbis, there is one chapter in the Bible that is so dangerous, it is forbidden to be taught to groups of disciples. It could be taught to no more than one student at a time, and only if he is a mature student. This chapter is so dangerous, it is forbidden to be read in the regular synagogue service. It led some of Israel's most famous rabbis to engage in strange mystical practices that killed one of them, made another crazy, and led another to heresy. For hundreds of years, even the name of this chapter caused knowledgeable Jews to shudder. What chapter is this? They call it Merkabah: The Chariot [Ezekiel Chapter 1]...
>
> The chariot was a powerful religious symbol for ancient Israel: not the ordinary chariots used for war, but what the Bible calls "chariots of fire."[168]

Harrison notes how the concept of God's chariot has caused so much confusion in Jewish scholarship that it is considered a subject area of extreme danger. Since Jewish scholars have not been able to reconcile their scriptures with any tangible reality, some of them have abandoned their faith altogether. How is it that one Biblical concept can be so confusing that rabbis consider it a "dangerous" subject and approach it with such apprehensions? Maybe this is primarily due to the fact that so much of the Jewish faith is predicated on a concept that God's people are to be guided and protected from these heavenly vessels. Therefore, a requisite indication of the true people of God is their connection to a God who operates from such a wheel-like craft. This criterion is one of many that debunks the Jewish claim of being the chosen people of God. Simultaneously this criteria solidifies the Nation of Islam's argument that Black people of America are indeed the people of God's choice.

This foretold requirement has caused Jewish scholars to relegate their studies of these crafts into secretive mysticism. In fact, Jewish historians admit that the earliest forms of mysticism among Jews relates to God's prophetic

---

[168] Jeffrey J. Harrison, "The Chariot," *To The Ends Of The Earth* (2008).

throne-chariot. According to Gershom Scholem, "the earliest Jewish mysticism is throne mysticism."[169] Rabbis have studied the prophecies concerning an anthropomorphic God who will appear to his chosen people and protect them from what would seem to be an insurmountable enemy. Rabbinical scholars know that this predestined people will have undergone a dilemma that only God himself could rectify. The NOI proves that no people in history have undergone the type of slavery and oppression as the Black man and woman of America. It is this fundamental theological argument that lies at the root of controversy between Caucasian Jews and the Nation of Islam.

The Nation of Islam's inherent UFO theology further solidifies this argument, which is why Jewish scholars have refused to have an open dialogue or debate on these pressing topics. Instead, powerful Jews have used their influence over media and education to besmirch the character of the NOI and its leadership. These efforts are used to prevent the public from realizing that the NOI answers and fulfills the prophecies that Jews have secretly studied regarding God's chosen people and his throne-chariot. Minister Farrakhan has publicly challenged all religious scholars and theologians on this very subject. **"Today we are prepared to call out the scholars of Christianity, Judaism, and Islam. If you can disprove what we say today, then I will pay with my life!"**[170] The Minister has publicly dared the scholarship of the world to challenge the NOI on this issue. He even put his life on the line if anyone can disprove the NOI's position on this subject. As much as many Jews vehemently hate Minister Farrakhan and the Black Muslims, wouldn't this be an opportunity for them to justifiably kill the man they have wanted dead for years? The same Jews who publicly chanted for the death of Farrakhan have not accepted the opportunity to do so. All they would have to do is accept Minister Farrakhan's dare that if they can disprove the NOI's position regarding God's chosen people, then he would give his life. NO JEWISH SCHOLAR HAS PUT FORTH A CHALLENGE TO THIS THEOLOGICAL ARGUMENT! What is it that Jewish scholars know about the Nation of Islam and Black people that they don't want the public to know?

In a feeble effort to avoid dealing with this topic, Jewish scholars like Dr. Harold Brackman, PhD wrote a diatribe against Minister Farrakhan with a nonsensical outburst besmirching the NOI's belief in the Mother Plane:

---

[169] *Major Trends in Jewish Mysticism* (New York, New York: Shocken Books Inc., 1995).
[170] "Who Are The Real Children Of Israel?" (Atlanta, GA: The Final Call, June 26, 2010).

> With a backward-looking message of hate, Farrakhan's UFO-"mother ship" navigates cyberspace spewing noxious emissions designed to poke a hole in the ozone layer protecting tolerance.[171]

The hypocrisy and incompetency of many Jewish leaders to challenge this truth is plainly evident. Knowing this prophetic vessel's relationship to God's chosen people, some Jews like Dr. Brackman totally avoid approaching this topic with scholarly acumen. Rather, they resort to childish mockery hoping that others will not investigate this subject with reason. This type of reaction from Jewish leaders toward the NOI's connection to UFOs has become commonplace. It seems this is the best response they can render against the truth.

The Jews' hatred of Minister Farrakhan strangely resembles the hatred that Jews had for Jesus 2000 years earlier. Citing words from the Honorable Elijah Muhammad, Minister Farrakhan has expressed how part of the Jewish hatred of Jesus stems from the fact that Jesus' role was to end the rule of the so-called Jews[172]—the ones he called the Synagogue of Satan (Revelation 2:9, 3:9). The same reason those Jews hated Jesus yesterday entails why certain Jews hate Farrakhan and the NOI today.

While Jesus did not end the rule of the Jews 2000 years ago, the promised Messiah embodies the same principles and fulfills these expectations. This explains much of the Jewish hatred against Minister Farrakhan who shares in this messianic role. The Messiah's destruction of Satan's civilization does not begin with the use of arms or weapons; instead it starts as a revelatory truth that exposes the Synagogue of Satan, which enlightens the people to Satan's true identity. The Honorable Elijah Muhammad revealed the 'man of sin' as it was written (2 Thessalonians 2:3) and he left Minister Farrakhan to fulfill the more specific assignment of exposing Satan's inner-workings. This is not a job relegated for anyone—these jobs are reserved for the Messiah. That huge Wheel in the sky signals proof of the Messiah's presence in the world and the destruction of Satan's domination.

The reason why Minister Farrakhan can speak so boldly to power without fear of consequences is because of this sure truth, which is further substantiated by that human-built planet. This God-centered plane explains why the unarmed Muslims of the NOI have always been required NOT to possess carnal weapons. The Muslims are not allowed to carry as much as a penknife on their persons. Yet they have been the most vocal proponents in

---

[171] Harold Brackman, "Louis Farrakhan at 80: A Needless Legacy of Hate," *Brandeis Center Blog*, May 3, 2013.

[172] Elijah Muhammad, *Our Saviour Has Arrived* (Chicago, IL: MUHAMMAD'S TEMPLE No. 2, 1974).166. ...he was ahead of the time of the Jews to preach the doctrine of the destruction or judgment and the setting up of a New Kingdom of Heaven after the destruction of the Jew's civilization.

exposing the wicked atrocities of the most powerful world governments and their military forces. Common sense should allow even the skeptical onlooker to conclude that either the Muslims are totally insane or they are certain of the power of Master Fard Muhammad's supreme host of weapons.

GOD HAS FLYING CHARIOTS OF FIRE

The prophecies of the Hebrew Bible clearly indicate the coming of God, his messiah, and his means of operation from heavenly vessels that would be used to guide and protect the people of his choice—a people so vulnerable and destroyed that God would utilize flying vessels to contend with their enemies. Ironically, most contemporary Jewish leaders do not accept the belief of a physical God, with physical angels who operate from a flying object. Again, the NOI is quite distinct in this area as far as religious communities are concerned.

One of the most promising passages of God's chariot is found in the Bible's Book of 2 Kings. It is from this scripture that the major prophet Elijah is seen taken up on a fiery chariot via a whirlwind to heaven:

> *And it came to pass, as they still went on, and talked, that, behold, there appeared a chariot of fire, and horses of fire, and parted them both asunder; and Elijah went up by a whirlwind into heaven.* – 2 Kings 2:11

This epic Biblical story plays a monumental role in the Jewish tradition whereas certain customs surround this prophetic passage. Because the prophet Elijah was taken upon this chariot and never tasted death, Jews await the return of Elijah during their ritual of *Seder*. This expectation is also rooted in the Book of Malachi 4:5 whereas it is predicted that Elijah would be sent by God "before the great and dreadful day of the Lord". The Seder ritual during the Passover is observed by preparing a feast at a table and leaving a door slightly ajar as Jews await Elijah's eminent return.

Considering that Jews expect Elijah's return, would they accept him if he really appeared? Would they accept him if he were a Black man from the despised and the rejected people who have been loathed by many Caucasian Jews?[173] Would they accept Elijah if he brought proof of his connection to a

---

[173] Jewish Historian, Dr. Harold Brackman notes, "There is no denying that the Babylonian Talmud was the first source to read a Negrophobic content into the episode by stressing Canaan's fraternal connections with Cush . . . The Talmudic glosses of the episode added the stigma of blackness to the fate of

modern fiery chariot that fulfills what was predicted? Evidence shows that there is a high likelihood that Caucasian Jews would NOT accept the fulfillment of the prophecies when they come into fruition. The proof is found in the Jewish treatment of Elijah Muhammad, Louis Farrakhan, and the Nation of Islam who represent an evidential materialization of what Jewish Rabbis have long studied.

Interestingly, the scriptural story of Elijah's ascension upon God's heavenly chariot has an uncanny relationship to Ezekiel's Wheel. Before Elijah was taken up, he and his protégé Elisha left from a recondite location known in Hebrew as **Gilgal**. The etymological meaning of this term is rooted in a *wheel*. Gilgal stems from the Hebrew term ***galgal***, which is one of the singular terms used to identify Ezekiel's wheel. The name Gilgal is said to mean *a wheel or rolling thing*.[174] It is this same root that has been used to signify a whirlwind (due to its rolling nature). Hence, there remains an inherent etymological connection with the wheels prophesied by Ezekiel, Elijah's chariot, and the whirlwind from whence it appeared. When examining the etymological signs of God's flying vehicles, the Honorable Elijah Muhammad's truth about the Mother Wheel becomes crystallized today.

Elijah Muhammad admits that he represents the materialized fulfillment of the Biblical Elijah who had an intrinsic relationship to God's heavenly chariot:

> It is up to you to listen, and as you listen, read and remember. If God says in the Bible, before that dreadful day shall come I will send you Elijah, I am Elijah!
> …I am Elijah of your Bible![175]

Since there is no valid historical evidence that the Elijah of the past ever really saw a spaceship capable of carrying him into the heavens, it stands to reason that the prophet Elijah gives us a prophetic glimpse of what the *Elijah* of the last days would experience. This is why Elijah Muhammad did not refer to himself as a prophet because prophets tell of things to come. Instead, he referred to himself as God's messenger who fulfills what the former prophets envisioned.

Just as the Honorable Elijah Muhammad recognized his divine role in light of scripture, those near to him also share in this divine light. In the Bible, Elijah had a designated representative, Elisha, who was granted a double

---

enslavement that Noah predicted for Ham's progeny" ("The Ebb and Flow of Conflict: A History of Black-Jewish Relations Through 1900" pages 79-81).
[174] Arie Uittenbogaard, "Meaning and etymology of the Hebrew name Gilgal" (Abarim Publications, 2011).
[175] "The Theology of Time (Lecture Series)," Vols. June 4, 1972 (Chicago, IL: MUHAMMAD Mosque No. 2, 1972).

portion of Elijah's spirit. Elisha was appointed to uphold the mission of Elijah during his absence. Similarly, Elijah Muhammad appointed Minister Louis Farrakhan as his National Representative who, like Elisha, was publicly commissioned by Elijah to carry on his divine work. Before his departure, the Honorable Elijah Muhammad gave these instructions to the believing community of the Nation of Islam:

> I want you to pay good attention to his preaching. His preaching is a bearing of witness to me and what God has given to me. This is one of the strongest national preachers that I have in the bounds of North America. Everywhere you hear him, listen to him. Everywhere you see him, look at him. Everywhere he advises you to go, go. Everywhere he advises you to stay from, stay from... He's not a proud man. He's a very humble man. If he can carry you across the lake without dropping you in, he doesn't say when he gets on the other side, " See what I have done?" He tells you, " See what Allah has done." ...and I say, continue to hear our Minister Farrakhan.[176]

Minister Farrakhan has been the number one propagator of the Mother Wheel and baby planes that his teacher introduced to the world. He manifests aspects of the Biblical Elisha who too had experiences with God's chariots of fire. After Elijah had ascended, the Biblical Elisha witnessed the glory of the Lord during a vulnerable moment. The enemies of Elisha were out to capture him because he kept exposing their secret war plans. Just when the enemy's army seemed to trap him in the small town of Dothan, Elisha prayed, then he and his servant witnessed God's power over his enemies (2 Kings 6:17).

Like Elisha, the Honorable Minister Louis Farrakhan has been in a heated controversy with the most powerful entities in the world. The American Government, under the influence of Zionists pressure, has sought to destroy Minister Farrakhan, the Nation of Islam, and the lost people of God. In the mid 1980s during a time when Jews were calling for his death, Farrakhan had a vision-like experience whereas he was carried from a smaller (baby) plane, spoke with Elijah Muhammad (who was supposed to be dead), and witnessed that huge Mother Plane that Elijah Muhammad so often spoke of. The Minister has continuously exclaimed this experience to the world since the mid-1980s.

With Farrakhan at the helm, the unarmed Muslims in the NOI continue to propagate the reality of the Mother Plane in the physical absence of the Honorable Elijah Muhammad. Amidst their controversy with powerful Jews, the Minister made these daring claims before the American people, the

---

[176] "The Theology of Time (Lecture Series)," Vols. July 30, 1972 (Chicago, IL: MUHAMMAD Mosque No. 2, 1972).

Government, and their powerful cohorts who wished to destroy him and the work of the Nation of Islam:

> That which you call "Unidentified Flying Objects"; that which you and white people put "Above Top Secret": that is real. There is a plane out there made like a wheel... It has 1500 little planes on it. They follow me everywhere I go. You can take it or leave it. I am not trying to impress you![177]

Like Elisha's ordeal in the Bible, Farrakhan's firsthand experience with the power of these wheels has proven to him and those who observe his work that there is a power behind him that Jews and world leaders refuse to openly acknowledge.

Although the scriptures use slightly different terminology to describe God's flying vessels, they all seem to point to the wheel-like planes that the NOI introduced to the modern world. In many cases the term chariot used in the Bible stems from the Hebrew word **rekeb**. While this term often refers to a chariot, it also refers to a millstone, which is a circular stone shaped like a wheel. It is from the same root of *rekeb* that the Hebrew word **Merkabah** is derived. Both Merkabah and rekeb stem from the same trilliteral root [178] **R-K-B**, which denotes a circular object. Therefore, at the root of Merkabah mysticism is the essence of God's heavenly throne-chariot, which is circular in nature. The Merkabah that mystic Jews have been studying turns out to be the Mother Wheel operated by the God of Elijah Muhammad to save his people.

Since the fulfillment of God's celestial Merkabah has been revealed to the children of slaves (Black people), many powerful Jews have increased their enmity toward the Nation of Islam and its leadership. This is one of many reasons why most Jews do not openly mock Minister Farrakhan or the NOI for their intrinsic belief in these wheels. Instead, they have used their influence in the media and government to discredit the NOI to prevent potential listeners from ever hearing such a truth.

THE AIRCRAFT OF ANGELS

In many scriptural passages, angels and flying vessels are described in ways that depict them as one in the same. It often seems as though mysterious angels fly on wings much like the super heroes in today's Hollywood movies. One likely reason for this imagery is because the strange vessels envisioned by

---

[177] "Public Lecture Delivered at Christ Universal Temple" (Chicago, IL: The Final Call, February 24, 1989).

[178] A **billiteral** or **trilliteral** root refers to the basic two or three consonant letters of Semitic words (absent the vowels) that can often be used to determine the root meaning of words.

the prophets would be piloted by the angels. This explains why there seems to be a direct connection between angels and flight. As the Messenger stated, angels are humans who are highly advanced scientists well-beyond the grasp of this world's intelligence. Humans do not fly without necessary vessels, nor do those planes fly without intelligent control. Like the planes they control, the angels have different purposes, attributes, and characteristics.

One of the terms used throughout the Bible to indicate a certain angel of God is a *cherub* (plural *cherubs* or *cherubim*). This concept has yielded tremendous confusion to the Judeo-Christian scholarship because scriptures don't give any definitive facts about them. Only symbolic characteristics are given throughout the Bible. Most of these descriptions associate cherubs with humans, guardians, angels, and flying vehicles. The theological confusion about cherubim led to the depiction of cherubim to the cupid styled beings found in European art. This is the imagery that has commonly been attributed to angels throughout the world. Cherubs serve as both guards (hosts) and as part of God's chariots (pilots). Genesis 3:24 describes them as earthly beings who guarded the way to the tree of life. They also guard God's throne (2 Samuel 6:2, 1 Chronicles 13:6, Isaiah 37:16). Cherubs are also described as flying vehicles (2 Samuel 22:11, Psalms 18:10).

While religious exegeses do not satisfy rational explanations for these mysterious cherubs, the descriptions become more practical when considering Elijah Muhammad's teachings:

> Out of that wheel, he said, he saw something come down from it. He called them Cherubims. We thought that he was talking about angels, but that was not angels, that was another plane coming out of this plane.[179]

These cherubim are not angels alone; instead, they are the wheel-like planes that people describe as UFOs today, which are controlled by angels. This explanation demystifies the notion of angels as cupid-like creatures with wings protruding from their backs. Just as the Bible describes the cherubim surrounding the throne of God, there are frequent UFO sightings that describe a large circular object surrounded by smaller circular crafts.

Biblical theologians may agree that cherubs serve in somewhat of a guardian capacity related to God's throne. Elijah Muhammad offers more specificity regarding these angels by noting that they not only protect the righteous, but the planes they control also have the prophetic capabilities of destroying America's wicked powers over the world.

---

[179] "The Theology of Time (Lecture Series)," Vols. July 9, 1972 (Chicago, IL: MUHAMMAD Mosque No. 2, 1972).

> This plane carries 1,500 of these small bombing planes. Each one of the bombing planes carries three bombs, and will take these bombs over a designated area, dropping them for covering destroying 50 miles where they're dropped.[180]

These are the vessels that God and his angels are to use to protect his chosen people from their deceitful oppressors. Secretly aware of Muhammad's representation of these planes, the U.S. Defense Department has frequently viewed these planes in an antagonistic light. This attitude was subtly exemplified in President Ronald Reagan's words during his address to the United Nations 42nd General Assembly on September 21, 1987.

> In our obsession with antagonisms of the moment, we often forget how much unites all the members of humanity. Perhaps we need some outside, universal threat to make us recognize this common bond. I occasionally think how quickly our differences worldwide would vanish if we were facing an alien threat from outside this world.

Although world governments are aware of what the NOI propagates, there remains a persistent goal to never openly acknowledge what Elijah Muhammad first brought to the modern world's attention. This unwelcoming attitude is shared by governments and religious systems alike.

The Honorable Elijah Muhammad spoke of his direct relationship with some of the angels of God whom he called scientists. He mentioned that different scientists have different roles and functions related to God's will. Similarly, the Bible describes angels under different titles and roles. One of the terms that prophet Ezekiel and John the Revelator used to describe those living creatures (beings) was **chayot.** Stemming from the Hebrew word *khayyot*, this refers to a category of angels associated with God's heavenly chariots. These are the *living beings* described in the first chapter of Ezekiel as having the shape of a man with faces that resemble various creatures. Although shrouded in symbolism, this obvious characteristic indicates the humanly nature of these angelic beings. They are associated with flight, being described as traveling *like lightning*. This description bears witness to the modern UFO characteristics whereas witnesses report disc-shaped objects that take off at enormous speeds. Revelation 4:6 identifies these creatures as angels of God.

Considering that mainstream religion has no clear explanation for angels or UFOs, some religious bodies have asserted that UFOs represent a demonic element. Some Christian apologists have asserted that UFOs are "machinations" that are "simply designed to prevent as many human beings as

---

[180] "The Theology of Time (Lecture Series)," Vols. July 2, 1972 (Chicago, IL: MUHAMMAD Mosque No. 2, 1972).

possible from accepting the gospel of Jesus Christ."[181] Other religious commentators suggest that UFOs are Satanic entities that have been cast down to earth to persuade humanity against the Bible:

> Satan's plan involves deceiving humans into accepting aliens and ufos, and a global religion based on the occult which will pave the way for antichrist. The main focus of this deception will be to convince humans that the Bible was wrong.[182]

If UFOs are Satanic beings designed to convince people that the Bible is wrong, they would be much more successful by encouraging anyone to study the history of the Bible, a subject which would clearly prove that the Bible has been tampered with. Besides, how is it that the Bible gives clear pictures that God and his angels would be seen up on heavenly vessels, yet some Christians attribute such heavenly vessels as demonic? Irrational explanations such as these are a testament that the religious world cannot make sense of the real-life UFO phenomenon with their understanding of divine scripture. Outside of the Nation of Islam and those who study their teachings, no religious scholars have been able to accurately rationalize UFOs with religious scriptures.

Elijah Muhammad gave clarity to the concept of angels and the wheel-like planes they pilot—a concept that still perplexes the religious world. As one delves into the etymology of many of the Biblical names related to God's flying vessels, it becomes evident that the prophetic utterances were directed toward the wheels propagated by Muhammad's Nation of Islam. The Hebrew word *ophanim* means wheels, particularly those related to the throne of God as described in the Book of Ezekiel. Bible scholars have no solidified answer regarding what these wheels are. Some attribute them as angelic beings while others assume them to be crafts that uphold the throne of God as mentioned in the Book of Daniel 7:9. Again, Muhammad synthesized and concretized the meaning of these mysteries since his early 1930s witness of the Mother Wheel.

THE NEW JERUSALEM

---

[181] Bob Hamrick and Suzanne Hamrick, "Exposing Satan's 'Left Behind' Chapter 16," *UFOs - Demonic Deception? Crop Circles, UFOs & Animal Mutilations Signs Of The Beginning Of The End?* (02 21, 2011).

[182] David Flynn, "Satan's Counterfeits: Judgment Day - UFOs, Angels & End Time Prophecy" (Watcher Website, 2012).

So he took me in the Spirit to a great, high mountain, and he showed me the holy city, Jerusalem, descending out of heaven from God. – Revelation 21:10

The Honorable Elijah Muhammad expressed the dual nature of the Mother Wheel. It is said to have two natures. Both the prophets and Elijah Muhammad gave descriptions about the destructive capabilities of God's planes that will be used to bring down the satanic powers of this world. He gave numerous warnings about how they will be witnessed over America's cities and how their pilot-scientists know all about the chicanery within the minds of world leaders. He spoke of how they would drop bombs in strategic places throughout America that would render her into oblivion because of her evils done to God's lost people. However, this only denotes one side of the plane's nature. The other side of the Mother Plane represents everlasting life, healing, and peace forevermore—a plane that represents salvation from the wisdom of God. While the concept of a real utopia may seem unrealistic to this world, it makes sense that the inexplicable capabilities demonstrated by such a plane can render a type of peace unimaginable to contemporary standards. This other side of the Mother Plane's purpose is why the Bible describes it as The *New Jerusalem*.

The *New Jerusalem* is among the many scriptural names used to describe that great Mother Plane taught by Elijah Muhammad and Minister Farrakhan. This is a heavenly city that prophets envisaged as a place so holy that it would be where God resides. This picture is synonymous with countless other Judeo-Christian and Islamic texts that speak of God in a celestial material station.

The fact that prophets foresaw this New Jerusalem is indicative of its prophetic, yet tangible qualities. The adjective *New* denotes that it had not yet come into the world during the time such prophecies were given. It would be a place that had never been seen before, yet it would have some of the qualities of the original Jerusalem, which was a city founded in peace.[183] Whereas the Jerusalem of yesterday was founded in God's peace, the New Jerusalem would be a place founded directly by God himself. This is one of the reasons why it is described as "the city of the living God, the heavenly Jerusalem" (Hebrews 12:22).

Unlike the old Jerusalem, which was limited to the earth's geography, the New Jerusalem will be one that resides in the heavenly skies. Hence, it is described in Galatians 4:26 as "the Jerusalem above." All of these demarcations

---

[183] The etymological meaning of **Jerusalem** is from the Semitic roots *yeru* meaning founded and *salem*, which is the peace of God. Hence, the name Jerusalem literally means founded in peace. This is further connoted in *The Supreme Wisdom Lessons* of the Nation of Islam in question 5 of "Lost Found Muslim Lesson No. 1".

indicate a physical place stationed in the skies that contains the physical embodiment of God himself. These characteristics delineate the Mother Plane that Elijah Muhammad daringly professed as the fulfillment of such prophecies. Muhammad's teachings regarding the specifics of this plane are the answer to what the prophecies described under varying terms. Unlike other hypotheses, tafsirs, and exegeses, Muhammad's claims are clearly distinguished in that he provided tangible evidence to substantiate his monumental claims. Moreover, he was the first and most accurate to describe these saucer-styled objects before they even became a public concern. He answered the questions before the questions were ever raised.

The Mother Wheel as the New Jerusalem represents the new order, the new paradigm, and the new way of life that will become established on earth after the destruction of this present world of Satanic rule. Prophets prayed for the day when this plane would become a reality. *The Lord's Prayer* petitions God that his will be done on earth as it is in heaven. Similarly the life and perfection upon the wheel will one day become manifest on the earth. This is one of the reasons why it is depicted as "the holy city" that "comes down out of heaven from God" (Revelation 21:2, 10). John the Revelator envisioned it as a city, Elijah Muhammad similarly described it as a man-made planet and as a new civilization:

> You will see this plane one day because it has a civilization on it. They stay up there a year and sometimes a year and a half in that plane. It's a wonderful thing.[184]

Elijah Muhammad and his appointed representative, Louis Farrakhan, have consistently taught that the Wheel contains the cure for any and every ailment, disease, or disorder that currently plagues the world. This is one of the many reasons why the title *mother* is given to this particular plane. It is from this craft that the new world will come into existence. Just as a mother produces new life from her womb, the Mother Plane contains the love and wisdom of Allah (God) that eternity will be founded upon. This is why the scriptures describe it in this manner:

> *But Jerusalem which is above is free, which is the mother of us all.* – Galatians 4:26

Interestingly, the word *above* in this passage is translated from the

---

[184] "The Theology of Time (Lecture Series)," Vols. July 2, 1972 (Chicago, IL: MUHAMMAD Mosque No. 2, 1972).

Greek ανω ano⊠, which actually means 'up above.' So here is a Jerusalem stationed up in the sky that is free from all the problems, sicknesses, and troubles that characterize the present world. Elijah Muhammad explained that this Wheel was created by a 'perfect' God who came in the person of Master Fard Muhammad to whom praise is due forever. Elijah Muhammad noted that his God's wisdom is so perfect that the foundation of the hereafter will be based on what he establishes in the world. The Mother Wheel is indicative of that new heaven and new earth that has not fully been introduced to this world yet. Minister Farrakhan notes how the Wheel has the answer to everything that is needed on the earth:

> There's another part to that Wheel—**The New Jerusalem**. In a toxic planet with toxic air, toxic water and toxic earth—[but] up there, everything we've got down here, they got it up there.[185]

The Minister explained that the earth below has become poisoned and toxic because the powers of the world have been in the hands of unscrupulous stewards who have corrupted the air, water, and land. Contrastingly the Wheel has the healing and solutions that trouble this world. In earlier lectures, the Minister spoke of the type of abundant life on the Wheel:

> There's a new vegetation on the Wheel. There are new feed on the Wheel. There is new life on the Wheel. You don't age on the Wheel.[186]

These words have been validated in numerous UFO case histories. During Sid Padrick's historic 1965 encounter on a UFO, he shared how the people on the ship communicated to him about their lifestyle. According to Padrick, one of those *persons* shared these words with him:

> As you know it, we have no sickness, we have no crimes, we have no police force. We have no schools – our young are taught at an early age to do a job, which they do very well. Because of our long life expectancy we have a very strict birth control. We have no money. We live as one.[187]

Whether one acknowledges Padrick's encounter or not, it cannot be denied that the most credible UFO case histories have striking resemblances to the characteristics that were first given by Elijah Muhammad. These

---

[185] "The Time And What Must Be Done," *Saviours' Day 2010 Keynote Address by The Honorable Minister Louis Farrakhan* (Chicago, IL: The Final Call, 2010 йил 28-February).
[186] "The Shock of The Hour" (Chicago, IL: The Final Call, 1992 26-April).
[187] Timothy Good, *Need to Know: UFOs, the Military, and Intelligence*, First Pegasus Edition (New York, NY: Pegasus Books, 2007). 250.

characteristics are just some of the fulfilling elements of what the Bible calls the New Jerusalem. The answer to every problem, every disease, and every issue is present on the Wheel. On this plane there is no deviousness, no lies, no poverty or want. This New Jerusalem contains the true freedom, justice, and equality that will reign for eternity. It holds the throne of the Supreme Being where the angels sing his praises. This is what Elijah Muhammad and the Nation of Islam introduced to the world before any others began making postulations relating the scriptural prophecies to the modern UFO phenomenon.

7. HISTORY AND THE NEW ERA

WHERE WERE UFOS BEFORE ELIJAH MUHAMMAD?

Who in America, who in the world was teaching about these unidentified flying objects fifty-five years ago [from 1987]? Nobody! But a man taught it and stuck by it, and here comes now the revelation that it's real! And even if you think the man was mistaken, soon you're going to see them![188]
– The Honorable Minister Louis Farrakhan

While the term UFO (unidentified flying object) has been commonly thought to signify some type of extraterrestrial life from other planets, the term actually refers to any type of unexplained aerial phenomenon. Strange activities have been taking place in the skies and on the earth since history has been recorded. However, there is a huge distinction between those strange occurrences that have taken place before the Mother Plane's construction and the UFO phenomenon that has caught the attention of the world afterwards. As previously stated, this research does not equate just any UFO with the planes that Elijah Muhammad propagated as the work of God in the person of Master Fard Muhammad.

Through a careful study of history and UFOs, it becomes increasingly clear that the strange occurrences that took place before Elijah Muhammad's advent are not the same as the planes that dominated the UFO frenzy afterwards. The huge circular craft along with the many smaller wheel-like planes that Master Fard Muhammad revealed to Elijah Muhammad comprise the preponderance of today's authentic sightings, reports, and encounters. For this reason it should be understood that most of the unexplained disc-shaped planes that people call UFOs are evidences that Elijah Muhammad was taught by the Supreme Being.

The modern UFO phenomenon began when Master Fard Muhammad developed the construction of what Elijah Muhammad described as a man-made planet. By 1929 amidst the islands of Japan, Master Fard Muhammad's host of guided scientists constructed a huge spacecraft unlike any technological feat witnessed in human history. This huge circular plane was made to fulfill the prophecies and offer tangible evidence of the superiority of a realistic God who has remained a mystery for millions of years. This craft hosts a multitude

---

[188] "The Reality Of The Mother Plane" (Chicago, IL: The Final Call Inc., January 4, 1987).

of 1500 smaller planes with similar capabilities. They travel with unfathomable speeds and maneuverability. Those who have witnessed some of their capabilities find it hard to acknowledge that humans were responsible for its construction, which is why many attempt to attribute the UFO phenomenon to extraterrestrial aliens.

Shortly after Elijah Muhammad's encounter with Master Fard Muhammad in 1931, Elijah was taught by this very light-skinned man from the East. Elijah Muhammad recognized this man as that long-awaited one whom the scriptures prophesied would come in the last days. This conception began the relationship that is synonymous with the physical appearances of God to his messengers. Elijah Muhammad recognized this man as the physical manifestation of Allah (God) in the person of Master Fard Muhammad. This Master taught Elijah Muhammad the wisdom of prophecies, the unknown sciences of the universe, the forgotten histories of man, and the secrets of the inner-sanctum of God. One of the most obvious and intriguing of these teachings involve the reality of that Mother Plane. Some time after their meeting in 1931, Master Fard Muhammad pointed out to Elijah Muhammad that huge man-made planet in the sky.

Scientists, engineers, scholars, researchers, and theologians have not been able to explain UFOs, which is obviously why they are called **unidentified flying objects**. However, the Honorable Elijah Muhammad has been able to identify and answer the most pressing questions and concerns about these crafts because he was shown this reality by the very Supreme Being responsible for its construction. Muhammad's firsthand orientation of these crafts and the God that pointed it out to him, have been the foundational principles on which the Nation of Islam (NOI) exists. Despite the Muslims continuous propagation of these *vehicles of God*, researchers and authorities refuse to publicly acknowledge the truth of what Master Fard Muhammad introduced to the world through Elijah Muhammad. It should be noted that the Muslims in the Nation of Islam don't just believe in what are called UFOs; instead, the Nation of Islam is responsible for the promulgation of these objects into the modern world. A careful look through history further proves this position.

As this research offers historical insight into the history of UFOs, the prophecies of the sacred scriptures of the Bible and Holy Qur'an are not included as historical events. This is because there remains hardly any evidence or indication that the UFO-like occurrences of the scriptures actually took place in history. As previously explained, those scriptures are comprised of visions and prophecies that are often shrouded in symbolism, which do not represent actual events of the past, but instead they represent images of *what will come*. Prophets are not historians and historians are not prophets. Therefore, this writing accepts the prophetic scriptures for what they are intended to represent—prophecies, not history. Confusing history and prophecy is a mistake that many ufologists have made. Many UFO scholars have taken Ezekiel's vision of the wheels, and other visions of heavenly vehicles as events in history despite the fact that they are prophecies. Again, there is no evidence that any of such occurrences ever took place in history, which is why this research does not use the scriptures for its historicity.

As previously stated, there were strange aerial phenomena in the world prior to the time of the Mother Plane's construction. There are cases of unidentified things or events that took place before 1929. However, those activities do not coincide with the wheel-like objects that constitute the majority of UFO sightings in this day and time. An examination of UFO history shows that there may only be about three cases before the Wheel's construction that offer a resemblance to the planes described by Elijah Muhammad. Even among these cases, there is evidence that suggests that they were likely natural astronomical occurrences (meteors, debris, etc.), attempted aircraft, pranks, hoaxes, or other creative figments that were frequently found in fictional literature of the times. Moreover, it was not until the 1950s that any credible UFO abduction case was reported.[189] So the influx of authentic UFO cases of the wheels became manifest after Elijah Muhammad's acquaintance with them.

In January of 1878, there was a case that could have been labeled a UFO sighting, but the specifics of this case do not add up to the sightings of today. Information about this particular case was found in the January 25, 1878 edition of *The Denison Daily News* where it was stated that a local farmer reported seeing a balloon-shaped object. BJ Booth writes about this scenario in his article:

> A Texas farmer, John Martin, was credited with one of the first uses of the term "flying saucer." Martin had actually seen a "balloon-shaped" UFO, but used the saucer term to describe the size of the object from his perspective. Martin's sighting was on January 2. What he saw was a dark object high in the sky. The object was moving closer to him all the while. Because the object maintained a dark color, there was speculation that the object was solid and backlit.[190]

Even though this account is said to be the first to use the term *saucer* to describe a UFO, the term did not apply to the shape of what Mr. Martin saw. Instead, it was said to be the size of a small saucer, which are only a few inches. The actual shape was said to be "balloon-shaped." It should be noted that

---

[189] Jacques Vallee, *Forbidden Science: Journals 1957-1969* (Marlowe & Co, 1993). 225.
[190] "Before the Wright Brothers... There Were UFOs," *American Chronicle*, December 8, 2006.

HISTORY AND THE NEW ERA

balloons were quite prevalent in the world at that time. Considering the small size and the balloon-shape, this account does not measure up to the wheels that have been witnessed by millions today.

There have been claims that the first documented encounter with a UFO occurred on July 3, 1893. This alleged encounter was reported in the *Tacoma Ledger Newspaper* headlined as *"An Electric Monster, Flashes of light and Terrible Sounds Emitted by One in the Bay."* These loud sounds and flashes of light were said to leave two men unconscious. While this report appears to resemble lightning and thunder, it was said to come from a type of monster with horns on its head, which is why it was described as an "electric monster."[191] This vague account does not give specific delineations concerning any vehicle or craft that resembles the circular crafts seen today. In fact, the fictional-like descriptions of this account make it questionable to even be considered as an actual event. Thus, this alleged *encounter* cannot be equated with the credible UFO encounters described in the post-1930s world.

In 1904, Lt. Frank Schofield stated that he saw three egg-shaped objects moving across the sky. The largest of these three objects he described as being the size of about "six suns."[192] While contemporary UFO enthusiasts may label this as a UFO sighting, it should be understood that these objects were also reported as *meteors*. Only recently have researchers attributed this sighting to be a UFO. During the time of the event, the actual witness recognized and reported it as "three meteors", which are natural astronomical occurrences. Contemporary theorists often inaccurately assert that these reported "meteors" were the UFOs of today. Moreover, Lt. Schofield described the enormity of its size, which would surpass that of the present Mother Plane. For these reasons, this event does not meet the criteria of the so-called UFOs represented by Muhammad.

The conglomeration of UFO sightings did not arise until after they had been propagated by the Nation of Islam. Even the most avid UFO researchers admit how the mass phenomenon of UFOs did not take off until after the 1930s. Internationally respected UFO researcher and author, Timothy Good initiates his documentation of credible UFO case histories as beginning in the 1930s. Moreover, he does not document major Government concerns about these crafts until the 1940s.[193] Good initiates the first chapter of his book

---

[191] Tacoma Ledger, "AN ELECTRIC MONSTER Flashes of light and Terrible Sounds Emitted by One in the Bay," *Tacoma Ledger*, July 3, 1893.
[192] The New York Times, "NAVY OFFICER SEES METEORS They Were Red Ones, the Largest About Six Suns Big. ," *New York Times*, March 19, 1904.
[193] *Need to Know: UFOs, the Military, and Intelligence*, First Pegasus Edition (New York, NY: Pegasus Books, 2007).

Above Top Secret: The Worldwide U.F.O. Cover-Up by showing how government concerns and investigations about UFOs did not arise until the 1940s:

> If the late American journalist Frank Edwards is to be believed, British government research into mysterious flying objects began as early as 1943 with Lieutenant General Massey's small organization in the War Office to investigate foo-fighters.[194]

Dr. Bruce Maccabee in his book *UFO FBI Connection* begins his study of significant UFO concerns in the post-1930s era.[195] According to *The UFO Conspiracy* by Jenny Randles, the first forty years of UFO history did not begin until the late 1940s.[196] The research of prominent surgical ufologist Dr. Roger Lier is limited to only the last few decades because all the legitimate UFO encounters and abductions have taken place after these planes were revealed to Elijah Muhammad.

Historian Dolan M. Richard admits that there were strange aerial sightings that have taken place over the last hundreds of years, but the most definitive of UFO reports did not emerge until the 1940s.

> The Second World War changed all this. Before the war, airplanes were scarce and radar nonexistent—by the war's end, both were global. In other words, it became much, much easier to detect strange aerial phenomena after 1940. Since military personnel were the main users of radar and airplanes, they might naturally be expected to encounter more UFOs than the average person—and they most certainly did.[197]

Internationally respected nuclear physicist and UFO Researcher, Stanton T. Friedman has rendered the conclusion that major knowledge about UFO activity did not arise until 1947. This position was summarized in the following manner:

> A few people in the U.S. and other governments have known the above since at least 1947 and employ a "need-to-know" policy regarding this knowledge;

---

[194] (New York, NY: Quill William Morrow, 1988). 27.
[195] Bruce Maccabee, *UFO/FBI Connection: The Secret History of the Government's Cover-Up*, First (St. Paul, MN: Llewellyn Publications, 2000).
[196] *UFO Conspiracy From the Official Case Files of the World's Leading Nations* (New York, NY: Barnes & Noble Books, 1987).
[197] Richard M. Dolan, *UFOs and the National Security State: Chronology of a Coverup, 1941-1973*, Kindel Edition (Charlottesville, VA: Keyhole Publishing Company, 2000). 2-3.

that is, the knowledge is highly classified largely as sensitive military information.[198]

The Mutual UFO Network (MUFON), one of the oldest and largest UFO-investigative organizations in America, makes the following assertion, "The modern era of UFO sightings began in 1947."[199] With the mass emergence of UFOs being sighted after Elijah Muhammad brought this to the world's attention, why is it that he and his teachings are not publicly consulted on this subject? Minister Farrakhan has blatantly answered this question on several occasions:

> Since 1930 they have known that this plane exists, but why won't they tell the American people? It is because the White man does not want to admit that there is a technology in the world, and a power in the world that makes his power look like that jumbo jet in comparison to that huge plane [the Mother Wheel]! He doesn't want to admit that he doesn't have what it takes to deal with what they called that walnut-shaped object in the sky![200]

For this reason it is highly unlikely that the powers of this world will ever openly admit that Elijah Muhammad was right and exact. Rather, they will continue to spin the truth about UFOs to fit their objectives. While these authorities may not openly admit to Muhammad's introduction of the wheel-like crafts known as flying saucers, practically every ufologist acknowledges that definitive UFO evidence did not arise until the 1930s and afterwards.

Is it a coincidence that world governments did not become concerned with UFOs until after the advent of Elijah Muhammad? While knowing that Muhammad gave full details of these disc-shaped crafts before major sightings occurred, most UFO researchers beat around the bush and attribute the June 1947 sighting of Kenneth Arnold as being the beginning of the modern UFO phenomenon:

---

[198] *Flying Saucers and Science: A Scientist Investigates the Mysteries of UFOs: Interstellar Travel, Crashes, and Government Cover-Ups* (New Page Books, 2008).

[199] John F. Schuessler, *Public Opinion Surveys and Unidentified Flying Objects 50+ years of Sampling Public Opinions*, UFO Statistics, International Director's Office, Mutual UFO Network, Inc. (MUFON) (Morrison, CO: MUFON, 2000).

[200] Louis Farrakhan, "The Reality Of The Mother Plane" (Chicago, IL: The Final Call Inc., January 4, 1987).

> Why all of this special attention to the search of intelligent life beyond earth? Some argue that it is the bi-product of what has become known as the modern flying saucer era, which began on June 24, 1947.[201]

Even though Kenneth Arnold's 1947 sighting came nearly two decades after Muhammad, his sighting and those that followed have been widely deemed as the dawn of the UFO era. Some have even considered Arnold as 'the man who started it all':

> In history, Kenneth Arnold is considered to be "The Man Who Started It All" and "The Father of the Modern Era of UFOs". He was a respected Idaho businessman and pilot. His historical sighting of flying saucers on June 24, 1947 ushered in the modern era of UFOs. [202]

Arnold is credited by mainstream UFO researchers as coining the term 'flying saucers'. Arnold simply described the same wheel-like planes that Elijah Muhammad heralded to the world several years earlier, yet Arnold is somehow credited as the figure whose sighting sparked the modern era of UFO phenomena. Simple mathematics prove that Muhammad already taught the specifics about these crafts nearly 20 years earlier. Despite this obvious reality, UFO researchers deliberately omit and ignore the truth that Elijah Muhammad brought to save his people. They continue to ignore the connection that these so-called UFOs have with Minister Farrakhan and the Nation of Islam.

Is it strange that practically every UFO researcher acknowledges that the phenomena did not become a serious concern until several years after Muhammad made his authentic advent? Even theorists who believe that similar phenomena have taken place for several centuries have to admit that all serious UFO activities and concerns arose in the 1940s. Here is an official statement from the United States Air Force regarding the sudden rise in UFO sightings and reports:

> The modern preoccupation with what ultimately came to be called Unidentified Flying Objects (UFOs) actually began in June, 1947. Although some pro-UFO researchers argue that sightings of UFOs go back to Biblical times, most researchers will not dispute that anything in UFO history can compare with the phenomenon that began in 1947. What was later characterized as "the UFO Wave of 1947" began with 16 alleged sightings that

---

[201] Brian Barkley, *UFO Conspiracy*, directed by Brian Barkley, 2004.
[202] Saucers Incorporated, *Kenneth A. Arnold*, 2011, http://www.kennetharnoldufo.com/kenneth-arnold.html (2012).

occurred between May 17 and July 12, 1947, (although some researchers claim there were as many as 800 sightings during that period).[203]

Nearly every historian, researcher, and even governmental agency has to admit that concerns over the circular UFOs did not occur until after the Nation of Islam introduced the manifestation of what the prophet Ezekiel described as *wheels*.

Every official book concerning UFOs were written years after Elijah Muhammad warned about this reality to the world! This does not include any fictional novels or publications; instead this refers to the non-fictional studies, observations, and publications about the sudden rise of the wheel-like aerial phenomena—all of which came after Muhammad's inaugural teachings about them. Marine Corps officer and author, Major Donald Keyhoe, published one of the first public books about flying saucers (UFOs) in 1950 where he contended that the U.S. Air Force had been covering up evidence of UFOs since at least the 1940s.[204] Major Keyhoe would later become one of the most significant players among military personnel who was bold enough not to play along with the government's script of hiding their knowledge and aims about UFOs. Quite naturally he was somewhat castigated by USAF and government officials despite his very compelling arguments and documentation.

Much of Major Keyhoe's research became vindicated in subsequent decades as it had been discovered that the U.S. Government had been officially investigating and deliberately withholding vital information concerning UFOs from the American public. Although Keyhoe could only assume that these planes may have been around for several years, he admitted with great certainty that their "observation suddenly increased in 1947, following the series of A-bomb explosions in 1945."[205]

Major Keyhoe and USAF Captain Edward J. Ruppelt are some of the first military officers to take the unpopular stance of publishing official documents that acknowledged the possibility or reality of these wheels despite the consequences of being antagonized by the powerful government. Captain Ruppelt was the first head of *Project Blue Book*, which was a government agency that sought to study and investigate the new UFO waves that began sweeping America in the late 1940s. He was responsible for the official

---

[203] Richard L. Weaver, *Report of Air Force Research Regarding the 'Roswell Incident'*, Research, Security And Special Program Oversight, UNITED STATES AIR FORCE (USAF, 1994).
[204] Donald Keyhoe, *The Flying Saucers Are Real*, Reprinted 2004 (Cosimo Classics, 1950).
[205] Ibid. 174.

document, *Report On Unidentified Flying Objects*, published in 1956 where he admitted that the Air Force's response to the UFO question "was tackled with organized confusion."[206] Obviously this 'organized confusion' with the Government's UFO concerns would continue for decades.

ANCIENT ALIENS OR THE ORIGINAL MAN?

When discussing the progress of human flight, historians will likely bring up the failed efforts of Leonardo da Vinci's designs, the French brothers who took off in a balloon, and of course, the Wright Brothers. Based on conventionally understood history, the first recorded human flight took place in France in 1783 when the Montgolfier brothers (Joseph-Michel and Jacques-Étienne) designed a lighter-than-air balloon that lifted Jacques-Étienne off the earth.[207] Then the Wright Brothers (Orville and Wilbur) came along in the early 1900s and demonstrated the first recorded powered-flight at Kitty Hawk.[208] While commonly accepted history records these persons as being the first proponents of human flight, it should be understood that these are *Johnny-come-lately* efforts when compared to the less-known history of the darker original people.

Human Flight is nothing new to the earth despite the generally understood notion that human flight began with hot-air balloons and later with the Wright Brothers. Human flight technology has been in the world for millions of years. Before the establishment of the present world of Caucasian dominance. Muhammad explained that there existed similar flight technology used by the original people of the earth. He acknowledges that there are differences between the planes of the past, those used in conventional aircraft today, and the wheel-like planes orchestrated by Allah and his host of scientists:

> The same type of plane was used by the Original God to put mountains on His planets...
> There are planes in various nations today, but this is the mother of them all. Why? Because this type of plane was used before the making of this world.[209]

---

[206] Edward J. Ruppelt, *THE REPORT ON UNIDENTIFIED FLYING OBJECTS*, public domain, Former Head of the Air Force Project Blue Book (Garden City, NY: DOUBLEDAY & COMPANY, INC., 1956).
[207] Charles Coulston Gillispie, *The Montgolfier Brothers and the Invention of Aviation, 1783-1784*, First Edition (Princeton University Press, 1983).
[208] Russell Freedman, *The Wright Brothers: How They Invented the Airplane* (Holiday House, 1994).
[209] Elijah Muhammad, *The Fall Of America* (Chicago, IL: Elijah Muhammad, 1973). 236.

HISTORY AND THE NEW ERA

Although these flight technologies were prevalent among the ancient people, the Honorable Elijah Muhammad explained that such wisdom had to be temporarily buried during the fall of the Original Black man and the advent of the Caucasian race whose rule on the earth would last for approximately 6000 years:

> The knowledge of how to do this has not been given to the world (white race), nor will they ever get this kind of knowledge. The knowledge of the world is limited. If the devil would get this type of knowledge we could just say that we are goners. However, they are not able to attain this type of knowledge.[210]

The fact that the intelligence and scholarship of this world have not been able to grasp the power of so-called UFOs is proof that there is a knowledge that has not been fully granted to the modern world.

Over the last few decades, scientists and historians have crept upon knowledge that illustrates that there were many ancient, yet highly advanced civilizations that existed on earth. As this type of knowledge becomes more manifest to the public, many wonder exactly how these civilizations thrived, and more importantly, what made them almost disappear? Archeological artifacts, monuments like the pyramids, and inscriptions of antiquity indicate that several ancient civilizations existed that were more advanced than those of the modern world. This included human flight technology.

Both the Bible and the Holy Qur'an attest to the notion that humanity has fallen from a previously godly state. It is called the *fall from grace* or the *fall of man* in Christian theology. The Holy Qur'an states that man was made to depart from the state from whence they once were (Al-Baqarah 2:36). The details regarding this fall and the destined resurrection of this original people was revealed to Elijah Muhammad by Master Fard Muhammad. According to Muhammad's teachings, the fall of the original Black man was initiated nearly 50,000 years ago. Since that time, the Black man had lost the knowledge of himself and devolved into a savage state. The fall of the original man became even more exacerbated in the last 6000 years under the imperial rise of the Caucasian race. The true knowledge of God and his wisdom had been deliberately withdrawn from the world while the relatively new Caucasian people would dominate the earth. Minister Farrakhan offered a fitting analogy to describe the original people's fall, the rise of the Caucasian, and the eventual awakening of the original people:

---

[210] Ibid. 241.

> May I humbly suggest, no matter how brilliant we are, doctor, when you go to sleep at night, all your brilliance sleeps with you—and your four-year old child that wakes up in the night can run the house while you are asleep. So you cannot judge a sleeping person in their time of rest and sleep![211]

By likening the fall of the original people to a sleeping doctor, Minister Farrakhan indicates how the true potential of a people cannot be determined by their temporary condition. Just as a toddler could reign dominance over the house of a sleeping physician, so have the relatively new Caucasian race exuded dominance over the darker original people who have declined into a dead-like state. However, this apparent dead-like state serves as grounds for the prophesied *Resurrection of the Dead*. The Honorable Elijah Muhammad explained that the much anticipated Resurrection in religion refers to the resurgence of the spiritually, morally, socially, and mentally dead people back to their rightful position on this earth.

> WE BELIEVE in the resurrection of the dead—not in physical resurrection—but in mental resurrection. We believe that the so-called Negroes are most in need of mental resurrection; therefore they will be resurrected first. Furthermore, we believe we are the people of God's choice, as it has been written, that God would choose the rejected and the despised. We can find no other persons fitting this description in these last days more than the so-called Negroes in America. We believe in the resurrection of the righteous.[212]

The inevitable resurrection of the original people amidst their oppressors serves as one of the primary reasons behind the UFO cover-up. It is necessary that those who rule the world prevent the realization that the original people are the ones responsible for this supremely high intelligence. It is imperative that those Caucasians and others who rule the world do not allow the darker people of the earth to realize that there is a power on their side that is far greater than the powers that have subjugated them. The secret concerning the true identity, potential, and destiny of the original Black people has been the underlying secret that most influential secret societies are based upon. If the lost original Black people ever wake up to their true potential, which is connected to the power of the Wheel, then those who have unjustly ruled over them will have to be removed from their position as world authorities. Elijah Muhammad summed up this horrific dilemma in simplistic terms:

---

[211] "Guidance For Our President & Our Nation" (Chicago, IL: The Final Call, October 21, 2012).

[212] Elijah Muhammad, *MESSAGE TO THE BLACKMAN In America*, Original Published by MUHAMMAD'S Temple No. 2 in Chicago 1965 (Chicago, IL: The Final Call Inc., 1965). 163.

HISTORY AND THE NEW ERA

> We have been so long separated from each other that we have lost the knowledge of each other. Even today the white American slave-masters are ever on the watch to keep out any Asiatic influence that might come among the so-called Negroes to teach them the truth.[213]

Under Caucasian domination, the darker original people have been disenfranchised from the ancient wisdom, knowledge, and abilities that once permeated the earth. This even includes the ancient technology of aerial flight.

Elijah Muhammad answers the questions regarding the fall from these ancient civilizations and why this type of technological wisdom had been kept away from the present world and its powers. That supreme wisdom had been secured by Allah, his Exalted Assembly, and his host of human angels. The Holy Qur'an maintains that such knowledge is in a book that is safely guarded: "And verily, it is in the Mother of the Book, in Our Presence, high (in dignity), full of wisdom." (Az-Zukhruf 43:4). Amazingly, the truth of this hidden wisdom was revealed to a man who didn't even have a full elementary school education. The wisdom of God and the ancient technology of supreme flight was revealed directly to the Honorable Elijah Muhammad. This is the reality that scholars have found too controversial to openly address.

Since this type of supreme wisdom has not been made available to this world, present-day scholars are left to guess, speculate, and theorize on subjects such as UFOs and ancient history. This is why their definitive knowledge of concrete history barely surpasses the last 6000 year period. Anything before then consists primarily of hypotheses and speculative theories. Nonetheless, historical and archeological evidences prove that the ancient original people were highly advanced in civilizations, lifestyles, and technologies just as the Honorable Elijah Muhammad taught. Evidences have surfaced authenticating that the original people of antiquity were astute in flight technology. As these truths are still being unearthed, many scholars are left puzzled by the fact that ancient people manifested highly advanced civilizations. This notion contradicts with Euro-centric ideologies that have downplayed the contributions of the darker people and highlighted the contributions of Caucasian dominance.

Several artifacts and archeological relics have been discovered indicating ancient flight technologies. For the past decades these relics have been found from ancient African, Indian, and South American civilizations. Scientists and historians have tried to make sense out of these discoveries:

---

[213] Ibid. 20.

...it seems rather incredible that someone, more than 2,000 years ago, for any reason, devised a model of a flying device with such advanced features, requiring quite extensive knowledge of aerodynamics. There were no such things as airplanes in these times, we are told by archeologists and historians. But this case seems to be an exception, living in the midst of the rather unimaginative and rigid paradigm of contemporary science. It is also necessary to point out that Egyptians are known to have nearly always made scale-models of projects and objects which they planned to create or build.

The ancient Pyramid of Khufu in Giza (Africa) gives clear proof of an advanced technology that existed before the industrialized world today. This is one of the reasons why it is considered the first *Wonder of the World* due to its advanced architecture and the mysteries surrounding it. Scientists and historians are left to speculate exactly when and how such a highly mathematically sound monument was developed during a time when advanced technology was not supposed to exist. Nonetheless, the Pyramids of Khufu are standing testimonies that the original people of Africa were highly advanced before their sudden decline.

In recent decades, findings have been made that correlate the pyramids geographical location with certain astronomical constellations. Even though these discoveries were initially shunned by some mainstream scientists, it has gained significant credibility among scientists and historians today. Inscriptions found in the ceiling beams in the ancient temple of Seti I at Abydos have shown what appear to be engraved images of modern day flight technology. These engravings show what could easily be identified as a modern helicopter, and other flying vehicles including the disc-shaped flying saucer.[214] Like interpretive art, there can be no definite proof that these are what they appear to be. However, such an obvious resemblance to modern aircraft makes it difficult to argue with the notion.

Still today, so-called experts cannot give any definitive explanation regarding how the pyramids were constructed or the inscriptions of the ancient temples. Only speculations and theories are given. Because of the majestic wisdom involved in the construction of these monuments, some theorists have postulated that humans were not involved in their construction at all. Some suggest that this was the work of ancient aliens astronauts from outer space. Regardless of the conclusion, the technology involved in the building of those pyramids only proves that there was an intelligence, a wisdom, and a civilization that was far more advanced than what conventional history has taught. Obviously racism is so deeply ingrained in the scholarship,

---

[214] Crystal Links, *Ancient Aircraft*, December 2000, http://crystalinks.com/ancientaircraft.html (accessed April 28, 2010). Images shown from Ceiling Beams of Temple of Seti I at Abydos.

that some would rather give credit to fictitious alien beings before giving due credit to the original Black man and woman of Africa.

One of the clearest marks of the original Black man's once majestic existence is symbolized in the architecture of the African Sphinx near the pyramids of Giza. Here the sphinx has the body of a royal lion with the head of the original Black man—an image that is reminiscent of the symbolic lion of Judah mentioned in the Bible. The Lion of Judah represents a once great people who have fallen into a dead-like sleeping state. The truth about who the original man is has been the core secret of the world's secret societies and world leaders.

It has been promised that one by the definitive name *Elijah* would be sent by the Supreme Being who would turn the children back to the original mind and heart of their ancient fathers (Malachi 4:5). Today, the promise has been fulfilled and the Supreme Being has sent Elijah Muhammad with the necessary wisdom to raise his lost people back to their original capabilities. The proof that Elijah Muhammad was taught by the best knower is validated by his unparalleled accomplishments amidst the most powerful opposition. Muhammad credits his success to the same power behind the wheel-shaped crafts now called UFOs. The models of aircraft found from ancient African, Indian, and South American artifacts have shown that flight capabilities were not only possible, but highly likely.

WHO IS THE ORIGINAL MAN?

"Who is the Original Man? The original man is the Asiatic Black man; the Maker; the Owner; the Cream of the planet Earth - God of the Universe." Every registered member of the Nation of Islam has been required to recite the aforementioned question and the answer that followed. This brief response gives only a small glimpse into the majestic wisdom of what was revealed to Elijah Muhammad regarding the original people of the earth—their highly advanced civilizations, technology, and capabilities.

In essence, these Original people represent the ancient Black people who once existed in their godly state before an intense devolution that rendered them near complete opposites of their former glory. The Honorable Elijah Muhammad described these original people today as the indigenous Black, Brown, Red, and Yellow man. These are the people of God today—some of whom are responsible for the construction of the Mother Plane and who operate the accompanying wheel-like planes.

> It will be the work of the wheel. The wheel is the power of the four creatures, namely the four colors of the Black man (Black, brown, yellow and red). The

red Indian is to benefit also from the judgment of the world.[215]

Since many scientists and historians have discovered the remarkable abilities of these ancient people, they are now forced to battle with the realization that the original man is who Elijah Muhammad said he is. Scientists are left to battle with the fact that the dark original people of the earth are responsible for advanced technology that once permeated the earth and is now present in the UFO phenomenon. This knowledge is largely the reason why they attribute UFO activity to extraterrestrial aliens. The racism infused throughout the world's academic scholarship makes it difficult to acknowledge the superior contributions of non-Caucasian entities. They would rather give credit to unknown far-distant aliens from other galaxies than admit that the original people are responsible for such remarkable wheel-like UFOs.

Historical and archeological evidences confirm Muhammad's assertions that the ancient original people were highly advanced in civilizations, technology, and lifestyles. In the Far East, many of the common people believe that those responsible for UFOs are in some way connected to human beings on earth. Forty percent of those polled from India and China believe that aliens (UFO beings) are disguised as humans since both countries have ancient relics of aerial craft.[216]

With the proof that ancient flight existed, researchers from around the world have now postulated what these discoveries mean. Instead of recognizing the truth of what Elijah Muhammad taught concerning the original people, theories have been put forth to suggest that those ancient technological wonders were the works of ancient aliens. These theories postulate that extraterrestrial alien astronauts visited the Earth in ancient times and that these aliens are somehow responsible for UFOs and the advancement of human civilization. Some of the leading proponents of this theory include Erich von Däniken, Zecharia Sitchin, and Robert Temple to name a few.

Von Däniken admits that ancient art and artifacts that show advanced technology cannot be explained by conventional historic interpretations. Hence he interprets that those past relics along with Biblical themes such as Ezekiel's wheel had to be the work of some other beings outside of humans. Instead of admitting the obvious truth that the darker indigenous people were responsible for those civilizations, Von Däniken renders the conclusion that these must have been the work of ancient alien astronauts:

> ...ancient Egypt appears suddenly and without transition with a fantastic ready- made civilisation. Great cities and enormous temples, colossal statues with tremendous expressive power, splendid streets flanked by magnificent

---

[215] Elijah Muhammad, *The Fall Of America* (Chicago, IL: Elijah Muhammad, 1973). 239.
[216] Reuters, "Reuters Ipsos Poll" (Reuters, April 2010).

sculptures, perfect drainage systems, luxurious tombs carved out of the rock, pyramids of overwhelming size—these and many other wonderful things shot out of the ground, so to speak. Genuine miracles in a country that is suddenly capable of such achievements without recognisable prehistory![217]

The subtle implications made by Von Däniken is that the Black African could not have been responsible for such civilizations, which is why they render the implausible conclusion that beings from outer space must have established them. Von Däniken has not been able to reconcile the idea that the Black people of Africa were once capable of such splendor. This racist attitude remains commonplace among the world's scholarship.

Zecharia Sitchin shares similar attitudes as Von Däniken whereas they have assumed that other beings outside of human beings are responsible for the advanced technology witnessed in ancient history as well as in modern UFOs.[218] Although astronomical science does not support their claims regarding ancient aliens being responsible for advancing human civilizations, the one valid aspect about Von Däniken and Sitchin's work is that there were highly advanced civilizations and flight technology in the indigenous world among the original people. Just as scholars, researchers, and authors find it difficult to admit that the darker people were responsible for ancient civilizations, they have more difficulties accepting the fact that darker humans are responsible for UFOs today. Even though Muhammad already made it clear, their observations have led them to conclude that the God of the sacred scriptures flies something in the sky, which is why they have postulated that God must be some kind of astronaut. If these researchers consulted the man who brought this wisdom to the modern world, they would have a much more accurate understanding about UFOs, their pilots, and the God responsible for them. Rather, these theorists have benefited from their writings that contradict logic and promote subtly racist views.

The Honorable Elijah Muhammad solved the puzzles that still baffle archeologists and historians. The Original Black man, as he calls them, are in fact the *ancient beings* that the aforementioned observers often depict as ancient alien astronauts. These are the same people who occupy and pilot the wheel-like crafts known as UFOs today. They are the indigenous people of the earth consisting of the Black, Brown, Red, and Yellow people who act at the behest of Allah (God) in the person of Master Fard Muhammad. Elijah Muhammad's knowledge of these matters is not derived from hypotheses or

---

[217] Erich Von Däniken, *Chariots Of The Gods?*, English translation 1984 (Berkley, 1968).
[218] Zecharia Sitchin, *Twelfth Planet: Book I of the Earth Chronicles (The Earth Chronicles)*, 0030 (Harper, 2007).

theories. Instead, his knowledge of these crafts and their human occupants come from his direct relationship with them. Muhammad is distinguished from all others on this matter for he has no need to speculate or postulate about UFOs and the power that operates them.

Questions and concerns about the origin and purpose of UFOs and their occupants continue to perplex scientists and ufologists. As they move closer to retrieving answers, they move closer to the authority of the Honorable Elijah Muhammad. While early assumptions attributed UFOs to other galactic intelligence, researchers like Michael Bara, author of *Dark Mission*, have questioned those previous theories:

> So, the question is, 'are those guys the extraterrestrials or is it possible that we, in fact, are extraterrestrial?' We did not come from here and it's simply an older version of humanity taking care of the younger version that they are going to leave the planet to.[219]

These type of hypotheses show that UFO researchers are realizing what the Nation of Islam has already known—that there is an *older version of humanity* (the Black original people) who gave a younger version (Caucasians) a certain time to rule until the coming of Allah (God). So Bara's hypothesis implicitly bears witness to the NOI's teachings. Elijah Muhammad clarified that today's pilots of the wheels consist of Black, Brown, Red, and Yellow original people from the planet earth—many that he personally knew as scientists-angels. According to Muhammad, "These [angels] are not spooks. They are men!"[220] They are like other people except for their highly advanced education, training, and capabilities, which stem directly from Allah (God) who appeared in the person of Master Fard Muhammad.

Timothy Good, notable UFO researcher and author, further recognizes the direct link between the humans and the so-called aliens from UFOs:

> They are not just aliens visiting. I'm convinced that many of them have been living here or based here perhaps longer than we have… All the aliens whose encounters with people have been reported do confirm that there is a genetic link between them and us, and that we are a hybridized species.[221]

Timothy Good has dedicated years of research and observations studying sightings, encounters, and abductions and he noticed a certain

---

[219] History, "Mysterious Places," *Ancient Aliens* (History.com, October 28, 2010).
[220] "The Theology of Time (Lecture Series)," Vols. July 9, 1972 (Chicago, IL: MUHAMMAD Mosque No. 2, 1972).
[221] Timothy Good, interview by Henrik Palmgren, *Secret Space Program, UFOs, ET & Coverup*, Red Ice Radio, February 24, 2011.

consistency in many of these cases. Consistent patterns show that the people from these crafts are described in human terms; hence they are called humanoids. Good recognizes that *they are not just aliens visiting us* and that *there is a genetic link between them and us.* Well, the Honorable Elijah Muhammad answered this concern before it ever became a mystery. His servant, the Honorable Minister Farrakhan continues to proclaim this truth, yet researchers continue to avoid the presence of these men and what they represent. The NOI's position that those who pilot the wheel-like crafts are human scientists has gone virtually unchallenged. Instead, several researchers have acted as though the human connection with UFO pilots is a newly realized concept. In any case, they avoid crediting the NOI as being the initial proponents of this truth.

It is highly unlikely that researchers and scientists have studied the UFO phenomenon for decades without knowing anything about this integral part of the NOI's teaching. Moreover, it is nearly impossible to undergo a thorough research of this subject without realizing the primary contributions from the Nation of Islam. For this reason, it is apparent that there remains a calculated cover-up that spans across government agencies, media, educational institutions, and even scientific circles. The History Channel has been one of the major entities that run programs that promote the ancient alien theory before the American people and the world. Yet, the History Channel has not responded to any of the NOI's requests to share information about this worthy subject on a mainstream platform. When a Christian evangelist, Minister Derrick Reese, asked Minister Farrakhan has he ever watched the television show entitled *Ancient Aliens* on the History Channel, the Minister kindly responded with these words:

> Well, I sometimes watch the History Channel but there are no Ancient Aliens. There are ancient people that existed before this world came into existence with a greater wisdom than this world has experienced. And this is why Solomon said: "There is nothing new under the sun."[222]

Minister Farrakhan's words remain virtually uncontested by those who continuously convey the deceptive notions that such UFO technology is the result of foreign aliens. Instead Farrakhan makes it plain that this wisdom stems from the original Black people under the auspices of the Supreme Being.

Even UFO believers and paranormal researchers have used the reality of UFOs to divert attention from their realistic source. Ignoring the NOIs

---

[222] Louis Farrakhan, "#AskFarrakhan Tweets," *Twitter Response to Minister Derrick Reese @HolyTabernacleU regarding Ancient Aliens on History Channel* (#AskFarrakhan via Twitter, January 26, 2013).

introduction of these planes, many UFO authors lead observers to believe that these are crafts controlled by extraterrestrial beings and the mainstream media has helped flood the market with such ideas.

David Icke published *The Biggest Secret: The Book that Will Change the World*, in 1999. He and several others have found creatively delusive ways to spin factual data about UFOs into fanciful insubstantial conclusions. Icke's theories are reminiscent of the 1980s science fiction mini-series *V*, where reptilians posing as humans attempt to conquer humanity. He associates UFOs with reptilian-type creatures. Similarly many other UFO related publications have depicted the intelligence behind UFOs as inherently evil and demonic. This idea has been frequently promoted throughout the media. Even some religious denominations have spread these ideas. These depictions of UFOs as being other than what Muhammad introduced them as is merely part of a plot to maintain an ongoing mass deception. The biggest secret is not the fact that UFOs exist; rather the biggest secret involves the persons and powers controlling these crafts—the original people guided by the Supreme Being.

These miraculous planes and the people who control them offer tangible proof of what the right knowledge and living conditions can yield, which is a sign of supreme human potential. Unfortunately the world's contemporary systems, paradigms, and theories have been tainted under Satanic rule, which makes it nearly impossible to manifest ones divine potential under such circumstances. This is why it is fundamentally necessary for humanity to obtain a new way of thinking from a new knowledge source outside of the current paradigm. The basis of this new paradigm is embedded in the strangeness of the Nation of Islam's teachings. The divine wisdom revealed to Elijah Muhammad lays the base for the establishment of a new world, which is why so much effort has been put forth to conceal the truth that the NOI has explicated for decades. The teachings and training espoused within the NOI represent an initial phase of the kingdom of Allah (God) on earth.

HISTORY AND THE NEW ERA

Figure 4: WONDERS OF THE ORIGINAL MAN

Clockwise from top left: Ancient African Egyptian pyramids, The Great Sphinx of Giza, Ancient encryptions of futuristic flight vehicles from the African ceiling beams of a 3000 year old New Kingdom Temple, at Abydos, Ancient flight artifact from the Chimú culture that existed in present day Colombia over 2,000 years ago. Ancient Quimbaya gold aircraft model artifact ~300CE.

8. THE ENCOUNTER, THE ARREST, AND THE AFTERMATH

A NEW AUTHORITY

They fly circles around anything we've got flying. Their strange behavior includes the ability to both hover and move at extremely high velocity, to make right angle turns at high speeds, to go straight up, straight down—all of this typically without any noise, without any visible external engines, without any wings, without any tail. We simply could not do that back fifty years ago.[223]

The term *unidentified flying object*, or *UFO*, is said to have been coined by the United States Air Force (USAF) Captain Edward J. Ruppelt in the mid 1950s.[224] Others have suggested that former U.S. Marine Corps Naval Aviator Donald Keyhoe coined the term around the same time.[225] Regardless to who said it first, it is strange how the U.S. military has been involved in coining terms about crafts that are not even supposed to exist. Since the U.S. military has been one of the primary witnesses of these crafts, their officials saw fit to name the objects that have caused so much commotion to their world. Prior to *UFO* becoming the officially used term, other labels were used such as *unidentified flying discs, flying flapjacks*, and of course, *flying saucers*. It is not by happenstance that all of these terms signify wheel-like shapes, nor is it a coincidence that that all of these official terms were applied after Muhammad's inaugural teaching about these crafts.

The main reason for the new nomenclature is because the mass sightings and witness accounts of these planes were new to the world at that time. The Government never had a serious need to investigate, study, or be concerned about UFOs until after Elijah Muhammad was made acquainted with the power from those type of planes. The American Government has been in existence for hundreds of years, but it wasn't until the 1940s that

---

[223] James Fox, Tim Coleman, Boris Zubov and Charles Fox, *Out Of The Blue - The Definitive Investigation of the UFO Phenomenon*, directed by James Fox, Tim Coleman and Boris Zubov, Hannover House, 2002.
[224] Edward J. Ruppelt, *THE REPORT ON UNIDENTIFIED FLYING OBJECTS*, public domain, Former Head of the Air Force Project Blue Book (Garden City, NY: DOUBLEDAY & COMPANY, INC., 1956).
[225] Oxford English Dictionary, "UFO," *OED Online* (Oxford University Press, 2012).

THE ENCOUNTER, THE ARREST, AND THE AFTERMATH

governments saw fit to begin investigating a phenomenon on UFOs. Various programs and agencies were established within the U.S. Government to investigate and possibly attack the sudden accumulation of sightings that started to arise in America during the 1940s.[226] **Before then, there were no serious UFO concerns that warranted this type of attention from the American Government!**

During the time that Master Fard Muhammad showed the Mother Wheel to Elijah Muhammad in the early 1930s, Black people were only a few decades up from chattel slavery. As America was suffering from the Great Depression, Black America was feeling the brunt of America's sickness. The thought of an unarmed, uneducated Black man standing up against the most powerful government in the world would seem like a fairy tale. The thought of such a man living through such a stance is even more bewildering. Black leaders before and after Muhammad's rise were targeted and destroyed by the powers of the American Government. It was commonplace for white mobs to lynch Blacks who said or acted outside of their approval. Even today, the U.S. Government targets any persons who think, speak, or act outside of the boundaries of white supremacy. This is one of the reasons why the unarmed Muslims of the Nation of Islam (NOI) have been victims of Government plots to discredit and destroy independent Black movements.[227]

The unabashed expression of white supremacy during the 1930s was so evident, that many Whites felt no need to hide their feelings. If Whites mobilized to protest Black people from attending their schools and businesses in the 1960s, how racist were their actions in the 1930s? The prevalent attitude of white supremacy and the new liberation theology of the NOI yielded an inevitable encounter from the police department of Detroit.

In 1934 the Honorable Elijah Muhammad and many of the early Muslim followers of the NOI were arrested for teaching this new strange doctrine to their children—a doctrine that was not approved by White America. This new teaching involved the fact that God has come to clean them up and free them from the people who oppress them. This teaching aimed to free the darker people from the physical and mental bounds that have contained them since their sojourn through slavery. Muhammad gives a glimpse of this teaching:

---

[226] *Project Sign, Project Grudge*, and *Project Blue Book* are just a few known agencies initiated by U.S. Government entities to investigate the UFO phenomena.

[227] Ward Churchill and Jim Vander Wall, *The COINTELPRO Papers: Documents from the FBI's Secret Wars Against Dissent in the United States* (South End Press, 1990).

> But on the coming and appearance of Allah in 1930 – who taught me a thorough knowledge of the devils, the time, the resurrection and end and the judgment of the devils and their followers and the danger of being called by devil names and believing what they teach as religion.[228]

This type of teaching caught the attention of the American Government, the Michigan State Board of Education, and the Detroit Police Department who raided the Muslims' school and arrested their teachers on the false charges that they were causing the delinquency of minors. Muhammad stated, "This false charge was dropped, and the teachers were freed. I was at that time given 6 months probation to put our Muslim children back in the public schools under Christian teachers. This I did not do..."[229] This would not be the last time Elijah Muhammad and the Muslims would be attacked by governmental agencies.

This encounter led to a physical confrontation between the outnumbered and unarmed Muslims and the armed Detroit Police Department—a brawl that grew the Muslims' confidence in the power of their God. Elijah Muhammad shares some of the results of that confrontation:

> This was the cause of the attack at that time and Allah was with us and we had been peaceful there all the while. However, it was said after the battle with my followers who had nothing to fight with but their hands, that there was hospitalization on both sides.
>
> There was no loss of lives on the side of the Muslims and not a gun was fired by them. The Lieutenant of police, the Captain and Commissioner of Police, had warned them to not use firearms against us because we were not armed -- this was true. But when the battle was over there were more of them hospitalized than there were of us.[230]

This was one of those events that sent an alarm throughout the U.S. Government, which caused the Government and its agencies to step up their surveillance and attacks against the NOI. Never before since the early slave rebellions had White American powers witnessed an audacious stance from Black people against their oppressors. With Elijah Muhammad at the helm, Muslim men, women, and children demonstrated a certainty that a greater power was with them to the point that they were willing to die for the truth.

The authorities of the 1930s categorized the NOI as a cult, as radicals, and a potential threat. E.D. Beynon wrote, "As a result of the teaching of this

---

[228] Elijah Muhammad, *MESSAGE TO THE BLACKMAN In America*, Original Published by MUHAMMAD'S Temple No. 2 in Chicago 1965 (Chicago, IL: The Final Call Inc., 1965). 179.
[229] Ibid. 179.
[230] Ibid. 213.

cult, they have gained a new conception of themselves and regard themselves as superior, rather than inferior, to other people."[231] The strangeness of the NOI with its teachings of a Mother Plane, put this group under the watchful eye of the Government who labeled the Muslims as a "Voodoo cult."[232] Muhammad's teaching about the Mother Plane seemed highly fictitious at the time, which is one of the reasons why the authorities castigated the Muslims as a cultist group. There were no groups or persons officially advocating the existence these type of planes at the time. Initially, Muhammad's Mother Plane teachings were dismissed as mythical enchantment, but what authorities once thought to be a make-believe spaceship would later be a primary reason for the U.S. Government's second arrest of Elijah Muhammad a few years later.

After Muhammad's arrest in 1934, the number of UFO sightings, encounters, and widespread concerns began to rise exponentially in America. A report from one of the largest UFO research programs gave the following conclusion:

> For more than 50 years surveys of public opinions about Unidentified Flying Objects (UFO) have been conducted to satisfy a variety of customers. While the numbers have fluctuated from time to time, the general results of these surveys showed the public to be very aware of UFO sightings, interested in what may be causing them, and concerned that the government was not doing enough to resolve the mystery.[233]

This report was prepared by MUFON based on a collection of polls and statistics about UFOs from a fifty-year period between 1940 and 2000. Obviously MUFON did not see the need to begin their research before the 1930s because they realized there were no UFO concerns worth seriously investigating before then.

After one of the first major waves of UFO sightings in 1947, 90% of people had heard of flying saucers (as they were most frequently called then). By 1957, a growing number of Americans believed in the possibility of flying saucers. Among those who believed, 25.3% believed they were from outer

---

[231] Erdmann Doane Beynon, "The Voodoo Cult Among Negro Migrants in Detroit," *The American Journal of Sociology* (The University of Chicago Press) 43, no. 6 (May 1938): 894.
[232] Ibid.
[233] John F. Schuessler, *Public Opinion Surveys and Unidentified Flying Objects 50+ years of Sampling Public Opinions*, UFO Statistics, International Director's Office, Mutual UFO Network, Inc. (MUFON) (Morrison, CO: MUFON, 2000).

space while a larger number believed they originated from earth.[234] Nearly a decade later, statistics showed that some 46% of Americans believed that flying saucers (UFOs) were real.[235] During the mid 1970s, the Canadian Gallup Poll reported that 36% of people believed that UFOs were something real.[236] By 1984, Psychology Today Magazine reported that 50% of Americans said they believed in UFOs.[237] If these type of numbers are taken into consideration, this suggests that a substantial amount of people began to realize the seriousness about UFOs. In light of these statistics, would it make sense to disregard all the evidence? Are all the millions of people who've witnessed these crafts hallucinating about the same thing?

THE BATTLE OF LOS ANGELES – FEBRUARY 25, 1942

It was not quite a decade after the first arrest of Elijah Muhammad that the American Government experienced a direct confrontation with those so-called mythical planes that Elijah Muhammad preached about. For many years, conventional history has covered-up what has been dubbed the *Battle of Los Angeles*. This is not to be confused with fictional movies with similar titles, but the real Battle of Los Angeles refers to one of the first major encounters between the American military and the wheel-like planes that were revealed to Elijah Muhammad.

On February 25, 1942 hundreds of residents were disturbed by sounds of artillery being fired at unknown aircraft. A large circular object accompanied by smaller wheel-like planes was spotted 120 miles off the coast of Los Angeles. "At 3:18 am on February 25, 1942, the 37th Coast Artillery Brigade's anti-aircraft artillery (AAA) began firing batteries of 12-15 pound shells at the 'unidentified aircraft' coming in over the ocean."[238] Naturally, the initial suspicion was that these crafts were of Japanese origin (which is kind of true when considering that the wheels were constructed among Japanese islands). America was just three months or so into the war with Japan after the attack on Pearl Harbor. As the objects came closer and shots were fired at them, it became overwhelmingly clear that these were not any type of conventional aircraft ever seen in this world before.

---

[234] TRENDEX POLL, *Do you believe there is some possibility that they (saucers) may be objects from outer space?*, TRENDEX POLL (St. Louis Globe Democrat, 1957).
[235] GALLUP POLL, (Des Moines, IA: Des Moines, 1966).
[236] Statistical Report (The Toronto Star - 1978, 1974).
[237] "Do you believe in UFOs?," *Psychology Today Magazine*, June 1984.
[238] Timothy Good, *Above Top Secret: The Worldwide U.F.O. Cover-Up* (New York, NY: Quill William Morrow, 1988). 15.

THE ENCOUNTER, THE ARREST, AND THE AFTERMATH

During this attack, a blackout was ordered, which rendered the city in the dark. Thousands of Californians were alarmed by the loud rounds of ammunitions being shot at the unidentified objects. As the Military fired some of its most advanced artillery at the objects, they were dumbfounded at the results. Witnesses reported that there was one "enormous UFO" and several smaller ones and the U.S.'s anti-aircraft rounds had no affect on the objects. The *Herald Express* reported that many shells burst directly in the middle of the object and it was not moved.[239] While America's heaviest weaponry was fired at the huge wheel-like craft, the object did not budge, as if to say "your power and intelligence is no match for what is on this wheel." The Wheel did not fire anything back at the now frantic military. As America continued to fire rounds at the objects, the smaller wheel-like crafts simply danced around at terrific speeds and dodged the ammunition.[240] Do these characteristics sound familiar? If so, that is because Elijah Muhammad had been teaching about this large circular plane and the smaller ones that God would use to empower his chosen people and to destroy his enemies, which included the oppressive powers of America. The Battle of Los Angeles rendered perhaps the first major encounter between the Mother Wheel and the U.S. powers.

As numerous pictures and video footage of this incident indicate, the Wheel remained stationed in the clouds amidst the smoke while the shots fired at it simply bounced off of it like a child throwing marbles at a well-constructed bulldozer. With searchlight beams aimed at the craft during the blackout, the missiles exploded upon impact showing flashes of light once it hit the object. The so-called unidentified object remained somewhat stationary amidst the smoke and clouds as though it had an invisible force field that shielded it from America's weaponry. The Honorable Elijah Muhammad spoke of this "protective coating" that the Wheel has that serves as a shield, much like the earth's atmospheric coating. He also spoke of the scientists aboard the wheels who will rush in when America tries to attack the Wheel. These scientists make it so that "she [America] can't come forward to the plane, then she can't shoot it."[241] The Messenger's words ring true as the Battle of Los Angeles demonstrated.

The morning following the encounter resulted in thousands of frantic Californians with questions unanswered. Six or more civilian deaths were reported from the fallen shrapnel that came back down from being fired at the

---

[239] Ibid.
[240] Peter Brookesmith, *UFO the Government Files* (Barnes Noble Books, 1996). Peter Brookesmith, *UFO the Government Files* (Barnes Noble Books, 1996). 15.
[241] "The Theology of Time (Lecture Series)," Vols. July 2, 1972 (Chicago, IL: MUHAMMAD Mosque No. 2, 1972).

UFOs. Other deaths were due to heart attacks resulting from the barrage. Houses and buildings were left with damages from the attempted air attack. The encounter also left the American Military with some explaining to do. People wanted answers. What did the Government give them?

Hours after the spectacle of an attack, Secretary of the Navy Frank Knox held a press conference in an attempt to quell the public. Knox suggested that the whole thing was just a "false alarm" due to the recently engaged war with Japan. Of course Secretary Knox's explanations did not satisfy residents or the press at that time. The local press began to suspect that some form of censorship was trying to halt discussions related to the incident.[242] The aftermath of the barrage left the whole nation in suspicion that the military had encountered something that they could not or would not explain to the public:

> The New York Times on 28 February expressed a belief that the more the incident was studied, the more incredible it became: "If the batteries were firing on nothing at all, as Secretary Knox implies, it is a sign of expensive incompetence and jitters. If the batteries were firing on real planes, some of them as low as 9,000 feet, as Secretary Stimson declares, why were they completely ineffective? Why did no American planes go up to engage them, or even to identify them?[243]

The U.S. Government has yet to provide a rational explanation to those practical questions. Where did the objects fly off to after the barrage? Since it was concluded that none of the UFOs were shot down, the question must be asked, where did they go? The Honorable Elijah Muhammad gave characteristics of the elusive capabilities of the Wheel. He stated, "If America's bombers are over California, the Scientist on the Wheel just sneak away into another place."[244]

The day following the incident, Chief of Staff General George Marshall sent President Franklin D. Roosevelt a memorandum regarding the event, which stated that "Unidentified airplanes, other than American Army and Navy planes, were *probably* over Los Angeles, and were fired on by elements of

---

[242] Long Beach Independent, "MYSTERY RAID! TWO WAVES OF PLANES SWEEP OVER CITY AS ANTI-AIRCRAFT GUNS ROAR," *Long Beach Independent*, February 1942.

[243] California State Military Department Office of Air Force History, "California and the Second World War: The Battle of Los Angeles," *The Army Air Forces in World War II*, ed. Wesley Frank Craven and James Lea Cate (Washington, DC: The California State Military Museum, 1983), 277-286.

[244] "The Theology of Time (Lecture Series)," Vols. July 9, 1972 (Chicago, IL: MUHAMMAD Mosque No. 2, 1972).

THE ENCOUNTER, THE ARREST, AND THE AFTERMATH

the 37th CA Brigade (AA) between 3:12 and 4:15 am."[245] Obviously, the military could not explain exactly what these planes were, which was grounds to engage in a serious investigation. The initial thought was that these were some highly advanced Japanese aircraft since this event occurred during a newly-ensued war with Japan. However, as much as Japan would have wanted credit for such technology, they officially acknowledged that they were not responsible for such a craft. If Japan did not back down from their attack on Pearl Harbor, they would have no reason to back away from such an encounter over Los Angeles if they did it. Besides, if the Japanese military was capable of such technology, they would have been able to conquer America and the known world. The Honorable Elijah Muhammad made the distinction between what Japan can do compared to what his God can do:

> You thought Pearl Harbor was terrible. Pearl Harbor would be like a gang of boys playing compared to what the God plans to do to America. I know that, but I can't tell you all of these things lest you go and talk too much.[246]

Chief of Staff Marshall's memo to Roosevelt concluded that the "unidentified airplanes *may have been* from commercial sources, operated by enemy agents for the purpose of spreading alarm." With such uncertainty about what was witnessed by thousands on the West Coast, the U.S. Government was in an embarrassingly vulnerable position. The military's implausible explanations left citizens more concerned and left the press raising more eyebrows. The Government saw fit to take certain actions before things got out of hand. Once it was realized that Japan was not responsible for the impenetrable objects in the sky, the Government and its Defense Department began looking for solid answers. President Roosevelt's administration realized something that the common American people had very little knowledge about. Their investigations led to a mild-mannered Black man who had already been preaching about those planes for the past decade.

THE ARREST OF THE MESSENGER

---

[245] General George Marshall's secret Memo to President Roosevelt about the unidentified objects over Los Angeles on February 25, 1942 were declassified and made available by the Freedom of Information Act.
[246] "The Theology of Time (Lecture Series)," Vols. July 2, 1972 (Chicago, IL: MUHAMMAD Mosque No. 2, 1972).

> *He has seen it. The white man admitted to me they have seen it, but they can't get to her [the Mother Wheel].*[247] – The Honorable Elijah Muhammad

It was not even three months after the Battle of Los Angeles that an Executive Decision was made by President Roosevelt's administration to arrest the Honorable Elijah Muhammad. On May 8, 1942 in Washington, DC, the FBI arrested Elijah Muhammad with no justifiable reasoning for doing so. During this arrest, they probed Muhammad's possessions and confiscated his materials concerning the Mother Plane that he so adamantly preached about. In a 1972 lecture, Muhammad warned his listeners about the reality of the Mother Plane and why the Government arrested him:

> Write in the paper if you want and tell the devil what I'm telling you! See if he'll try to deny it. They know it's out there! I sat down and I talked with them years ago about it. They asked me questions. They have the drawing on a blackboard that they'd taken from us when they arrested us and I had drawn the plane and written explanations on the blackboard, and they took it to the FBI office. They have it there today. They know this to be true and they admitted to me that it is true![248]

The Messenger's claims have gone unchallenged. It is public record that he was arrested less than two and a half months after the Battle of Los Angeles. It is also no coincidence that Elijah Muhammad and the Nation of Islam were the only group of people who propagated the existence of these wheel-like planes and their specific capabilities like those witnessed over California. This provided justification for America to remove Elijah Muhammad from the streets and interrogate him about the Mother Plane.

The interrogation of Elijah Muhammad and the surveillance that followed could be considered some of the first serious investigative studies that the Government has conducted about so-called UFOs. Before *Project Sign*, *Project Grudge* or *Project Blue Book*,[249] the U.S. Government engaged in a project to investigate and suppress the truth about these planes that Elijah Muhammad enlightened the modern world about. Although a few authorities were familiarized with Muhammad's teaching about these crafts when they

---

[247] Elijah Muhammad, "The Theology of Time (Lecture Series)," Vols. July 9, 1972 (Chicago, IL: MUHAMMAD Mosque No. 2, 1972).
[248] "The Theology of Time (Lecture Series)," Vols. July 2, 1972 (Chicago, IL: MUHAMMAD Mosque No. 2, 1972).
[249] **Project Sign** was one of the first official governmental studies on UFOs beginning in 1947, followed by **Project Grudge** in 1949. **Project Blue Book** was a collective study of unidentified flying objects (UFOs) conducted by the United States Air Force started in 1952 and said to have ended in 1969.

THE ENCOUNTER, THE ARREST, AND THE AFTERMATH

arrested him in the 1930s, they didn't take his wisdom as urgently until they encountered this craft during the Battle of Los Angeles. The circular planes Muhammad preached about was synonymous with the planes America encountered off the West Coast. The information and illustrations about the planes that the FBI took from Muhammad has also been what Government and scientists have used for reverse engineering technologies. John Lear (whose father developed the *Lear Jet*) admitted that their knowledge from observing UFOs is what sparked the development of the engineering technology associated with the Lear Jet. His family's wealth is predicated on their observance of UFOs. John Lear states, "the aliens give us technology and we use that technology... We tried to reverse engineer it, but it's millions of years ahead of us."[250] Lear is one of many who admitted that their study of UFOs give reasons for the advancement of technology today. Much of the technological advancements of America sprang exponentially after Elijah Muhammad's arrest and the Governments confiscation of his material about the Wheel in 1942.

The Government had no valid reason for arresting Elijah Muhammad. His arrest was the result of an Executive Decision from President Roosevelt's administration. The Selective Service Act of 1940 was used as a pretext to arrest him, but the Act required men between the ages of 18 to 45 and Muhammad was already beyond the drafting age. There was not even a formal trial to convict him of any wrong. Muhammad's bold stance against White American powers (which was uncommon at the time) alerted authorities to take action. Considering that America was engaged in a war with Japan at the time, Muhammad's Asian-like features coupled with his unabashed confidence in Allah (God) made him a unique target. Many of his critics described his Asian-like features as added grounds for U.S. Governmental concerns:

> To some, Muhammad's thin lips, pronounced cheekbones, and deep-set brown eyes were reminiscent of Oriental features. His appearances in fezzes, indeed, gave him a decidedly Eastern look.[251]

Why would the most powerful government in the world arrest a mild-mannered Black man who did not even believe in possessing as much as a pin knife? Why would a world superpower find it necessary to arrest a harmless man for preaching what he believed about the Wheel if it was not real? When has the U.S. Government ever arrested someone for such a teaching without a

---

[250] Brad Meltzer's Decoded, "UFO," *Brad Meltzer's Decoded*, Vol. Season 2 (History Channel, 2011 30-November).
[251] Claude Andrew Clegg, *An Original Man: The Life and Times of Elijah Muhammad* (Macmillan, 1998). 177.

formal trial or hearing? Furthermore, one should ask, 'What was Elijah Muhammad teaching that prompted an Executive decision to have him arrested and questioned about these crafts?' Why would the FBI confiscate Muhammad's documents and illustrations concerning the Wheel if this teaching were just some occult dogma? Why don't UFO researchers even mention these documented truths? The answers to all of these questions lead to the fact that the Honorable Elijah Muhammad was divinely appointed by the same power that controls those wheels—the same power that backs the Honorable Minister Louis Farrakhan today. This truth is the primary reason behind the whole UFO cover-up.

Since the U.S. Government recognized that Elijah Muhammad had firsthand knowledge about these crafts, they had to use the false charge of *draft evasion* to justify arresting him. Muhammad gives another account of the false charge:

> When the call was made for all males between 18 and 44, I refused (NOT EVADING) on the grounds that, first, I was a Muslim and would not take part in war and especially not on the side with the infidels. Second, I was 45 years of age and was NOT according to the law required to register.
> The above can be verified with the court records in Detroit and Washington D.C.[252]

U.S. Authorities realized that Elijah Muhammad was unlike any Black man witnessed in history. This strange man with a relatively small stature boldly asserted his position as the Messenger of Allah (God) who was taught directly by the Supreme Being. The FBI agents admitted to Muhammad that they witnessed and knew of the Mother Plane's reality and he assured the Government that they were no match for the power behind that Wheel. The FBI knew that this represented a seemingly incomprehensible intelligence and a power beyond their grasp. They recognized that they could not have Elijah Muhammad on the streets of America preaching this doctrine amidst America's ongoing war with Japan. They realized that Elijah Muhammad represented a higher power beyond their comprehension. As a result, the Messenger was unjustly incarcerated for five years.

While Muhammad remained incarcerated, UFO activities continued to plague both sides of the war. The advent of what became known as *foo-fighters* were frequently seen by pilots and military personnel during the 1940s. These were mostly orbital-shaped UFOs that were frequently seen around the globe, especially where military activities were taking place. These sightings, reported by mostly military personnel, were not a coincidence. The Honorable Elijah

---

[252] *MESSAGE TO THE BLACKMAN In America*, Original Published by MUHAMMAD'S Temple No. 2 in Chicago 1965 (Chicago, IL: The Final Call Inc., 1965).

THE ENCOUNTER, THE ARREST, AND THE AFTERMATH

Muhammad taught that the scientists who pilot the baby planes are very aware of all the plans and schemes of the world's powers. Minister Farrakhan reiterates Muhammad's teachings in these words:

> Those people are the angels. They are up there. They know what you think and before you can execute, they know it. These are the people from God...
>
> ...Those planes know everything about your military installations. You've caught them over all the military installations not only here, but in England, in France, in Germany, in Russia, in China, in India.[253]

The growing concern of the baby planes (foo-fighters) was expressed in the press during the 1940s:

> If it was not a hoax or an optical illusion, it was certainly the most puzzling secret weapon that Allied fighters have yet encountered. Last week U.S. night fighter pilots based in France told a strange story of balls of fire which for more than a month have been following their planes at night over Germany. No one seemed to know what, if anything, the fireballs were supposed to accomplish. Pilots, guessing that it was a new psychological weapon, named it the "foo-fighter."[254]

Even though they had Muhammad behind bars, there was nothing any world power could do about the UFOs that became rather ubiquitous during the tumultuous atmosphere in the world. This coupled with Muhammad's growing influence within the prisons established an avenue for authorities to become concerned enough to release Muhammad in August 1946. The UFO activities around the world did not stop then. In fact, many ufologists would say that sightings increased exponentially after Muhammad's release. Even after his release, the U.S. Government worked diligently to monitor and stifle the progress of the Honorable Elijah Muhammad and his followers.[255] The Messenger exposed the Governments attempts to cover-up the truth of his teachings as well as their attacks on his followers:

---

[253] "The Time And What Must Be Done," *Saviours' Day 2010 Keynote Address by The Honorable Minister Louis Farrakhan* (Chicago, IL: The Final Call, 2010 28-February).
[254] Time Magazine, "Foo-Fighter," *Time*, January 15, 1945.
[255] Ward Churchill and Jim Vander Wall, *The COINTELPRO Papers: Documents from the FBI's Secret Wars Against Dissent in the United States* (South End Press, 1990).

They call the truth and salvation of Allah, that He has brought to us, false and trouble-making. They call in both men and women who believe for questioning just for the sole purpose of trying to frighten them away.
They are trying to frighten them from that which they know is their so-called Negroes' salvation and universal recognition, friendship in all walks of life, money and good homes.[256]

The Government's harassment of the Nation of Islam has continued for decades. This has been compounded by the media's negative depictions of the Muslims in order to cover-up the truth that they convey about UFOs and the time of prophetic fulfillment. Part of the UFO cover-up involves discrediting the source of information behind them. In other words, if the NOI is made to appear as a wild-eyed cult, intelligent people would never accept their message of truth.

The Battle of Los Angeles sparked tremendous concerns as well as embarrassment to the U.S. Government that they never wanted to experience again. What happened during that encounter had virtually been kept from the public for decades. Ironically, one of the most significant modern accounts of a mass public UFO sighting had become one of the least remembered. It was as though this history was deliberately swept under the rug, but ufologists, historians, and researchers have not let this monumental event go unnoticed. Since this subject has resurfaced over the last years, the U.S. Government still has not offered a plausible explanation to the public about what happened over California in 1942. The explanations they have offered have caused more suspicion that the Government and the mainstream media are involved in a decades-long UFO cover-up.

Over forty years after that shocking event in California, the Office of Air Force History's analysis suggests that meteorological balloons were the initial cause of alarm:

> …a balloon carrying a red flare was seen over Santa Monica and four batteries of anti-aircraft artillery opened fire, whereupon "the air over Los Angeles erupted like a volcano." From this point on reports were hopelessly at variance.
> Probably much of the confusion came from the fact that anti-aircraft shell bursts, caught by the searchlights, were themselves mistaken for enemy planes.[257]

---

[256] *MESSAGE TO THE BLACKMAN In America*, Original Published by MUHAMMAD'S Temple No. 2 in Chicago 1965 (Chicago, IL: The Final Call Inc., 1965).
[257] California State Military Department Office of Air Force History, "California and the Second World War: The Battle of Los Angeles," *The Army Air Forces in World War II*, ed. Wesley Frank Craven and James Lea Cate (Washington, DC: The California State Military Museum, 1983), 277-286.

THE ENCOUNTER, THE ARREST, AND THE AFTERMATH

Of course this *weather balloon* theory does not satisfy hardly any thinker, whether they are a UFO believer or a staunch skeptic. How is it that over 1400 rounds of fired artillery could not bring down a weather balloon? What kind of weather balloon or any conventional aircraft can remain unshaken by such an attack? The more that governments try to cover-up the UFO phenomena, the more they make it known that they are hiding something by their absurd explanations. Since there have been no rational explanations, the U.S. Government and the mainstream media have worked diligently to cover-up the reality of the Wheel as represented by the Nation of Islam. Some historians suggest that the scenario surrounding the Battle of Los Angeles was the beginning of the Government's UFO cover-up:

> If they can't bring down a weather balloon with over 1500 rounds of anti-aircraft shrapnel of twelve-pound weaponry, what are they going to do against a real enemy target? That's when they decided, "What do we do? Do we tell the American and the world public there is something among us that we cannot bring down, that we cannot control? We don't know where they're from and we don't know what they're doing here." No they didn't want to say that, so the next best thing to do was to officially deny their existence. That's when the first official denial on UFOs started.[258]

Since decades of insurmountable evidence shows that UFOs exist, the ruling powers of the world refuse to acknowledge the source of this reality. This also includes many UFO researchers and believers. The embarrassing experience from the UFO encounter over Los Angeles County was a learning experience for the Government's Intelligence. Since more encounters were likely imminent, the Government, with help from the media, would ensure that they would make provisions not to allow the public to be alarmed by this higher intelligence that makes their world look like child's-play.

The America Government and the media began to develop more methods of swaying public opinion to the point where they could persuade people to believe official governmental reports instead of the people believing what they saw with their own eyes. These efforts could not be successful without the cooperation of the mainstream media. Media campaigns to sway public opinion have always been used by governments and militaries to achieve certain objectives. In the case of UFOs, diligent efforts have been used to depict the concept of UFOs and flying saucers as figments of people's imaginations. After the UFO encounter and Muhammad's arrest in 1942,

---

[258] Jose Escamilla, interview by Dara Brown, "The 65th Anniversary of The Battle of Los Angeles," *MSNBC News*, MSNBC (2007).

several movies and films were subsequently produced that propagandized the ideas that made UFOs more of a fictitious fad of pop culture.

Figure 5: THE ENCOUNTER & THE ARREST

Clockwise from top left: Lights shined and missiles fired during the Battle of Los Angeles on February 25-26, 1942, LA Times cover after the UFO encounter, Los Angeles Examiner after the Battle of LA 1942, General George C. Marshall, Elijah Muhammad handcuffed and arrested by FBI after the Battle of LA in 1942, President Franklin D. Roosevelt.

It took nearly 70 years for the CIA to even admit that Area 51 officially existed.[259] The fact that the U.S. Government has concealed and denied the truth about one of their secret military locations is proof that they have lied about their knowledge of UFOs and the real power behind them. If it took that long just to acknowledge such a place exists, then what other vital knowledge are they withholding from the public?

---

[259] Central Intelligence Agency History Staff, "The Central Intelligence Agency and Overhead Reconnaissance. The U-2 and OXCART Programs, 1954-1974," Declassified CIA Documents, History Staff: Pedlow, Gregory W.; Welzenbach, Donald E., Central Intelligence Agency (Washington, DC, 1992), 407.

THE ENCOUNTER, THE ARREST, AND THE AFTERMATH

THE COVER-UP BEGINS

In studying the UFO phenomenon I am always stuck by the results of the most recent surveys. Recall the argument that there would be wide spread panic if the government announced that there was an extraterrestrial presence visiting earth. Well every polling result in the last 10 years simply doesn't support that argument.[260] – Alberta UFO Study Group Report

If the truth about UFOs became widely known to Americans and the rest of the world, this could lead to a global admission that Elijah Muhammad was taught by a most intelligent entity. This is perhaps the primary reason for the blatant cover-up. Drastic measures have been taken to ensure that the masses of the people never come to this realization, even if it means deceiving the people before they ever witness these crafts for themselves. The strategy of leading people against the reality of UFOs before they ever witness them for themselves is what can be termed *pre-emptive propaganda*.[261] This is only one of many tactics used to deceive the public from accepting the authenticity of these planes and to deter them from the designated persons representing the power of those planes.

Official sightings and reports ensued drastically after the FBI arrested the Honorable Elijah Muhammad as all the most famous sightings and UFO cases arose exponentially over subsequent decades. Despite continuous attempts to deceive the public about these planes, the evidence concerning UFOs has become increasingly lucid among common Americans. By 1996, 48% of Americans believed UFOs were real and that the government has been concealing information about them.[262] This represents nearly half of the American people who acknowledged that all UFOs are not just figments of people's imaginations as portrayed in much of the media. The numbers didn't change nearly five years later where a Life Magazine poll showed that 49% of Americans believed the Government was withholding vital information about UFOs.[263] The Roper Poll in 2002 reflected that 56% of the American public thinks that UFOs are something real and not just in people's imagination.

---

[260] Alberta UFO Study Group, "Summaries of Some Recent Opinion Polls on UFOs," *UFO Evidence* (ufoevidence.org, 2011).
[261] **Pre-emptive propaganda** is a term coined by Ilia Rashad Muhammad that refers to the use of deceiving the public about UFOs before they have the opportunity to witness the truth about them for themselves.
[262] Newsweek Magazine, "Alien Invasion!," *Newsweek*, July 7, 1996.
[263] "UFO's: Why do we believe?," *Life Magazine*, March 2000.

Since then, the numbers have remained generally the same whereas nearly half or more of the American people believe in the existence of UFOs.

In 2008, 14% of the American people have sighted a UFO.[264] If 14% of the American people have literally seen UFOs and there are over 300 million Americans, then well over forty-two million Americans have seen UFOs. Is it mere coincides or fictitious thinking that has caused over forty million people in America to witness UFOs for themselves? Is it by happenstance that tens of millions of Americans have witnessed virtually the same type of crafts and described them in practically the same manner? Are tens of millions of witnesses all hallucinating or playing hoaxes about the same thing? How much would the testimonies of forty-two million witnesses in a court of law have? There is absolutely no possible way that the reality of UFOs can continue to remain withheld in light of the overwhelming evidence.

Figure 6: STATISTICAL DATA

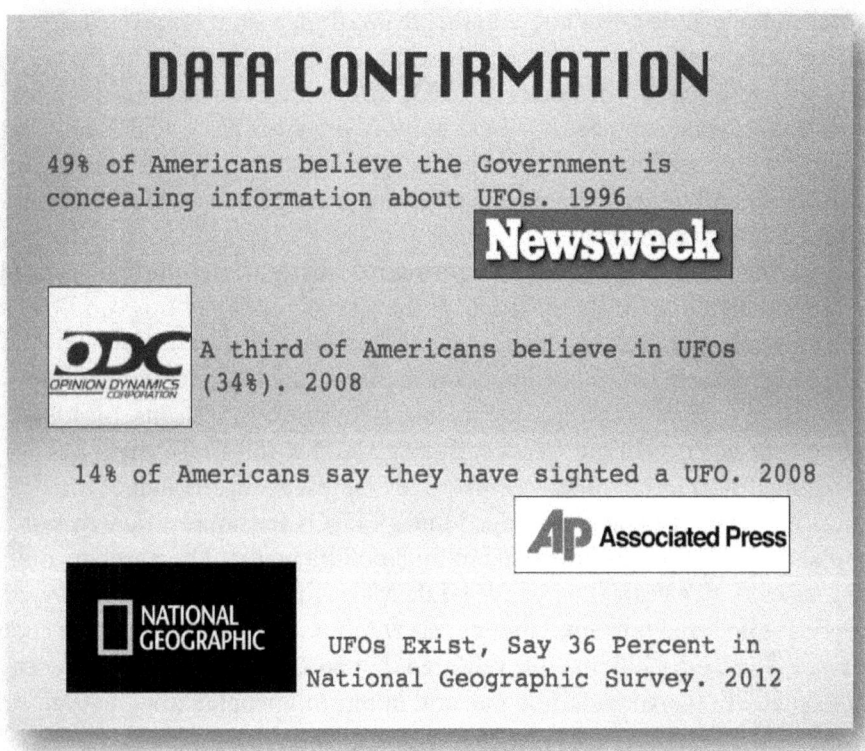

Tens of millions of Americans have witnessed a UFO and over a hundred million believe in them.

---

[264] AP/Ipsos Poll, "Majority of Americans Believe in Ghosts (57%) and UFOs (52%)," *Associated Press/Ipsos* (Washington, DC, October 31, 2008).

THE ENCOUNTER, THE ARREST, AND THE AFTERMATH

In light of all the evidence, official reports, millions of sightings, and governmental investigations, would it make sense to deny the existence of these planes? Moreover, would it make sense to ignore the person who brought this truth to the modern world? Ironically, this is exactly what continues to take place. Instead of associating the wheel-like UFOs with the entities responsible for them, the mainstream media works to spin the concept of UFOs into some kind of non-human extraterrestrial entity. Through movie depictions and fantasy television shows, they have often spun the image of UFO personnel to be monstrous antagonistic creatures who seek to destroy humanity. This type of pre-emptive propaganda is used to induce fear and hatred against something that could represent salvation.

THE HOLLYWOOD ACCOMPLICE

Minister Farrakhan expressed, "I don't believe people make movies just to entertain. Wise people make movies to move people in certain directions."[265] History bears witness that most movies are not made for the sole purpose of entertainment. Wise people produce movies, songs, and entertainment to influence public opinion. Minister Farrakhan and several others have valid reasons for maintaining such a belief. He explained that during the early 1970s, a Jewish film producer asked to meet with him while he was in Jamaica during the same time that the movie *Lost in the Stars* was being produced. Upon meeting with the Minister, this Jewish producer/director acknowledged that it was not the Minister himself whom Whites feared; instead, it was the idea that he represented that they feared. He further shared with Minister Farrakhan that a clandestine group of Whites (primarily Jews) meet annually to plan and initiate how they will continue to influence public opinion by way of film, music, fashion, food and a host of other avenues.[266]

The idea that certain Jews convene to manipulate the public should not sound unrealistic or absurd. It is a known fact that since the early Twentieth-Century, Jews have annually convened to do just that. The World Zionist Organization (WZO) has been meeting since 1897 with the objective to summon enough world influence to form and maintain a Jewish state of

---

[265] Louis Farrakhan, interview by Ashahed Muhammad, Starla Muhammad, Richard Muhammad, "Farrakhan Speaks On The Year 2012 & The New Year 2013," *Farrakhan Speaks*, FCN, Chicago, January 2013.
[266] Ibid.

Israel.[267] The WZO is only one of many influential Jewish entities that host a number of other groups, congresses, and entities that influence public opinion and public policies.

With this in mind, Minister Farrakhan's words are proven true. Years later, a highly influential Jewish business mogul, Edgar Bronfman Sr., invited Minister Farrakhan to his New York Penthouse. During this private meeting, Mr. Bronfman boasted of his people's influence over aspects of American life with the intention to impress the Minister to stop preaching the truth that Elijah Muhammad revealed to him. Needless to say, Minister Farrakhan pleasantly declined their offer and has continued to preach the truth against those who keep his people oppressed as well as the truth about these wheel-like planes that have been personally revealed to him by his experience with the Honorable Elijah Muhammad.

Those who have tremendous influence over the entertainment industry have motives and agendas that extend far beyond entertainment or financial purposes alone. Hollywood has served as an arm of the Government's Intelligence agencies to manipulate the public's perception about UFOs. This explains why so many UFO related movies have sought to mystify and spin the idea that these wheel-shaped planes are either fictitious, monstrous, villainous, or altogether of some alien origin. There have been no known movies or big screen documentaries that incorporate the fact that Elijah Muhammad, Louis Farrakhan, and the Nation of Islam are those responsible for representing this reality to the modern world. It is overwhelmingly obvious that Hollywood has another motive behind their release of these type of films.

Diligent efforts are put forth to ensure that the public is not made aware of the truth about so-called UFOs. Anything within grasp is done to distract the masses from realizing there is a power more superior to America's. Governmental and military Intelligence have covered-up most of the known UFO activities and encounters with their military operations. The mainstream media has been used to fictionalize the credible UFO cases through satirical movies and television shows. Hollywood has helped people to believe that the credible UFO cases are from extraterrestrial alien sources. Religion has even played its part in the deception by not having any plausible explanation about the sudden rise of these mysterious planes around the globe. Having no justifiable way to rationalize these wheel-like planes, some religious schools of thought have begun teaching that these planes are of demonic origin. It seems that almost anything is done to hinder the truth about Muhammad's teachings.

One of the most commonly used tactics the media uses to sway the public against the reality of UFOs is through *pre-emptive propaganda*—a strategy that leads people to disbelieve in the idea that these wheel-like planes

---

[267] Mordecai Naor, *Zionism: The First 120 Years, 1882-2002* (Jerusalem: The Zionist Library, 2002).

THE ENCOUNTER, THE ARREST, AND THE AFTERMATH

(UFOs) exist before they get a chance to witness the evidence of these planes for themselves. By highlighting the foiled hoaxes and the creative imagination of Hollywood cinema, and by downplaying the credible UFO related cases, many people are led to believe that all possible cases are mistaken imaginations or hoaxes.

Perhaps one of the most effective tools in the pre-emptive propaganda campaign against UFOs has been the movie and film industry. After the fiasco over Los Angeles and the subsequent arrest of Elijah Muhammad in 1942, the movie industry went to work to sensationalize the growing sightings and beliefs in flying saucers. Starting mostly in the 1950s, many movies were released depicting the flying saucers as alien monsters from another planet or galaxy. Such depictions have diverted the reality that these planes and their intelligence stem from earth. These frequent depictions have become so embedded in America's cultural psyche that even most UFO believers attribute these wheels to some extraterrestrial beings. Of course this idea contradicts the accurate descriptions given by the primary source of the modern UFO era, the Most Honorable Elijah Muhammad. He made it clear what those planes are and who controls them before the world ever had concerns about such aerial phenomena.

All major UFO-centered films came years after Elijah Muhammad had already preached this reality to the world. Historians have admitted to this truth that cinematic attention on flying saucers began well over a decade past Muhammad's introduction:

> Arnold's sighting [1947]–combined with a highly publicized UFO incident that took place later that summer near Roswell, New Mexico – a frenzy of interest in otherworldly visitors and an entire new subculture, known as "ufology," that would be vividly represented in movies in the decades to come.[268]

One of the first UFO related films to hit the big screen included *The Day the Earth Stood Still* (1951). In this film, aliens from a huge spaceship represented a power sent to hold the earth spellbound. The humanoid aliens from the ship are ultimately antagonized because America was given the choice of living in peace or being utterly destroyed. If they chose to live in peace, they would have to do so under the rule of this new foreign power, which many critics have argued was indicative of the anti-Communist sentiments that pervaded the U.S. at that time. Needless to say, movie critics have pointed out that the subtle vilification of the aliens was part of Government's propaganda

---

[268] History - UFO Hunters, *Aliens in the Movies: UFOs and Alien Invasions in Film* (History.com, 2012).

against Communism and any foreign powers that threatened white supremacy, especially during the era of *McCarthyism*.[269] Movies such as *The Day the Earth Stood Still* helped initiate the pre-emptive propaganda against the power associated with the wheels.

As people became more intrigued with UFOs due to increased sightings and reports, many in the public also became embittered with the powers associated with those planes. This was greatly due to the rise in movie depictions. Another early film that portrayed UFO related powers as villainous included the film adaptation of Orson Wells' *The War of the Worlds* in 1953. This movie improvised Orson Wells' novel to fit the newly arisen UFO phenomenon. Again the inhabitants of the spaceships are depicted as a threat to earth. Other researchers have acknowledged the sudden growth of interest in UFOs that sprang up from the 1950s:

> The popularity of *The War of the Worlds* and *The Day the Earth Stood Still*, as well as that of a number of other films, including *The Thing From Another World* (1951), *Earth Versus the Flying Saucers* (1956) and *Invasion of the Body Snatchers* (1956) helped make the 1950s a watershed decade for ufology.[270]

Such films and the television depictions that followed have been significant factors that have kept the public in the dark about the wheels. Several blockbuster films have come and gone since the fifties that continue with the same theme of counteracting Elijah Muhammad's teachings by sensationalizing the purpose and origin of the wheel-like spacecraft. More and more movies have been released in the years and decades following Muhammad's heralding of these planes.

The 1960s yielded one of the most popular television shows related to UFOs, *Star Trek: The Original Series*. This American pop culture classic depicted the famous Starship Enterprise, which was a huge wheel-shaped spaceship that traveled at terrific speeds throughout the galaxies. Where did that idea come from? There is a reason why so many depictions of wheel-like planes entered the vernacular of popular culture after the 1930s. The primary reason is the Honorable Elijah Muhammad and the Supreme Being who showed him the reality of these planes.

Steven Speilberg has been credited for his involvement in some of the most notable UFO movies of recent decades. He directed *Close Encounters of the Third Kind* (1977) and the famous movie *E.T.* (1982). Both movies depicted aliens who appear from space on a circular wheel-like ship. In *Close Encounters of the Third Kind*, an huge mother ship returns to earth with people who had

---

[269] McCarthyism refers to the vitriolic campaign against alleged communists in the U.S. Government and other institutions carried out under Senator Joseph McCarthy in the early 1950s.
[270] Op. cit. History - UFO Hunters.

THE ENCOUNTER, THE ARREST, AND THE AFTERMATH

been abducted from previous decades—strangely the abductees had not aged since the times they were abducted. This depiction is based on Muhammad's descriptions of the technology and lifestyle upon those crafts. However, Hollywood would never credit the truth about their movie plots to the man who truly started it all.

V: The Original Miniseries of 1983 and the 2009 remake *V* were both series that depict human-looking aliens appearing on earth as outwardly peaceful. They arrive on wheel-shaped spaceships, one of which is dubbed the *Mother Ship*, which is commanded by a pleasantly deceitful commander. In both miniseries, the aliens' human appearance only served as a cover for their malevolent intentions to usurp humanity. Aside from the entertaining qualities of such programs, these type of shows instilled more animosity toward the wheels that Muhammad spoke of.

One year after the Honorable Minister Louis Farrakhan led over one million Black men in unity during the Million Man March, Hollywood released another UFO related film that sought to antagonize the powers of the Mother Wheel and the baby planes that the Honorable Elijah Muhammad taught and that Minister Farrakhan represents. Using A-list actors like Will Smith, *Independence Day* (1996) was a blockbuster hit that continued the idea of evil non-negotiating aliens appearing on huge wheels that were to be defeated by the U.S. and its allied forces. This is indicative of an attitude that is pervasive among government and military officials who seek to oppose the divine powers associated with the wheels. The evidence of their attitude lies in their treatment of the Nation of Islam which represents the power of those planes.

Men in Black I, II, and *III* (1997, 2002, and 2012) perpetuated the notion that UFO activities are derived from alien invasions and that many of the aliens secretly reside in human-form throughout society. Despite the entertaining qualities associated with all the Men in Black movies, it too sensationalizes the notion of UFOs and the pilots who operate them, thus prompting the false belief that UFOs are merely the result of creative imagination of the movie screen, not something that should be taken seriously.

The movie *Battle: LA* was released in March 2011. It seems that the title of this movie was deliberately intended to throw off potential observers since it is loosely titled after the more realistic Battle of Los Angeles event of 1942—the event that led to the arrest of the Honorable Elijah Muhammad the same year. The 2011 movie was a total diversion from the actual events of 1942. The movie portrayed UFOs with a monstrous extraterrestrial nature that invaded earth with the aim of destroying humanity. The U.S. Military was called upon to battle against these evil aliens who coincidentally appeared from wheel-shaped spacecrafts over Los Angeles. Nowadays, most people would probably relegate the Battle of Los Angeles to a movie rather than the actual event.

Acting as tentacles of governmental propaganda, mainstream media organizations have done their parts to deter potential believers from recognizing the truth about UFOs. Their frequently used cover-up techniques have been rather effective in keeping the public from knowing what these crafts are, who controls them, where they come from, and their purpose in this world. The truth about them had already been detailed by the Honorable Elijah Muhammad and the Nation of Islam. The result of such inaccurate depictions of the wheel-like planes on the big screen caused many people to mock the theology of the Nation of Islam for several decades. The NOI had been ridiculed for teaching about the Mother Wheel and the baby planes during a time when the average person had yet to be exposed to them. Take into consideration that these were times when the concept of sending a rocket outer space was considered unrealistic to most people. Nonetheless, the Nation of Islam stood strong in their recognition that Allah (God) revealed this truth to his appointed Messenger, Elijah Muhammad.

9. THE MESSENGER, THE PROOF, AND THE DENIALS

THE CRITICS' ROUTINE: OMIT FACTS, OFFER OPINIONS

It is extremely difficult, if not impossible to find the concept of an aerial *mothership* or *Mother Plane* prior to Muhammad's initial exegesis. Its flight-related jargon of a mothership-type craft can be linked to the advent of the Honorable Elijah Muhammad in the early 1930s. Now, this terminology has found its way into modern vernacular. Deliberately overlooking him, so-called "experts" on this subject have often attributed UFO related concepts of a mother ship to a California woman in 1947 who described what she and others saw as a "mother saucer" with a "bunch of little saucers playing around it."[271] Although she described something that Elijah Muhammad was shown nearly two decades earlier, the "experts" totally overlook the credence these reports give to the NOI. Several reports and video footage from around the globe have exemplified the same characteristics. In 2008, world-renown astrophysicist and UFO researcher Dr. Stanton Friedman used the same terminology to describe certain UFO sightings during his CNN interview with Larry King. Part of their discussion is as follows:

> FRIEDMAN: It reminds me of a case up in the Yukon in 1996, where a total of 31 witnesses were interviewed by a civil engineer -- that were in groups of two and three driving on the Klondike Highway in the middle of winter. And they all described this huge thing in the sky that was silent, that had very bright lights on it, that hung around for quite awhile. There was only one place to stop. A lot of them had stopped for gas and food. And so the investigator, Martin Jasek, a registered civil engineer, was able to triangulate. This thing was between half a mile and a mile big. So that rules out any conventional aircraft. The silence rules out, as you know, any airplanes, anything like that.
>
> KING: So, what's your conclusion?

---

[271] Michael D. Connors and Wendy Hall, *Alfred Loedding & the Great Flying Saucer Wave of 1947*, 1st (Rose Press, 1998). 55. Quote taken from the Palmdale South Antelope Valley Press, 10 July 1947, p. 1

FRIEDMAN: Probably -- I'll call it a mother ship.
KING: A mother ship?
FRIEDMAN: Well, a space carrier, does that sound better? You know, we have aircraft carriers which are huge and little small airplanes on it. We have a number of reports of huge craft -- big monsters, half a mile to a mile, that move silently and slowly and then fast.
KING: All right, what do you make of the military chasing it?
FRIEDMAN: Well, that's standard practice. Larry, I hate to say this and it sounds unpatriotic, but the Air Force has lied about UFOs for 50 -- more than 50 -- for 60 years, actually. And this would be in keeping with that.
KING: For what purpose?
FRIEDMAN: To keep us from knowing what's going on.[272]

Are Friedman and other acclaimed researchers aware that their reports vindicate the authority of the Honorable Elijah Muhammad or are they totally oblivious to the facts of the NOI's position on this subject? Unsurprisingly, no mention or reference to the source of this 'mother ship' phenomenon occurred during any part of their on-air discussions, yet these are considered qualified researchers on this subject. It is not a coincidence that most pundits, critics, and skeptics omit this vital information from their commentary. Even more interesting is how most critics follow the same deceptive patterns when discussing the NOI and the UFO phenomena. These patterns involve overlooking Muhammad's inaugural teachings, reinterpreting his words based on their opinions, and omitting vital facts.

Critics frequently throw Muhammad's firsthand data about these objects into a category of *mythology*. Ney Rieber, an evangelical critic, posted his review about the NOI's belief in the wheels:

> There is also a rather unique space man mythology associated with the Nation of Islam's teachings. Elijah Muhammad contended that it had been revealed to him by W. D. Fard, (Allah) that there was a great mother plane (aircraft/spaceship) which is really a small maneuverable planet that orbits as much as forty miles above the earth... This doctrine, again, is foreign to both the Bible and the Qur'an.[273]

Clearly such critics should conduct more research of the scriptures and of the Nation of Islam. Contrary to Rieber's claim, the teachings of God's heavenly vehicles are laced throughout the Bible and Qur'an. Yet Rieber who is supposed to be a Biblical preacher categorized this reality as 'space man mythology.' Would he categorize his Lord and Savior's alleged ascension into

---

[272] Stanton Friedman, interview by Larry King, "UFOS: Questions & Controversy," *CNN LARRY KING LIVE*, CNN, January 18, 2008.
[273] Ney Rieber, "The Nation of Islam - Islam: Truth or Myth?," *Bible.Ca* (Bible.ca, September 2002).

the clouds (without a vehicle) as a 'space man mythology'? Maybe he forgot to mention that the Bible describes the New Jerusalem in the sky, God's heavenly chariots, and of course those flying wheels. Maybe he never read how the Holy Qur'an describes Allah's Throne of Power and Allah's Exalted Assembly in the heavens. Elijah Muhammad's doctrine not only proved to be pragmatically consistent with the sacred scriptures, but it also exposed the incompetence of world scholars whose theologies and ideologies have not been able to explain the UFO phenomenon. Apparently this 'space man mythology' has prompted world governments to open their investigative files on UFOs.[274]

While most critics use diversionary mockery to discredit the Nation's 'Mother Wheel' theology, writer Amir Fatir on the other hand, is one of the few who credits Muhammad as bringing this reality to the world:

> Before UFOlogy became popular, the Honorable Elijah Muhammad taught that a large spaceship had been built "to destroy the white man's world." He called this spaceship "the Mother Plane." He also referred to it as "the Mother of Planes." The various parts of the ship were built in factories across the world, but the workers had no idea of what they were actually building. It was eventually assembled in Japan in 1929.[275]

Fatir acknowledges that Muhammad heralded this concept to the public; however, his interpretation of Muhammad's teaching is rather delusive. Fatir gives his own reinterpretation that mystifies the NOI's teachings by implying that the Wheel is only a symbolic metaphor, not to be taken literally:

> In Nation of Islam esoteric symbolism, white, black, red and yellow "people" were symbols of states of mind. Very few people in the Nation, however, knew that most of the doctrine was given metaphorically and symbolically. The rank-and-file membership considers the teachings to be "actual facts."[276]

If Muhammad's teachings concerning the Mother Wheel and baby planes are strictly metaphoric, how is it that millions of sightings and decades of governmental investigations have proven otherwise? Even though there are deeply spiritual principles involved in his teachings of the wheels, Elijah Muhammad elucidated the blatant physical reality of these planes in the physical world as well as their spiritual significance. Besides, the Honorable

---

[274] The Disclosure Project, *UFO FILES - COUNTRIES RELEASING*, 2010, http://www.disclosureproject.org/ (accessed March 11, 2013).
[275] Amir Fatir, "Nation of Islam: Mothership Connection" (Amir Fatir - Astrologer, Healer and Author, April 2002).
[276] Ibid.

Elijah Muhammad never relegated the Wheel as just a metaphor; he spoke of it as a physical manifestation of the prophetic utterances. Again, countless thousands of photos, reports, video footage, and Muhammad's own words prove this to be accurate.

Instead of giving just credit to Muhammad, some of his critics and detractors openly discard the facts while rendering their opinion-based reinterpretations of his teachings. Following the normal routine of NOI critics, Professor Claude Clegg continues the same nonsensical pattern:

> Perhaps second only to the Yacub myth, the Mother Plane story was the most peculiar element of the theology of the Nation. Unless one was predisposed to believe in flying saucers, this tale could hardly be told without raising doubts even among the most open-minded of listeners…
>
> This aerial aircraft carrier of Fard Muhammad's played into both the science fiction films that, as mentioned earlier, were extremely popular during the early twentieth century and actual technological developments…
>
> In essence, Fard Muhammad's fictional plane simply combined the mythical spaceships of the Martian movies with the superbattleships and aircraft carriers that were filling the ranks of every major navy in a weapon of divine retribution that was virtually invincible.[277]

While Clegg rendered his skeptical 'opinion' of the Mother Plane as a fictional tale, he omits the facts concerning the vast proof and evidence of these circular planes that have been a major focal point of military concerns and investigations around the globe. Clegg says nothing about the hundreds of military officials from around the globe whose reports and eyewitness testimonies[278] bear witness to Elijah Muhammad's teachings. Were 'myths' seen by hundreds of military airmen or were wheel-shaped planes seen and reported by them? Did real wheels interfere with some of the world's most sophisticated weaponry or were those fictional tales? The answers to these questions prove that Elijah Muhammad and Louis Farrakhan represent an authentically supreme authority. Claude Clegg and those pundits who unjustly castigate the truth of the NOI have not been able to reconcile their own critiques with realistic data. Obviously this is why these critics can only render outright lies, warped interpretations, and 'opinions' instead of clear evidence. The Nation of Islam, on the other hand, has brought a truth that is

---

[277] Claude Andrew Clegg, *An Original Man: The Life and Times of Elijah Muhammad* (Macmillan, 1998). 66.
[278] Robert Hastings, et al., "UFO Press Conference from The National Press Club," *Robert Hastings Presents* (Washiington, DC: CNN, 2010 йил 27-September).

substantiated with practical evidence in the real world. That evidence is documented and sighted nearly every week.[279]

A MAN LIKE MOSES, A TYRANT LIKE PHARAOH

I met with Allah as Moses met with Jehovah. Allah has revealed the truth unto me. It is up to you to believe it or let it alone. But this does not negate the fact that I know the end of it all. I know tomorrow. I would be happy to tell it to you if you will believe it. I want you to know that our oppressors are exerting every effort to prevent you and me from uniting.[280] – The Honorable Elijah Muhammad

The Nation of Islam continued to proclaim that Allah (God) appeared in person and raised Elijah Muhammad as his divine messenger. This message did not resonate well with the religious and political leadership of America. In fact, Muhammad's unpopular teaching of the Mother Plane and the 1500 smaller wheels brought charges of blasphemy and sedition from America's leadership. While the NOI withstood the attacks, many of the high-ranking officials within America's military and government began to witness these crafts for themselves. Ironically, this did little to humble their oppressive attitudes. Rather, Western powers remained steadfast in their efforts to deceive the public about the Nation of Islam and the wheels that were now being sighted in waves across America. The wheels had not only been sighted by common people, but these wheels had been witnessed by some of those who would later become the world's most influential figures.[281]

The idea of this majestic power being witnessed by policy-makers and influencers is not a mere coincidence. This idea is consistent with the divine forecasting of the scriptures. Throughout the sacred texts, God has frequently revealed majestic signs of his power to his enemies in order to see how they

---

[279] John F. Schuessler, *Public Opinion Surveys and Unidentified Flying Objects 50+ years of Sampling Public Opinions*, UFO Statistics, International Director's Office, Mutual UFO Network, Inc. (MUFON) (Morrison, CO: MUFON, 2000).
[280] Elijah Muhammad, *The Fall Of America* (Chicago, IL: Elijah Muhammad, 1973). Excerpted from his speech at the Uline Arena. Washington, DC, Sunday, May 29, 1959.
[281] Grant Cameron and T. Crain, *UFOs, Area 51, and Government Informants*, Kindle (Keyhole Publishing Company, 2013). Numerous Presidents, heads of state, and government officials have secretly known about UFOs, but have frequently shielded this truth from the public.

respond to his divine will. Most of the scriptures indicate that the oppressive enemies of God hardly ever took heed to his divine warnings, despite the clear evidence of God's power. Pharaoh became even more embittered by the warning signs of God as represented by Moses and Aaron. Herod took offense to the celestial signs of God's power. Instead of submitting to the power behind the heavenly signs, Herod sought to counteract the will of God by destroying the person sent by God for their salvation. These prophetic scenarios give clear insight into the mindset that is prevalent among the leadership of America and the world.

Just as God revealed his power to his enemies in the scriptures, he continues the same pattern today. He gives everyone a chance before his destruction, but history and prophecy show that hardly any of the ruling powers would take heed to the divine warnings of God despite his clear presence. The coming of Allah (God) in person, the raising of Elijah Muhammad as his messenger, and the revelation of the Mother Plane (and smaller wheel-like planes) are fulfillments of the prophetic patterns of God. This scenario is depicted in this prophetic glimpse into Pharaoh's mind.

> *And he [Pharaoh] said to his people, "Look, the people of the children of Israel are more and mightier than we; come, let us deal shrewdly with them, lest they multiply, and it happen, in the event of war, that they also join our enemies and fight against us, and so go up out of the land." –* Exodus 1:9-10

America's attempt to suppress the words of Elijah Muhammad and Louis Farrakhan is synonymous with Pharaoh's fears toward Moses and Aaron. Obviously Pharaoh's counsel realized that God's representation through Moses and Aaron would free the people from their oppressors. According to both the Bible and the Holy Qur'an, Pharaoh's counsel feared that God's servants would free the people from bondage. They feared that Moses and Aaron would turn the former slaves against them and unite with a foreign power against Pharaoh's people. This dichotomy led Pharaoh and his military powers to challenge God's authority—the same efforts that the U.S. Government has exhibited towards the Nation of Islam.

Elijah Muhammad acknowledged that he fulfills the prophetic mission of that man like Moses spoken of in *Deuteronomy 18:18*. This represents a man whom God promises to raise up and teach himself—a man whom God would befriend and speak with *face to face* as a man speaks to a friend (Exodus 33:11). Perhaps no significant leader in the last century has even claimed such a position. Certainly no leader has provided the evidence that Muhammad used to substantiate his claims.

Interestingly, the promise that God would raise a man like Moses to a future generation would not make sense unless the circumstances and

THE MESSENGER, THE PROOF, AND THE DENIALS

conditions warranted it. Moses was raised by God to deliver his enslaved people from the oppressive powers of Pharaoh's regime. Moses and his spokesperson, Aaron, had the unpopular task of preaching a doctrine of separation from Pharaoh's power. Moses and Aaron had the arduous task of making known the presence of a God whose identity was previously unknown to the people whom they were sent to liberate—a God who was also unknown to their oppressor's people. The Honorable Elijah Muhammad proclaimed that this is a reason for God's visit to America:

> In this country, Allah desired to make Himself known as He did (for example) in Egypt, only this time it is universal, coming first to the lost and found members of the Black Nation of America. That prophecy of the Bible from Moses to Jesus must be fulfilled.[282]

Similarly, Elijah Muhammad and Louis Farrakhan have had the burdensome task of representing the supreme God who came in person to set justice in the world. This task has been extremely unpopular in a world where God is said to be a formless shapeless spirit. Elijah Muhammad (the Messenger) and Louis Farrakhan (the Minister) represent a God who appeared in person. Like the God of Moses and Aaron, the God of the Nation of Islam pointed out a power in the sky that appeared as a cloud by day and as fire by night (Exodus 13:21) that would guide the chosen people through their journey for liberation.

This *fire in the sky* has been witnessed by more than average citizens. Some of the most distinctive sightings have been experienced by some of the world's most influential personalities. Presidents, world leaders, astronauts, elected officials, pilots, and celebrities, have been perplexed by these flying objects. Unsurprisingly, many of the leaders reacted with the same attitudes of leaders in the sacred scriptures. Very seldom did the oppressive powers take heed to the divine call of God or his messengers, even though they were shown clear signs from their Lord. This has certainly been the case in America's leadership.

The Bible and the Holy Qur'an illustrate how Pharaoh and his army ignored the warnings of Moses and Aaron. Pharaoh did not see the connection between the warnings of Moses and Aaron with the plagues that were taking place in the land until it was nearly too late. He finally realized that it was the God of Moses responsible for these horrific events. Likewise, the people today have not readily accepted the connection that Elijah Muhammad and Louis

---

[282] *MESSAGE TO THE BLACKMAN In America*, Original Published by MUHAMMAD'S Temple No. 2 in Chicago 1965 (Chicago, IL: The Final Call Inc., 1965). 187.

Farrakhan have with the UFO phenomena. Despite several decades of preaching and teaching about the existence of these planes, the American public has not fully made the connection between these planes and the men who represent them. This failure to realize and yield to God's warnings may cost America her country just as it cost Pharaoh his kingdom.

Even though Minister Farrakhan has proclaimed his relationship and experiences with the power of those wheels, the media is extremely hesitant to even question him about it. When a Twitter question was posed to Minister Farrakhan about why the media does not question him about his experience on the Wheel, he responded in these words:

> I am not a person made by the media. They have decided that it is not in their interest to bring me to the media and ask me questions that they know that I am quite capable of answering. So they would rather keep me away from the media and make people to think that the minister has passed away.[283]

The FBI's arrest of the Messenger and the government's ongoing attempts to suppress the words of the Nation of Islam are just a few examples of their efforts to cover-up the UFO phenomenon. Even if millions of people saw these objects for themselves, most have already been preconditioned to believe they are of extraterrestrial origin. With all of the notable cases, reports, and sightings that have arisen, there has still never been a formal acknowledgement concerning the Nation of Islam's direct representation of this phenomenon. Considering the dominant attitude in leadership, there will likely never be such an acknowledgement.

ROSWELL: THE KNOWN, THE UNKNOWN, AND THE POSSIBILITY

After the fiasco that occurred off the coast of Los Angeles in 1942, more sightings began to take place. The mid 1940s were brimmed with sightings of *foo-fighters*, which were unidentified orbs frequently observed by American, European, and Asian military personnel, especially in areas designated for war activity. The foo-fighters were often seen in ranks, but never seemed to demonstrate aggressive behaviors. They were frequently seen pacing around airplanes at varying speeds. Some were observed hovering in a stationary position before darting off at terrific speeds in any direction. Aside from an occasional interference with radar and radio frequencies, no satisfactory theory was ever given that could explain the sudden sightings amidst international

---

[283] Louis Farrakhan, "#AskFarrakhan Tweets," *Minister Louis Farrakhan responds to tweet from Ilia Rashad Muhammad @iliarashad*, comp. Ilia Rashad Muhammad (#AskFarrakhan via Twitter, January 13, 2013).

THE MESSENGER, THE PROOF, AND THE DENIALS

theaters of war. These planes brought heavy concerns across the globe. Meanwhile, American authorities held Elijah Muhammad behind bars hoping to silence his voice during a time when America was engaged in wars across the Pacific.

Trailing the foo-fighter epidemic was a wave of UFO sightings styled as *ghost rockets*. These were unexplained aerial phenomena witnessed by over 1500 people over Sweden and neighboring countries. The first reports of ghost rockets were made on February 26, 1946, by Finnish observers.[284] Coincidentally, the 26th of February is the birth anniversary of Master Fard Muhammad and it is considered the most revered time for Muslims in the Nation of Islam. It seems this date was a fitting time to reintroduce his planes to that part of the world. Perhaps Master Fard Muhammad was sending a message to certain world leaders.

Following the wave of foo-fighters and ghost rockets along with the release of the Messenger from prison in 1946, one of the most famous UFO sightings took place with pilot Kenneth Arnold over Mt. Rainier in 1947. Historians and researchers often credit Arnold with being the man who started the flying saucer frenzy, which later became known as the modern era of UFOs. Historians fail to acknowledge the fact that the Honorable Elijah Muhammad brought this reality to the world much earlier.

Nearly a thousand sightings of disc-shaped planes were reported in weeks following Arnold's report. Just as the sightings increased, the attempts to explain away this phenomena increased. It was during the same time of Kenneth Arnold's sighting that the **Roswell UFO Incident** was said to take place. The Roswell incident alleges that a UFO crashed near Roswell, New Mexico in June or July of 1947. This has been perhaps one of the most controversial UFO related events in history, mostly because it is shrouded in secrecy, suspicion, and mixed reports.

According to most ufological reports, a UFO crashed near Roswell, New Mexico during the wave of the 1947 sightings. It was headlined in a local newspaper, that a flying saucer was captured on a Roswell ranch. It was circulated that Roswell AAF Intelligence Officer, Major Jesse A. Marcel, had recovered a "flying disc" from the land of an unidentified rancher in the vicinity of Roswell and that the disc had been "flown to higher headquarters."[285]

The Roswell incident was almost completely forgotten from history until it resurfaced in 1980 when *The National Enquirer* tabloid ran an

---

[284] Kevin D. Randle and Russ Estes, *The Spaceships of the Visitors: An Illustrated Guide to Alien Spacecraft* (Touchstone, 2000).
[285] Roswell Daily Record, "RAAF Captures Flying Saucer On Ranch in Roswell Region," *Roswell Daily Record*, July 08, 1947.

interview with Major Jesse Marcel who was involved in the recovery of the debris from the 1947 incident. This interview, along with another publicized work in 1978, helped bring the Roswell Incident back into the national spotlight. Since then, the speculations and theories have catapulted in mainstream media.

Although many people associate this incident with a UFO crash, it should be noted that the initial reports suggested that the alleged craft had *landed*, not crashed:

> Roswell army air base initially said that a "flying disc" had come down, but hours later, as government scientists arrived in the area, it was stated instead that a weather balloon had crashed.[286]

Somehow, reports developed from an object *coming down* to an object crashing. Such conflicting reports make it difficult to arrive at a definite conclusion.

Despite its highly publicized content, the Roswell Incident still remains highly ambiguous regarding what, if anything, happened. Several theories and reports indicate that something crashed or landed near Roswell that has caused the Government of America and its military agencies to treat the alleged incident with some of the most classified secrecy. Since limited knowledge has been divulged on this matter, one can only make rational postulations based on the limited data given. Before rushing into hasty conclusions with limited data, it is much wiser to make rational speculations based on what is *known*. Therefore this writing offers postulations about the alleged Roswell Incident based on the known, not the unknown.

What can be classified as *known*? The disc-shaped planes developed by Master Fard Muhammad (and his host of scientists) are known to exist and they have been witnessed by millions since being revealed to the Honorable Elijah Muhammad. Since these planes are known to exist, then there is a possibility that some type of UFO-related encounter could have taken place near Roswell at that time. However, it has also been established that the technological capabilities of the wheels are eons ahead of this world's grasp. Therefore, a crashed wheel could indicate an inferior technology. This definitely would not be congruent with the acknowledged capabilities of the wheels. It would seem highly implausible that the same planes that are capable of interstellar flight would suddenly crash amidst the earth's atmosphere. This idea becomes even more incongruous when considering that the scientists who pilot the planes are familiar with every square inch of the earth. Consider these words from Messenger Elijah Muhammad:

---

[286] Thomas Harding, "Roswell 'was Soviet plot to create US panic," *The Telegraph*, May 13, 2011.

THE MESSENGER, THE PROOF, AND THE DENIALS

I have given you a description of what is in the sky. There's a scientist or two on it that knows every spot where America has got her dreadful planes, which are scouting around with bombs that is capable of ripping the Wheel apart, but they can't get to her.[287]

It is also a known fact that U.S. scientists have tried to emulate the technology of the wheels, which is largely responsible for the advancement of reverse engineering technology. Reverse engineering refers to the process of attempting to reproduce the construction and capabilities of another product or system. Some of the most accomplished aviators in modern history have openly confirmed that military and aviation technology have advanced because of attempts to reverse engineer what has been observed from UFOs. John Lear (the son of Bill Lear who invented the Learjet) is one of those highly-respected persons who know that disc-shaped UFOs exist. The mechanics of the Learjet is predicated upon his family's observance of UFOs. John Lear stated that he and his father would frequently observe UFOs, which served as a basis for the development of the Learjet's technologies: "The aliens give us technology and we use that technology." He continued, "We tried to reverse engineer it, but it's millions of years ahead of us."[288] He admitted that their study of UFOs gives reasons for the advancement of technology today. It should also be noted that John Lear is one of the most decorated aviators in history. Few people today have more knowledge on air travel. He is the only pilot ever to earn every Airman Certificate issued by the FAA. He held 18 world speed records and has flown over 150 different types of aircraft.

During the same era as the Learjet's development, the wheel-shaped Avro Car was developed in Canada as part of a secret U.S. military project.[289] Its style and design was intended to simulate the flight abilities of the wheels and it was to be used for military warfare. After years of failed attempts, the Avro Car project was cancelled in September 1961. The Honorable Elijah Muhammad guaranteed that America's knowledge is limited and could never make a plane that is comparable to the Mother Plane or its smaller wheels.

---

[287] "The Theology of Time (Lecture Series)," Vols. July 9, 1972 (Chicago, IL: MUHAMMAD Mosque No. 2, 1972).
[288] Brad Meltzer's Decoded, "UFO," *Brad Meltzer's Decoded*, Vol. Season 2 (History Channel, 2011 30-November).
[289] William Yenne, *Weapons of World War II: The Techno-Military Breakthroughs That Changed History* (New York, NY: Berkley Books, 2003).

> "The like of this wheel-like plane was never seen before. You cannot build one like it and get the same results. Your brains are limited. If you would make one to look like it, you could not get it up off the earth into outer space."[290]

Considering the numerous attempts to engineer technology similar to the baby planes, the alleged crash of an unknown object could have likely been one of their failed attempts to imitate the wheels. This could be a plausible explanation, especially since the U.S. Military reported that the object that crashed was from one of their own projects known as Project Mogul. According to B. D. Gildenberg, "Project Mogul was eventually declassified in 1972, almost a decade before the first stirrings of popular literature about the Roswell Incident."[291] Was the Roswell Incident the result of a failed attempt to imitate the technology of the real disc-shaped UFOs? This may be a rational explanation since it has been acknowledged in an official message from the U.S. Armed Forces that the Roswell Incident was from debris left over from one of their own high-altitude surveillance projects.[292]

It is a recorded fact that the U.S. Government has investigated and attempted to monitor as much UFO activity as possible. After all, this is a major reason why they arrested and interrogated Elijah Muhammad in 1942. This has been initiated through various agencies, projects, programs, and operations. Unlike the average layman, governmental scientists use their findings with the intention to imitate it through reverse engineering. Much of America's technological and mechanical advancements have been patterned after America's observation of UFOs.

> Computer company chief Jack Shulman argues that the transistor could never have been invented so suddenly at AT&T in late 1947 without input from top secret Government projects, that some have identified to him as being from alien spacecraft.[293]

U.S. Government knows that these planes exist, but have consistently lied, deceived, and denied the existence of Master Fard Muhammad's wheels. They have used erroneous reports, propaganda, and misleading information. They have deliberately disseminated misleading reports to divert attention

---

[290] *MESSAGE TO THE BLACKMAN In America*, Original Published by MUHAMMAD'S Temple No. 2 in Chicago 1965 (Chicago, IL: The Final Call Inc., 1965). 290.
[291] "A Roswell Requiem," *Skeptic*, March 22, 2003.
[292] Richard L. Weaver and James McAndrew, *The Roswell Report Fact vs. Fiction in the New Mexico Desert*, Executive Summary, Headquarters, United States Air Force (United States Air Force, 1995).
[293] UFO Evidence, "Reverse-Engineering Roswell UFO Technology. A summary of Jack Shulman's speech at the Global Sciences Congress in 1999," *Nexus Magazine*, June-July 1999.

THE MESSENGER, THE PROOF, AND THE DENIALS

away from the truth about Elijah Muhammad, Master Fard Muhammad, the Nation of Islam, and their direct connection to the sudden rise in UFO activity. If America's Military Intelligence had to choose, it would seem less threatening for the public to accept little green aliens than to accept a little Black man as the Messenger of Allah (God). After all, little green aliens cannot hold the world's oppressors responsible for their evils done to humanity, especially against the darker nations. Extraterrestrial aliens cannot hold anyone accountable for the Trans-Atlantic Slave Trade as a Black man would. Extraterrestrial aliens would not expose the deceit that oppressive regimes have used to maintain influence over world affairs. However, it would be perceived as a threat to Caucasian dominance if it became widely known that the power of those UFOs was directly connected to the children of slaves.

Again, it would be far less threatening to associate little grey beings with UFOs than to associate them with the Black man who introduced them to the world. This has been an ongoing strategy to misdirect the public away from Elijah Muhammad's practical teachings. For decades, the fictitious ideas of little greys or monstrous aliens have been promoted as a diversionary tactic. The same propaganda used against the Honorable Elijah Muhammad has been used to discredit Minister Farrakhan's connection to the worldwide UFO phenomena. Despite his direct connection to Elijah Muhammad and the wheels, Minister Farrakhan is seldom referenced with these planes—at least not in mainstream media.

Simply put, the wheels represented by Elijah Muhammad are far superior than any technology known to this world. It would be extremely irrational to assume that such a plane would have accidentally crashed on the earth. It is also unreasonable to assume that America's limited capabilities could have captured one of these crafts with such impunity. However, there is a possibility that Master Fard Muhammad may have allowed some of his technology to reach the grasp of America's arrogant leadership. Remember, God has often revealed aspects of his power to his enemies to see how they will respond. Could this have been one of those cases?

If Master Fard Muhammad allowed one of the lesser-developed wheels into the hands of America's powers, this idea would be in keeping with the Holy Qur'an. It is written that Allah (God) would allow the devil to snatch away a glimpse of Allah's heavenly activities:

> *Surely We have adorned the lower heaven with an adornment, the stars,*
> *And (there is) a safeguard against every rebellious devil.*
> *They cannot listen to the exalted assembly and they are reproached from every side,*
> *Driven off; and for them is a perpetual chastisement,*

> *Except him who snatches away but once, then there follows him a brightly shining flame.* – Surah Al-Saffat (Those Ranging in Ranks) 37:6-10

This manifest passage from the Muslims' holy book reiterates the power that Allah (God) has over the heavens and the earth. It also illustrates the mindset of the devil who frequently tries to monitor the activities of Allah's *Exalted Assembly* who reside in the lower heavens. In so doing, the Qur'an suggests that the devil has limitations to his heavenly pursuits. However, the passage also indicates that Allah will allow the devil to snatch away something. After snatching something away, the devil would be frequently pursued by a flaming fire of piercing brightness. In the Holy Qur'an, the term for flaming fire comes from the Arabic phrase **shihab mubin**, which is a *brightly visible flame* that will pursue Satan. The brightly visible flames have a piercing quality as noted from the Arabic word **thaqib**, which describes that which pierces through the darkness. Such descriptions are congruent with the wheel-like planes that appear as brightly shining flames that travel at speeds capable of piercing the night skies.

Could it be that Allah allowed the devil (American leadership) to snatch away a glimpse of his majestic wisdom? While no definitive answer to this question can be provided here, such a hypothesis may well explain the Roswell rumors of some type of UFO incident. The advancement of reverse engineering technology may further make this hypothesis plausible. If Master Fard Muhammad allowed a part of his craft to reach the devils' hands, it would likely have been an earlier (less-advanced) model of a much more advanced style of wheels now. It is known that the technological capabilities witnessed on those planes have prompted governments and militaries to improve their technology. Again, with limited data on this alleged case, one can only put forth rational hypotheses based on the knowledge given.

It can be argued that the development of the National Security Administration and the Central Intelligence Agency were likely in response to the accumulating sightings and reports that had escalated by 1947. On July 26 of that year, President Harry Truman signed the National Security Act.[294] This act served to restructure the U.S. Armed Forces, its foreign policies, and its Intelligence agencies. It was out of these efforts that the Central Intelligence Agency (CIA) was formed on September 18, 1947.[295] The CIA was developed to serve as an independent wing of the government to collect and use vital data gathered from various sources.

Understandably these Acts and agencies were developed in the wake of World War II, but the increased UFO activity provided additional reasons for

---

[294] (Pub.L. 80-253, 61 Stat. 495, codified at 50 U.S.C. ch.15)
[295] CIA, "About CIA" (Central Intelligence Agency (CIA), December 19, 2006).

THE MESSENGER, THE PROOF, AND THE DENIALS

the U.S. Government to reappraise its own sovereignty. After all, these disc-shaped planes were now being spotted over America's military bases, weapons sites and by thousands of people around the country. A seemingly new and overwhelmingly superior power was making its presence felt through the advent of UFOs and there was hardly anything the government could do about it. It seemed the best they could do was to restructure their military and Intelligence agencies.

These agencies have served as arms of the U.S. Government dedicated to enacting covert defense operations and maintaining secrecy of certain information. It has become quite apparent that information about UFOs has been a priority on their list of covert intelligence operations. Hence, it stands to reason that the seemingly insignificant Nation of Islam would be at the top of their targeted list since this group was responsible for representing the wheel-like planes to the modern world. Unsurprisingly the unarmed Nation of Islam has been the target of covert Government investigations and attacks. The FBI's Counter Intelligence Program worked to discredit and destabilize the noble efforts of the Nation of Islam to uplift their people from the grave of ignorance. The Government viewed this group as a subversive "hate group".[296] As recently as 2007 it was discovered that Homeland Security had been improperly spying on the Nation of Islam.[297] This was no shock to the Muslims who understood that it has been the *devil*'s job to enact mischief towards the righteous.

Reports have surfaced from firsthand witnesses of the alleged Roswell Incident that reveal the type of being(s) found on the craft. Annie Jacobsen in her book *Area 51* offers reports from certain scientists and engineers who worked in Area 51. According to these reports, it was not any little green men, nor was it any grey aliens that were controlling the disc-shaped object. Instead, the witness reports express that to the surprise of all, it involved humans of what seemed to be young ages. Jacobsen reports from her interviews with witnesses: "They found bodies alongside the crashed craft. These were not aliens. Nor were they consenting airmen. They were human guinea pigs. Unusually petite for pilots, they appeared to be children. Each was under five feet tall."[298] While some of the scientists and engineers believed the craft to be some kind of Russian military ploy intended to strike fear in Americans, Russian and German militaries denied any involvement with such.

---

[296] Ward Churchill and Jim Vander Wall, *The COINTELPRO Papers: Documents from the FBI's Secret Wars Against Dissent in the United States* (South End Press, 1990).
[297] Spencer S. Hsu and Carrie Johnson, "Documents show DHS improperly spied on Nation of Islam in 2007," *The Washington Post*, December 17, 2009.
[298] Annie Jacobsen, *Area 51: An Uncensored History of America's Top Secret Military Base* (Back Bay Books, 2012).

Furthermore, none of the world powers have comparable technologies in their arsenals today, so certainly these nations could not have produced the likes of these wheels back then.

If there is any credibility to these reports of alleged Roswell Incident, it totally debunks the theory that the pilots of UFOs are of extraterrestrial origin. More importantly it would further prove that Elijah Muhammad's teachings concerning the youthful appearing pilots is exact! If any truth is contained in these reports, it would further confirm what the Government already knew about the power that commissioned Elijah Muhammad. This was already authenticated after the Battle of Los Angeles and their subsequent interrogation of Muhammad in 1942. The cardinal reason behind the Government's cover-up about UFOs is more than fear of a public hysteria. After all, over a hundred million Americans already believe in UFOs,[299] so it would be foolish to assume that the public is incapable of handling this truth. Hence, the fundamental reason behind the UFO denial is the proof that a little Black man from Georgia met Allah (God) in person.

According to the Holy Qur'an, Allah gives everyone a chance to submit and benefit from his guidance, even the devil (Al-Ĥijr 15:36-37). Did Master Fard Muhammad give America's devilish leadership a chance to submit to his authority by showing them a snippet of his supreme wisdom and power? If so, how has America responded? Whether a plane landing in Roswell or not, it remains evident that America has been exposed to the majesty of Master Fard Muhammad's wheel-shaped planes as represented by his Messenger, Elijah Muhammad and his representative, Minister Louis Farrakhan. Fully aware of these realities, America has not taken heed to the divine guidance that Master Fard Muhammad has offered through these clear signs of his power.

TOO MUCH EVIDENCE TO IGNORE

In the Holy Qur'an (37:6-10), Allah promises to have certain devils pursued by his brightly shining piercing flames. Interestingly, military officials have come forth and admitted that these wheels of brightly shining lights and colors have been seen and witnessed over major military bases and have interfered with nuclear weapons programs across the globe. Dozens of military personnel have come forth and admitted that these UFOs have been monitoring and destabilizing U.S. Defense activities for decades.[300]

---

[299] AP/Ipsos Poll, "Majority of Americans Believe in Ghosts (57%) and UFOs (52%)," *Associated Press/Ipsos* (Washington, DC, October 31, 2008).
[300] Steven M. Greer, "Project Background" (Crozet, VA: The Disclosure Project, April 2001). The Disclosure Project reported from "over 500 government, military, and intelligence community witnesses testifying to their

THE MESSENGER, THE PROOF, AND THE DENIALS

One of the first notable individuals within the U.S. Government to make the bold and unpopular admission that these disc-like planes exist was American Marine Corps Naval Aviator, Major **Donald Keyhoe**. Having worked in various military and governmental programs and projects, Keyhoe was initially a skeptic about the saucer-shaped objects that were so much talked about in the late 1940s. Through his open-minded investigations and his direct involvement with the U.S. Government and Military, he became overwhelmingly convinced that these planes existed. His direct involvement with military officials and certain case files privileged him with information that was inaccessible to the American public. Keyhoe's firsthand data made him a credible source of information as well as a potential threat to his colleagues within the government.

Amidst Keyhoe's investigations into the newfound UFO concerns, he became increasingly aware that the American Government was the primary culprit in covering up vital information from the American public. In fact he realized that despite several witness reports and encounters from credible pilots and military officials, the U.S. government was adamant in their denial of these planes.

The Government's unrelenting denial of these objects prompted Major Keyhoe to compose what became one of his most famous books, *The Flying Saucers Are Real*. This publication argued that these planes were in fact real using empirical evidence from credible witness reports and government activities. He published more books on related subjects and became somewhat disenchanted with the Government and military for whom he once worked. His popularity increased in the public eye, but his relationship among governmental entities became less than stellar. This was due to Keyhoe's arguments that various government agencies were involved in a blatant deception concerning the truth about these saucers.

In the late 1950s, Keyhoe's image became more frequent on mainstream television as he discussed this matter on some of the popular shows at that time. In January of 1958, he appeared on the live CBS television show *the Armstrong Circle Theatre* to discuss these issues. As he offered his arguments concerning the reality of UFOs on live television, CBS deliberately cut off the sound.

> Keyhoe announced that a congressional committee was evaluating evidence which, if made public, "will absolutely prove that the UFOs are machines under intelligent control." But viewers never heard the message, because CBS had worked out a prearranged deal with the Air Force. As Herbert A.

direct, personal, first hand experience with UFOs, ETs, ET technology, and the cover-up that keeps this information secret."

Carlborg, CBS director of editing, later explained, "This program had been carefully cleared for security reasons."[301]

This event raised serious speculations concerning the government and the media's blatant attempts to conceal the truth about the flying saucers—the same planes that Elijah Muhammad explained are the product of his God.

Nearly two months after the Armstrong Circle Theatre appearance, Keyhoe was interviewed by Mike Wallace on national television. Wallace, being a trained journalist interrogated Keyhoe concerning his position about UFOs and the attempted cover-ups. It seemed that Wallace attempted to make the UFO phenomena as the fanciful thinking of certain disillusioned persons. Keyhoe, however, provided sobering details to substantiate his claims. When Mike Wallace questioned him about the notion that a respected journalist suggested that "pranksters, half-wits and screwballs are responsible for the stories about flying saucers." Keyhoe responded accordingly:

> Well, I wish I could show him, at anytime, a list of about 800 witnesses, some of the big names of aviation including, up to the rank of colonel in the Air Force. They're still flying, and they're still carrying passengers; they've never been grounded. They're still guiding airliners in the radar, night after night in bad weather. If they're screwballs and incompetents, why are they still on the job?[302]

Of course Mike Wallace did not respond directly to Keyhoe's counter question. Keyhoe held strong to his position without backing down. It seemed that his arguments were more valid than the mixed reports coming from government. What made Keyhoe have the audacity to stand up and acknowledge this unpopular truth despite its unpopularity? What allowed Keyhoe to stand up against his former colleagues and a much more powerful government? Why didn't he work to cover-up this truth like several others who knew the truth?

Minister Jabril Muhammad stated "the Honorable Elijah Muhammad wrote publicly in 1962 that Master Fard Muhammad forced this man [Major Donald Keyhoe] to write the book."[303] Could this explain Keyhoe's unexplained boldness toward this subject during a time when he could have been charged with sedition, especially during the McCarthy era? While the exact methods of how Master Fard Muhammad did such is unknown to the

---

[301] Billy Cox, "The limits of libertarianism?," *Herald-Tribune*, January 11, 2008.
[302] Donald Keyhoe, interview by Mike Wallace, *The Mike Wallace Interview*, ABC, March 8, 1958.
[303] Jabril Muhammad, "The Wheel," *Lecture by Minister Jabril Muhammad* (Phoenix, AZ, September 18, 1985).

public, it stands to reason that he permitted the circumstances whereby Keyhoe would feel prompted to act as he did.

THE WASHINGTON D.C. UFO INCIDENT

For a while it seemed that Keyhoe was a lone ranger among government personnel who was willing to publicly acknowledge the reality of the wheels. Even though the Government offered mixed reports and denials about these crafts, it has been verified that the Government was undergoing official investigations on the subject matter. These investigations (under various names) give clear indications that they gave serious attention to UFOs. One of the persons responsible for these investigations included notable astrophysicist J. Allen Hynek. He was hired by the United States Air Force under their UFO investigation programs (Project Sign, Project Grudge, and Project Blue Book).

Like Keyhoe, Hynek was initially skeptical of the UFO frenzy. During his first few years of investigations he was rather cynical about the subject, but as a scientist he approached it with a certain level of objectivity. He described the UFO fascination as a mere fad that would eventually pass away. He even described it as an "utterly ridiculous" subject matter.[304] However as his investigations progressed, he became convinced that the empirical evidence associated with many reports were too credible to dismiss. Hynek also came to the realization that his government was involved in concealing the authenticity of these reports. He later stated that there were two main reasons for his change of heart, some of which he shared in this statement:

> One was the completely negative and unyielding attitude of the Air Force. They wouldn't give UFOs the chance of existing, even if they were flying up and down the street in broad daylight. Everything had to have an explanation. I began to resent that, even though I basically felt the same way, because I still thought they weren't going about it in the right way. You can't assume that everything is black no matter what. Secondly, the caliber of the witnesses began to trouble me. Quite a few instances were reported by military pilots, for example, and I knew them to be fairly well-trained, so this is when I first began to think that, well, maybe there was something to all this.[305]

---

[304] Sara Daniels and Pat Schneidman, *Mysteries Of The Unknown: The UFO Phenomenon* (Time-Life, 1987).
[305] J. Allen Hynek, interview by Dennis Stacy, , *CLOSE ENCOUNTER WITH DR. J. ALLEN HYNEK*ed. Dale Goudie, The Dean 1985, CUFON 1991 (1985).

As an analytical thinker, Hynek became increasingly disturbed by the lack of scientific application that the USAF used to reach their conclusions about UFOs. Physicists of his stature don't simply accept data based on emotional hype. Instead they apply intense scrutiny, tests, and analysis based on known laws of the universe. The USAF's treatment of the subject and their relentless pursuits to debunk UFOs in the public was enough to make Hynek question the motives of their investigations.

Although Hynek was never as bold as Major Donald Keyhoe in his stance, he still deserves credit for acknowledging the controversial reality of these planes. He grew to resent his previous position that sought to debunk the concept of UFOs, especially in light of the tremendous amount of evidence that manifested over the years. The simple way of conveying Hynek's realization is that he initially went along with the Government's objectives until he realized that they were lying. At a certain point he was compelled to acknowledge this, albeit ambiguously.

One of the very notable events that drew tremendous concerns about UFOs was the wave of sightings in the Washington D.C. area during the weeks of July 1952. This culminated in what became known as the *1952 Washington D.C. UFO Incident*. As early as July 12th of that year, waves of sightings were reported by commoners as well as air-traffic personnel and radar detections. At a certain point, the brightly shining crafts were seen piercing across Washington's most significant edifices, The White House and the U.S. Capitol Building. These sightings were witnessed by hundreds of residents as well as numerous Washington National Airport personnel. After all, these wheels were picked up on radarscope (off and on). The wave of sightings hit local and national headlines. Neither the airport nor the Military could account for what was taking place as all government and military entities admitted that they had no known airplanes or devices in the airspace during the times of the sightings, except for the jets that were scrambled to investigate the unknown crafts.

Many UFO researchers have considered this event one of the most important cases that made the UFO phenomena most evident to the public:

> During the dawn of Ufology in the United States, unidentified flying objects made themselves known to the leaders of the free world in 1952, buzzing over the White House, the Capitol building, and the Pentagon. Seemingly the unknown objects were defying the very governmental agencies sworn to protect the United States from foreign powers.
>
> Washington National Airport and Andrews Air Force Base picked up a number of UFOs on their radar screens on July 19, 1952, beginning a wave of sightings still unexplained to this day.

THE MESSENGER, THE PROOF, AND THE DENIALS

These blips were objects traveling at about 100 m.p.h. but with the ability to accelerate to the unbelievable speed of 7,200 m.p.h. The Washington National sighting was confirmed by other local radar, and then Andrews Air Force Base was contacted.[306]

The brightly shining wheels audaciously flew over America's most powerful seat of power with impunity. This event was not only picked up by radar, but it was captured in photographs and recorded on video. Just as the Holy Qur'an states that the rebellious devil would be "pursued by a flaming fire of piercing brightness" (37:7-10), the occurrences over D.C. seemed to clearly manifest this prophetic description. It was not the first time these crafts have displayed their authority over America's power and it would later prove not to be the last.

Jet interceptors were scrambled to seek out the objects that appeared as unknown blips[307] on radar. The blips vanished from radar and shortly after the jets landed, the UFOs returned, only to be publicly seen over America's seat of power. Since this event took place over Washington, it quickly became of widespread interest. Like the Battle of Los Angeles in 1942, the Washington D.C. UFO Incident left the American powers embarrassed and frustrated. This time it was witnessed by hundreds of residents amidst the seat of America's power. These crafts flew in ranks across what was supposed to be the most secured airspace in America and the world. How would America respond this time? Would they be able to explain away this event as they tried before? Following the D.C. incident the public demanded answers and the U.S. Government was not prepared to deliver.

---

[306] UFO Casebook, "1952 Washington D.C. Sightings" (UFOCasesbook.com).
[307] **blip:** a spot of light on a radar or sonar screen indicating the position of a detected object

Figure 7: THE SURE TRUTH & AUTHORITY

Clockwise from top left: General John Samford's UFO press conference at the Pentagon on July 29, 1952. Luminous UFO discs fly in ranks over the U.S. Capital Building in July 1952, J. Allen Hynek in a March 1966 news conference, Former FBI Director J. Edgar Hoover, President Jimmy Carter, USAF's Project Blue Book staff members, Former American Marine Corps naval aviator Donald Keyhoe, Former President Ronald Reagan witnessed UFOs as Governor of California.
Center: The Most Honorable Elijah Muhammad

On July 29, 1952 during the aftermath of the D.C. sightings, Air Force Major General and Director of Intelligence John Samford and USAF Director of Operations Roger Ramey held what became one of the largest Pentagon press conferences at the time. The attempt was to respond to the lingering questions that the public was demanding. During the press conference, Samford concluded, "it does not contain any pattern of purpose or consistency

THE MESSENGER, THE PROOF, AND THE DENIALS

that we can relate to any conceivable threat to the United States."[308] Later Samford and other Air Force officials within Project Blue Book concluded that the radar that picked up these planes were mirage effects caused by temperature inversions along with "meteors coupled with the normal excitement of witnesses."[309] These explanations suggested that radar detections, photographs, video recordings, and hundreds of eyewitnesses were basically hyped-up illusions and strange weather patterns.

Once again, the official reports appeared to be irrational attempts to explain-away what people actually saw and witnessed for themselves. The official explanations did not sit well with the public. The mixed reports resulting in an absurd official explanation is what made this incident also known as the *Washington Flap*. The U.S. Government was in another embarrassing situation resulting from how officials handled the UFO sightings. Ten years after the Battle of Los Angeles, the American Government continued to offer the same type of conflicting reports that made it more evident that a major cover-up was taking place.

After the 1952 Washington UFO incident, the government and the press became far less prone to publicize any wave of UFO sightings. Any promotion of UFO activity in the news could have potentially validated Mr. Muhammad and his growing Nation of Islam in the public. This has been considered a threat to National Security since government agencies set objectives to discredit the Nation of Islam anyway.[310] Decades following the Washington Flap seemed to bring a quietness of UFO activity, not because UFOs weren't being sighted, but because these sightings were not being publicized in the press as much. Instead, movies and television shows that fictionalized the concept of UFOs began to flood the media. All of the major motion pictures related to flying discs took off around this time (the early 1950s). After several decades of alien monsters and Martians being depicted on the big screen, many people automatically began to associate UFOs as mere products of creative imagination.

---

[308] Bruce Maccabee, *UFO/FBI Connection: The Secret History of the Government's Cover-Up*, First (St. Paul, MN: Llewellyn Publications, 2000). 224-225.
[309] Jerome Clark, *The UFO Book: Encyclopedia of the Extraterrestrial* (Visible Ink Press, 1997).
[310] Ward Churchill and Jim Vander Wall, *The COINTELPRO Papers: Documents from the FBI's Secret Wars Against Dissent in the United States* (South End Press, 1990).

10. THE TRUTH IS OUT THERE

TIME REVEALS THE TRUTH

Whether those in power think it's time or not—is immaterial or irrelevant because these wheels are now being seen over the major cities and when human beings of intelligence can look up and see this phenomenon, how can you keep hiding it in the midst of thousands upon thousands of people now seeing them? [311]

During what seemed to be the quiet years of UFOs when governments became better at concealing reports and sightings, the Honorable Elijah Muhammad recruited a young brother from prison whom he would groom to become his National Spokesman, Minister Malcolm X. After Malcolm's release from prison in August of 1952, he fled directly into the fold of the Nation of Islam and into the arms of his teacher, the Honorable Elijah Muhammad. Throughout his tenure as Elijah Muhammad's top Minister, Malcolm seldom spoke about this inherent part of the NOI theology in the public. However, he did preach this reality within the private NOI Temple meetings. Although Minister Malcolm X gained notoriety for his bold and cogent defense of the NOI's theology and program, he probably limited his public talks about the Mother Wheel and baby planes because there was very little being reported in the press that would clearly substantiate this truth. After all, Malcolm's reign as the NOI's spokesman was during the quiet era of UFOs in the press. By this time the NOI was already being mocked in the press and labeled as a cult for their untraditional theology, which included the belief that Allah (God) had these wheel-shaped planes made to protect the righteous and destroy the wicked.

After Malcolm's defection from the NOI, he acknowledged that his religion was still Islam and that his political and social views remained Black Nationalism. Questions remain whether or not he abandoned Muhammad's teachings about the Mother Plane altogether. This is especially intriguing when considering the 'nationalistic' purpose of this plane, which will be used in the protection and salvation of the chosen people, the Black man and woman of America. Perhaps no teaching exudes Black Nationalism and Black Universalism more than Muhammad's teachings. After all, he propagated the

---

[311] Louis Farrakhan, interview by Jaimie Maussan, "The Islamic Minister Louis Farrakhan speaks openly about UFO disclosure," *FULL ALIEN DISCLOSURE*, Chicago, IL (April 13, 2011).

intrinsic belief that such a plane was constructed for the benefit of the original Black nation of the earth. If Malcolm's religious and political ideologies encompassed the nationalistic notion of Allah's chosen people, it stands to reason that true Black Nationalism would include such a concept as this Mother Plane.

Critics of both Malcolm and Muhammad have questioned Malcolm's views on this unique part of the NOI theology:

> Most of his public life had been devoted to propagating what he finally scorned as "some of the most fantastic things that you could ever imagine": the Nation of Islam's bizarre mélange of theology, science fiction and racial chauvinism. Although in his last months he was breaking away from those beliefs – and died because of that break - he did so only in ambiguous ways. His ideological evolution was rapid, and was cut brutally short, enabling admirers to project onto him multiple imaginings about where it was going. But it had not (yet?) included clear-cut rejection of ideas he had once propounded: like the inherent evil of white people and especially Jews, the natural inferiority of women, the desirability not just of armed revolution but of political murder, or for that matter that black Gods were circling the Earth in giant spaceships.[312]

Whether Malcolm X abandoned the truth about the wheels remains questionable. If he did, he would be like thousands of others who abandoned a truth that has now been realized as authentically accurate.

If only Malcolm could have lived to realize that those wheels taught to him by the Honorable Elijah Muhammad have become more evident as technology and time have allowed. Unfortunately Malcolm's life was tragically cut short by several shots to the body in February of 1965, after nearly one year of defecting from the Nation of Islam. Malcolm defected from some aspects of the NOI theology that didn't seem as believable at the time. After all, that was a few years before *mankind* was known to land on the moon. Since then, so much evidence has manifested that prove Elijah Muhammad was right and exact all along. Statistical polls have shown that more people recognize and believe in UFOs than ever before. A *National Geographic* study in 2012 found that "80 million Americans are certain UFOs exist and that one in 10 believe they've spotted one."[313] This is likely due to the advancements in modern technology that allow events from around the world to be photographed,

---

[312] Stephen Howe, "Malcolm X: A Life of Reinvention, By Manning Marable - Book Review," *The Independent*, May 13, 2011.
[313] Natalie DiBlasio, "A third of Earthlings believe in UFOs, would befriend aliens," *USA Today*, June 06, 2012. Based on a National Geographic poll.

filmed, and recorded by the common man. This is quite the contrast to previous decades when certain technological capabilities such as computers, mobile phones and other technological gizmos were only accessible by high-ranking governmental agencies. Now, those things that once would have seemed impossible have become commonplace in society. Such is the case with UFOs.

Outside of those in the upper echelons of Government and those exposed to the teachings of Elijah Muhammad, very few people had been aware of the Nation of Islam's direct connection to the so-called UFO phenomenon. This was primarily due to numerous attempts to silence the message and the Messenger. During the decades of Muhammad's ministry, the accessibility of information was not as vast as it presently is. It would take several years before his teaching about these wheels would become more obvious to the public. Muhammad's National Representative, Minister Louis Farrakhan shared that this emerging technology has "created now the means by which the masses of the planet are quickly awakening—escaping the controlled media by the elite and oligarchs of the world."[314] Statistical data confirms Minister Farrakhan's assessment:

> Since then, reports have been getting better and more numerous. The "claims" of sightings from polls seem more or less the same in number, however. There's no way to be certain; statistics vary slightly from each place. Photo and video recordings of UFOs have undoubtedly increased significantly, due to the much larger number of owned digital cameras and implementation of cameras in every day devices. Along with the rise of technology of course also comes the rise in inevitable fakes and hoaxes, but there is no way to cancel out a particular percentage. For the moment, keeping track of the number of UFO sightings remains quite difficult. It's now expected to be around 100,000,000 Worldwide today.[315]

The explosion of communicational technology has allowed the average person to share information, photographs, data, sound and video recordings with the world within milliseconds. This surge of technology has enabled people to share their sightings and recordings of UFOs before Government Intelligence could have a chance to seize the footage and silence the witnesses as they have often done. Email, YouTube and numerous online sources have made it almost impossible not to accept the reality of UFOs. However, since authentic UFO footage can be shared so easily, this has also made it just as

---

[314] Louis Farrakhan, interview by Ashahed Muhammad, Starla Muhammad, Richard Muhammad, "Farrakhan Speaks On The Year 2012 & The New Year 2013," *Farrakhan Speaks*, FCN, Chicago, January 2013.
[315] Answers, "How many people have seen a UFO?," *Answers.com* (Answers Corporation, 2010).

feasible to share and promote the hoaxes and computer generated images (CGI). It seems that the less credible videos are intentionally highlighted and promoted over the Internet so that potential observers would be discouraged from pursuing this topic altogether.

The acceleration in modern technology is likely why the Honorable Elijah Muhammad exhorted his listeners to have patience with him as he delved into the subject concerning these wheels that his God showed him:

> I am very happy, at times, to go into great depths of the wisdom of God. If you have the patience to wait and..., it's here. All you have to do is get it. There's so much that we need to know, but we get impatient before we ever learn what we should. We get too impatient.[316]

Obviously Muhammad understood that the technology to capture images of these crafts were not available to the average person as it is now. There was no Internet, Email, YouTube, Facebook, or any similar type of social media available during the Messenger's public ministry. Therefore, his preaching of the Mother Wheel may have appeared like fantasy to a public who did not have these capabilities. During Muhammad's time of preaching, the average person did not have access to video files, or photographs that they could use to measure the authenticity of his claims because U.S. Officials would often confiscate materials and muzzle those who acquired such. It was for these same reasons that U.S. Officials arrested the Messenger and confiscated his drawings of the Mother Plane in 1942.

One may ask, "So why didn't Master Fard Muhammad just reveal it all at once and get it over with?" According to the Holy Qur'an, Allah (God) raises humanity in stages and degrees (Al-Mujadilah, 58:11). This suggests that there are gradients of time, knowledge, and circumstances involving the wisdom of God just as there are gradients to practically everything in the natural world. The Holy Qur'an also speaks of The Ways of Ascent, which is also the title of the 70th chapter (Al-Ma'arij in Arabic). This title may explain the methods that Master Fard Muhammad uses to make the reality of his wisdom known. Maulana Muhammad Ali, in his translation of The Holy Qur'an mentions these words in the opening description of this chapter:

> While holding out the certainty of the punishment, this chapter points out at first that great ends are achieved in a long period of time. Towards the close of the first section we are told that the ways or means of Ascent are those by which the faithful attain nearness to the Divine Being. The second section

---

[316] Elijah Muhammad, "The Theology of Time (Lecture Series)," Vols. October 8, 1972 (Chicago, IL: MUHAMMAD Mosque No. 2, 1972).

speaks very clearly of the disgrace which the opponents shall meet with, a new nation being raised in their place.

From monthly newspapers to the information highway, the world has advanced significantly since the visitations of Master Fard Muhammad and the launching of his Mother Plane in 1929. Since that time the world's cultures, industries, and technologies have advanced in unprecedented ways. The mere thought of revealing a mass spacecraft and its accompanying planes at once could have shocked the people to death in the 1930s! - Consider the hysteria caused by the 1938 radio broadcast of *War of the Worlds* by Orson Welles. Here, the fictional story of a fake Martian invasion caused enough social panic across the nation. Imagine what would have happened if Master Fard Muhammad had flaunted this technology back then.

Perhaps this is why Allah (God) suggests that He advances man by stages and degrees. It would not have seemed proper to bombard this reality upon the world at once, especially during a time when the concept of a mobile phone or Internet would have seemed insanely absurd. Instead, the reality of the wheels was able to become more and more evident to the people as technology, information, and the intelligence of the people grew.

Even contemporary manufacturers of computer technologies don't reveal the pinnacle of their capabilities to the public until several years after such technology has been used and mastered by those within the upper echelon of the corporation. This is a common pattern used by industries, militaries, and governments alike. This may also explain why these planes have often been witnessed by those who represent the upper echelon of governments – to serve as a fair warning to those who rule over the masses. This is consistent with the prophetic patterns of God's warnings to the kings and rulers. Similarly the Bible speaks of the wisdom in the book being sealed until the end (Daniel 12:4), which suggests that the true wisdom and mysteries of the book would not be made available until a time when the people could possibly handle such truths.

The present era qualifies as an appropriate time when these magnificent realities are to become more manifest. In an era referred to as the Information Age when the masses of the people have mobile devices that can capture and record phenomena unlike ever before, in a era when the intelligence of this world is able to send contraptions to the planet Mars and sneak a peak into the heavens, and in an era where information and data can be spread all over the globe within seconds, it would seem that the people of this day would be more prone to accept the notion of a Mother Plane and the baby planes; especially when millions of people have sighted, reported, and shared recordings of these crafts.

THE TRUTH IS OUT THERE

Today there is more computing power in smart phone than there was in NASA's Apollo 11.[317] It would not seem as absurd to accept that more supremely built planes exist outside of the conventional power structure of this world. It stands to reason that the intelligence that controls those crafts have advanced timing and calculations regarding when and how they should be revealed to the public. The Honorable Elijah Muhammad stated, *"the more we know about this world of technology, the more advanced we would be in The Hereafter."*[318]

Mother Tynnetta Muhammad, wife of the Honorable Elijah Muhammad, shared these insightful words concerning the gradual recognition of these planes and the powers thereof:

> It has long been speculated since the recording of an incident of a crashed UFO in Roswell, New Mexico in 1947, that the United States government guided by branches of the CIA Intelligence Agencies and the military have been gathering information on UFO phenomenon and were exposed to advanced technology of a new civilization heretofore unknown. Continual sightings of UFOs have been reported near military installations. None of the purported centers of UFO investigation is named as the Wright Patterson Military Base in Dayton, Ohio, with subsequent covert operations exhibited at Site 51 in the Nevada Desert. Whether there exists such an exchange of technology from more advanced beings with the United States government and military remains to be proven. However, records of the Nation of Islam's early history in the 1930s, as reported in Detroit, Michigan, shows evidence that a break-in of our temple properties ended up with the confiscating of drawings and literature pertaining to the advanced technology of the operations of our Great "Mother's Wheel" and her contents of 1,500 in numbers of baby planes has been diligently studied, along with our Nation's Sacred Book or Supreme Wisdom writings of Lessons. It would not be surprising to learn that some of these archives in possession of the United States intelligence forces and the Executive branch of the United States government have laid the base for their scientific research and studies of such phenomenon that they identify as UFO, Top Secret investigation files.[319]

---

[317] Craig Nelson, "Ten Things You Didn't Know About the Apollo 11 Moon Landing," *Popular Science*, July 7, 2009.
[318] Tynnetta Muhammad, "A visit with Study Group 19, Dayton, Ohio and the National Museum of the United States Air Force," *The Final Call*, June 11, 2007.
[319] Tynnetta Muhammad, ""Woe to the Inhabitants of the Earth and of the Sea For the Devil is Come Down Unto You, Having Great Wrath Because He Knoweth that he Hath But a Short Time!" -Revelations 12:12," *The Final Call*, July 30, 2010.

Time has revealed that numerous scientists, engineers, and government officials have admitted that much of today's technology has resulted from their study and observation of UFOs. These observations grew exponentially since U.S. Officials confiscated Elijah Muhammad's firsthand documents and illustrations about the wheels. Time has ultimately revealed that Elijah Muhammad was accurate all along.

ENCOUNTERS CONFIRM MUHAMMAD'S AUTHORITY

After the 1952 debacle in D.C., most of the famous abduction cases began to arise. Some of these cases did not gain widespread attention until years after their respected happenings, especially since the U.S. Armed Forces did not want to be further embarrassed in the media. Many of the UFO abduction cases would further credit that these planes are definitely real and are operated by intelligent beings from this earth. This does not include those cases that were deliberate hoaxes, pranks, and outright lies. The press would often call attention to the artificial cases, which made it difficult for the average person to distinguish the truth from falsehood.

One of the first credible abduction cases associated with the modern UFO era occurred in the late 1950s. The case of **Antonio Villas Boas** took place in mid October of 1957. This was considered one of the first recorded UFO-related abduction cases in the field of ufology. Boas was a young Brazilian farmer who witnessed what appeared to be a brightly shining star in the sky. As it moved closer he could see that it was a circular craft with a dome shape at the top—the same wheel shape as most other flying saucer sightings. Being somewhat terrified, he hopped on his tractor to get away when the lights and engine went out (likely due to the craft). He then took off on foot when the oblong craft landed. He was captured by four humanoids.[320]

Researchers frequently use the term humanoid because the inhabitants of these crafts are apparently human in nature although their attire and mannerisms make it difficult for witnesses to give definite clarity. Imagine trying to give definitive descriptions of a robber's characteristics when the robber has on a mask and costume. It would be quite difficult to describe what cannot be seen. At best, one could give vivid descriptions of the external characteristics. After all, the angelic scientists on those crafts can project certain thoughts into the minds of onlookers to see what they want them to see, not necessarily what is. This could be the case with many close encounters. Witnesses have described the *beings* who inhabit these planes as *humanoids* for this reason. Some are described as clearly human altogether.

---

[320] Bruce Rux, *Architects of the Underworld: Unriddling Atlantis, Anomalies of Mars, and the Mystery of the Sphinx* (Frog Books, 1996). 110.

Villas Boas described each abductor and everyone aboard the craft as wearing a grey "very tight-fitting siren-suit"[321] that covered their whole bodies. These type of descriptions became commonplace among many of the plausible reports. The *little grey men* characteristics that have often been attributed to UFO aliens may likely be sensationalized descriptions of the people whose form-fitting outfits have often been grey colored. As the people brought Villas Boas toward the craft, they boarded via a metallic retractable-like ladder that he described as "so neatly that no seam was visible to the naked eye."[322] He described their headgear as double the size of a normal human head, which he assumed was because "there was something else hidden under those helmets".[323]

This research does not automatically assume that the Villas Boas case is fully credible; however, it is mentioned because of its interesting correlations to the truth that Muhammad already provided. Villas Boas believed that his encounter was for scientific breeding purposes.[324] Many other UFO abductees reported similar encounters involving scientific procedures that involved extractions from internal fluids and organs, especially within the reproductive system. UFO researcher Timothy Good gave his hypothesis about this common pattern among UFO abductions:

> There is a requirement on the part of certain species of aliens for our ovum and sperm. And the object of the exercise is to produce a hybrid. That's what most of them say... Generally speaking, I would say the object of the exercise is to produce a hybridized species.[325]

Good recognizes that there are frequent scientific undertakings associated with many UFO abductions. His analysis arrives closer to the Honorable Elijah Muhammad's authority on this subject. The fact that the so-called aliens are highly scientific in their affairs confirms the notion that these beings are actual scientists who perform highly advanced scientific procedures. This is the truth Muhammad had already identified.

Similarly, the **Betty and Barney Hill** abduction case, which began on September 19, 1961, involved controlled extractions from the reproductive areas of both Betty and Barney. As perhaps the most famous of the early abduction cases, the Hills (an interracial couple from New Hampshire)

---

[321] Ibid. 111.
[322] Ibid. 112.
[323] Ibid. 111.
[324] Ibid. 115.
[325] Timothy Good, interview by Red Ice Radio, , *Secret Space Program, UFOs, ET & Coverup*, Red Ice Creations (February 2, 2011).

reported that *little men* summoned them aboard a circular craft and telepathically communicated to them before performing scientific procedures upon them both. The Hills described the men as being humanly with matching uniforms. They stood from about five feet to five and a half feet tall with military styled headgear.[326]

The men separated Betty and Barney into separate "operating rooms" before running a series of tests on them. The men took samples of skin, hair, and other internal specimens during highly advanced examinations. Barney recalled the men placing a cup on his groin area where he believed they extracted his semen. Betty, who recognized one of the crewmembers as "the leader" and another as a "doctor", recalled that they ran somewhat of a "pregnancy test" on her using a needle that was inserted through her naval.[327] These procedures greatly involved the reproductive organs. Regardless what the people did with their samples, the procedure left Barney Hill with reoccurring pains in the bodily areas that were sampled. His wife, Betty, had evidence of a pinkish powder that was left on her torn garment from the examination.

Like many of the more 'credible' abduction cases, the Hills did not recall their encounter until days after their incident. The reality of their experience became more delineated through their reoccurring dreams and their subsequent hypnosis sessions. Under separate hypnosis sessions, Betty and Barney's accounts of the incident were shockingly similar to one another's. These sessions revealed more evidence that the couple's experience was an actual event. The Hill's incident, like several other authentic abduction cases, revealed what researchers have labeled as *missing time*.[328] **Missing time** generally refers to a certain period of time that goes unaccounted for, especially during UFO encounters.

Notable cases like Villas Boas', the Hills', and several others follow similar patterns of an unexplained loss of time. When Antonio Villas Boas returned from his abduction, "he discovered that four hours had passed."[329] This normally results from the abductors placing the abductees in a trance-like state as they undergo scientific procedures—much like a doctor would sedate a patient before undergoing an operation. The Honorable Minister Louis Farrakhan is a firsthand witness to this type of activity. After his experience upon the huge Mother Wheel in September of 1985, Minister Farrakhan did

---

[326] Stanton Friedman and Kathleen Marden, *Captured! The Betty and Barney Hill UFO Experience* (Franklin Lakes, NJ: New Page Books, 2007).
[327] Richard M. Dolan, *UFOs and the National Security State: Chronology of a Coverup, 1941-1973* (Charlottesville, VA: Keyhole Publishing Company, 2000). 255.
[328] Op. Cit. Stanton Friedman and Kathleen Marden.
[329] Pablo Villarrubia Mauso, *Antonio Villas Boas: "Total Abduction"* (Pablo Villarrubia Mauso, 2007).

not fully recall his encounter until it crystallized with him nearly two days afterwards. These consistent patterns and behaviors offer clear indication that the intelligence of these so-called UFOs all stem from the same source. Despite slightly different uniforms, sizes of the wheels, different colors and lights shown from these planes, they all manifest the same basic functions—the same qualities Elijah Muhammad presented decades earlier.

The scientific practices and observations like these confirm the Honorable Elijah Muhammad's teachings to be quite accurate. He recognized these beings as *scientists* with applicable reasons. The aforementioned encounters don't describe *magic* or *sorcery*. Rather, these UFO related encounters demonstrate a supremely high level of science and mathematics beyond this world's comprehension. The profundity regarding these close encounters is that the Honorable Elijah Muhammad had already described these beings and their capabilities before these cases occurred.

The *beings* that have occasionally encountered and abducted civilians are the *humans* that the Honorable Elijah Muhammad spoke of as *scientists*. They are the ones who control these crafts and perform skillful examinations on abductees. Hence, they are called scientists because they perform scientific tests and acts. These are the same type of people described in the sacred texts as angels. They are human beings differing from most other humans only in their extraordinary intelligence and power. Having been groomed under Master Fard Muhammad's direction since they were small children, many of these scientists carry out miraculous feats. This is the result of their special training, teaching, diet, and lifestyle that allow them to perform in ways that would seem impossible for the average person. They manifest telepathic and telekinetic talents, which Muhammad simplistically described as "tuning-in" and the "radio in the head."[330]

Although some of the angels may have appearances that slightly differ from the average person, they are humans nonetheless. Just as the Honorable Elijah Muhammad acknowledged his firsthand relationship with the Supreme Being, he also spoke of his direct relationship with some of these angels. Some would visit him and assure him of their allegiance to him.[331] Muhammad explained that these scientists have different roles, but they all act and perform at the behest of Allah (God) who appeared in the person of Master Fard Muhammad.

---

[330] Elijah Muhammad, *The True History of Jesus* (Chicago, IL: C.R.O.E., 1992).
[331] Elijah Muhammad, "The Theology of Time (Lecture Series)," Vols. July 9, 1972 (Chicago, IL: MUHAMMAD Mosque No. 2, 1972).

More and more ufologists are coming closer to the truth that the Messenger brought to the world. Whereas many observers attributed UFO activity with extraterrestrial aliens, newer findings arrive closer to the teachings of the Honorable Elijah Muhammad. UFO researcher and author, Timothy Good gives his analysis on the origin of these beings based on years of studies and observations:

> They are not just aliens visiting. I'm convinced that many of them have been living here or based here perhaps longer than we have... All the aliens whose encounters with people have been reported do confirm that there is a genetic link between them and us, and that we are a hybridized species.[332]

Good's hypothesis show that there is a direct connection between the inhabitants of UFOs and humanity. His realization about the so-called aliens come closer to the Nation of Islam's authoritative position. Although Good does not openly acknowledge that Muhammad already gave firsthand details of these beings, his analysis draws the same conclusion as many other ufologists—that there is a direct relationship between those beings who pilot UFOs and humanity. While these findings may seem new to the public, they are not new to researchers and scientists who have knowingly kept this truth concealed from the public. Many have been extremely reluctant to clearly express the earthly origins of UFOs because it would likely validate the teachings of the Honorable Elijah Muhammad and the authority of his servant, the Honorable Minister Louis Farrakhan.

Like his teacher, Minister Farrakhan has a direct connection with the power of the wheels, which he has frequently explained before the public. In the face of his bold claims, UFO researchers avoid acknowledging that this is the same power that guides, directs, and protects Minister Farrakhan and the NOI under his leadership. This blatant omission about the origins of modern UFOs has become commonplace, even among ufologists.

Not only does Minister Farrakhan uphold the divine authority granted to him by the Honorable Elijah Muhammad, but Minister Farrakhan represents the same sovereignty associated with those wheel-shaped planes commonly called UFOs. The Minister has publically and continuously proclaimed his experience with the Honorable Elijah Muhammad upon the Mother Plane as well as his experiences with the smaller wheels. Surprising to some, Minister Farrakhan's claims have gone virtually unchallenged by even his staunchest critics. What does this reveal about the power that supports and protects him? Furthermore, what does this reveal about those in power who won't challenge him on this principle?

---

[332] Timothy Good, interview by Henrik Palmgren, *Secret Space Program, UFOs, ET & Coverup*, Red Ice Radio, February 24, 2011.

THE TRUTH IS OUT THERE

The little known case of the **Sid Padrick Abduction** gives additional credence to the Nation of Islam's exactness concerning UFOs. On January 30, 1965 Sid Padrick encountered a wheel-shaped object that landed near Watsonville, California. Padrick reported that the plane looked like "two real thick saucers inverted" when a voice communicated to him, "Do not be frightened, we are not hostile."[333] Padrick cautiously entered the craft where he was met by a man he described as "no different than me in basic appearance" with "clean-cut features." On board, Padrick saw seven other men of similar appearance along with a very beautiful woman. They were all about five feet eight to five feet nine inches tall and they all wore fully covered outfits that had "no buttons or zippers."[334]

While on board, the scientists showed Padrick a three-dimensional magnifying lens that allowed him to see a large object that resembled a blimp. Padrick believed the object to be about 1,000 miles away from the plane they were aboard. The people told him that it was a "navigation craft" that Padrick described in these words:

> I didn't see any markings or portholes in it... he told me that the power source [of the craft he was in] was transferred to them from the other craft, and that it did all the navigation and manipulation through space.[335]

This is the same relationship that the Honorable Elijah Muhammad described concerning the Mother Wheel and the baby planes. The Mother Wheel is the source of power that empowers and guides the smaller wheels. It is from the huge Wheel that the 1500 smaller wheels travel to and fro throughout the universe. While aboard, "The being asked Padrick if he wanted to pay his respects to the supreme deity, and Padrick reported having a deep spiritual experience."[336] The Padrick case further bears witness to Muhammad's authority as one of the scientists from the craft explained this to Padrick:

> As you know it, we have no sickness, we have no crimes, we have no police force. We have no schools—our young are taught at an early age to do a job,

---

[333] Timothy Good, *Above Top Secret: The Worldwide U.F.O. Cover-Up* (New York, NY: Quill William Morrow, 1988). 293.
[334] Ibid. 294.
[335] Ibid. 295.
[336] Richard M. Dolan, *UFOs and the National Security State: Chronology of a Coverup, 1941-1973* (Charlottesville, VA: Keyhole Publishing Company, 2000). 280

which they do very well. Because of our long life expectancy we have a very strict birth control. We have no money. We live as one.[337]

This is exactly what the Honorable Elijah Muhammad taught about the Mother Plane, which is the New Jerusalem, the city of the living God, the place where Allah (God) dwells. Muhammad made it clear for years that he was taught by Allah (God) who came in the person of Master Fard Muhammad. Elijah Muhammad was authorized by the Supreme Being to divinely represent him as his Messenger. The Supreme Being personally showed Elijah Muhammad this craft and gave him the particulars about it. This has become a primary reality that UFO researchers, enthusiasts, and critics avoid altogether. The argument that Elijah Muhammad met the Supreme Being who showed him the Mother Wheel seems to be deliberately avoided in ufological circles. This is a major reason why many of the credible sightings, encounters, and abduction cases have been withheld from public attention—because it confirms the truth that the Honorable Elijah Muhammad and the Honorable Minister Louis Farrakhan are the primary representatives of those wheel-like objects. This has been that *elephant in the boardroom* that scientists, theologians, educators, and officials continue to shy away from.

During Sid Padrick's encounter, the people from the plane telepathically communicated with one another and heavily impressed him, to say the least. Padrick stated that he had never felt the presence of the Supreme Being until that night. His experience vindicates Muhammad's position that these beings are human scientists and not the type of extraterrestrial aliens that Hollywood would make them out to be. Here are some of Padrick's firsthand observations from his encounter:

> It's obvious that they are on a very high scientific level, but their relation with the Supreme Being means a lot more to them than their technical and scientific ability and knowledge. I would say that their religion and their science are all in one.[338]

This is the highly scientific religion that Messenger Muhammad represented as salvation for his people who have become blind, deaf, and dumb to the true knowledge of themselves and their relationship to the Supreme Being. There is no wonder why the Sid Padrick case has found little attention outside of ufological circles. The religion that the Messenger represented to his people is one with science and mathematics. This is rooted in the Nation of

---

[337] Op. Cit. Good, 296.
[338] Timothy Good, *Above Top Secret: The Worldwide U.F.O. Cover-Up* (New York, NY: Quill William Morrow, 1988). 297.

THE TRUTH IS OUT THERE

Islam's core curriculum, which emphasizes that "Islam is Mathematics."[339] Even Muhammad's critics acknowledge, "he saw the need for 20th-century religions to declare themselves based on science, not faith. Islam was a science and a "way of life," not a religion."[340] This pragmatically precise teaching revealed to Elijah Muhammad stems from the same supreme source that Padrick witnessed aboard the UFO.

Mindful of Padrick's reputable background, his encounter was taken rather seriously, which led U.S. Defense Officials from Hamilton Air Force Base to carefully observe and interrogate him:

> According to Padrick, "they wanted my account of it, word for word." He said there were certain details which they asked him not to talk about publicly, but he talked anyway. Reporters found that Padrick was backed up by everyone who knew him; he was not a nut, nor a religious fanatic, nor interested in UFOs.[341]

What were the "certain details" that officials did not want Padrick to disclose to the public? Did it have anything to do with the fact that Padrick's descriptions would give public credence to the Nation of Islam whom U.S. Officials sought to discredit? Knowing the plausibility of his encounter, officials all but silenced Sid Padrick's case from the public. It was not until researchers revisited this episode in recent decades that people can now read about it. Like many of the plausible UFO abduction cases, several of them had been intentionally withheld from the public or deliberately drifted into oblivion. Meanwhile, the mainstream press highlighted the preposterous claims, hoaxes, and fanciful images in order to nullify the idea that these wheels exist.

BROTHERS FROM ANOTHER

Far too many reported UFO-related encounters have strikingly similar commonalities, especially regarding the beings who occupy these miraculous

---

[339] The Supreme Wisdom, "Lessons by Master Fard Muhammad to his servant, The Honorable Elijah Muhammad," *THE SUPREME WISDOM* (Detroit, MI: The Nation Of Islam, 1930-1934).
[340] C. Gerald Fraser, "Elijah Muhammad Dead; Black Muslim Leader, 77," *The New York Times*, February 26, 1975.
[341] Richard M. Dolan, *UFOs and the National Security State: Chronology of a Coverup, 1941-1973* (Charlottesville, VA: Keyhole Publishing Company, 2000). 280-281.

crafts. Even more strangely is that those commonalities further buttress and validate Elijah Muhammad's claim that he met the Supreme Being. It becomes easier to deduce exactly why governments, media, and world powers have misled the public about UFOs. Simply knowing that a higher power exists would not be as shocking to the world as finding out those powers are connected to the true Chosen people of God, which happen to be the oppressed Black and original people of the earth.

Unbeknownst to most, many reported UFO encounters have confirmed this connection to Black people. One of the early, yet less known encounters involved two Caucasian sisters, Betty and Helen Mitchell, who claimed to have numerous encounters with the occupants of wheel-shaped UFOs in the late 1950s. Their accounts further corroborate Muhammad's description of the people and purposes of these crafts. They shared these words:

> While in the coffee shop we were approached in a very mannerly way by two gentlemen dressed in grey suits, who managed to interrupt into our private conversation. As they spoke to us we found that they were from a huge mother-craft orbiting the planet Earth, and that their names were Elen and Zelas...
> ...They told us of the reasons why the space people were coming to Earth and that they were here to guide Earth along the lines of Brotherhood and Science.[342]

The sisters offered very lucid descriptions of these 'space people'. The fact that they did not describe Hollywood-styled aliens is probably why their accounts find little popularity outside of ufological circles. Instead they described men and gave further descriptions of their range of dark complexions:

> I was then introduced to three men and learned that one was Alna, the commander of all craft operation upon Earth. Alna spoke with a very heavy accent, and was much darker than any of the others. His skin had a high bronze tint to it, as compared with the lighter complexions of the others.[343]

This account is no different from what Messenger Muhammad revealed decades earlier. These dark-skinned men that Betty and Helen encountered were frequently described as "the Brothers"—the same terminology that Elijah Muhammad and the Nation of Islam have used to describe the occupants on the wheels. He taught that the scientists (angels) who pilot and occupy the wheels are original people from earth who are of

---

[342] Betty Mitchell and Helen Mitchell, *We Met The Space People*, Kindle (Clarksburg, WV: Saucerian Books, 1959). 24-25
[343] Ibid. 65-68

different complexions ranging from very dark to very light-skinned. Of course, Muhammad used much plainer terms such as the *Black, Brown, Red, and Yellow man*. These variations of hues enable 'the Brothers' to access resources without alarming 'the enemy' just as the very light-skinned (white-looking) Master Fard Muhammad was able to do so. These are the same type of people who had an ongoing working relationship with the Honorable Elijah Muhammad.

Instead of outright admitting that Elijah Muhammad's Nation of Islam is right and exact about these entities, some researchers have re-labeled the human UFO occupants and pilots from *extra-terrestrials* to *ultra-terrestrials*,[344] which is merely a fancy term to describe the supremely advanced (darker) people from these crafts who happen to be from earth.

These brothers and sisters aboard the wheels are not from another planet or galaxy (although they have interplanetary travel capabilities); rather they are from the same earth as those reading this book. However, they are certainly from a different social, educational, mental, and spiritual world. Earth simply serves as the primary base whereby they can access other parts of the universe. After all, the power of Allah (God) and his angels are not limited to earth; the earth is His footstool while his throne and wisdom encompasses all within the heavens. Hence, the Holy Qur'an denotes Allah (God) as *the Lord of all the worlds* (*Rab-bil aa-la-meen*). These worlds include the life on this planet as well as the life that exists throughout the universe.

The association of the wheels with the darker people gives another reason why world powers have secretive UFO concerns, which is why many have never even heard of the UFO sighting near Ariel School on September 16, 1994. Here, dozens of school children (ages 5-12) of various ethnicities witnessed one of the most evident, yet seldom talked about UFO encounters. This event occurred in Ruwa, Zimbabwe during recess when 62 school children witnessed a circular UFO land behind trees near their playground. From this craft, short Black men were seen with straight black hair. One of them came out relatively close to the playground before going back to the circular silvery craft.[345]

The children described these people as wearing fitting outfits (which is commonplace among credible UFO encounters) with very dark skin. One of the school girls who witnessed the encounter said that she felt that God was

---

[344] Timothy Green Beckley, *The Authentic Book Of Ultra-Terrestrial Contacts: From The Secret Alien Files of UFO Researcher Timothy Green Beckley*, trans. Jorge J. Martin (Contributor) (Inner Light - Global Communications, 2012).

[345] Cynthia Hind, "The Children of Ariel School - Case No. #96. Ruwa, Zimbabwe," *UFO AFRINEWS*, 1994.

coming. Whether she understood it or not, those planes and the people associated with them are indeed practical evidences of God's presence in the world. Little did those children know that they witnessed tangible signs of a realistic Supreme Being. Strangely there had been reports of UFOs in the skies over Zimbabwe only two days before. [346]

Nearly a dozen of the older children were recorded on BBC television giving their accounts of this sighting. Some of their reports and drawings can be easily accessed from various online sites. Unsurprisingly, this major sighting and encounter has caught very little attention by U.S. media, likely because the children's descriptions of their sighting bear witness to the truth the Nation of Islam has been explicating for decades.

Black people being sighted and reported as UFO occupants is nothing new or strange. In fact this has been a common thread among many witnesses who have seen or encountered these 'beings' from UFO crafts. The Black and original people's connection to these planes explains an important reason behind the cover-up. Messenger Elijah Muhammad fervently explained the messianic purpose of the Mother Plane and the baby planes and their purpose for protecting Allah's chosen people from their open enemies. Since the destroyed Black nation has no military institutions strong enough to overcome the White Western powers of the world, Allah (God) has orchestrated his supreme technology, which has contemporary world powers in awe. The fact that these highly advanced crafts are operated by a supreme power associated with dark people shatters the fiber of white supremacy—an idea that has poisoned and influenced the entire world. If this truth about so-called UFOs became known, the very foundation upon which global militaries operate would be crumbled. Hence, a major factor of world governments' attempts to conceal the UFO reality involves these planes connections to Elijah Muhammad, Louis Farrakhan, the Nation of Islam, and the Black (and Original) people of God's choice.

With all the red tape associated with disclosing information about UFO sightings, some former military and government workers have used radio broadcasts to anonymously share information that would otherwise bring trouble to them. Some nationally syndicated radio programs have become a hotbed for UFO reports. While some calls and reports are clearly outlandish, there tends to be some accounts that convey a sense of credibility. One caller who was simply identified as *Charles from Echo Park, California* described himself as a 67-year old former Vietnam Aero Vet who now has a 'Red File'. He narrated what he believed is the reason behind the U.S. Government's UFO investigations cover-up. Charles, whose voice connoted that of a Caucasian male, disclosed what he claims to have witnessed during the 1980s.

---

[346] Ibid.

THE TRUTH IS OUT THERE

While on a U.S. Air Force base, three cigar-shaped spaceships were sighted. One of the ships, which he described as over a mile long, landed on this base. Several hundred young Black men came out the back of the craft standing in military-styled ranks. When describing what he saw, Charles exclaimed, "This particular race that landed those ships and that are seen in these huge cigar-shaped ships—they are a Black race, they looked like African Americans!"[347] He continued that they had a look about them as though "they had never been conquered." Much to the surprise of George Knapp (the radio announcer), Charles continued that while on America's military base, these impune Black men were said to have met with unnamed U.S. Commanders. Charles even suggested that Ronald Reagan's UN address where he encouraged humanity to band together against a common 'alien enemy' was in reaction to this encounter at a US Air Force Base. While this research does not assume that Charles' account is fully credible, it does stand to reason that such an encounter would not be too farfetched. After all, the U.S. Government has, on several occasions, officially denied and lied about their UFO encounters and the reality of this phenomenon because of its connection to the darker people of the earth.

---

[347] George Knapp in for George Noory, *Coast To Coast AM with George Noory* (Premiere Networks Inc., May 24, 2013).

11. THE WHEELS AND DIVINE JUDGMENT

THE CHANGING OF WORLDS

If the intelligence behind these planes represents the healing and salvation of the world's problems, why is there so much fear of their presence? Much of America's UFO fears exist because of the divine significance of these planes. The Honorable Elijah Muhammad made known that these planes were divinely crafted in fulfillment of the prophecies. While these planes represent the peace and salvation of Allah (God), they also represent the other end of the spectrum, which is the divine destruction of the present world of wickedness. Since the present world order has been subjugated under satanic authorities, the clear signs of God's presence have been the greatest fear among world powers.

The Honorable Elijah Muhammad made it clear that the wheels are tools of God that will be used in the destruction of the world's oppressive powers, with America at the helm of wickedness and oppression. He stated, "The Mother Plane was made to destroy this world of evil and to show the wisdom and mighty power of the God Whom came to destroy an old world and set up a new world."[348] Since America's powers have witnessed these planes and their superior capabilities, U.S. Defense understands that the wheels are thousands of years more advanced than their weaponry. However, history and prophecy show that arrogant leadership do not heed to divine warnings. For example, Pharaoh of the Bible was shown the divine plagues of God, yet he still desired to fight against God's messenger and the chosen people.

While most American people have been kept in the dark concerning the prophetic purpose of these planes, America's hierarchal leaders are well aware of the divine power of Master Fard Muhammad and his host of angelic scientists who control these wheel-like planes. Believe it or not, the Government is not as ignorant as they make themselves seem. The Messenger taught that the American Government retains certain theological scholars whose purpose is to study prophecy in relation to modern events. Jabril Muhammad recounted what the Honorable Elijah Muhammad shared with him:

> There are wise white men who are paid by Government to study prophecy—not for divine guidance, but to see how they can try to get around it. There are

---

[348] Elijah Muhammad, *The Fall Of America* (Chicago, IL: Elijah Muhammad, 1973). 236.

some Whites who are humbled by it, but those ones [in power] are arrogant and they are trying to figure out how to get around it.[349]

If such clandestine groups exist as Elijah Muhammad proclaimed, how have they responded to the power of Master Fard Muhammad demonstrated through so-called UFOs? Have they acknowledged that Elijah Muhammad was right or have they worked to discredit him and his teachings? Reality shows that U.S. authorities have NOT publicly acknowledged the fact that Elijah Muhammad brought this truth to the modern world. In fact U.S. authorities have barely even acknowledged that the NOI teaches about these so-called UFOs. Since the American Government has proven to attack the Messenger and the Nation of Islam, it stands to reason that they are arrogant enough to try to challenge the divine power of God's wheels. This should come to no surprise to anyone who studies the prophecies for it was already written that such would take place. This is the type of racist arrogant leadership that is leading America into her own doom.

The Bible and the Holy Qur'an give several symbolic and prophetic scenarios that indicate the type of mind that occupies present day leadership. Even with knowledge of the scriptural prophecies and clear signs, it is a mind that refuses to heed the warnings of God. According to the Bible, Herod had such men on his staff whose purpose was to study the prophecies—not with the intention to follow divine guidance, but with the evil intention of subduing the written will of God (Matthew 2:1-18). King Herod saw clear signs in the heavens, but he sought to kill the one who represented those heavenly signs. He gave the false impression that he desired to give homage to God's designated messenger, but all the while he was planning to kill the destined savior. This is the mindset of America's present rulers who have deceitfully misled the people from the truth of God's Messenger—Elijah Muhammad, his servant—Louis Farrakhan, and the clearly identified objects they represent. The FBI under the direction of J. Edgar Hoover demonstrated this wicked mindset for it was their objectives that sought to "Prevent the RISE OF A "MESSIAH" who could unify, and electrify, the militant black nationalist movement."[350] Among the many Black leaders and groups targeted by the U.S. Government, Elijah Muhammad's Nation of Islam is the only one who has consistently proclaimed the reality of these wheel-like planes and their direct

---

[349] Jabril Muhammad, "The Wheel," *Lecture by Minister Jabril Muhammad* (Phoenix, AZ, September 18, 1985).
[350] Ward Churchill and Jim Vander Wall, *The COINTELPRO Papers: Documents from the FBI's Secret Wars Against Dissent in the United States* (South End Press, 1990). 110.

connection to the messiah. This is just one of the many attributes that set the NOI apart from all other groups, theologies, and societies.

Why won't White American powers just accept the truth about these wheel-shaped UFOs and allow the truth to flourish so that peace can truly be established on earth? Wouldn't this seem to be the right thing to do since they know that these wheels have a divine purpose? Those who understand prophecy and eschatology know that certain prophecies are 'conditional' and some are 'written in stone.' In other words, there are some scriptural scenarios and principles that must be fulfilled and there are certain individuals and groups that must fulfill these roles. The Honorable Minister Louis Farrakhan is such a man who has been taught the meaning of prophecies by the Messenger of Allah (God). Hence, he has been given the keys to understand the time, world events, and different people as they relate to the prophecies. Farrakhan has frequently answered exactly why America refuses to tell the truth about so-called UFOs:

> Since 1930 they have known that this plane exists, but why won't they tell the American people? It is because the White man does not want to admit that there is a technology in the world, and a power in the world that makes his power look like jumbo jet in comparison to that huge plane [the Mother Wheel]! He doesn't want to admit that he doesn't have what it takes to deal with what they called that walnut-shaped object in the sky![351]

White supremacy breeds a type of arrogance that blinds even those who are considered brilliant in their respected disciplines. America's leadership and those under their dominance have rejected the divine warnings coming from Elijah Muhammad and Minister Farrakhan. This type of racist and arrogant attitude was foreseen, which is why the scriptures predict a divine judgment and the inevitable War of Armageddon, which renders the ultimate destruction of this world's paradigms. **It's not the 'unknown' quality about UFOs that prompt U.S. Defense concerns. It's the 'known' power associated with those wheel-like planes that have them troubled.** American powers and world leaders have been shown the power of Allah (God) via so-called UFOs. They know that these wheels are real, but racism and arrogance have clouded the minds of American and world leaders. Their continued mistreatment of God's people justifies the destruction of America's powers.

Several Presidents and world leaders have witnessed these crafts for themselves. In 1969 Jimmy Carter and several others witnessed that huge Mother Wheel that Muhammad represented to the world for years. Some four years later as Governor of Georgia, Carter reported his sighting to the

---

[351] "The Reality Of The Mother Plane" (Chicago, IL: The Final Call Inc., 1987 4-January).

THE WHEELS AND DIVINE JUDGMENT

International UFO Bureau Inc. During his Presidential campaign trail in 1976, Carter reported these words regarding his sighting and intentions as President:

> It was the darndest thing I've ever seen. It was big, it was very bright, it changed colors and it was about the size of the moon... We watched it for ten minutes, but none of us could figure out what it was. One thing's for sure, I'll never make fun of people who say they've seen unidentified objects in the sky. If I become President, I'll make every piece of information this country has about UFO sightings available to the public and the scientists.[352]

Of course, Carter was never able to make such information available as he initially intended because there are forces in Government that even Presidents must answer to. Those forces have continued to conceal the truth and mislead the public. Although President Jimmy Carter could not implement his intentions, he was able to create two new cabinet-level departments: the Department of Energy and the Department of Education. He established a national energy policy that included conservation, price control, and 'new technology'. Carter's previous UFO sighting was a major motivation behind this drive to discover new technologies because he was a witness of the most advanced technology in the world.

It has become commonplace for Presidents and high-ranking officials to witness this awesome power of Allah (God). In fact this follows the scriptural patterns whereas God has always shown his power to the wicked rulers to give them a chance to submit to his divine will. Hence their rejection of the clear truth serves as justification for God to execute his Judgment upon them. Ronald Reagan was another figure who witnessed Master Fard Muhammad's technology. As Governor of California in 1974, he witnessed a 'baby plane' while on a Cessna Citation airplane. He shared his experience with journalist Norman C. Miller who was the Washington Bureau chief for the Wall Street Journal. Reagan told Miller these words:

> We followed it for several minutes. It was a bright white light. We followed it to Bakersfield, and all of a sudden to our utter amazement it went straight up into the heavens.[353]

Ever since his encounter, Reagan had been fascinated with UFOs. He took his fascination and UFO concerns to office with him as he became President of the United States nearly six years later. He made several references

---

[352] Timothy Good, *Above Top Secret: The Worldwide U.F.O. Cover-Up* (New York, NY: Quill William Morrow, 1988). 368.
[353] Stephen Spignesi, *The UFO Book Of Lists* (Citadel, 2000). 72.

to uniting the world against a "threat to this world from some other species from another planet outside of the universe".[354] In his address to the United Nations, President Ronald Reagan made the following comments:

> Perhaps we need some outside universal threat… Our differences worldwide would vanish if we were facing an alien threat from outside this world. And yet I ask you, "is not an alien threat already among us?"[355]

President Reagan did not demonstrate the slightest willingness to accept guidance from a technology that was obviously supreme in power. Instead, Reagan showed an antagonistic position toward these wheels, which he described as "an alien threat." Under his Presidency, he developed the Strategic Defense Initiative (SDI), a project that would construct a space-based anti-missile system. This program was perhaps better known in the mid 1980s as Reagan's "Star Wars." What was Reagan so concerned and worried about that he felt the need to propose such an ambitious project that would shoot and combat deadly missiles into space? What was in the heavens that countless billions of dollars would go into such an initiative? What was the perceived 'alien threat' that caused the Government to be so adamantly concerned? There was no need to shoot missiles into space when fighting against other nations on earth. The U.S. Government literally had the audacity and the willingness to go to war with the power of Allah (God)! This has remained the pervasive attitude and position of the U.S. Government, which is exactly why a divine judgment against America and her cohorts are warranted. Only a satanic mind would allow them to try to contend with a power that is obviously more capable than anything in this world.

THE BATTLE IN THE SKY

According to the Honorable Elijah Muhammad, the presence of the Wheel is indicative of the inevitable war that is to take place between good and evil. The very presence of this craft signifies the changing of worlds. Messenger Muhammad gives an analysis on this final war:

> The final war between Allah (God) and the devils is dangerously close. The very least amount of friction can bring it into action within minutes. There is no such thing as getting ready for this most terrible and dreadful war; they are

---

[354] Ronald Reagan, "Remarks of the President to Fallston High School Students and Faculty," *White House Transcripts* (The White House, December 4, 1985).
[355] Ronald Reagan, "Speech to the United Nations General Assembly" (42nd General Assembly, September 21, 1987).

THE WHEELS AND DIVINE JUDGMENT

ready. Preparation for the battle between man and man or nations has been made and carried out on land and water for the past 6,000 years. Man has now become very wise and has learned many of the secrets of nature, which make the old battles with swords and bows and arrows look like child's play.[356]

As America has grown in military prowess and nuclear weaponry, so has America's arrogance. With the world's nations under her control and influence, this leaves America as the primary contender against the power of Allah's wheels. The Honorable Elijah Muhammad was given insight as to how this battle would unravel. He stated that the technology on the wheels is such that it will shut down the capabilities of America's aircraft before they even get a chance to come close to attacking the Wheel or the smaller planes:

> When America thinks that she's going after this plane… those scientists on the plane go to rush in and charge America so that she can't come forward to the plane, then she can't shoot it.[357]

Aside from the powerful bombs carried by the smaller baby planes, the scientists who maneuver these wheels are inherently capable of calculating the thoughts of people before the thought even comes to their minds. Plus, the scientists have the technology of manipulating America's weaponry from afar. Muhammad further gives this hint regarding the capabilities of Allah's scientists who operate the smaller baby (bomber) planes:

> When this plane unloads here deadly destruction, you won't have no planes up there. No. They won't fly up there with your jets. They're going to get rid of your jets on the ground first. "How are they going to do that, Mr. Muhammad?" They'll do it like this: First thing they will do is destroy all of America's airplane bases. They will also destroy her planes that you see flying at the speed of sound. They will get rid of them first.[358]

The reports of military airmen from around the globe confirm these capabilities that Muhammad warned the world about. In 2010 UFO researcher Robert Hastings assembled a host of decorated military airmen who came forth to admit that the U.S. Armed Forces have been witnessing UFO activity since

---

[356] *MESSAGE TO THE BLACKMAN In America*, Original Published by MUHAMMAD'S Temple No. 2 in Chicago 1965 (Chicago, IL: The Final Call Inc., 1965). 293.
[357] "The Theology of Time (Lecture Series)," Vols. July 2, 1972 (Chicago, IL: MUHAMMAD Mosque No. 2, 1972).
[358] "The Theology of Time (Lecture Series)," Vols. July 9, 1972 (Chicago, IL: MUHAMMAD Mosque No. 9, 1972).

the 1940s and have been working to keep this information from the public. These planes have interfered with some of the world's most advanced artillery. Because of the known UFO activity with America's military weaponry, Hastings made the obvious conclusion that these planes "have taken an interest in the nuclear arms race."[359] For those who follow the teachings of the Honorable Elijah Muhammad and the guidance of Minister Louis Farrakhan, this conclusion is nothing new. After all, the Messenger had been explaining the purpose and capabilities behind these objects for decades. Hastings' research from military personnel has shown that disc-shaped UFOs have been seen hovering over and apparently monitoring the activities of the United States' most advanced weapons installation sites. He gave the following related report:

> Declassified U.S. government documents and the testimony of more than 120 former or retired military personnel have established, beyond doubt, the reality of ongoing UFO incursions at American nuclear weapons sites. While most of the incidents apparently involved mere surveillance, in a few cases a significant number of nuclear missiles suddenly and simultaneously malfunctioned, just as USAF Security Policemen reported seeing disc-shaped craft hovering nearby.[360]

Among these respected military airmen who took the bold step to break their government-imposed silence were retired USAF Captain Robert Salas, retired USAF Col. Charles Halt, USAF Nuclear Missile Launch Officer Jerome Nelson, and a host of others. All of these men and several more have admitted that UFOs have monitored and often tampered with America's nuclear weapons. Unsurprisingly, this type of UFO activity is not limited toward America's weaponry. Just a few years earlier in 2007, another conference took place where high-ranking officials, pilots, and military officers from around the world came forth about UFOs in their respective countries. This press conference was assembled by the Disclosure Project who claims to have "over 500 government, military, and intelligence community witnesses testifying to their direct, personal, firsthand experience with UFOs, ETs, ET technology, and the cover-up that keeps this information secret."[361] Moderating this panel of world-renowned officials was former Arizona Governor Fife Symington.

---

[359] "Major UFO Press Conference - National Press Club," *Nuclear Weapons Have Been Compromised by Unidentified Aerial Objects* (Washington D.C.: Robert Hastings, September 27, 2010).
[360] "UFO-Nukes Press Conference Line-Up," *The Upcoming UFO-Nukes Connection Press Conference* (Toronto: UFO UpDates, Septmber 17, 2010).
[361] The Disclosure Project, *The Discolsure Project*, 2010, http://www.disclosureproject.org/ (accessed March 11, 2013).

THE WHEELS AND DIVINE JUDGMENT

Under Symington's gubernatorial reign, one of the most widespread sightings in recent history took place in what has been dubbed **The Phoenix Lights**. This event, which occurred on March 13, 1997, involved a massive UFO said to be nearly a mile long with lights shining in a V formation. It was witnessed by thousands of residents in the areas surrounding Phoenix, Arizona. As Governor, Symington initially followed the normal governmental protocol, which involves denying or explaining such events away in some sort. It wasn't until years after the mass sighting and after Symington left office that he was brave enough to come forth and admit that what he saw was not anything of this world's intelligence. During an interview with CNN, Symington gave the following recollections:

> To my astonishment this apparition appeared; this dramatically large, very distinctive leading edge with some enormous lights was traveling through the Arizona sky.
> As a pilot and a former Air Force Officer, I can definitively say that this craft did not resemble any man-made object I'd ever seen. And it was certainly not high-altitude flares because flares don't fly in formation.[362]

Aside from the fact that a Governor witnessed this huge vessel, thousands more saw this craft at the same time and it has been recorded on video. How is it that such a blatant showing of aerial majesty can be swept under the rug, even after the Governor came forth and admitted that this object is in fact a reality? Several more U.S. military officers have expressed their willingness to speak out and give more details about their sightings and experiences, but they are still under certain military obligations of secrecy. They have sought immunity from their security oaths, but Congress has yet to help in such an area, which is consistent with America's protocols on UFO sightings—muzzle those credible persons from going public with evidence that supports the notion of Muhammad's wheels.

Many of these cases clearly demonstrate the accuracy of the Nation of Islam's theology. On September 15, 1964 U.S. Air Force Lieutenant Robert Jacobs filmed a UFO intercepting and disabling a missile warhead. While reviewing the film of the missile launch in slow motion, Jacobs and fellow officers saw a luminous disc-shaped object fly to the missile, shoot a beam of light on it, and dismantle it within milliseconds. After reviewing the film, two CIA agents took the video footage and Jacobs was told to never speak of it

---

[362] "Symington: I saw a UFO in the Arizona sky," *CNN.com*, November 9, 2007.

again. Needless to say, the footage was never to be seen again either.[363] How is it that Elijah Muhammad already knew and reported the exact characteristics of these planes before such documented reports ever took place? These cases are clear indicators that prove Elijah Muhammad's firsthand knowledge to be absolutely correct. Since it is proven that U.S. Government Intelligence knows the reality of Muhammad's connection to these objects, they have not acted amicably to him, Minister Louis Farrakhan, or the truth they represent. This characterizes the great fear among America's leadership—that white supremacy and corruption will ultimately be overthrown by the same power associated with those wheels. The architects and stewards of this world's deception are at their wits end and are fighting to sustain their domination of the masses. The U.S. Government, its mainstream media, its military have displayed their antagonism toward Master Fard Muhammad's wheels that they have wrongfully classified as UFOs. America has proven to deceive the public and even attempt to battle against these majestic objects and the God responsible for them. This conflict is what brings about the inevitable *Battle in the Sky* that the Messenger and his Minister have so adamantly proclaimed. The Book of Revelation describes this scenario as the devil attempting to attack the people of God because they realize their time is up:

> *Therefore rejoice, you heavens, and you that dwell in them. Woe to the inhabitants of the earth and of the sea! for the devil is come down to you, having great wrath, because he knows that he has but a short time.* – Revelation 12:12, American King James Version

Since Muhammad's teachings and character have been intentionally distorted for decades, most Black Americans have no idea that Allah (God) has intervened for their salvation and protection against the world's most vicious and deceitful oppressors. For the most part, the darker aboriginal people are not cognizant that these wheel-like planes are direct indications of God's power that will be used to save and protect his chosen people. This teaching is at the core of the Nation of Islam's theology. Conversely, this is the same reason why Western powers have deemed Elijah Muhammad and his unarmed followers as primary threats.[364] The Black Muslims are not threats to the U.S. Government because of any violence; instead, the Caucasian-dominated power

---

[363] James Fox, Tim Coleman, Boris Zubov and Charles Fox, *Out Of The Blue - The Definitive Investigation of the UFO Phenomenon*, directed by James Fox, Tim Coleman and Boris Zubov, Hannover House, 2002.
[364] Ward Churchill and Jim Vander Wall, *The COINTELPRO Papers: Documents from the FBI's Secret Wars Against Dissent in the United States* (South End Press, 1990).

structure is threatened by the bold truths born out of the NOI's 'Mathematical Theology'[365] and the proven power of the wheels represented by the Muslims.

IT'S ABOVE THEIR HEADS

The Battle in The Sky that the Honorable Elijah Muhammad frequently described clearly delineated the ultimate battle between the forces of good, represented by Allah's circular planes, and the military weaponry of this world's powers led by America. Although this inevitable conflict is expected to physically take place, the battle in the sky also signifies the spiritual battle over the hearts and minds of the people. It has both literal and figurative connotations. While the sacred scriptures depict Satan as being the temporary ruler of this world, the end of Satan's dominance is signified by the coming of God who makes himself known and exposes Satan for who and what he truly is. This is the other battle that has been taking place. Just as the sky is above the heads of the people, so is the spiritual war that is taking place. The masses of the people are in total oblivion as it relates to the truth about God's coming and the wheel-like planes. The U.S. and world powers have worked tirelessly to keep this truth away from the people's conscious.

The reality of the Mother Plane and the smaller wheels is above the people's heads, literally and figuratively. Since the masses have been strategically kept in the dark about this subject, there is no wonder why there is a war taking place that they are unaware of. While discussing how America intentionally keeps her citizens distracted from the truth, Minister Farrakhan likened America to the wicked rulers of the scriptures wherein he stated, "The wicked king of Babylon Nebuchadnezzar, used music, art, and culture to dumb-down the people so they would not be mindful of how God was wreaking his wrath on Babylon."[366] These methods of mass distraction involve keeping the people preoccupied with sport and play. As long as they are occupied with frivolity and want, the masses are generally unable to take time to reflect on the truth being conveyed by the Honorable Elijah Muhammad and the Honorable Minister Farrakhan.

---

[365] **Mathematical Theology** is a term derived from the Nation of Islam's Lessons called *The Supreme Wisdom*. Mathematical Theology indicates the soundness and applicable accuracy of the wisdom that Master Fard Muhammad revealed to the Honorable Elijah Muhammad.

[366] "On The Year 2012 & The New Year 2013," *A Special Roundtable edition of Farrakhan Speaks* (The Final Call, January 7, 2013).

Knowing that the masses of the people have been deceived by the Satanic forces who influence policies, media, and finance, the God of the scriptures uses his influence over nature along with his messenger to warn the people in order to avoid a destined chastisement. Allah offers these words in the Holy Qur'an:

> *And indeed We sent (messengers) to nations before thee then We seized them with distress and affliction that they might humble themselves.* (Al-An`am 6:42)

The Honorable Elijah Muhammad and the Honorable Minister Farrakhan have virtually been lone voices crying in the wilderness. These men have continuously challenged and fought against the wiles of Satan while the masses of the people have been totally unaware that the Supreme Being has intervened in the affairs of humanity. Since many people have turned a deaf ear to Muhammad's truth, Allah (God) permits various occurrences to afflict America so that hopefully their attention can be redirected to heed the truth.

Aside from the weather, earthquakes and famine, Allah (God) has frequently used his heavenly signs to capture the attention of his people as well as the attention of his enemies. Sometimes it becomes necessary to capture their attention in ways that clearly show that a superior power is on the scene. This is why the scriptures depict God showcasing his heavenly vehicles and weaponry to leave no excuse that his power is on the scene. Since America has not heeded the truth spoken by Elijah Muhammad and Louis Farrakhan, will America respond to the wheel-shaped UFOs they represent?

ELIJAH'S GOD MUST BE GOD!

The conflicts between Messenger Elijah Muhammad and the ruling powers of this world are synonymous to the prophetic narratives of the prophets and messengers of old. The scriptures of the Bible and Holy Qur'an are filled with God's messengers being attacked, lied on, and even killed by the opposing Satanic forces and those under Satan's influence. The mission of the Honorable Elijah Muhammad is no different. In fact, his mission can be described as a manifestation of all the prophetic assignments put together. The enemies of Elijah Muhammad are more technologically and militarily advanced than any of those ancient powers. Modern America's hegemony reel a type of power and influence that would make all of the past nations pale in comparison. According to the scriptures, Moses' enemies were the oppressive ruling powers of his day, Jesus' enemies were the secretive ruling body of Jews in his day, and Prophet Muhammad's enemies were the idolatrous ruling class of Mecca during his advent. The same principle is applied today on a level unlike ever before.

Unsurprisingly, those divine messengers relied on a celestial power to aid them in what would otherwise be an impossible mission. This is commonplace in the divine texts of the Torah, Gospel, and the Qur'an. Moses and Aaron's followers were protected by a heavenly vehicle described as a cloud by day and a pillar of fire by night. Jesus' ascension and his predicted return takes place by way of a vehicular cloud. Even Prophet Muhammad's Night Journey holds that he was transported overnight by a heavenly steed. There is much symbolism and substance related to these and numerous more accounts of God's messengers.

The Honorable Elijah Muhammad made it clear that the scriptures are not ancient history books. Instead, much of what is read is actually symbolic prophecy. He demonstrated how most of the prophetic figures in some way point to him and his divine mission in America. This includes the Biblical account of the major prophet Elijah and his battle to prove the reality of his living God. The name *Elijah* gives indications to his relationship with the Supreme Being. Elijah stems from the Semitic name *Eliyah*. The first part *Eli* is an abbreviated possessive form of *Elohi* or *Allahi*, which means 'my God'. The second half of Elijah's name stems from *Jah/Yah*, which is an abbreviated name for *YHWH*, another personal name of God. So together the name Elijah is a declaration suggesting, "My God is God!" Abarim Publications offer the following commentary related to the etymology of the name Elijah:

> The name Elijah is truly fabulous; a junction of two of the most common appellatives of God in the Bible: the word (El), the common abbreviation of Elohim (Elohim), meaning God (or gods), but most fundamentally possibly meaning power or strength and God's personal name (YHWH), or Yahweh.[367]

Similarly, the 19th Century theologian, Adam Clarke, rendered this assertion regarding the significance of Elijah's name:

> His Hebrew name, which we have corrupted into Elijah and Elias, is אליהו Alihu, or, according to the vowel points, Eliyahu; and signifies he is my God. Does this give countenance to the supposition that this great personage was a manifestation in the flesh of the Supreme Being?[368]

---

[367] Arie Uittenbogaard, "Meaning and etymology of the Hebrew name Elijah" (Abarim Publications, 2011).
[368] Adam Clarke, *Clarke's Commentary on the Bible 1 Kings 17:1*, trans. Text Courtesy of Internet Sacred Texts Archive (Biblos.com, 1831).

Despite slightly varying interpretations on the exact etymology of the name Elijah, it is clear that the name and personage of Elijah represents the presence of the divine Supreme Being.

The name of Elijah signifies his direct connection to the true and living God. Just as interesting is the fact that the story of Elijah in the Bible offers a striking resemblance to the mission of the Honorable Elijah Muhammad and his servant the Honorable Louis Farrakhan. The Biblical Elijah was a major prophet of obscure origin. Little is known about his background and upbringing. He is introduced in the 17th Chapter of 1 Kings as Elijah "The Tishbite". Unlike some of the minor prophets of old, Elijah's appearance shows a man backed by God to disturb the idolatrous society that had lost their way from the path and identity of God. It was Elijah's job to introduce the people to the true God and to contend with the kings and rulers on this point. Consequently he was labeled the 'troubler of Israel' because of his radical preaching of a God who controlled the forces of the heavens and earth. This troubled the society who worshiped their own ideas of God, which were contrary to what Elijah had been shown. Hence, the representatives of the false god *Baal*, known as Baal prophets, sought to contend with Elijah at the behest of the king.

The 18th Chapter of Kings narrates this epic showdown where one man, Elijah, challenges the Baal prophets at Mount Carmel because he wanted to prove to Israel that his God is indeed the true and living God. Elijah dared King Ahab and the Baal prophets to see whose God would respond from the heavens, which would prove whose God is God. Elijah promised that his God would send down signs of fire from heaven as a clear indication of his power (this indicates a Godly power that operates from a celestial position). First the Baal prophets would pray to their God to send down fire to consume their offering. While they prayed, there was no response from heaven, which prompted God's prophet to seemingly taunt them, showing that Baal was not God. The Baalites went into a frenzy becoming louder and more frantic to no avail. Then it was Elijah's turn. Elijah prayed for fire that it would be known that his God is God and that he is the appointed man of God. As he prayed, fire descended from heaven consuming even the watery alter. After this dare proved that Elijah represented the true and living God, the Baal prophets were taken to the Kishon stream and executed.

The fate of the rulers and their cohorts who have deceived the people from the truth of Elijah Muhammad and the wheel-like planes that back him are synonymous with the fate of the King Ahab and Baal prophets. This is the fear of those who control and influence the world today. There is a power in the world that aims to set down the tyrants and deceivers and to establish the kingdom of righteousness on earth. That power is clearly demonstrated in those fiery chariots from heaven represented by the Honorable Elijah Muhammad and Minister Louis Farrakhan. Unlike any other leaders in

THE WHEELS AND DIVINE JUDGMENT

American history, these unarmed men challenge the kings and ruling powers that Allah (God) has come and is present in the world. Unlike any social, educational, political, or religious leaders, these men have preached of God's presence and the wheel-like planes that he is using to prove his power and presence in the world. The fact that these planes exist is clear proof that Elijah's God must be God!

It was after the epic showdown at Mount Carmel that Elijah the prophet anointed Elisha with a double portion of the spirit to carry on after his departure (2 Kings 2:9). Elijah was destined to leave because he had a heavenly rendezvous with the Lord who would sweep him away on a strange fiery chariot that would carry him away on a heavenly whirlwind. This mysterious departure took place as Elijah and his representative were on their way from Gilgal (2 Kings 2:1-1). Interestingly both the chariot of fire (**rekeb**-*esh*) and the location (*Gilgal*) have etymological roots that signify a circular wheel-type object. Hence, the authority of the Man of God is distinguished by his relationship to circular objects and their connection to heavenly travel, thus proving that Elijah's God must be God!

12. UFOS AND THE MESSIANIC CONNECTION

HE COMES IN THE VOLUME OF THE BOOK

Then said I, Lo, I come: in the volume of the book it is written of me, – Psalm 40: 7, KJV

Not only do the wheel-like UFOs affirm that Elijah Muhammad met the Supreme Being, this reality offers clear indication to the divinity associated with this man. Like the Baal prophets against Elijah and Elisha, Ufologists and researchers will become obviously hypocritical if they continue to negate the direct affiliation of Elijah Muhammad, Louis Farrakhan, and the NOI with the UFO phenomenon. Elijah Muhammad never backed down from his claim of being taught by God, being the anointed representative of God, and being backed by the Mother Plane and the smaller wheels. Scholars and academics continue to avoid this reality because these planes serve as proof that such men are divinely guided. Furthermore, theological scholars realize that these planes are vivid indicators of the messianic prophecies.

Theologians and scholars have stumbled upon the notion that more than one messiah is expected to arise during this prophetic time. The discovery of the Dead Sea Scrolls in the 1940s and 1950s brought about a shift in theological thinking. These ancient texts show that Jews had prophesies of two messiahs. The first was best known to them for his "priestly" works, while the second was best known to them for his "kingly" works.[369] Other scholars of the Dead Sea Scrolls render similar statements concerning the expected two messiahs and the messianic community they shall lead:

> According to the dominant view in the sectarian texts from Qumran, two messiahs were to lead the congregation in the End of Days, one priestly, and the other lay.[370]

Another study of the scrolls gives this assertion:

---

[369] Robert H. Eisenman and Michael Wise, *The Dead Sea Scrolls Uncovered: The First Complete Translation and Interpretation of 50 Key Documents withheld for Over 35 Years* (Penguin Books, 1993).
[370] Lawrence H. Schiffman, *Reclaiming the Dead Sea Scrolls: The History of Judaism, the Background of Christianity, the Lost Library of Qumran* (Yale University Press, 1995). 321-322.

UFOS AND THE MESSIANIC CONNECTION

Several texts are considered to be written by members of the sect: the Damascus document for example, and the Messianic rule. In these texts, we may expect to find the sect's own messianology. The distinguishing characteristic is that the Qumranites expected the coming of not one, but two Messiahs.[371]

While much confusion still exists concerning the expected messiah, most Jewish traditions await the messiah's advent, which is signified by the return of Elijah. Elijah's presence answers the authenticity of the true messiah. Dr. Wesley Muhammad of the Nation of Islam Research Department makes the following observation:

> Justin Martyr, a Christian Apologist who lived approximately 100 CE, wrote a book entitled "The Dialogue with Trypho the Jew," which is a record of a discussion between he and a Jewish rabbi. This dialogue begins with Justin telling the rabbi he believes Jesus was the long awaited Messiah. The rabbi responds in part:
>
> "... But Christ - if he has indeed been born, and exists anywhere ... has no power until Elijah comes to anoint him, and make him manifest to all. And you, having accepted a groundless report, invent a Christ for yourselves, and for his sake are inconsiderately perishing."
>
> The rabbi here reveals the reason Jews 2,000 years ago and today reject the historical Jesus as the prophesied Messiah: Elijah is expected to herald the Messiah and make his presence known to the people. Jews know 2,000 years ago Jesus was not made manifest to all by the work of Elijah (John the Baptist denied being Elijah, John 1:21, 25).[372]

As Elijah's presence signifies the messianic age, Elijah is also directly associated with heavenly vehicles that have the ability to aid him and his appointed servant in times of need (2 Kings 2:11, 2 Kings 6:17). There can be no way of separating Elijah's messianic connection from the heavenly chariots that he is directly associated with. Hence, Elijah, the Messiah, and the flying fiery chariots (now called UFOs) are all interconnected.

The term *messiah* is a title that refers to the prophesied savior and deliverer who is divinely anointed to crush the wicked and establish the eternal kingdom of peace on earth. The messiah is expected to lead and liberate the

---

[371] Jona Lendering, "Messiah (14) Qumran's two Messiahs," *LIVIUS* (2013).
[372] Wesley Muhammad, "The Wise of this World Awaited Elijah," *The Final Call*, December 10, 2012.

chosen people of God. This one title refers to different persons who will fulfill these roles within a certain span of time. Some of these roles are fulfilled by God himself, while other messianic duties are fulfilled by God's messenger. Many of the prophets and messengers of old were prototypes of this anticipated messiah who will appear during the 'fullness of time.' Hence it is written that he comes "in the volume of the book" (Psalm 40:7, Hebrews 10:7) because the Messiah's functions are an amalgamation of all the prophets' missions rolled into one. This is why many of the messianic prophecies have common characteristics. These characteristics show God's messengers being rescued, taken away on aerial objects, and escaping death: Elijah's ascension on the fiery chariot (2 Kings 2:11), Jesus' rise into the clouds (Acts 1:9), and the messiah's strange exaltation to Allah (Holy Qur'an, An-Nisa` 4:158). These prophecies refer to a time when God and his messiah would make their presence known in the world. During such time, God would ensure that various prophecies concerning the Messiah are fulfilled—whether by God himself or if carried out by his Messenger, which explains why there is more than one expected messiah.

While most people's ideas and concepts of the destined messiah may be perceived as a young man in his mid thirties, this image poses conflicts with many of the Biblical and Qur'anic prophecies. Most of the messianic prophecies depict an aged man. The Old Testament describes him as the "Ancient of Days" with white hair:

> *As I looked, "thrones were set in place, and the Ancient of Days took his seat. His clothing was as white as snow; the hair of his head was white like wool. His throne was flaming with fire, and its wheels were all ablaze. – Daniel 7:9*

Too, the New Testament states, "The hairs of his head were white, like white wool, like snow. His eyes were like a flame of fire." (Revelation 1:14). Moreover, the Holy Qur'an describes this one as speaking wisdom to the people in "old age." Surely this could not refer to a man who was crucified in his 30s:

> *When Allah will say: O Jesus, son of Mary, remember My favour to thee and to thy mother, when I strengthened thee with the Holy Spirit; thou spokest to people in the cradle and in old age, and when I taught thee the Book and the Wisdom and the Torah and the Gospel, and... – Al-Ma`idah 5:110*

These scriptures give strong clues to the appearance of that destined deliverer—clues that lead to an older man who would be taught by Allah (God) and confound the world with a uniquely supreme wisdom. Elijah Muhammad is such a man.

During a dinner dialogue with his close followers, the Honorable Elijah Muhammad and Minister Farrakhan discussed that prophesied one who comes in the end:

> **Elijah Muhammad:** So, the Bible gives it to you beautifully… It's just talking about him all over—all the way through, everywhere you look.
> You may start reading a piece and you think it's referring to some other man. When you get through reading it, you change your mind. Ain't this the same man talking to you?
> **Louis Farrakhan:** They give you many names, but it's all talking about you.
> **Elijah Muhammad:** See, that's why it's said, the Messenger says, "Behold I came in the volume of the Book," because it is written of him. Very beautiful, well, that's what the Book says. This is a marvelous thing.[373]

The Honorable Elijah Muhammad did not hesitate to acknowledge that he is the one designated by God to carry out the messianic mission. He did not shy away from expressing that he fulfills much of what is written about Moses, Jesus, Elijah, and several other messianic prototypes. Like Moses, who had a speech impediment, Elijah Muhammad claims he met God face to face (Exodus 33:11). At a certain point, Moses' function was promoted from being a simple prophet into a god while his brother Aaron was made his messenger (Exodus 7:1). Similarly Elijah Muhammad evolved into his messiah-ship and appointed Minister Louis Farrakhan as his National Representative (messenger). Notice that both Moses and Aaron's mission involved the existence of a heavenly power appearing in the clouds and in the night skies that protected and guided the people of God. These prophetic figures and the aerial objects connected to them are indicators of the messianic age wherein a man like Moses would appear with a spokesman like Aaron. This is analogous to the relationship of the Honorable Elijah Muhammad and the Honorable Louis Farrakhan.

The scriptural passages frequently depict a changing of roles among God's messengers: Moses and Aaron evolve into a God and a messenger. Jesus evolves from a messenger into the Christ and his disciples become apostles. Elijah transcends up into God's heavenly chariot and Elisha is granted a double portion of the spirit. These changing of roles and functions are shown to occur after a divine ascension or heavenly meeting. Similarly, the divine roles of

---

[373] Sultan R. Muhammad, *Table Talks of the Honorable Elijah Muhammad - The Transcripts: Volume One*, Second, ed. Table Talks Project Editorial Board (Chicago, IL: MUI Press, 2013). 132.

Messenger Elijah Muhammad and his spokesman Louis Farrakhan would undergo their own evolutions.

It was Louis Farrakhan who discovered that his teacher was more than just a divine messenger, but in fact the Christ/Messiah figure that the world of religion has been expecting. Although Elijah Muhammad proclaimed that Master Fard Muhammad was the Messiah (and God in person), he did not deny the fact that he too would share that divine title of messiah. Aside from outright stating that he is the Christ,[374] Elijah Muhammad made it painfully clear that he was to become that Christ/Messiah who would be rescued from death. His direct connection to Allah (God), his scientists/angels, and the wheel-like UFOs would all play a part in this messianic picture.

THE MESSENGER PREDICTS HIS DEPARTURE UPON THE WHEEL

It cannot be denied that Elijah Muhammad spoke of his escape from death and his destined exaltation to Master Fard Muhammad. Even his son Wallace (Imam Warith Deen Mohammed) acknowledged his father's statements about this exaltation. Imam Mohammed stated, "He did, however, mention his passing, but as hints to the wise. He also said that he would not die, that he would live and be with his God in the end."[375] Like many, Imam Mohammed denounced his father's divinity and his teachings of the Wheel, but time and evidence have now shown that these realities exist just as his father proclaimed.

Elijah Muhammad acknowledged that he fulfills the prophetic roles of those who would be taken away to a celestial position with the Lord, the Supreme Being. This strange occurrence would take place by way of these wheels that he taught about for decades. Muhammad's divine insight into things to come allowed him to forecast and forewarn some of his followers of the near future. He knew that a time would come when he would go away and that his followers would turn to disbelief in his absence. He shared these sentiments during a dinner at his home in December 1973:

> **Elijah Muhammad:** Yes, many… all… you be careful during that time. Yes all of you be careful during that time. Right. You will feel like calling the Messenger a liar.
> **Louis Farrakhan:** But the Book said, "Because of a long delay in the Lord, they went back."

---

[374] Sultan R. Muhammad, *Table Talks of the Honorable Elijah Muhammad – (currently undisclosed from public access)*, Table Talks Project Editorial Board (Chicago, IL: MUI Press, 2013).
[375] Wallace D. Muhammad, *The Teachings of W.D. Muhammad Book I Elementary Level* (Chicago, IL: Mosque No. 2, 1976).

UFOS AND THE MESSIANIC CONNECTION

> **Elijah Muhammad:** This is the time [inaudible] because he's beared witness in such time... that all of you all will walk away and leave me alone. The Messenger[376] told me that outright. He said, "Brother, they will all go back and leave you alone. Alone... Just imagine, in a bout one year, I say about one year, I don't believe it will go over that... one year coming... that you will not care to hear this Teaching. From now, in the coming year. And then your mind will begin to change and shift and you'll think that there's nothing to what he said. That just meant for that time and I think things is going back... and when you start thinking like that, then you'll start slipping.[377]

Clearly Muhammad knew that an ugly period of disbelief in his teachings would arise. He obviously understood and accepted what the prophecies predicted concerning his departure and the slanderous hypocrisy that would overcome his name and the revelation that was revealed to him by the Supreme Being.

Elijah Muhammad's foretelling of what would happen after his departure proved to be true. In two months, he gave what became known as his last sermon in February 1974. The subsequent months were followed with Muhammad stepping back from day to day activities of governing the NOI. In turn, this was a time when hypocrites and government agents would step up their agendas to infiltrate the NOI with disbelief in Muhammad's teachings. This happened exactly as he predicted.

Muhammad knew that his practical teachings about a real God and his wheel-shaped planes would be thrown out of the window. His understanding of the prophecies and his direct communications with Master Fard Muhammad allowed him to know that such a time would come. As a result, the Honorable Elijah Muhammad came out nearly three years before his departure to make known who he would designate to sit in his seat during his absence. In 1972, he called up his faithful servant to come before the believing community, then he shared these words about him:

> I want you to remember, today, I have one of my greatest preachers here. ... What are you hiding behind the sycamore tree for brother? [chuckling]. C'mon around here where they can see you! [A rousing round of applause ensued].

---

[376] The Honorable Elijah Muhammad would sometimes refer to Master Fard Muhammad using the title 'Messenger'. Refer to Problem No. 32 of The Supreme Wisdom, "The Problem Book," (The Nation Of Islam, 1930-1934).
[377] Sultan R. Muhammad, *Table Talks of the Honorable Elijah Muhammad - The Transcripts: Volume One*, Second, ed. Table Talks Project Editorial Board (Chicago, IL: MUI Press, 2013). 136-137.

We have with us today... our great national preacher. The preacher who don't mind going into Harlem, New York, one of the most worst towns in our nation or cities. It is our brother in Detroit and Chicago or New York. But, I want you to remember every week he's on the air helping me to reach those people that I can't get out of my house and go reach them like he.

I want you to pay good attention to his preaching. His preaching is a bearing of witness to me and what God has given to me... This is one of the strongest national preachers that I have in the bounds of North America. Everywhere you hear him, listen to him. Everywhere you see him, look at him. Everywhere he advises you to go, go. Everywhere he advises you to stay from, stay from. For we are thankful to Allah for this great helper of mine, Minister Farrakhan [Another rousing round of applause ensued]...

He's not a proud man. He's a very humble man. If he can carry you across the lake without dropping you in; he don't say when you get on the other side, 'You see what I have done?' He tells you, 'You see what Allah has done.' He doesn't take it upon himself. He's a mighty fine preacher. We hear him every week, and I say continue to hear our Minister Farrakhan...[378]

The Messenger knew that he would leave under strange circumstances and he knew that he had prepared Minister Farrakhan to take his place during his absence (despite a temporary fall that Farrakhan would endure). His foresight undoubtedly made him to know that he would depart in a way that most would assume that he is dead. He made various references to his departure and the effects it would have on his followers who would resort back to disbelief. While many people anticipated his death, Muhammad instead asserted that he would leave to meet with the Supreme Being again.

Like Moses who left and disappeared into a cloud as he went upon the mountain, the Honorable Elijah Muhammad expressed that he would one day leave under similar circumstances. With some of his top officials and followers present at his table, he is recorded discussing his destined departure and how his followers would react after he is gone:

So Moses is a sign that if I was to go away from you for a while, up in the mount of God—in the Mount of God there means that Moses stepped aside to listen to Him. God was the mountain... no imaginary mountain of nature to go up...

The man Moses went up into the mount of God—not just to get the knowledge. It meant that it was up in the height of the wisdom of God...

And I'm saying mount... I didn't say mount-ain. It's up in the mount...

---

[378] Elijah Muhammad, "The Theology of Time (Lecture Series)," Vols. July 30, 1972 (Chicago, IL: MUHAMMAD Mosque No. 2, 1972).

See if the Messenger is missing for a little while and the children down there will be ripping down all his work when they get the chance. Well, that's the same way it will be with my followers... if I go and stay away from you for six months or a year. Whenever I come back, I will hardly know where to come find you.[379]

It is a scenario that is almost surreal to see a man foretelling things that play out exactly as he stated. Either he put forth some extremely lucky guesses or he was, in fact, divinely guided by the Supreme Being. Whether the people understood him or not, the Honorable Elijah Muhammad made numerous public references that he was destined to meet with his teacher, Master Fard Muhammad, upon the Wheel:

Then He [Master Fard Muhammad] told me, "I will give you a Holy Qur'an when you learn how to read Arabic, then I will give you a Holy Qur'an in Arabic." He said, "I made it myself." He showed me that Holy Qur'an in Arabic in September last, but I couldn't read it. I could only recognize one letter in it. I expected Him within a year to come back with that same book.[380]

These quotes show that Elijah Muhammad anticipated and foretold that he would meet again with the Supreme Being who resides on that huge so-called UFO. On several occasions, Minister Farrakhan has cited words that the Honorable Elijah Muhammad shared with him concerning his departure and subsequent return. Muhammad told him, "When you see me again, the power that you will see me exercising, if I did not tell you that I was not God, you would be found worshiping at my feet." These type of comments show how certain Elijah Muhammad was concerning his leaving, his exaltation, and his being empowered by Allah (God). What's even more shocking is that this man foretold how he would escape amidst what seems to be his death.

ELIJAH TAKEN ON A CLOUD

In a letter dated November 25, 1966, the Honorable Elijah Muhammad responded to questions posed by his student, Bernard Cushmeer (now Jabril

---

[379] Sultan R. Muhammad, *Table Talks of the Honorable Elijah Muhammad - The Transcripts: Volume One*, Second, ed. Table Talks Project Editorial Board (Chicago, IL: MUI Press, 2013). 142-143.
[380] Elijah Muhammad, "The Theology of Time (Lecture Series)," Vols. August 20, 1972 (Chicago, IL: MUHAMMAD Mosque No. 2, 1972).

Muhammad) regarding his inevitable departure under strange circumstances. The Messenger responded with these words:

> Remember, Brother, that Daniel said there are 70 weeks for the term upon thy people. The 69th week is something similar to the attack on the woman in Revelations; and it is hinted in the Quran, in symbolic language, and again in Daniel it says in the night they came and they took the prey away; and, to Isaiah he makes mention not of death, but of a taking away and escape of the Messenger from a death plot against him, by the angels (smile).[381]

Here the Messenger expressed his knowledge that after an appointed term among the people, he would be rescued by a band of angels under what some may think is his death. He further makes it clear that this rescue would be orchestrated by God who would accomplish this feat through a dark heavenly cloud:

> In the Psalms prophecy, he was taken under a cover of darkness. While the enemies were after him, God made the heavens a dark thickness of clouds, and under cover of this darkness, God came down and picked him up.[382]

This scenario is in sync with the Holy Qur'an's prophecies concerning the Messiah who would be exalted to Allah under the presumption of death (An-Nisa` 4:157) and the Lamb mentioned in the Book of Revelation who appeared as though he was slain from the earth. This Lamb of God is suddenly found within the heavenly throne among the four creatures, the elders, and the seven spirits—whom Elijah Muhammad described as angels (Revelation 5:6). Strangely the symbolic Lamb is a person who appears to have been dead on earth, but is somehow brought to an exalted assembly, which takes place upon the New Jerusalem (Revelation 21). The New Jerusalem is what Elijah Muhammad and Minister Louis Farrakhan have described synonymously with that colossal Mother Wheel, the heavenly city of God.

The Honorable Elijah Muhammad elucidated this symbolism by stating exactly who and what the Lamb represents. He proclaimed these recorded words in 1972:

> I am that little fellow that He [Allah (God)] had taken off aside and taught. Why I say, 'little fellow'? The Bible makes him little; He didn't make him a big sheep; He said a little lamb.[383]

---

[381] Jabril Muhammad, *Is It Possible That The Honorable Elijah Muhammad Is Still Physically Alive???*, Fourth (Phoenix, AZ: Nuevo Books LLC, 2007). 102-103

[382] Ibid. 103.

[383] Elijah Muhammad, "The Theology of Time (Lecture Series)," Vols. June 4, 1972 (Chicago, IL: MUHAMMAD Mosque No. 2, 1972).

UFOS AND THE MESSIANIC CONNECTION

Two weeks after making that statement, he boldly issued these words in another related address:

> I don't want you to think you're playing with no light boy at all. My size is very small, that's why they symbolically prophesied of me as being a little Lamb instead of a grown up Lamb.[384]

There is no denying that Elijah Muhammad recognized himself as fulfilling the role of the Lamb of God. Is it a coincidence that this man uttered the circumstances surrounding his departure before it took place? What is even more convincing is that he showed the prophetic utterances that substantiated his position. Even those totally opposed to religion, theology, and scriptures would have to bear witness that Elijah Muhammad was given unparalleled insight into matters that the wisest persons in this world could have never imagined. His proclaiming the reality of the wheel-like planes before they were ever a public concern, his bold challenges to authorities to dispute his divine authority, and his comprehensible foretelling of his own departure are just a few reasons why the learned of this world have deceptively withdrawn the truth about Elijah Muhammad and UFOs from the public.

Like many prophets and messengers depicted as being taken away on clouds and winds, Elijah Muhammad likened his mission to that of the Biblical Elijah. Interestingly Elijah of the Bible was a major prophet who challenged the kings and rulers of his day. This prophet is depicted as a radical preacher who challenged the public's false idea of God and contended to a showdown to prove whose God was actually the real God. The criteria to measure this reality was contingent upon whose God would respond from a heavenly source. In the end, Elijah's God proved to be the true and living God. Amazingly, God would show his power by whisking him away on a fiery chariot that takes him to heaven on a whirlwind. Similarly, Elijah Muhammad would do the same. In fact Muhammad exemplified that this biblical picture refers to him:

> It is up to you to listen, and as you listen, read and remember. If God says in the Bible, "before that dreadful day shall come, I will send you Elijah," I am Elijah![385]

---

[384] Elijah Muhammad, "The Theology of Time (Lecture Series)," Vols. June 18, 1972 (Chicago, IL: MUHAMMAD Mosque No. 2, 1972).

[385] Elijah Muhammad, "The Theology of Time (Lecture Series)," Vols. June 4, 1972 (Chicago, IL: MUHAMMAD Mosque No. 2, 1972).

If Elijah Muhammad demonstrated that he fulfils this prophetic role of Elijah, then was he too taken away to that wheel, symbolized in the prophecies as a fiery chariot from heaven? Regardless if anyone believes in the prophetic utterances or not, the facts have proven that the huge Mother Plane and smaller wheels do exist just as Elijah Muhammad represented. Therefore, the possibility of Elijah Muhammad being stealthily rescued by the proven technology of these planes is highly likely. The fact that his situation parallels the prophetic scenario of the Biblical Elijah only adds to the theological proof of his divine role. Even theologians agree that the Biblical Elijah is said to have 'never tasted death.' This means that his time was significantly extended because of his heavenly relevance.

Muhammad's wisdom continues to astound those who measure his profound teachings. He didn't simply preach of Bible stories; instead, he illustrated how his divine mission aligns with the sacred scriptures, leaving no room for naysayers to refute his practicality. He showed how his God-authored wheel-like planes were in the world as a fulfillment of prophecies. Whether one believes in scriptures or not, they cannot deny the existence of these UFOs in the modern world. Therefore, the most cynical pundit would be hypocritical to deny the profundity in Muhammad's message.

MADE TO 'APPEAR' DEAD

Is it a coincidence that practically all of the prophetic figures that the Honorable Elijah Muhammad fulfilled ascended to a celestial position by way of strange vehicles? Isn't it even more perplexing that most of these characters escaped an apparent death, only to be brought in the presence of God Almighty? Did Elijah Muhammad's teacher who is responsible for the phenomenal wheel-shaped UFOs have the power to rescue him from what seemed to be his death? Is the power behind those circular objects capable of such technology? According to Elijah Muhammad, absolutely! He gave more clarifying words concerning his fulfillment of these persons who had experiences of being taken away:

> I am Elijah of your Bible. I am the Muhammad of your Holy Qur'an, not the Muhammad that was here near 1,400 years ago. I am the one that the Holy Qur'an is referring to![386]

The "one that the Holy Qur'an is referring to" happens to be the promised messiah. He is the one who will be directly taught by God himself. This messiah would be given the deeper wisdom of the sacred texts: the Torah,

---

[386] Ibid.

the Gospel, and the Qur'an (Al-Imran 3:48). The Holy Qur'an gives candid descriptions of the messiah, along with the situations surrounding what would appear to be his death. Consider what Allah (God) promises about his messiah:

> *And for their saying: We have killed the Messiah, Jesus, son of Mary, the messenger of Allah, and they killed him not, nor did they cause his death on the cross, but he was made to appear to them as such. And certainly those who differ therein are in doubt about it. They have no knowledge about it, but only follow a conjecture, and they killed him not for certain:*
> – An Nisa` 4:157

Allah (God) offers a certainty that even though it would seem that this person dies, another plan was taking place all along. According to this passage, the Messiah was made to appear as though he was dead, but God used this scenario as a cover for his Messiah's rescue and subsequent exaltation.

It is not impossible for someone to fake his or her own death. There have been many cases of persons successfully doing such. Some have been exposed while other cases remain unsolved. Nonetheless, it would be highly illogical to believe that people of significantly less technology can fool authorities into believing they are dead, then deny that the supreme technology of the wheels are incapable of such.

Interestingly, the Qur'anic phrase *made to appear dead* is translated from the Arabic term *shubbiha*. This term stems from the triliteral root *shīn bā hā* (ش ب ه) or (S-B-H), which signifies the appearance, similarity, or resemblance of something. Here it is made evident that the escape of the Messiah would resemble an apparent death. Perhaps this is why other English translations of this verse state that *"a likeness to him of another was shown to them"*.[387] The methods by which Allah would enact this promise are endless. One could guess that a decoy body was used as some translations suggest, or one could hypothesize that the Messiah was placed in a temporary coma-like state before being revived. After all, many of the reputable UFO abduction cases have reported that the people aboard those crafts have the ability to effectuate inexplicable trances upon abductees that could last for hours or even days.

Is it wise to ignore Muhammad's claims even though his words, deeds, and actions fulfill these characteristics? No other leader of prominence has made the bold claims of being directly taught by Allah (God) and having a direct relationship with these planes (so-called UFOs) as the Honorable Elijah

---

[387] Phrase taken from An Nisa` 4:157, Dr. Laleh Bakhtiar's English translation of the Holy Qur'an.

Muhammad. Furthermore no others have taught that the Supreme Being would use this technology to rescue him in fulfillment of what is written. Not only is there no other leader to make such claims, but there are certainly no others who have offered the practical evidence that Elijah Muhammad presented.

Muhammad provided consistent teachings about his role in Allah's divine scheme and he foretold of a situation that no one but his God could save him from. Only a technology as advanced as the wheel-like planes (UFOs) would be able to rescue him from such a vulnerable predicament. Since it is proven that such highly advanced aerial technology exists, then there is no question that such has the capabilities of rescuing Elijah Muhammad from what seemed to have been his death.

THE MESSENGER OUT OF SIGHT, THE WHEELS OUT OF MIND

> *So when Elijah Muhammad left us, it was said that his teaching of a Mother Plane was a joke, that it was false—it had other meanings, and it was explained away. The very heart of his teaching was ripped out!*[388] – The Honorable Minister Louis Farrakhan

The decades following Muhammad's public ministry have been filled with countless UFO sightings, experiences, and abductions. As more UFO activity took place, the more U.S. Authorities shielded the public from the knowledge of these planes and their direct connection to the Honorable Elijah Muhammad and the Nation of Islam. At a certain point, it seemed as though America's deceitful agenda would prevail. On February 25, 1975, it was reported that the Honorable Elijah Muhammad had passed away at Mercy Hospital in Chicago, Illinois.

Reports immediately ran throughout the world that Elijah Muhammad was dead. These obituary-type reports were released as though the press had already anticipated or planned his death. The mainstream media did not hesitate to express a subtle sense of triumph with news of Elijah Muhammad being dead. Within 24 hours of his assumed death, mainstream journalists mocked his teachings about the Mother Plane. The New York Times ran the following excerpt from their obituary within a day of Muhammad's believed passing:

> Elijah Muhammad was a mystic. But his mysticism was applied; it always had a quite earthly purpose. Forerunning transcendental meditation and other

---

[388] Louis Farrakhan, "The Reality Of The Mother Plane" (Chicago, IL: The Final Call Inc., January 4, 1987).

modern popular sects, he saw the need for 20th-century religions to declare themselves based on science, not faith. Islam was a science and a "way of life," not a religion, he said. Yet, he would refer to the Mother Plane, a mysterious space ship with superior beings, giant black gods or something like that, that patrolled the universe, keeping an eye on the devil and ready to rescue Black Muslims from Armageddon.[389]

This was a time for American powers and their controlled media to gloat in the idea that the anointed representative of those wheel-like planes was no longer around to preach his controversial theology. They used it as an opportunity to discredit his teachings of the Mother Plane by falsely attributing giant creatures that have no place in Muhammad's teachings concerning the Wheel. The media had already begun twisting the truth about the wheels before a funeral arrangement had even taken place. There had to have already been a deliberate plan afoot—a plan that involved the highest echelons of the U.S. Government.

The absence of the Messenger posed numerous challenges within the Nation of Islam and Black people in general. The U.S. Government seized upon this time as an opportunity to sway the public and the NOI away from the core truths it was founded upon. The FBI's Counter Intelligence Program sought to misdirect the Nation of Islam from its 'nationalistic' efforts and teachings and to focus the NOI's attention to a strictly religious movement. The FBI anticipated the departure of the Messenger and documented their evil intentions to subdue the movement:

> We should plan how to change the philosophy of the NOI to one of the strictly religious and self-improvement orientation, deleting the race hatred and separate nationhood aspects.
>
> In this connection Chicago should consider what counterintelligence action might be needed now or at the time of Elijah Muhammad's death to bring about such a change in NOI philosophy. Important considerations should include the identity, strengths, and weaknesses, of any contenders for NOI leadership. What are the positions of our [BUREAU DELETION] informants in regard to leadership? How could potential leaders be turned or neutralized?
>
> The alternative to changing the philosophy of the NOI is the destruction of the organization. This might be accomplished through generating factionalism among the contenders for Elijah Muhammad's leadership or through legal action in probate court on his death. Chicago should consider

---

[389] C. Gerald Fraser, "Elijah Muhammad Dead; Black Muslim Leader, 77," *The New York Times*, February 26, 1975.

the question of how to generate the factionalism necessary to destroy the NOI by splitting into several groups.[390]

The Government's plot to destroy Elijah Muhammad and the NOI seemed to have succeeded. Despite the Honorable Elijah Muhammad's obvious choice of Minister Louis Farrakhan to sit in his seat as father over the house, the FBI's selection found its way into the leadership capacity instead. Upon what appeared to be the death of Elijah Muhammad in February 1975, his son, Wallace D. Muhammad (now known as Imam Warith Deen Mohammed), assumed leadership over the Nation of Islam. Shortly after Imam Mohammed's assumption of leadership, numerous changes began to take place within the Nation of Islam. Coincidentally, these changes occurred just as the FBI intended. Considering the rocky relationship Imam Mohammed had with his father, having been put in 'bad standings' with the Muslim community on several occasions, the Imam was a fitting candidate to facilitate the FBI's objectives to misdirect the NOI from its 'nationhood aspects'. Those 'nationhood aspects' include the belief that God intervened into human affairs by appearing in the person of Master Fard Muhammad who rendered a gigantic plane called the Mother Wheel, which would be used for the salvation of his chosen people—the Black people of America.

Teachings of God appearing in person, the Mother Wheel, and the baby planes were literally mocked and ridiculed by the new leadership of the NOI. The vast body of wisdom that was revealed to the Honorable Elijah Muhammad was abandoned just as he foretold. The very character and person of Elijah Muhammad was defamed. Louis Farrakhan, the National Representative of the Honorable Elijah Muhammad was eventually demoted and relegated to preaching at a small mosque on the Westside of Chicago. For all practical purposes, the objectives of the U.S. Government to misdirect, destroy, and dismantle the Nation of Islam were achieved... so it seemed.

The departure of the Messenger left many in doubt about his teachings and he was no longer there to answer their questions: *Did he really meet God? How could God allow the Messenger to die and let the Nation of Islam fall from its core principles? Is the Mother Plane real or was it just a myth that Elijah Muhammad created to make himself seem divine?* With many of the Believers startled and confused over Muhammad's departure, these questions and many more were left unanswered. Consequently, the NOI took a turn away from its core teachings. The NOI had lost nearly all of the material gains it had acquired and unfortunately lost the spiritual core that had carried this group to its heights. With the Honorable Elijah Muhammad now gone, the hypocrites

---

[390] FBI COUNTERINTELLIGENCE PROGRAM, "RACIAL INTELLIGENCE (NATION OF ISLAM)," *BLACK NATIONALIST - HATE GROUPS* (FBI Counter Intelligence Program, January 7, 1969).

and government agents were able to manipulate the direction of the NOI. The U.S. Government played a significant role in redirecting the NOI as FBI programs sought to destroy the NOI for years anyway. The physical absence of the Messenger appeared to be a perfect opportunity to destroy the Muslims, the good name of Elijah Muhammad, and his controversially unorthodox teachings. The inherent teachings about the Mother Plane and its smaller wheels were explained away. The Nation of Islam that once was, seemed to be no more. The world believed Elijah Muhammad was dead and there was no more talk of the Mother Plane.

As Louis Farrakhan struggled to make sense out of the new direction the NOI had gone, it came to a point when he could no longer tolerate the disrespect of Elijah Muhammad, his supreme wisdom, and the God he represents. After almost two years of attempting to go along with the newly selected leadership of the NOI, Minister Farrakhan had to peacefully walk away. This era would be a serious trial for Farrakhan as he became rather lost without the physical presence of his Messenger to guide him. He traveled the Muslim world, performed Hajj[391] and tried to find guidance through the traditional Islamic ways of devotion, but it did little to fulfill the void of guidance he now lacked with his leader absent. It was in this state of confusion and struggle that he was visited by one of his colleagues, Minister Bernard Cushmeer. Cushmeer (now known as Jabril Muhammad) presented Minister Farrakhan with a book he had written pertaining to the Honorable Elijah Muhammad's divine exaltation. Minister Farrakhan gives an account of the significance of this book and its reawakening affect on him:

> He (Jabril) gave me what I would call a commentary or something that you would add to a book that's not in the book and he gave it to me to read on the Honorable Elijah Muhammad possibly being alive. And I didn't even want to waste time with something like that. Because at that time I said, "Oh poor fella, you know, well we're going to go on and rebuild the work of the Honorable Elijah Muhammad."

> One day, almost two years later, he was in my Lincoln Continental in Chicago, and he saw what he had given me, kind of ground up a little under the front driver's seat. So he took it out and smoothed it out, like one would do a wrinkled coat or shirt and knew that it wasn't destroyed. And he put it back in my hands.

---

[391] **Hajj** is the pilgrimage to the holy city of Mecca, which every able-bodied Muslim is expected to perform at least once in his or her lifetime.

I finally decided I'll entertain him. I'll read it. And as I began to read what he wrote, the words of the Honorable Elijah Muhammad began to make sense. They couldn't make sense if he were dead. But, if he escaped a death plot, then the words that he shared with me made almost perfect sense.[392]

Once he finally began reading the book, the scales were removed from his eyes and he realized the Messenger's words to him were completely true. It became painfully obvious again that the Honorable Elijah Muhammad's words and mission were not in vain. Of the many Believers who fell away from truth after the departure, Louis Farrakhan became the first to awaken to the reality that Elijah Muhammad is physically alive. He became what the Bible describes as one of "the first fruits of those who have fallen asleep" (1 Corinthians 15:20).

The Minister's transition was much like the transitory period between Peter's fall and the sudden rise of the Apostle Paul. Peter signifies Jesus' chief disciple who represented Jesus before his ascension to meet with God. The Apostle Paul represents the chief representative of Jesus on earth after Jesus' ascension. Minister Farrakhan's tenure as the Messenger's National Representative before the departure is indicative of Peter's chief discipleship because his leader was present to guide him. The Minister's temporary fall after the Honorable Elijah Muhammad's departure also parallels Peter's role. Like Peter, Minister Farrakhan underwent a temporary state of confusion after his Messenger left the scene. But as it was prayed, his faith did not totally leave him. After thirty months away from the Messenger, Minister Farrakhan's faith was restored. His eyes became opened. His sudden reawakening to the truth of Elijah Muhammad's messianic role and the wheels that accompany his messianic mission removed the scales from his eyes like Paul's epiphany on the road to Damascus (Acts 26). Like Paul who rose to prominence after Jesus' departure and made Christ's resurrection known, Minister Farrakhan rose from his slump of faith to make the commission and resurrection of his savior, the Honorable, known to the world. It was Paul's unpopular preaching of a resurrection that made his job uniquely distinguished in the Bible. Likewise, Farrakhan's unpopular preaching that Elijah Muhammad escaped death and serves as the right hand of God clearly distinguishes him as fulfilling Paul's prophetic role.

These prophetic figures are indicative of Minister Farrakhan's roles before and after the departure of the Honorable Elijah Muhammad. It was the Apostle Paul who asserted, "And if Christ be not raised, your faith is in vain…" (1 Corinthians 15:17, AKJV). Minister Farrakhan makes this same plea, but with more practicality. If Muhammad introduced the reality of these highly advanced wheel-like planes that are capable of accomplishing unfathomable

---

[392] Jabril Muhammad, *Closing The Gap: Inner Views of the Heart, Mind & Sprit of the Honorable Minister Louis Farrakhan* (Chicago, IL: FCN Publishing Company, 2006). 326-332.

UFOS AND THE MESSIANIC CONNECTION

feats, would not these crafts have the capabilities to rescue their representative as promised? If these crafts do not exist or do not have the ability to save him, then everything the NOI teaches would be in vain. After all, everything the Honorable Elijah Muhammad and Minister Farrakhan preach is predicated upon the notion that Elijah Muhammad met God in person who showed him these planes, which would be used to reign destruction on his enemies and save the righteous. This is the work of the much-anticipated Messenger-Messiah.

Figure 8: THE DEPARTURE & RESCUE

Clockwise from top: A thick darkening cloud, Minister Louis Farrakhan (1970s), A gravesite for Elijah Muhammad, A death certificate for the 'assumed dead' Elijah Muhammad, Messenger Elijah Muhammad.

THEY PLAN AND ALLAH PLANS

And they planned and Allah (also) planned, and Allah is the best of planners.—The Holy Qur'an, Al-Imran 3:54

If Elijah Muhammad made accurate predictions about UFOs, his departure, how his followers would abandon his teaching, and even his rescue, then is it possible that Elijah Muhammad is physically alive? Furthermore, do those UFOs that he introduced to the world have the capabilities of rescuing him from an apparent death?

The Honorable Elijah Muhammad's 1966 letter to Jabril Muhammad played out as he noted. There he referenced his anticipated departure under the cover of death. He made strong references to the 70 weeks mentioned in the apocalyptic Book of Daniel, wherein he states, "Remember, Brother, that Daniel said there are 70 weeks for the term upon thy people." The number seven (7) and its multiples bear significant meanings related to the time he would spend before being rescued. Stemming from the Arabic word *sab'a* (سبع), Ancient Arabs thought this to be a "perfect" number. It is from the same Semitic root that the word *Sabbath* is derived, which happens to be the era when God would usher in his perfect world. Fittingly, the Honorable Elijah Muhammad was **77** years old during the end of his term among the people.

In Jewish Talmudic traditions, the seventh heaven known in Hebrew as **Araboth** (ערבות) is where the throne of the Lord is located surrounded by flying wheels called **ofanim** (אופנים) and other angels. This perfect celestial place is further described in this manner:

> Arabot, where justice and righteousness, the treasures of life and of blessing, the souls of the righteous and the dew of resurrection are to be found. There are the ofanim, the seraphim, and the hayyot of holiness, the ministering angels and the throne of glory; and over them is enthroned the great King.[393]

Muhammad's age during the time of his departure (77), it seems, has a far too interesting correlation with the perfect time and place where one can be resurrected to the presence of God, his angels, and flying wheels (ofanim).

Aside from the numerical signs of his age, the date of his departure plays another significant factor in his prophetic exaltation. Of all the days of the year for such an act to occur, how is it that Elijah Muhammad's reported death took place on the eve of Saviour's Day, the most revered day in the NOI? Saviour's Day is the 26th of February when the Nation of Islam celebrates the birth anniversary of Master Fard Muhammad who was on born that day in

---

[393] Jewish Encyclopedia, "ANGELOLOGY," *The unedited full-text of the 1906 Jewish Encyclopedia* (JewishEncyclopedia.com, 1906).

UFOS AND THE MESSIANIC CONNECTION

1877. He is known as the Mahdi and he is the ultimate power behind the wheel-shaped UFOs. Is it just a coincidence or is this an obvious sign of the divine scheme that Elijah Muhammad alluded to?

In the previously mentioned 1966 letter to Jabril Muhammad (then known as Bernard Cushmeer), Elijah Muhammad alluded to how God's angels would covertly save him through a thickening dark cloud, which would take him up to God.[394] The eyewitness account of Joshua Farrakhan sheds more light on this matter. Joshua, who is a son of Minister Farrakhan, was present at the hospital room during the exact time of the alleged death of Muhammad. He shared numerous accounts of the eerie events and circumstances occurring at the hospital. This included the sudden emergence and vanishing of a huge thick dark cloud that covered the area surrounding Mercy Hospital. Here are words from Joshua's firsthand account:

> I walked to the end of the corridor back to where the lounge area is, and all of a sudden, from an early nice sunny day, all of a sudden, out of nowhere, there was this huge, black monstrous-looking cloud, almost like the kind you see in Poltergeist, where rolling clouds—I don't know if that's what you call them—but it was a scary-looking monster, the cloud. And it was very dark, and it was carrying a storm with it. You know, rain, and electricity...

> I saw a little lightning. The lightning seemed like it traveled in the cloud, instead of striking down or out. You know, right across the cloud. Very thick—Coming from over the lake. Coming towards—I could see the lake, and I could see part of, you know, downtown.[395]

Joshua's recollection of this event holds an uncanny similarity to the Messenger's letter to Jabril concerning the use of a thickening dark cloud. Elijah Muhammad spoke of his personal relationship with the angels who would use this darkening cloud for his rescue. He again openly declared that these angels (whom he interchangeably referred to as scientists) assured him of their assistance during this special part of his mission:

> There was two of that type of people visiting my home. They both look like brothers. Whenever there is a God-raised man or prophet to do a big job, these type of scientists [angels] visits him to assure him of their friendship, that whenever the right time comes, they will be with him. "We will take care of you". These are the type of Scientists that you read of in the Bible who

---

[394] Jabril Muhammad, *Is It Possible That The Honorable Elijah Muhammad Is Still Physically Alive???*, Fourth (Phoenix, AZ: Nuevo Books LLC, 2007).

[395] Jabril Muhammad, "How well do we understand the Minister and his work?," *The Final Call*, November 15, 2010.

wanted to go forth and do this and another one do that. These are the ones I'm telling you about who visited me at my home. They have orders by Allah to do a certain job.[396]

Mother Tynnetta Muhammad, wife of the Honorable Elijah Muhammad attests to this visit. She has spoken and written of these accounts:

> It was from this country [Turkey] that the Honorable Elijah Muhammad described the appearance of one of the scientists (angels) who had a twin brother who visited his home (National Palace) in the year 1974, just prior to his departure. He is the one who sat at his dinner table next to him at his left side, who was described to us as having power over the fire in the atmosphere. I interpreted this as one who came to inform the Honorable Elijah Muhammad of the time that was approaching and preparation for his departure. The rest is now a part of history. [397]

Tynnetta Muhammad also described the ubiquitous presence of this light-skinned scientist during and after The Messenger's alleged death. He was seen at the Messenger's last sermon—Saviour's Day 1974. He was seen praying over the Messenger at the hospital during the alleged death and he appeared at the Messenger's home within days afterward. What would this angel be doing hanging around at such a critical time unless he was acting according to the covert rescue and exaltation of the Messenger as promised? Remember, these angelic scientists assured him that they would take care of him at the right time.

As the Messenger's wife, Tynnetta Muhammad also serves as a firsthand witness to the majesty surrounding the Messenger. After all, she was actually there to witness these events herself. Her children, Ishmael and Rasul, have also given accounts and testimonies about how they never believed that the body they saw in the casket was that of their father, Elijah Muhammad. They and others like Jabril Muhammad had knowledgeable insight regarding when the Messenger would leave and who he would choose to lead the NOI in his absence.

As it turned out, Messenger Muhammad knew that his enemies and the hypocrites would rise, causing the NOI to fall, which is why he came out three years before the enemies could gain a stronghold over the NOI. Here, the Messenger let the world know who his choice was by instructing the NOI to follow Minister Farrakhan. This was like Jesus laying the keys of authority on Peter who was the rock upon whom his temple would be built (Matthew

---

[396] Elijah Muhammad, "The Theology of Time (Lecture Series)," Vols. July 9, 1972 (Chicago, IL: MUHAMMAD Mosque No. 2, 1972).
[397] Tynnetta Muhammad, "The Mystical Link between The Whirling Dervishes and the Mongolian People of Central Asia," *The Final Call,* January 08, 2008.

16:18). This act was similar to David coming before Israel to solidify Solomon as the one to sit in his seat over the kingdom (1 Chronicles 28:5). Elijah Muhammad actually foretold of this plot because he told Minister Farrakhan that there would be a time when the believers would abandon him, call him a liar, and would not care to even hear his teachings after he leaves.[398] Even though the U.S. Government and internal enemies worked to misdirect and destroy the NOI, their plan was no match for Allah's plan. Just when it seemed that the Nation of Islam was all but conquered, Minister Farrakhan was divinely prepared to uplift and rebuild the name, works, and teachings of the Honorable Elijah Muhammad. Regardless to one's attitude toward him, Minister Farrakhan is by far the number one proponent of Elijah Muhammad's mission and the wheel-shaped planes that were promised to save him.

---

[398] Sultan R. Muhammad, *Table Talks of the Honorable Elijah Muhammad - The Transcripts: Volume One*, Second, ed. Table Talks Project Editorial Board (Chicago, IL: MUI Press, 2013). 136-137.

13. THE VISION-LIKE EXPERIENCE

THE NIGHT JOURNEY

Once Farrakhan was reawakened to see his teacher's divine exaltation, he did not skip a beat to resume building the work of the Nation of Islam after it had been usurped (as Muhammad foretold). It was Saviours' Day, February 22, 1981 that Minister Farrakhan shocked the world by publicly revealing that Elijah Muhammad is physically alive. This occurred to the dismay of many supporters. Yet despite the inevitable ridicule and scorn, he has not deterred from his position. Many supporters and believers were disappointed at the Minister's revelation and assumed that he had reached a level of insanity. It was reported that some people left out of the assembly at that very moment. Yet Farrakhan has continued preaching such an unpopular truth at the risk of appearing insane. After all, the whole world believed that Elijah Muhammad died in 1975. At least that's what the news reported throughout the world.

In 1984 the Minister published an article in The Final Call Newspaper wherein he wrote these daring words:

"I, Louis Farrakhan, am saying to the world that the Honorable Elijah Muhammad is not physically dead. I am further stating that he was made to appear as such as written in the Bible and in the Holy Qur'an, in order that the scriptures might be fulfilled.

"We stand ready, at any time, to pay for the exhuming of the 'body' of the Honorable Elijah Muhammad and we stand ready to pay for the two dentists who worked on his teeth to compare their dental records with the dental records obtained from examination of the 'body.' We will also pay for two other dentists to make an examination and give their findings.

"I am willing to go before the world to be seen as one whose belief that the Honorable Elijah Muhammad is physically alive is false; or, be manifested as the true representative of the Mahdi and the Messiah, the Christ that the world is now looking for and whose return is imminent."[399]

Certainly, if Minister Farrakhan is an insane man, then his enemies could easily take advantage of this opportunity to invalidate his character and

---

[399] Jabril Muhammad, *Is It Possible That The Honorable Elijah Muhammad Is Still Physically Alive???*, Fourth (Phoenix, AZ: Nuevo Books LLC, 2007). Back cover.

THE VISION-LIKE EXPERIENCE

his claims. Be mindful that these words have been spoken and printed on a global platform. He has welcomed world scrutiny to disprove his position that the Honorable Elijah Muhammad is physically alive due to the power of those wheels. With all of the ridicule that Minister Farrakhan has endured, no power has stepped up to accept his challenge. The Minister has even promised to pay for the exhumation process.

For a man to make such claims indicates that he is either insane or he knows the truth about something. Like his father, the Honorable Elijah Muhammad, Farrakhan has challenged the Presidents, kings, rulers, and governments of the world to contend with the truth that Allah (God) revealed. In other words, this is no feeble showdown that Farrakhan is calling for. This is the ultimate battle between God and Satan. How is it that an unarmed Black man can challenge the world's rulers to determine who is right and who is wrong, yet none have accepted the challenge?

Although no power has taken the Minister up on his offer, this has not stopped them from plotting against him and the NOI. As Farrakhan continuously worked to rebuild the NOI, he unintentionally stumbled upon a heated controversy with members of the Jewish community in 1984. Farrakhan defended Reverend Jesse Jackson when Jews threatened him during his Presidential campaign. Since then, the Jews have wrongfully forwarded their attacks against the Minister. This controversy has ensued and exacerbated for decades as Jews have falsely labeled Minister Farrakhan and the Nation of Islam as *anti-Semitic* and have used their power and influence to dissuade resources from the NOI. Of course, the root of this controversy stems from the fact that Elijah Muhammad proved that Black people in America fit the prophetic 'chosen people of God.' Farrakhan has continued that truth by exposing those whom Jesus called 'the Synagogue of Satan.'

Since 1984 the Jews have pursued any opportunity to defame and thwart Minister Farrakhan's efforts, much like they did Jesus in the New Testament. As the heated controversy with the Jews ensued, they eventually called for his death chanting, "Who do you want? Farrakhan! How do you want him? Dead!" The Minister traveled the country speaking while Jews were on his trail. During a time of international turmoil with Jews planning his death, government plots, and crack cocaine consuming Black communities, Minister Farrakhan took a detour of his rigorous schedule and resorted to Tepotzlan, Mexico. It was here that he would undergo an experience that would change the course of his life and the course of history. The power of the Supreme Being was made manifest in a vision-like experience where Minister Farrakhan communicated directly with the Honorable Elijah Muhammad—a man who was supposed to have died ten years earlier. The following is an excerpt of a press conference where Minister Farrakhan publicly details what took place during this vision-like experience:

> In a tiny town in Mexico, called Tepotzlan, there is a mountain on the top of which is the ruins of a temple dedicated to *Quetzacoatl*, the Christ-figure of Central and South America – a mountain which I have climbed several times. However, on the night of **September 17, 1985**, I was carried up on that mountain, in a vision, with a few friends of mine. As we reached the top of the mountain, a Wheel, or what you call an unidentified flying object (UFO), appeared at the side of the mountain and called to me to come up into the Wheel. Three metal legs appeared from the Wheel, giving me the impression that it was going to land, but it never came over the mountain.
>
> Being somewhat afraid, I called to the members of my party to come with me, but a voice came from the Wheel saying, "Not them; just you." I was told to relax and a beam of light came from the Wheel and I was carried up on this beam of light into the Wheel.
>
> I sat next to the pilot, however, I could not see him. I could only feel his presence. As the Wheel lifted off from the side of the mountain, moving at a terrific speed, I knew I was being transported to the Mother Wheel, which is a human-built planet, a half-mile by a half-mile that the Honorable Elijah Muhammad had taught us of for nearly 60 years. The pilot, knowing that I was fearful of seeing this great, mechanical object in the sky, maneuvered his craft in such a way that I would not see the Mother Wheel (Plane) and then backed quickly into it and docked in a tunnel. I was escorted by the pilot to a door and admitted into a room.
>
> I shall not bother you with a description of the room, but suffice it to say that at the center of the ceiling was a speaker and through this speaker I heard the voice of the Honorable Elijah Muhammad speaking to me as clearly as you are hearing my voice this morning.
>
> He spoke in short cryptic sentences and as he spoke a scroll full of cursive writing rolled down in front of my eyes, but it was a projection of what was being written in my mind. As I attempted to read the cursive writing, which was in English, the scroll disappeared and the Honorable Elijah Muhammad began to speak to me.
> He said, "President Reagan has met with the Joint Chiefs of Staff to plan a war. I want you to hold a press conference in Washington, D.C., and announce their plan and say to the world that you got the information from me, Elijah Muhammad, on the Wheel."
>
> He said to me that he would not permit me to see him at that time. However, he said that I had one more thing to do and when that one more thing was done that I could come again to the Wheel and I would be permitted to see him face to face.

THE VISION-LIKE EXPERIENCE

He then dismissed me. I entered the small wheel and the pilot whom I still could not see, moved the craft out of the tunnel and took it up to a terrific height and maneuvered his craft that I might look down upon the Mother Wheel. I saw a city in the sky. With great speed it brought me back to earth and dropped me off near Washington where I then proceeded into this city to make The Announcement.[400]

Figure 9: THE CLEAR EVIDENCE

Clockwise from top left: Betty and Barney Hill in 1960s, Pilot Kenneth Arnold who sighted flying saucers in 1947, Captain Kenju Terauchi (pilot of JAL Flight 1628) sighted a humongous walnut-shaped Mother Plane with two smaller ones in 1986, Former U.S. Government & Military officials disclose testimonials regarding UFOs and the Government's cover-up, President Kirsan Iliymzhinov was abducted by 'people' on a circular UFO on September 17, 1997. Center: The Honorable Minister Louis Farrakhan during a 1989 press conference where he revealed that he spoke with the Honorable Elijah Muhammad on the Wheel.

---

[400] Louis Farrakhan, "The Announcement: International Press Conference " (Washington, DC, October 24, 1989).

Up to this point, Minister Farrakhan's belief in his teacher being alive was based solely on his faith, his understanding in the prophecies and the words that Elijah Muhammad foretold would happen. Now Minister Farrakhan's faith became solidified even more because he witnessed this experience for himself. Although there was no doubt that this was real to the Minister, the ultimate test would be how others react to his experience.

A few years had passed before the Minister further confirmed that his experience was real. Several national newspapers eased-out reports that Reagan had actually met (around the time of the vision) with the Joint Chiefs of Staff to plan a war with Libya,[401][402] These articles and reports had occurred just as the Minister was told from the Honorable Elijah Muhammad during the vision-like experience

The vision that Minister Farrakhan experienced on September 17, 1985 parallels the Night Journey of Prophet Muhammad (PBUH) documented in the Holy Qur'an where it reads:

> *Glory to Him Who carried His servant by night from the Sacred Mosque to the Remote Mosque, whose precincts We blessed, that We might show him of Our signs! Surely He is the Hearing, the Seeing.* – Al-Isra` 17:1

This passage reflects one of the most significant episodes in the life of the Prophet and the history of Islam. In essence, the Prophet had an experience whereas he was carried away in the middle of the night from Arabia to Jerusalem. During this Night Journey, he ascended through the Seven Heavens greeting various prophets until he reached *Al-Bait al-Ma'mur* (Allah's house).[403] Here, he was escorted by the angel Jabril into the inner-sanctum of Allah (God) where he spoke with his Lord. It was here that Prophet Muhammad (PBUH) was given more instructive guidance from the Supreme Being. Like Minister Farrakhan's vision-like experience, this episode would pose a significant trial for the believers. If his experience did not occur, then he could justifiably be considered a mad man. However, if the experience proves true, then it would clearly pinpoint who the designated voice of Allah (God) is. This was the dilemma of the Prophet. This was the dilemma of the Minister.

Islamic scholars acknowledge that the Prophet's Night Journey posed a serious trial for the early Muslims. Dr. Tariq Ramadan, professor of Islamic Studies at Oxford University gives this commentary on the aftermath of the Prophet's Night Journey:

---

[401] The Atlanta Journal, "U.S. planned to invade Libya in '85," *The Washington Post*, February 20, 1987, The Atlanta Journal ed.: A/1.
[402] Stephen Engleberg, "Egypt-U.S. Plan to Raid Libya Reported," *The New York Times*, February 21, 1987: 3.
[403] Ṣaḥīḥ al-Bukhārī, "4.429 Narrated Malik bin Sasaa ," *Al-Hadith*.

THE VISION-LIKE EXPERIENCE

The trial that Muhammad's Night Journey presented for his fellow Muslims occurred at a moment when they were struggling with a most difficult situation. Tradition reports that a few Muslims left Islam, but most trusted Muhammad. A few weeks later, facts confirmed some elements of his account, for instance the arrival of caravans whose coming he had announced (having seen them on his way back) and of which he had given a precise description.[404]

Today, the world is faced with the trial of taking heed to the designated voice of God who represents the wheel-like planes as proof of his God's presence and power. That voice is echoed through the Honorable Minister Louis Farrakhan. His experience is only one of many factors that give credence to his divine support just as it did with the Holy Prophet Muhammad (PBUH) over 1400 years earlier. In fact, Farrakhan's experience was forecasted by the Night Journey of the Prophet.

The Prophet's strange experience took place on a flying steed known in Arabic as *Al-Buraq*. While the actual vehicle is described as a steed-like creature, the actual meaning of Al-Buraq refers to 'the lightning'. This too describes the modern UFOs that have been recorded and described as vessels of light that travel at speeds resembling lightning. Therefore, *Buraq* signifies an extremely fast vessel of light that has been designated by Allah (God) to aid his messengers. Ironically, some of the traditionalists Muslims have rejected Elijah Muhammad's teachings concerning the Mother Wheel and the accompanying baby planes, calling it 'mythical' and 'un-Islamic.' Yet some traditionalists will deny all the evidence that proves these modern wheels exist simply to hold on to traditions that they don't truly understand.

In the case of the Prophet 1400 years ago, it is said that his journey took him from his homeland of Arabia to the remote place in Jerusalem. Similarly, Minister Farrakhan's Night Journey led him to the NEW JERUSALEM where the throne of God is located.

A PRESIDENTIAL PROBLEM

President Ronald Reagan was in office during the Minister's vision-like experience when the voice of the Honorable Elijah Muhammad warned that the President had met with the Joint Chiefs of Staff to plan a war. The Minister understood this to mean a war against Libya, a small African Islamic nation, which was only a sign of the Government's planned war against Black people

---

[404] Tariq Ramadan, *In The Footsteps of The Prophet: Lessons from the Life of Muhammad* (Oxford University Press, 2009).

and the Nation of Islam. This is quite significant considering that Ronald Reagan witnessed a UFO while he was Governor of California. He described the UFO as moving very fast and that it "went up at a 45 degree angle," he continued these words to reporter Norman C. Miller about his 1974 sighting:

> We followed it for several minutes. It was a bright white light. We followed it to Bakersfield, and all of a sudden to our utter amazement it went straight up into the heavens.[405]

Reagan took his UFO fascination with him to the White House when he became President. However his fascination was not one of welcoming joy. Instead, Reagan expressed his antagonistic sentiments toward the wheel-like planes and the man who represents them. As President, he proposed the creation of the Strategic Defense Initiative (SDI), better known to the public as his Star Wars project. This initiative sought to produce military weaponry capable of fighting against powers beyond the earth's atmosphere. President Reagan quite frequently used international platforms to convey his attitude toward the power behind the UFOs referring to them as 'aliens' and 'extraterrestrials.' Here are his famous words from his address to the United Nations:

> Can we and all nations not live in peace? In our obsession with antagonisms of the moment, we often forget how much unites all the members of humanity. Perhaps we need some outside, universal threat to make us recognize this common bond. I occasionally think how quickly our differences worldwide would vanish if we were facing an alien threat from outside this world. And yet, I ask you, is not an alien force already among us? What could be more alien to the universal aspirations of our peoples than war and the threat of war?[406]

On other occasions Reagan expressed some of the same subtle sentiments about an outside alien attack:

> I couldn't help but say to him, just think how easy his task and mine might be in these meetings that we held if suddenly there was a threat to this world from some other species from another planet outside in the universe. We'd forget all the little local differences that we have between our countries and we

---

[405] Stephen J. Spignes, *The UFO Book of Lists* (Citadel Press, 2000). 72.
[406] Ronald Reagan, "Address to the 42nd Session of the United Nations General Assembly," *The United Nations General Assembly* (New York, NY, September 21, 1987).

THE VISION-LIKE EXPERIENCE

would find out once and for all that we really are all human beings here on this earth together.[407]

Farrakhan's public announcements about his vision further troubled the Reagan Administration. The vision exposed the President's war plans and thereby interfered with America's foreign and domestic policies. This intensified Reagan's efforts to develop space missile programs. Reagan's witness account of UFO technology worried him to rely heavily on his astrologer to make important decisions in the White House. His entire schedule is said to have been coordinated by his astrologer, Joan Quigley.[408] This further confirms the Honorable Elijah Muhammad's words that the U.S. Government retains scholars to study prophecy for the purpose of trying to see how they can get around their foretold chastisement.[409]

Clearly President Reagan perceived the reality of these wheel-like UFOs as an alien threat. Like King Herod in the Bible, he sought counsel from his astrologers to interpret the signs of the heavens. These signs denoted the presence of God's expected deliverer and savior, yet Herod devised an abominable scheme to kill God's servant. Like Herod, Reagan used beautiful words to cover his mischief toward Minister Louis Farrakhan and the Nation of Islam. It was during the Reagan Administration that the all-White U.S. Senate officially censured Minister Farrakhan for his truthful statements about Israel.[410] The Jewish-influenced media falsified Farrakhan's true statements and labeled them as anti-Semitic causing significant loss of friends and resources from the NOI. This calumny against Minister Farrakhan affected Black America altogether. The mere fact that the most powerful government in the world censured a man for speaking truth proves that they are threatened by his voice. It also signifies that the Government is influenced by a Satanic power. It is that same power that antagonizes Minister Farrakhan, the Nation of Islam, and the UFO reality today.

---

[407] Ronald Reagan, "Remarks of the President to Fallston High School Students and Faculty," *The White House Transcripts* (Fallston, MD, December 4, 1985).
[408] Barrett Seaman, "Good Heavens! An astrologer dictating the President's schedule?," *Time Magazine*, May 16, 1988.
[409] Jabril Muhammad, "The Wheel," *Lecture by Minister Jabril Muhammad* (Phoenix, AZ, September 18, 1985).
[410] United States Senate, "To express the sense of the Senate relating to Louis Farrakhan," *S.AMDT.3363 to H.R.5712*, Sponsor: Sen. Don Nickles [OK] (June 28, 1984). Status: Amendment SP 3363 agreed to in Senate by Yea-Nay Vote. 95-0. Record Vote No: 187.

The Minister's vision-like experience exposed the secret war plans of the U.S. Government towards Black people and the Muslim world. The CIA and other Government agencies worked to limit his influence in America and overseas. In 1986 Minister Farrakhan was banned from the United Kingdom on the notion that he was somehow subversive and anti-Semitic. Governments collaborated to ban the Minister from entering the UK strictly because the Jews labeled him Anti-Semitic, even though he has NO record of harming Jews or anyone else! Yet these same governments welcome nuclear arms, drugs, diseases, pornography, and all manner of filth. What is it about Minister Farrakhan that has the most powerful world governments afraid of an unarmed man with no record of violence? The words he speaks must have some truth and power to them! Though commoners may know little about its significance, world governments are well aware and cautious of Minister Farrakhan's connection to so-called UFOs.

The U.S. Government's position against Farrakhan has resembled the Bible's King Aram who sought after Elisha (Elijah's representative) because God revealed to Elisha what was taking place in the king's secret quarter (2 Kings 6:11-12). Similarly the Vision gave Minister Farrakhan direct insight into the secret plans taking place within the highest echelons of government. Just as God delivered Elisha from King Aram's army during what seemed to be a vulnerable moment, Farrakhan has withstood the vilest attacks from the most powerful government in the modern world. Perhaps what is most remarkable is that he claims that the power of the wheels (UFOs) is the power that guides and protects him:

> That which you call "Unidentified Flying Objects"; that which you and White people put "Above Top Secret"; that is real. There is a plane out there made like a wheel. Ezekiel saw it five hundred and fifty (550) years before Jesus was born. A wheel in the middle of the air, run by the Grace of God, with "eyes" all around it, meaning with people in it. It is not from another planet. It is made by the Son of man to destroy this world. It is up there now, forty (40) miles above us. It is like a city in the sky. "And I saw as it was a city come down from heaven." It has 1500 little planes on it. They follow me everywhere I go. You can take it or leave it. I am not trying to impress you. I know the Power that is behind that wheel and the Power of the wheel is the Power that Guides me.[411]

Around the same time that Minister Farrakhan was censured by the U.S. Senate and banned from the UK, Captain Kenju Terauchi of JAL Flight 1628 made headlines that shocked U.S. Authorities. A respected pilot for 29 years, Captain Terauchi reported seeing a large circular walnut-shaped plane

---

[411] Louis Farrakhan, "Who Is God?," *Saviours' Day Keynote Address* (Chicago, IL, February 24, 1991).

along with two smaller ones that moved around his plane in unconventional ways. He described the large one as being the size of two aircraft carriers (which amounts to roughly a half mile x half mile). Suddenly all of the planes took off at terrific speeds unimaginable by modern aircraft. The objects were also picked up on radar. Despite his credibility, he was grounded and no longer licensed to fly commercial planes. Terauchi's sighting further authenticates the Minister's public claims, which made it more difficult for the U.S. Government to continue hiding what Farrakhan has been proclaiming. Even UFO critics admitted that the Government tried to deter the public from this reality before it continued to gain acceptance:

> The Federal Aviation Administration launched an investigation that took months, attempting to make sure their system was not malfunctioning, even as the pilot's eye-witness account spread around the globe.
> The debunking of Kenju Terauchi began even before the wheels of the JAL flight #1628 landed in Anchorage. [412]

FARRAKHAN'S DARING PROOF

As attacks against Minister Farrakhan intensified, he decided it was time for a public showdown. On October 24, 1989 he held an international press conference where he shared his vision-like experience with the entire world. Knowing that some would not understand his motives, he remained steadfast in telling his account of what happened as he spoke with Elijah Muhammad on the Wheel. Toward the end of his announcement he offered this challenge to the world:

> Before you will be able to establish your mockery of me (if that is what you wish to do) for what was revealed to me in the Wheel you will see these wheels, or what you call UFOs, in abundance over the major cities of America and the calamities that America is presently experiencing will increase in number and in intensity that you might humble yourselves to the Warning contained in this Announcement. [413]

Within one day of those audacious words, these wheel-like UFOs were witnessed and reported in the local news where Farrakhan delivered his

---

[412] Scott Christiansen, "They really do want to believe: Alaska's enduring place in the literature of UFO sightings," *Anchorage Press*, October 25, 2012.
[413] Louis Farrakhan, "The Announcement: International Press Conference" (Washington, DC, October 24, 1989).

address.[414] These planes did not simply come and go after a few minutes. They stuck around for days. Local eyewitness television news reporters were flabbergasted over these UFOs that were filmed throughout the days and nights after Farrakhan's press conference. With video footage of these crafts showing, reporters spent several segments of the news broadcasts trying to determine what these crafts were that had been captivating the skies above them. Within the following weeks, several more UFOs were spotted and reported throughout the entire country. This time it was worthy of making national news.

A few weeks after Minister Farrakhan's address, the nationally syndicated television news show, *Hard Copy*, ran segments on Unidentified Flying Objects. Hard Copy reporter, Terry Murphy, began one program with these words:

> ...spending hundreds of millions of dollars to identify just what and just who is in outer space. Despite the skeptics and official denials, there are more and more sightings of UFOs and with the help of sophisticated new instruments, more and more evidence confirming those sightings. Today Hard Copy begins a two-part report on contact with alien beings, including the most recent sightings just last month.[415]

The news segment showed that some of those 'most recent sightings' included some from October 1989, which is the time of the Minister's announcement. Despite the national influx of UFO sightings surrounding his bold dare, none of the journalists, reporters, or speculators made any reference to Minister Farrakhan. None of the reports made any attribution to the man who dared them to mock his words and his connection with these wheels. These were deliberate attempts to prevent the public from knowing that there is a supreme power that bolsters this man.

The Holy Qur'an confirms the validity of the Night Journey wherein it assures the believers that the Messenger is not in error and that he is not speaking from arrogance, but instead he was shown majestic signs from his Lord in the highest part of the horizon. This confirmation is shown in the following verses:

> *1 By the star when it sets!*
> *2 Your companion errs not, nor does he deviate.*
> *3 Nor does he speak out of desire.*
> *4 It is naught but revelation that is revealed —*

---

[414] WDVM Eyewitness News 9 with Mike Buchanan & Andrea Roan (Washington, DC, October 25-26, 1989).
[415] Terry Murphy, "Unidentified Flying Objects," *Hard Copy*, ed. Janelle Balnicke (Santa Monica, CA, December 1989).

THE VISION-LIKE EXPERIENCE

5 One Mighty in Power has taught him,
6 The Lord of Strength. So he attained to perfection,
7 And he is in the highest part of the horizon.
8 Then he drew near, drew nearer yet,
9 So he was the measure of two bows or closer still.
10 So He revealed to His servant what He revealed.
11 The heart was not untrue in seeing what he saw.
12 Do you then dispute with him as to what he saw?
13 And certainly he saw Him in another descent,
14 At the farthest lote-tree.
15 Near it is the Garden of Abode.
16 When that which covers covered the lote-tree;
17 The eye turned not aside, nor did it exceed the limit.
18 Certainly he saw of the greatest signs of his Lord.— An-Najm 53:1-18

What was shown to the Holy Prophet Muhammad (PBUH), the Honorable Elijah Muhammad, and the Honorable Louis Farrakhan have been some of the greatest signs of Allah (God). These signs involve strange flying vehicles that travel to a larger heavenly abode where Allah (God) dwells. Since others were not there to witness the intricacies shown to Allah's servants, the question is asked, "Do you then dispute with him as to what he saw?" It's funny how the primary mockers are often the ones who have no firsthand knowledge to dispute what was shown to God's servants. After all, they were not there in the first place. Can the critics of Elijah Muhammad and Louis Farrakhan dispute something that was disclosed to them from Allah (God)? Were the critics there when Master Fard Muhammad pointed these planes out to Elijah Muhammad? Were they there in Tepotzlan, Mexico when Minister Farrakhan had his experience? How then can one dispute these majestic signs that have now proven themselves to be true in the physical world?

The *farthest lote-tree* mentioned in the aforementioned passage has much significance. Prophet Muhammad (PBUH) associated this symbolic tree with the heavenly dwelling of Allah (God). The following statement is attributed to the Holy Prophet:

> ....Then I was made to ascend to Sidrat–ul–Muntaha (i.e. the Lote Tree of the utmost boundary) Behold! Its fruits were like the jars of Hajr (i.e. a place near Medina) and its leaves were as big as the ears of elephants. Gabriel said, 'This is the Lote Tree of the utmost boundary). Behold! There ran four rivers, two were hidden and two were visible, I asked, 'What are these two kinds of rivers, O Gabriel?' He replied,' As for the hidden rivers, they are two rivers in Paradise and the visible rivers are the Nile and the Euphrates.' Then Al–Bait–ul–Ma'mur (i.e. the Sacred House) was shown to me and a container

full of wine and another full of milk and a third full of honey were brought to me...[416]

Al-Bait-ul-Ma'mur is also known as Allah's house. This is part of the Seventh Heaven where the Prophet met with Allah (God). The Holy Qur'an describes Allah's dwelling place as his Throne of Power (Al-'Arshi). This has tremendous spiritual significance, but it clearly maintains a strong physical reality as well. The angels will be seen traveling around this throne (Az-Zumar 39:75), it extended over the waters (Hud 11:7), and it even has leg-like apparatuses.[417]

Unfortunately, many Islamic scholars (*ulema*) have no *tafsir* (Qur'anic explanation) regarding Allah's Throne and it's relation to the modern UFO phenomenon. This is because such knowledge has been reserved for the Messiah whom Allah (God) will teach Himself (Al-Imran 3:48). Elijah Muhammad is recognized as that messianic figure spoken of in those Qur'anic verses. He is the only Islamic leader who makes the bold and audacious claims that he was taught directly by Allah (God) in person who controls this huge circular plane with his myriad angels who pilot hundreds of smaller ones. It is this very reason that he and the NOI have been misunderstood by many Islamic clerics. Yet it is for this same reason that the NOI offers a much more accurate tafsir for these Qura'nic passages. The Muslim world has no solidified explanation for Allah's 'arsh (throne of power) even though the book makes distinct descriptions of it. Unfortunately some traditional Muslims have lambasted Minister Louis Farrakhan and the Nation of Islam for acknowledging what Allah revealed in the Holy Qur'an, yet they charge the NOI with being un-Islamic. What could be worse than Muslims denouncing other Muslims for validating what the Holy Qur'an speaks of? Nevertheless, Farrakhan challenges the entire world of scholarship to disprove the reality of these Wheels.

THE WHEELS GUIDE FARRAKHAN

The Minister's 1985 experience on the Wheel would become even more solidified in subsequent years. His daring statements about these planes following him throughout his journeys have proven rather consistent. In October of 1985, the Minister left from Phoenix, Arizona in route to New York to culminate his historic *Power At Last Forever* tour. Just as he arrived in the city, the wheels soon followed. The Arizona Daily Star reported that a local air-traffic controller and police helicopter pilot tracked about 60 unidentified aircraft leaving from the southwestern skies of Arizona.[418] The controller

---

[416] Ṣaḥīḥ al-Bukhārī, "5.226 Narrated by Jabir bin 'Abdullah," *Al-Hadith*.
[417] Ṣaḥīḥ al-Bukhārī, "3.41.594 Narrated by Abu Huraira," *Al-Hadith*.
[418] Arizona Daily Star, *Arizona Daily Star*, October 09, 1985.

THE VISION-LIKE EXPERIENCE

reported that 15 groups of four to six objects were monitored on the radar traveling in a northeastern direction—the same route as the Minister who arrived in New York. On another occasion he, Jabril Muhammad, and about sixty or seventy others saw the Wheel in upstate Arizona while on Big Mountain in July 1986.[419] They were on an Indian Reservation during a time when White authorities were threatening the Native American Indians from their land. As the Minister visited to stand in support of his brothers and sisters, the Wheel also showed up.

Minister Farrakhan has remained in constant communication with the intelligence of the wheels. Throughout his overseas travels in the late 1980-1990s, he reported several events where the wheels guided him throughout his travels abroad. Strangely, many of these claims did not make headlines in the U.S. media.

The Bible teaches everywhere the son of man went, the wheel went. This has been exemplified in Minister Farrakhan's words and travels throughout the globe. Abdul Sharrieff Muhammad, one of the Minister's top aides gives some of his firsthand accounts about what he witnessed while traveling with Minister Farrakhan:

> Everywhere the Minister went, the Plane went. We were in Ghana and the bats came out in the daytime. You know, bats don't come out in the daytime. Bats come out at night. And it was so many of them that came out, it was like a cloud. The people in Africa were looking like they had never seen that before. So I asked the Minister, "Why are bats out in the daytime?" He said, "That Wheel—bats have very sensitive ears," so they heard the Wheel because everywhere he goes the Wheel is there! So the bats came out in the daytime because the Wheel stirred them![420]

Abdul Sharrieff continued:

> And when we left Ghana and went into Burkina Faso, the Minister called back to check with the Government to see if the bats were still out. The bats went away when he left. The book says everywhere he went, the Wheel went!

After his Vision-Like Experience, the Minister went to Africa during America's war-hungry plans against East Africa in 1986. While overseas, he

---

[419] Jabril Muhammad, "The Wheel: Is It Real or Reel?," *The Final Call*, March 31, 2010.
[420] Abdul-Sharrieff Muhammad, "Is The Honorable Louis Farrakhan Divinely Guided And Is He Connected To The Wheel?" (Nashville, TN: Muhammad Mosque 60, August 12, 2012).

traveled to Libya to warn Colonel Muammar Gadhafi about America's impending attack. Minister Farrakhan sent his whole delegation back to the states except two or three staff members (Abdul Sharrieff Muhammad and Salim Muhammad). While in Libya, Colonel Gadhafi's top officials visited the Minister's hotel suite. Being guided by the Messenger's words from the Wheel, it was here that Minister Farrakhan forthrightly explained to Libyan officials that America planned to destroy their military, airplanes, and infrastructure. After the Minister shared these words, those Libyan officials speedily left his hotel to tell Gadhafi of these impending plans. Once he received the Minister's warning, Gadhafi responded accordingly. Abdul Sharrieff Muhammad offers a first-hand narrative of these accounts:

> When the Minister finished speaking, all of them [Libyan officials] got up and ran out of the room and went to Gadhafi and told Brother Gadhafi what the Minister said to them! Bro Gadhafi took some of his planes out of Libya and took them to Chad. This is real because he knows that the Minister is a man of God![421]

Despite that Libya had shot down American F-14 bombers and knowing America was prepared to retaliate during his stay in Libya, the Minister remained uncannily calm. "The Minister was just as calm. In his suite there was a big plate window looking out over the ocean. The Minister walked over to the widow and he said, 'Out there is the plane. I'm not worried.'" The wheels communicated to him through various lights and movements, signaling when he should move, leave, or stay. This type of activity became quite frequent throughout the Minister's travels abroad.

The delegation left Libya and went to Saudi Arabia. While in Arabia the Minister and his small delegation (consisting of Abdul Sharrieff Muhammad and Salim Muhammad) came across a newspaper that stated how America's most sophisticated warship was going into Libya. It reported that a bright shiny object was spotted in the sky and somehow interfered with America's most sophisticated warship during the same time Minister Farrakhan was in Libya. The ship had to turn around and go back to Florida for repairs while a replacement ship was sent. It has later been revealed that unidentified maneuvering lights had been frequently seen from US Navy ships resulting in numerous malfunctions during the Spring and Summer of 1986.[422]

While overseas, Farrakhan's delegation received a communiqué that President Reagan ordered that when Farrakhan comes into the country, he was to be apprehended and arrested because no American citizen was to travel to Libya without Government approval. Upon learning that the President's

---

[421] Ibid.
[422] B.J. Booth, *1986-UFO Seen from Bridge of USS Edenton*, UFO Case Reports, CMS (Case Management System) , MUFON (MUFON, 2006).

THE VISION-LIKE EXPERIENCE

administration sought to apprehend him, the Minister decided to return to America anyway.

The U.S. Border Patrol had pictures and profiles of Minister Farrakhan posted with the anticipation of arresting him upon his arrival into the country. Abdul Sharrieff gave the following recollection when they arrived at the American borders:

> They've got pictures up looking for him. The Minister isn't worried about nothing... We got to the borders. I'm looking and they've got police everywhere... I'm nervous as all out doors. The Minister said, "I'm ready to go; you all stay back." And I'm watching the Minister walk... I watched the Minister walk right by Customs. They never saw him! But it's in the book. He walked right by and they never saw him! By the grace of God I bear witness that he is the Jesus in our midst!
>
> You go back and check out the newspapers. They wondered how did he get back into the country. To this very day, they don't even know! Now you know America, they have to be sharp. They pride themselves on being the best, and the Minister walked right past them! He got back into America, turned around, and saluted us. I said, "Good God almighty! Praise be to Allah!"[423]

Knowing the threats against him and anyone else who violated President Reagan's order to punish any American citizen visiting Libya at that time, the press went crazy once they realized the Minister was back in the states. How is it that America with all its power was unable to identify and apprehend the unarmed Farrakhan as he blatantly returned to America during such a volatile time? What type of power has control over people's thinking? What is the power that backs Minister Farrakhan that allows him to speak and act in such manners without fear of consequences? These type of events give more and more credence to the fact that Louis Farrakhan is divinely buttressed by the power of the living God who operates from that huge Wheel.

HE KNOWS WHAT THEY DON'T WANT KNOWN

History has proven that American powers know what those objects are; they just don't have any control over them. They are well aware of the messianic relationship these so-called UFOs have with the Honorable Elijah Muhammad and the Honorable Minister Louis Farrakhan. This has been the primary reasoning behind the U.S. Government's cover-up of these planes.

---

[423] Op. cit. Abdul-Sharrieff Muhammad.

Everything Farrakhan does and says has been based on the vision: his *Stop the Killing* tours around the country, the *Million Man March*, his *World Friendship Tours*, and a host of other major moves that have taken place. He speaks boldly to world powers unlike any living leader because he knows he has back up. Farrakhan is distinguished from any leader of influence, being the only one who promotes a fundamental belief in such crafts as an integral part of his theological, political, educational, and social position. Knowing this, why hasn't the media exploited this claim as much as they hate Farrakhan? After all, they are aware of his beliefs considering that he has fervently expressed his vision and his communication from the Wheel with the public. He even sat before the editorial board of the Washington Post to discuss certain matters when this topic arose:

> On April 30, 1990, Minister Farrakhan was interviewed by the editorial board and staff of The Washington Post - one of America's most prestigious newspapers. Towards the end of the unusual session, Minister Farrakhan answered a question about the great wheel like plane which the Honorable Elijah Muhammad spoke of for over four decades.
> The Minister stated in no uncertain terms the reality of these planes. In the course of his answer he reviewed his vision, which included the instructions he was given by the Honorable Elijah Muhammad. He also reviewed some of the national and international events which occurred in conjunction with his momentous experience.
> The Washington Post did a commendable job of accurately presenting Minister Farrakhan's words to the public. However, there was something that was not reported to the reading public. It was significant.
> Immediately after the Minister answered their question about the wheel-like-plane, the Minister, and some of those who came with him, heard one of the executives lean over and whisper these words to another: "He knows." I don't believe he intended to be heard. But he was.[424]

Why don't these highly influential media entities publicly question the Minister on such unpopular topics as his belief and relationship to these planes, along with his claim that Elijah Muhammad is alive? It would seem that his enemies would go overboard to publicly mock such an unpopular position. Surprisingly very few have dared to bring up this topic on an open forum. One should ask, why? It is because a true investigation of these topics will explain the truth about the God that backs Farrakhan and the Nation of Islam.

While most journalists avoid questioning the Minister on these items, one Jewish writer, Jonah Goldberg, mockingly brought up Farrakhan's belief in the wheels as it relates to Elijah Muhammad being alive. Though he never

---

[424] Cedric Muhammad, "Scripture, The Mother Plane, And Minister Farrakhan's Vision From Tepoztlan, Mexico," *Black Electorate* (BlackElectorate.com, July 23, 2002).

THE VISION-LIKE EXPERIENCE

offered a logical argument against the truth of this position, he only offered a mocking tone to question why other journalists are apprehensive to bring up this subject:

> But Russert et al. could do a lot more for the common good if they asked Farrakhan to explain why he thinks he has ridden in a flying saucer...
>
> Putting all that aside, Farrakhan believes Elijah Muhammad, the (by all accounts deceased) former leader of the Nation of Islam, is living on a spaceship circling the planet. Also, a few years after Elijah "died," the spaceship picked up Farrakhan and the two men had a nice chat with each other. Afterward, Farrakhan says the spaceship let him off near Washington, D.C.
>
> The only major television journalist I've ever seen query Farrakhan about this stuff was Ted Koppel, host of ABCs "Nightline," in 1996. Koppel asked him about the spaceship stuff, saying, "It sounds like gibberish, but maybe you can explain it."
>
> Farrakhan didn't back off. The spiritual leader explained that the huge spaceship is "over the heads of us in North America, and soon you shall see these (spaceships) over the major cities of America." This fact is being kept "above top-secret by the United States government."
>
> Farrakhan didn't stop there. Offended at the "gibberish" remark, he fell back on some hard science: "And if it were gibberish, they made an awful lot of money, Mr. Koppel, on that movie called 'Independence Day' --- it flooded the theaters..."[425]

Despite his foolish and misguided manner, Goldberg did admit that few journalists have dared to question the Minister on these issues. What he did not mention was that the Minister has pinpointed exactly why the media avoids dealing with him on such a topic:

> They have decided that it is not in their interest to bring me to the media and ask me questions that they know that I am quite capable of answering. So they would rather keep me away from the media and make people to think that the minister has passed away.[426]

---

[425] Jonah Goldberg, "Treatment of Farrakhan glosses over odd issues," *Jewish World Review*, October 20, 2000.

[426] Louis Farrakhan, "#AskFarrakhan Tweets," *Minister Louis Farrakhan responds to tweet from Ilia Rashad Muhammad @iliarashad*, comp. Ilia Rashad Muhammad (#AskFarrakhan via Twitter, January 13, 2013).

If any researcher actually gave a little time and energy into this subject, all roads will eventually lead to the fact that Elijah Muhammad introduced these wheel-shaped crafts (so-called UFOs) to the modern world and that he was acquainted with the supreme power behind those objects. Any worthy study of this topic will lead the student to discover that the Honorable Elijah Muhammad met the Supreme Being and that same power guides his servant, the Honorable Minister Louis Farrakhan. This is the ultimate reason why the UFO topic is either deliberately twisted to confuse the public or it is avoided altogether. The Nation of Islam respectfully challenges the world's scholarship, scientists, theologians, and academics to at least dialogue on this subject. Hardly any have stepped up. Instead, some have rendered frivolous insults that don't address the issue at hand. This is the manner of response for those who are bereft of adequate facts.

Some critics have even suggested that Minister Farrakhan makes claims about his experience on the Wheel as a ploy to gain more followers. To the contrary, it would be outright foolish to try to attract followers with such an unpopular claim. After all, it would seem more plausible in the eyes of most people to believe that Elijah Muhammad is dead and that he lives through the work of others. Instead, Minister Farrakhan has stood on the most unpopular and seemingly unbelievable truth that Elijah Muhammad is physically alive. He has done this at the risk of appearing insane before the world. If anything, many people would be more apt to assume he is crazy for such a belief… unless they have adequate knowledge and insight. Obviously Farrakhan knows something that others do not want made known to the public.

REMEMBER THE 17TH OF SEPTEMBER

The blessed night of Minister Farrakhan's vision occurred on September 17, 1985 in Tepotzlan, Mexico from a mountain that he had climbed many times throughout his visits there. Both the time and the location of this experience hold divine significance. It is from such mountainous settings that his vision was foretold:

> *And he carried me away in the spirit to a great and high mountain, and shewed me that great city, the holy Jerusalem, descending out of heaven from God,* – Revelation 21:10 (KJV)

After the Minister's vision in 1985, Tepotzlan became a haven for UFO sightings and activities. Several local inhabitants and tourists photographed and filmed some of the most credible images of these luminous circular crafts. One of such persons was Carlos Diaz who became internationally recognized

THE VISION-LIKE EXPERIENCE

for his recorded footage and photographs of these objects in and around Tepotzlan, Mexico. Diaz, who was also an abductee, has been examined by a number of UFO critics and researchers. Here is a brief analysis concerning research of Diaz's UFO photos:

> Mexican TV journalist and UFOlogist Jaime Maussan, who has been at the centre of UFO investigations in Mexico since the wave began in 1991, believes that Diaz's UFO photographs are among the most impressive he has seen. Maussan took Diaz's photographs to Jim Dilettoso, an image processing expert at Village Labs, in Tucson, Arizona, who concluded they were genuine. After satisfying himself he was not dealing with a hoaxer, Maussan visited Diaz at his home in Tepoztlan, Mexico. There, he spoke to a number of other witnesses who claimed to have seen exactly the same type of UFO. The apparent credibility of the Diaz case has also attracted UFO researchers from further afield, who have attempted to glean insights into the alien agenda from Diaz's contactee claims.[427]

Why Tepotzlan, Mexico? This location represents a spiritual journey to the ancient home of Quetzalcoatl who is considered the Christ-type figure to the indigenous people of that area. Hence, it is associated with a messianic-type figure and experience.

One of the most mindboggling factors associated with Minister Farrakhan's vision from Tepotzlan has to do with the Biblical calculations that signify its authenticity. Before modern Bible scholars were able to pinpoint the dates and times of Biblical events, Minister Farrakhan had been proclaiming the majesty of the vision-like experience, which occurred on September 17, 1985. One of the scriptures forecasting this vision-like experience occurs in the 8th Chapter of Ezekiel. The prophet Ezekiel, who is most commonly associated with these flying wheels, was given a vision that reads in traditional Bibles in this manner:

> *And it came to pass in the sixth year, in the sixth month, in the fifth day of the month, as I sat in mine house, and the elders of Judah sat before me, that the hand of the Lord GOD fell there upon me. Then I beheld, and lo a likeness as the appearance of fire: from the appearance of his loins even downward, fire; and from his loins even upward, as the appearance of brightness, as the colour of amber. And he put forth the form of an hand, and took me by a lock of mine head; and the spirit lifted*

---

[427] UFO Evidence, "Carlos Diaz - UFO Abductee," *UFO Evidence: Scientific Study of the UFO Phenomenon and the Search for Extraterrestrial Life* (The X Factor, Issue 89 (reprinted on Cosmic Conspiracies), 2011).

> *me up between the earth and the heaven, and brought me in the visions of God to Jerusalem, to the door of the inner gate that looketh toward the north; where was the seat of the image of jealousy, which provoketh to jealousy. And, behold, the glory of the God of Israel was there, according to the vision that I saw in the plain.* – Ezekiel 8:1-4, King James Version

This vision describes a man who is being lifted in the spirit and shown the heavenly signs of God in what is understood to be the New Jerusalem. Even more astonishing is that years after the Minister's vision on September 17th, Biblical scholars developed the *New Living Translation Bible* that was designed to offer more up-to-date calculations of Biblical dates. In this translation the same passage from Ezekiel reads as such:

> *Then on **September 17**, during the sixth year of King Jehoiachin's captivity, while the leaders of Judah were in my home, the Sovereign LORD took hold of me. I saw a figure that appeared to be a man. From what appeared to be his waist down, he looked like a burning flame. From the waist up he looked like gleaming amber. He reached out what seemed to be a hand and took me by the hair. Then the Spirit lifted me up into the sky and transported me to Jerusalem in a vision from God. I was taken to the north gate of the inner courtyard of the Temple, where there is a large idol that has made the LORD very jealous. Suddenly, the glory of the God of Israel was there, just as I had seen it before in the valley.* – Ezekiel 8:1-4, New Living Translation

Is this a coincidence that Ezekiel's foretold vision occurred on the exact same day (September 17th) as the Minister's vision? The first edition of the *New Living Translation* was published in 1996. This happened 11 years after Minister Farrakhan's vision-like experience. The theological developers of this Bible translation did not consult with the NOI for this calculation. Such mathematical precision only validates the awesome power of Allah's prophecies and the authenticity of his servant's experience.

Minister Farrakhan has never backed away from this *out of the body experience*. This should not appear strange for any researcher familiar with Biblical, Qur'anic, and scientific principles. The Honorable Elijah Muhammad explained the awesome capabilities of Allah and his angels who have the ability to tune-in and control the thinking of people. Numerous UFO abductees and witnesses have reported this type of behavior during their abductions. The Holy Qur'an further acknowledges this activity wherein it is written:

> *And He it is Who takes your souls at night, and He knows what you earn by day, then He raises you up therein that an appointed term may be*

THE VISION-LIKE EXPERIENCE

fulfilled. Then to Him is your return, then He will inform you of what you did. – Al-An`am 6:60

This verse attests to Allah's behavior and capabilities, which the Honorable Elijah Muhammad spoke heavily about. He taught that the prophet Jesus of 2000 years ago had these abilities, which allowed him to know the thinking of his enemies in order to avert danger.[428] According to the Honorable Elijah Muhammad, Jesus was an example that such technology can be utilized by the righteous:

> This is what Jesus was equipped with, the knowledge of thought. That's why he could always get away of his enemy before they got there. He had already tuned up on them. When he knew they were coming from this way, he'd go that way and they couldn't over take him, because they were not equipped with this instrument to tune in on the thoughts of other people. He could always evade them.[429]

This ability to tune-in and even control the thinking of people coincides with many other UFO related cases that show people being put in a trance-like state during UFO encounters. Other UFO Researchers have tried to make sense of this phenomenon and have offered their speculations concerning how these 'humanoids' have hypnotized, 'implanted memories,' and 'communicated telepathic messages' to those who have encountered UFOs. One of these reported messages offers a striking resemblance to Elijah Muhammad's teachings. The following is a sample of a reported message that was channeled by a so-called 'extraterrestrial being':

> We come from the interplanetary confederation of solar systems and our purpose is to aid our brother man on the planet earth as the new age dawns. The teacher that was known to you as Jesus was able to use many more of the abilities than the people of this planet. Unfortunately man upon planet Earth has misinterpreted the meaning of this man's life. He was no different than any of you; he was simply able to remember certain principles. These principles may be realized by anyone at any time. It is only necessary that you avail yourself to our contract through meditation in order to re-realize that which is rightfully yours, the truth of the creation, and the truth of your position in it. Know ye not that ye are Gods?...

---

[428] Elijah Muhammad, *The True History Of Jesus* (Secretarius MEMPS Publications, 2008).
[429] Elijah Muhammad, "The Theology of Time (Lecture Series)," Vols. June 18, 1972 (Chicago, IL: MUHAMMAD Mosque No. 2, 1972).

...Man is now in the transitional period before the dawn of a new age. With peace, love, brotherhood, and understanding on man's part, he will see a great new era begin to dawn.[430]

Whether a hoax or an actual report, the principles expressed in the aforementioned communication are the exact same teachings conveyed by the Honorable Elijah Muhammad since the 1930s. Is it simply a coincidence that several of the UFO encounters validate everything that Elijah Muhammad taught about them?

As if that was not enough, Minister Farrakhan's September 17th communication with the (believed dead) Honorable Elijah Muhammad would hold further significance. One of the most famous international UFO abduction cases occurred on this date 12 years after Minister Farrakhan's vision. Kirsan Ilyumzhinov, President of the Republic of Kalmykia in the Russian Federation from 1993 to 2010, made international headlines when he reported being abducted by people from a circular UFO. Aside from his reputation as an international leader, Ilyumzhinov is also the President of FIDE, also known as the *World Chess Federation*, the world's pre-eminent international chess organization since 1995. Therefore his friendly UFO abduction was not taken lightly. His encounter with these people occurred on September 17, 1997 while he was residing in his high-rise Moscow apartment. He told The Guardian newspaper some of this event:

> They took me from my apartment and we went aboard their ship... We flew to some kind of star. They put a spacesuit on me, told me many things and showed me around. They wanted to demonstrate that UFOs do exist.[431]

Clearly, if these UFO pilots whom Ilyumzhinov described as "people like us,"[432] wanted to show him that these planes exist, they picked a truly significant day. Obviously they used a credible international figure to offer more credence to the Minister's September 17th experience. These type of patterns show that the Minister does not speak out of vain desire, but that he was shown some of the mightiest signs from his Lord.

Although President Ilymzhinov has spoken publicly about his encounter to the world for several years, these reports have somehow not reached the pages of America's media. How is it that such internationally newsworthy information regarding an influential head of state has not reached

---

[430] *The UFO Conspiracy*, Video Documentary, directed by Brian Barkley, New Liberty Videos, 2004.
[431] Tom Parfitt, "King of Kalmykia," *The Guardian*, September 20, 2006.
[432] Antonio Huneeus, "Russian style Exopolitics – Kirsan Ilyumzhinov's alien abduction," *Open Minds TV*, June 16, 2010.

the American public? Is this part of the mainstream effort to withhold prominent UFO facts from the people in order to keep them unenlightened?

BIG MONEY SPENT ON UFO INVESTIGATIONS

While some may not see the significance that UFOs have on society, this may result from the fact that most of the important information about these crafts is not disclosed to the public. Few Americans are aware of the countless billions of dollars and multi-agency efforts placed on UFO research and investigations. There are highly contrasting perspectives about these crafts that differ between classes of people. Even though the average person may not spend much time, energy, or money into UFO research, the affluently powerful groups tend to be more adamant about this reality. Little is known about the billions of taxpayer dollars attached to UFO investigations. Researcher J. Antonio Huneeus states, "a significant amount of UFO-related research was funded by the billionaire philanthropist Laurance S. Rockefeller, yet with a few exceptions, this was mostly unknown by the general public, the media, and even the majority of the ufological community."[433] For entities as powerful and influential as the famous Rockefellers to allot their time, energy, and finances toward UFO research gives vivid indications that this is a topic deserving realistic attention. Wise persons with business acumen like the Rockefellers do not necessarily invest billions of dollars into unrealistic endeavors.

Huneeus contributed to some of the studies that were funded by the billionaire where Rockefeller is acknowledged as one of the primary financial contributors for the creation of *The UFO Briefing Document*[434], which served as a collaborative effort of individuals and organizations that show evidence that these planes exist. It's worth noting that Laurance Rockefeller's interest in UFOs heightened during the same time Minister Farrakhan publicized his vision-like experience aboard that huge circular plane. Huneeus makes this observation:

> Laurance Rockefeller's first forays into ufology started sometime in the late 1980s through Dr. Cecil B. Scott Jones, a parapsychologist and former U.S. Navy commander, who had worked as a naval attaché in Asia and at the Naval Scientific and Technical Intelligence Center. Between 1985 and 1991, Jones

---

[433] J. Antonio Huneeus, "The Laurance Rockefeller UFO Initiative," *Open Minds TV*, September 3, 2010: 54.
[434] Don Berliner, Marie Galbraith and Antonio Huneeus, *UFO Briefing Document: The Best Available Evidence* , Research, Presented by CUFONS, FUFOR, MUFON , UFO Research Coalition (UFO Research Coalition , 1995).

was special assistant to Senator Claiborne Pell (1918- 2009), the powerful Rhode Island Democrat Chairman of the Senate Foreign Relations Committee, who was deeply interested in parapsychology.[435]

Interestingly, **parapsychology** is the study of mental phenomena, such as telepathy, telekinesis, and other inexplicable occurrences—including vision-like experiences, which have been commonly associated with UFO activity. These are some of the capabilities of the scientists (angels and pilots of the wheels) that the Honorable Elijah Muhammad described—some of whom, he knew personally. This relationship continues to astound those within some of the highest echelons of the U.S. Government. Why else would there be a need for parapsychologists in these levels of government? Why would billionaires utilize the assistance of such persons to help in their UFO inquiries? Rockefeller's probing into UFO activities occurred during the same span of years (1985-1991) that the Honorable Minister Louis Farrakhan dared the U.S. Government and the world to contest that he was guided by the Honorable Elijah Muhammad from that huge Mother Wheel.[436] Is this simply a mere coincidence? Although the Minister has not backed down from his bold position, none of those powerful governmental or media entities have publicly challenged him on this point. Instead, they secretly investigate these crafts while leading the public to assume that those objects are the fictitious work of Hollywood.

Collaborating with military commanders and parapsychologists to study UFOs, Rockefeller was also connected to Senator Claiborne Pell, "the powerful Rhode Island Democrat" who coincidentally was a part of the 98th U.S. Congress that officially censored Minister Farrakhan for speaking the truth.[437] It is apparent that the rich and powerful of this nation have colluded and utilized their influence to suppress the voice and message of the only present leader who officially represents the power of the planes—the Honorable Minister Louis Farrakhan.

Perhaps one of the reasons why many people are oblivious to those highly-funded UFO investigations is because they have not been publicized as such. Instead, these investigations, projects, research, and monitoring systems are often shrouded under the guise of scientific exploration and military defense operations. President Reagan's Strategic Defense Initiative (Star Wars) and the U.S. Air Force Space Surveillance System (Space Fence) are such

---

[435] J. Antonio Huneeus, "The Laurance Rockefeller UFO Initiative," *Open Minds TV*, September 3, 2010: 56.
[436] Louis Farrakhan, "The Announcement: International Press Conference " (Washington, DC, October 24, 1989).
[437] United States Senate, "To express the sense of the Senate relating to Louis Farrakhan," *S.AMDT.3363 to H.R.5712*, comp. Sponsor: Sen. Don Nickles [OK] (Washington, D.C., 1984, 28-June).

THE VISION-LIKE EXPERIENCE

examples. While these programs don't readily use the term 'UFO' in their titles, they all have worked to investigate and even attempt to counter the activities of these wheel-shaped crafts—the ones that Elijah Muhammad had been representing for decades. Although hardly any of the publicly available UFO investigations reference Muhammad's responsibility for initiating this concept to the modern world, it stands to reason that those multi-billion dollar programs and investigations have clearly pinpointed him and the Nation of Islam as the primary sources of this worldwide phenomenon. This explains why the U.S. Government and its mainstream media cohorts have worked diligently to discredit the truth offered by the Honorable Minister Louis Farrakhan.

14. THE CLEAR EVIDENCE, THE SURE TRUTH

ELIJAH'S BOOK

There had been several occasions when the Honorable Elijah Muhammad spoke of his leaving and what would take place during his absence. Ultimately things have played out exactly as he foretold. Minister Louis Farrakhan has recounted, on numerous occasions, important words that the Honorable Elijah Muhammad said to him regarding his departure—words that involve a book that Elijah Muhammad would receive by Master Fard Muhammad. "A new book is coming into being and that new book is the thing to which the people must give ear!"[438]

The Honorable Elijah Muhammad shed light on this destined book that he was to acquire from Master Fard Muhammad:

> He gave me a Holy Qur'an in Arabic, but I couldn't read it. So, He got me one in Arabic and English translated by Muhammad Ali of Pakistan. Later He found one translated by Yusuf Ali of Egypt; He brought me that one. Then He told me, "I will give you a Holy Qur'an when you learn how to read Arabic, then I will give you a Holy Qur'an in Arabic." He said, "I made it myself." He showed me that Holy Qur'an in Arabic in September last, but I couldn't read it. I could only recognize one letter in it. So I expect Him within a year to come back with that same book.[439]

The same supreme power that is responsible for the UFO phenomenon is the same power that promised to offer Elijah Muhammad this book. Of course this could not take place if Elijah Muhammad died in 1975, so how and where could he be taught Arabic and obtain this book from Master Fard Muhammad unless it involved supreme capabilities?

As it turns out, these questions are answered in the prophetic passages of the Bible and Holy Qur'an. Elijah Muhammad receiving his book is cryptically depicted as the Lamb accepting a book from the one who sat on the throne (Revelation 5:7). This prophetic scenario occurs after the Lamb, who appeared to have died, is exalted into the heavenly presence of God and his

---

[438] Elijah Muhammad, "The Theology of Time (Lecture Series)," Vols. September 24, 1972 (Chicago, IL: MUHAMMAD Mosque No. 2, 1972).
[439] Elijah Muhammad, "The Theology of Time (Lecture Series)," Vols. August 20, 1972 (Chicago, IL: MUHAMMAD Mosque No. 2, 1972).

angels. In this celestial location, the Lamb is reacquainted with the divine power of his God. It is here that this messianic Lamb receives the book that was promised him.

This is the book that is described in Biblical terms as the *Lamb's Book of Life*. It is a portion of a larger canon called the *Book of Life* (Revelation 20:12) that contains the record of people according to how they will be judged. *The Book of Life* draws parallels to what the Holy Qur'an describes as the *Mother Book* (*Umm al-Kitab*), which is the source of all knowledge and scriptures. The Mother Book is said to be safely-guarded in the presence of Allah (God) (Az-Zukhruf 43:2-4)—the same God who dwells upon his Throne of Power.

This *Mother Book* and the Biblical *Book of Life* contain records of everyone and everything. It is from this canonical catalogue that all scriptures have been revealed. *The Lamb's Book of Life*, however, is only a portion of that greater book and it contains the names of those who are officially enlisted as righteous followers of the messianic Lamb of God. These are the ones who will be granted access to the New Jerusalem, the heavenly dwelling place of God (Revelation 21:27). These are they who will avert the divine destruction of God (Revelation 20:15).

The Holy Qur'an verifies that a select group of persons ask to be recorded as followers of the Messiah. The verse reads as follows:

> *Our Lord, we believe in that which Thou has revealed and we follow the messenger, so write us down with those who bear witness.*

The words *write us down* comes from the Arabic phrase *fauktubna*, which means to *write us, enlist us,* or *register us*. This criteria distinguishes those who bear witness to the man that Allah (God) has raised. It is an act that distinguishes the true adherents of God from those who merely sympathize or support God's designated representative. This reflects the process of those who become registered members of the Nation of Islam as followers of the Honorable Elijah Muhammad under the guidance of the Honorable Minister Louis Farrakhan. Elijah Muhammad blatantly preached that he is the fulfillment of this Lamb and those enlisted as his helpers signify the practical registration of those written in the Lamb's Book of Life.

The Honorable Elijah Muhammad verifies his position as that symbolic Lamb who receives this book:

> As the Bible teaches you back there in the last part of it, [Revelation], that he saw God give a man with a symbolic name [Lamb] a little book and that little book was enough to take care of all the big books. That is true. Allah gave me

a little book and HE'S PREPARING ANOTHER LITTLE BOOK. Well, He's got it prepared, but He's waiting for a certain time to give it to me.[440]

Here is a man that doesn't just preach prophecy; instead he illustrates how his actions fulfill what was written of him. This is a distinguishing testament to the quality of his divine role.

Elijah Muhammad promised to return and when he returned, he said that he would reveal a portion of this new book to Minister Farrakhan as the Minister recalled:

> Then later on he said to me, "Brother, I'm going away. I'm going away to study. I'll be gone for approximately three years. Don't change the teachings while I'm gone. And if you are faithful when I return, I will reveal the new teaching through you.[441]

During the vision-like experience, Elijah Muhammad told the Minister that he had another major assignment. After completing this assignment, Farrakhan would be able to see him face to face. He did not say exactly what that *one more thing* was that had to be done, but Minister Farrakhan was resolved that he would complete it and be granted access to see his messiah on the Wheel. If Muhammad promised Minister Farrakhan that he would reveal a portion of this book to him and that he would be able to see him on the Mother Wheel, then this suggests that Minister Farrakhan has another destiny aboard that huge wheel-shaped craft.

THE 33rd PARALLEL

And when this comes to pass, (lo, it will come,) then shall they know that a prophet has been among them – **Ezekiel 33:33**

Despite the practical evidence that Elijah Muhammad and Louis Farrakhan have brought—which proves the reality of their God, many people have found it difficult to accept such precise teachings. Knowing that many people won't grasp clear truths, Allah (God) has often provided signs and indicators to entice those who may not grasp the plain logic associated with his truth. The Holy Qur'an denotes that Allah (God) gives guidance and clues to those who reflect on the signs of his creation (Al-Jathiyah 45:3). Therefore, it is

---

[440] Elijah Muhammad, "The Theology of Time (Lecture Series)," Vols. June 11, 1972 (Chicago, IL: MUHAMMAD Mosque No. 2, 1972).
[441] Jabril Muhammad, *Closing The Gap: Inner Views of the Heart, Mind & Sprit of the Honorable Minister Louis Farrakhan* (Chicago, IL: FCN Publishing Company, 2006). 326-332.

incumbent upon readers to discover the principles of nature and see how they parallel with God's written will. These signs give dominant clues that indicate Elijah Muhammad and Louis Farrakhan's connection to the modern UFO phenomena.

The geographical 33rd Latitude Parallel North is a latitudinal line that circles 33 degrees north of the equator and runs through numerous countries throughout the earth including America, Japan, Libya, and Israel, just to name a few. Ufologists, numerologists, and other researchers have placed heavy significance on this number and the various locations around the 33rd parallel, associating them with divinity, mysticism, and frequent UFO activity. Numerologists often attribute this number with a highly spiritual bearing. Author Gary A. David contributed his analysis on this number:

> The number 33 enigmatically stretches as a latitude line across many diverse cultures in many different times. Known in numerology as the Master Teacher, 33 is the most influential of all numbers, indicating selfless devotion to the spiritual progress of humankind.[442]

David continued with more of his insight related to the 33rd latitudinal parallel denoting that it has "a number of provocative synchronicities[443]." Among these strange occurrences include the area where the mass UFO sighting dubbed the *Phoenix Lights* took place in March 1997. During this sighting, thousands of witnesses saw a massive UFO described as nearly a mile wide with lights dazzling in a triangular formation.

The 33rd latitude parallel is where Roswell, NM sits, which was the sight of the famous alleged UFO incident in 1947. The 33rd Parallel is also related closely to the 1975 Travis Walton UFO abduction around Snowflake Mountain in Arizona. Interestingly part of Japan is located on this parallel. It is no coincidence that this was the geographical location where the Mother Wheel and the smaller wheel-like planes were built.

On January 8, 2008, a mass UFO sighting took place in Stephenville, TX, which also happens to be located near the 33rd parallel north. After a series of investigations and data analysis, Robert Powell, Mutual UFO Network (MUFON) national research director, and Glen Schulze, retired radar analyst, have concluded that the UFOs witnessed over Stephenville, TX were not

---

[442] Gary A. David, "Along the 33rd Parallel: A Global Mystery Circle," in *Underground! The Disinformation Guide to Ancient Civilizations, Astonishing Archaeology and Hidden History* (New York, NY: Disinformation Books, 2005).

[443] **synchronicities:** *noun* things happening or being at same time or place.

military or commercial aircraft.[444] Witnesses of this sighting reported a huge circular craft that made no sounds before it traveled off at a terrific speed.

The Battle of Los Angeles, which occurred on February 25, 1942 off the coast of California, just so happened to take place around this parallel. This was considered the first major encounter that the U. S. Armed Forces had with that large round Mother Plane and several smaller ones. Some of America's most sophisticated arsenal (of that time) was fired at these UFOs to no avail. While America fired shots, the large plane remained stationary amidst a dark cloud while the smaller crafts dotted and dodged all of America's artillery. It was clear that the power of those crafts were thousands of years more advanced than what was being fired at them. The aftermath of this incident led U.S. Officials to arrest Elijah Muhammad where they questioned him about his knowledge of those planes. The FBI confiscated his illustrations and documents related to these wheel-like crafts and have deliberately covered-up the reality of these planes for decades. The February 25, 1942 Battle of Los Angeles can be considered the first major public encounter between the Wheel and America's military.

Just as this latitudinal line offers clues to the intelligence behind UFOs, it offers literal parallels with the numerical significance of Elijah Muhammad and Louis Farrakhan's relationship to these planes. Most Christians believe Jesus Christ to have been the "perfect age" of 33 years old when he ascended into the clouds to be with the Father. Likewise, a 33-year period would define the Honorable Elijah Muhammad's departure via a darkened cloud.

Just as Allah showed his power through the Wheel during the February 25, 1942 Battle of Los Angeles, it took 33 years to the exact date between that encounter and the departure of the Messenger on February 25, 1975. In 1942, the Wheel crept in amidst a cloud prompting U.S. Authorities to apprehend Elijah Muhammad. In 1975 the Wheel crept in amidst a cloud, then Allah (God) rescued Elijah Muhammad, just as it was promised. This is synonymous with the 33-year attribution to the ascension of Jesus Christ who was believed to be dead, but mysteriously rose into the clouds instead.

Just as the Honorable Elijah Muhammad made known his divine role in the prophecies, he also gave notice that another third (33%) of the book was to be fulfilled by another fellow. During a 1964 interview, Messenger Muhammad revealed these words concerning this other person's role in prophecy:

> Then he [Master Fard Muhammad] goes and gets me a Holy Qur'an in Arabic and English…

---

[444] Glen Shulze and Robert Powell, *Stephenville Lights: A Comprehensive Radar and Witness Report Study*, UFO Sighting, Research, MUFON (MUFON, 2010), 76.

THE CLEAR EVIDENCE, THE SURE TRUTH

And I have the Qur'an that he gave to me and he gave me two thirds [2/3] of it to study. The other third [33%] he said didn't amount to anything because that would be probably in some other man's time and not our time and we shouldn't be worried about what the other fellow has to do. Let him worry about that.[445]

This divine role was reserved for one born in the year 19 and 33. Strangely, of all those assumed leaders who claimed that they should be the leader of the NOI after Muhammad's departure, Louis Farrakhan is virtually the only one who proclaims the unpopular belief that Elijah Muhammad is physically alive. What does Farrakhan know that so many others have yet to realize? It was his insight into Elijah Muhammad's true identity that separated him from all other national officials of the NOI. Farrakhan was the apple of Muhammad's eye and the clear favorite as the Messenger distinguished him as such. On October 4, 1973, Elijah Muhammad shared these comments about Minister Farrakhan while reviewing one of his lectures:

> Allah couldn't have given me a better helper…
> They can't help but to follow a man like that! Got the whole big city New York all stirred up!…
> If I was all the other Ministers, I'd take pattern at 'em. Like the Disciples did Paul. Paul was one of the greatest preaches the Disciples had. Well, he wasn't one of the Disciples, but he came up and beat all the other disciples…[446]

Undoubtedly Minister Farrakhan was the Messenger's clear choice. It is no coincidence that Farrakhan remains the most vocal proponent of Muhammad's teachings about the Mother Wheel and his connection thereof. Time and actions have proven that the Honorable Minister Louis Farrakhan is indeed the other fellow who fulfills that other 33% of the book. Hence, he too has a certain destiny with the Mother Wheel and the powers thereof. However, if the prophecies prove themselves true, this destiny includes the ugly fait of suffering at the hands of the enemy before the wheels intervene.

---

[445] Elijah Muhammad, interview by Buzz Anderson, *The Buzz Anderson Interview*, National Educational Television Network, KQED, San Francisco, Phoenix, December 1964.
[446] Sultan R. Muhammad, *Table Talks of the Honorable Elijah Muhammad - The Transcripts: Volume One*, Second, ed. Table Talks Project Editorial Board (Chicago, IL: MUI Press, 2013).

HE CALLS FOR ELIJAH

Just as Elijah Muhammad was promised a book from Master Fard Muhammad, Minister Farrakhan was also promised a portion of a book from his teacher. This script is to represent part of a new teaching for a new world. Obtaining this text presupposes that Elijah Muhammad is not dead and that another meeting between the two will take place. The journey and circumstances to reach this meeting, however, may not seem too glorious.

The not-so joyous part of Minister Farrakhan's assignment is that he must fulfill certain aspects of the Book (since he too comes in the *volume of the book*). If he is to fulfill the other third (33%) of the book, then he too has to undergo some of the strife, crucifixion, and passion of the Christ. Minister Farrakhan understands and has accepted his divine role in the prophecies. He understands that the bulk of the biblical stories surrounding Jesus are both prophetic and heavily symbolic as he has taught for years. Despite what seems to be a gloomy prophecy, this assignment yields an ultimate good because the Mother Wheel and the powers thereof will play a direct role in this process.

The Jewish onslaught to have Jesus crucified involves using their influence to turn the people against him and thereby kill him on the cross. It is on this symbolic cross that Jesus is heard calling for Elijah:

> *About three in the afternoon Jesus cried out in a loud voice, "Eli, Eli, lemasabachthani?" (which means "My God, my God, why have you forsaken me?").*
> *When some of those standing there heard this, they said, "He's calling Elijah."*
> *Immediately one of them ran and got a sponge. He filled it with wine vinegar, put it on a staff, and offered it to Jesus to drink.*
> *The rest said, "Now leave him alone. Let's see if Elijah comes to save him."* – Matthew 27:46-49

Chronologically speaking, it would make no since for Jesus to call on a prophet who was departed hundreds of years before him. This has to be a prophetic description of the messiahs who would appear in the last days. Minister Farrakhan's painful destiny was already depicted in this prophecy. He is the one who, like Jesus, would undergo tremendous persecution from the enemy that only his heavenly father (Elijah Muhammad) and his God could rescue him from.

The Biblical setting representing the assumed death of Jesus actually has a significant meaning. The term *Golgotha* is known as the place where Jesus was allegedly buried. Scholars and historians are uncertain as to the exactitude of its whereabouts. In fact, many scholars are uncertain as to its exact meaning. However, with a careful study, one can derive the essence of these terms as it relates to the Mother Plane and the rescue of Allah's servants. The name **Golgotha** stems from the Semitic root ***galgal*** (גַּלְגַּל). This term signifies a circle or wheel. It is one of the same roots from whence Ezekiel's prophetic wheels (*galgal*) are derived.

Frequently throughout the Bible, wheels are described by the singular Hebraic term **Galgal**. Although Golgotha has become recognized as a place of death since it is associated with Jesus' crucifixion, it has more etymological connections to its association with wheels. The actual etymology of the word Golgotha does not indicate anything about a skull or death, which has left many linguists and theologians baffled. According to one Bible Dictionary, "It is uncertain why it received this name - possibly because it was a round bare spot, bearing some likeness to a bald head..."[447]

Other Theological linguists speculate, "The name of the place where the Lord was crucified is the Aramaic *Gulgoltha* which became *Golgotha* in Greek. It arose from *galal* through the Hebrew word for a skull, *gulgoluth*, so called because of its round form."[448] While others can only speculate, the actual root of the word gives direct clues to its meaning and significance. Since Golgotha represents a wheel and the location from whence Jesus ascended, this gives vivid indications that the wheels would be involved in what seems to be the crucifixion and exaltation of the messianic figure! Is this why Jesus would be heard calling for Elijah? An ugly portion of Minister Farrakhan's prophetic role involves him being apprehended by the enemy and being put in a position that only Elijah Muhammad, on the Wheel, can deliver him from. This illustrates how the destined roles of Jesus, Elijah, and the great Mother Wheel are interconnected.

HE LIVES, MORE THAN A POSSIBILITY

Is the power behind those planes capable of rescuing Elijah Muhammad from what would appear to be his death? Can the power from those planes save Elijah Muhammad as promised? Keep in mind that Muhammad demonstrated his affiliation with these planes and the intelligence thereof. He publicly verified some of the scientists who are capable of accomplishing such a seemingly arduous task. He stated that his God, Master Fard Muhammad, would rescue him from a death-like situation that only

---

[447] The Official Scriptures of The Church of Jesus Christ of Latter-day Saints, "GOLGOTHA," *Bible Dictionary* (Intellectual Reserve Inc., 2010).
[448] The Bible Wheel, "Golgotha - The Axis of the Wheel," *The Bible Wheel* (Richard Amiel McGough, 2012).

could be done by this power. In October 1967 he stated, "If Allah had not shown me how I was going to escape, I would have no hope."[449] So if the question is asked, "Is Elijah Muhammad physically alive?" there can be no in-between answer. The answer is either YES or NO!

Not only did Elijah Muhammad claim to fulfill various aspects of the messianic prophecies, he demonstrated how his works align with the scriptures he taught, especially those figures who would somehow escape death. Furthermore, he is on record as giving accurate predictions about his departure, the fall of the NOI, and significant events decades before they unfolded. Since his forecasts have unfolded as he stated, does this include his escape from what would appear to be his death?

While there is a death certificate and a gravesite on record for Elijah Muhammad, does this prove that he is dead? Logically speaking, a sheet of paper or a beautiful monument has never proven the quality of life or death, although they can give strong indications. On the other hand, people have skillfully faked their own deaths—some have been caught while others cases remain unsolved. Can those who faked their own deaths strategize their operations more effectively than the Supreme Being?

Is it scientifically likely that UFO technology aided in the covert rescue of Elijah Muhammad? Overwhelming evidence shows that the capabilities of these circular crafts have manipulated and destabilized the most sophisticated weaponry of the world's armed forces. Hundreds of military officials, officers, and witnesses have attested that these planes have disarmed the most advanced nuclear technologies from afar. Some of the best military and scientific authorities have admitted that the intelligence of these UFOs demonstrate telepathic and telekinetic capabilities that this world cannot grasp. Surely if these planes can baffle and manipulate nuclear arms from a distance, there is much more they can do to abduct a man from a public facility.

The UFO Abduction of President Kirsan Ilyumzhinov from a high-rise apartment building gives further evidence of Muhammad's escape. President Ilyumzhinov was whisked away from his balcony through a transparent tubular pathway within a matter of seconds. Take into consideration that as a head of state, his vicinity was guarded by Russian Intelligence. Yet, the people aboard these planes were able to apprehend this global diplomat and bring him back safely. This event, which occurred on September 17, 1997, was later investigated by Russian authorities. Their primary concern was not whether or not this event actually took place; instead they were more concerned with whether or not Ilyumzhinov disclosed Russia's private information. If the scientists who pilot the wheels can pull-off this feat, they can surely rescue the Messenger from what appears to be impossible circumstances.

---

[449] Jabril Author, "The Messenger, Minister Farrakhan and how Allah controls circumstances," *The Final Call*, October 26, 2010.

THE CLEAR EVIDENCE, THE SURE TRUTH

The Holy Qur'an, like the Bible, conveys the certainty that Allah's messiah would be made to appear as though he is dead, but Allah would secretly exalt him to his presence instead (An-Nisa 4:157-158). The Honorable Elijah Muhammad pointed out that he is that one the Holy Qur'an is referring to. Although it is certain that the Supreme Being has the capacity to enact such a task, the exact specifics of this situation were not disclosed. This leaves the reasonable thinker to speculate on the numerous possible methods that could have been used. Since Master Fard Muhammad was said to have communicated with various animals and creatures around the world, he was very familiar with the science of animal behaviors. One of such behaviors includes what is called **Thanatosis**. This refers to a behavior observed in certain animals in which they take on the appearance of being dead as a protective mechanism that literally fools the predator into believing that the animal is dead. If certain animals have the innate ability to appear dead, do supremely gifted humans have this ability too? Did Master Fard Muhammad use this or a similar science to fool the enemy into believing his Messenger-Messiah was dead?

The Arabic word *tawaffa* and its cognates are frequently used in the Holy Qur'an to convey the meaning of death, the state of being taken, or the state of being fulfilled as in the following verse:

> *When Allah said: O Jesus, I shall cause thee to die and exalt thee in My Presence and clear thee of those who disbelieve and make those who follow thee above those who disbelieve, to the day of Resurrection. Then to Me is your return, so I shall decide between you concerning that wherein you differ.* – Al-Imran 3:55

The Holy Qur'an bears witness that Allah has the ability to revive those who may experience a temporary dead state. The words of the Honorable Elijah Muhammad to his wife, Mother Tynnetta Muhammad bear witness to this reality. Mother Tynnetta Muhammad recounts her experience surrounding the departure of the Messenger and this dead-like state:

> It was on the day of February 25, 1975 when it was announced that the Honorable Elijah Muhammad died in Chicago's Mercy Hospital from congestive heart failure. I remembered going to my children reluctantly to tell them about this announcement. I then went to the telephone to make a call to the Mexican family who was caring for my two younger sons. The lady told me quite emphatically that she didn't believe that he was dead. She instructed me to go quickly to the funeral parlor and place my finger or thumb on his pulse and on his jugular vein. She further stated that if it was still warm then he was not dead. I then turned to Sister Ethel Sharrief, the Honorable Elijah

Muhammad's eldest daughter, now deceased, and to her husband Brother Raymond Sharrief, also deceased, to take me to the funeral parlor so I could view his body. I was permitted to go, even though we were told that no one was to officially visit at that time. They agreed to accompany me and we drove somberly to Griffith Funeral parlor where his body lay on the funeral bier. I asked for the sheet to be pulled back and I began my examination of the body with those instructions that I received. I placed my hand on his pulse and on his jugular vein and truly, as was stated, it was still quite warm to the touch. The funeral parlor director explained that it was considered normal and that within 24 hours, the temperature in the room would lower and his body would be cold.

Shortly thereafter, not being convinced with that answer, I departed and upon returning to his residence, I found one of the eldest sons of the Honorable Elijah Muhammad and prevailed upon him not to order the autopsy during the next two days, to which he agreed. It was my son, Ishmael, who had furnished me with another important key to the Honorable Elijah Muhammad's appearance of death. On one occasion he questioned his father, at the tender age of 8, to explain to him what happens to a person after they are pronounced dead and he answered saying that if a person is a good and righteous being and a true servant of God, that if He (Allah) reaches the body within a 24 to 48 hour period, He can restore that person back to life.[450]

The technology of temporarily suspending vital functions of life is a practice that is used by contemporary scientists and medical professionals. In a practice known as *suspended animation*, scientists know how to halt the life processes by external means without terminating the organism. For example a young girl named Laina Beasley was kept in suspended animation as a two-celled embryo for 13 years.[451] It wasn't until her parents decided to move forward with the life development process that her embryo was later revived to proceed with human life. If medical professionals can suspend human life for 13 years while in its most fragile state, certainly this can be done with a more developed adult. So the concept of making someone temporarily appear dead should not sound too surprising, especially since the Supreme Being already said he would do it.

Interestingly, the Holy Qur'an denotes that the Messiah was *made to appear dead* to the onlookers. Since its Arabic phrase *shubbiha* refers to the similitude and likeness of something, some Qur'anic translators convey that the "the matter was made obscure for them through mutual resemblance"[452] or

---

[450] Tynnetta Muhammad, "Thought Never Dies—The Science of God's True Religion," *The Final Call*, November 16, 2004.
[451] BBC News, "Longest frozen embryo baby born," *BBC*, July 6, 2005.
[452] Muhammad Mahmoud Ghali translation of The Holy Qur'an, An-Nisa` 4:157.

that "a likeness to him of another was shown to them."[453] Such phraseology connotes that another body could have been used to replace the Messiah's. This brings up the possibility of cloning being used to help facilitate this monumental escape. Certainly cloning is a scientific reality—the practice of which was understood by the scientists on the wheels long before current medical discoveries.

Intriguingly, UFO researchers are captivated with the belief that the people who control UFOs have an apparent interest in human genetics. This is based on several UFO abduction reports that show these 'advanced beings' conducting scientific tests on contactees. Cases like the Betty and Barney Hill abduction, the Travis Walton abduction, and the Antonio Villas Boas case are just a few that come to mind. The January 25, 1967 Betty Andreasson abduction case reflects this notion as well. She claimed to have been taken onto a spaceship while her family members were put into a state of suspended animation. Her case involves people who were able to communicate telepathically while she was being subjected to various forms of physiological tests.[454] Another indication that cloning technology could have been used in Elijah Muhammad's departure is the fact that several witnesses reported that the body in his casket looked "about twenty to twenty-five years younger"[455] Regardless whether cloning was used or not, the fact remains that the advanced technology that governs those wheel-like planes has proven abilities to rescue Elijah Muhammad from such a vulnerable situation.

NO ROOM FOR DOUBT!

How is it that the Honorable Elijah Muhammad and the Honorable Minister Louis Farrakhan have boldly proclaimed such unpopular truths for decades without fear of consequences? How have these truths remained virtually unchallenged even among the academics, scholars, and scientists of the world? At a certain point, the world's leadership and the general public must face the reality and purpose of these wheel-like planes that have been introduced to the modern world by Elijah Muhammad and his Nation of Islam.

---

[453] Dr. Laleh Bakhtiar translation of The Holy Qur'an, An-Nisa` 4:157.
[454] Betty Andreasson-Luca, "B J's Interview with Abductee Betty Andreasson Luca," *UFO Casebook*.
[455] Jabril Muhammad, *Closing The Gap: Inner Views of the Heart, Mind & Sprit of the Honorable Minister Louis Farrakhan* (Chicago, IL: FCN Publishing Company, 2006).

The spiritual and theological leadership has strategically avoided the UFO phenomenon and its prophetic relationship with the 'chosen people of God'—a discussion that seems to be constantly avoided by religious leaders and historians. The sacred scriptures give vivid criteria for determining the divine authenticity of God's representatives. This criteria is based on whether or not their sayings come to pass:

> *When a prophet speaks in the name of the LORD, if the thing follow not, nor come to pass, that is the thing which the LORD has not spoken, but the prophet has spoken it presumptuously: you shall not be afraid of him.*
> – Deuteronomy 18:22, AKJV

If Elijah Muhammad and Louis Farrakhan spew meaningless rhetoric then perhaps no one should be concerned. However, the decades-long teachings of Elijah Muhammad's NOI has not only come to pass, but are continuously being enacted and unfolded before the public. Unlike other philosophers and teachers, Elijah Muhammad and Louis Farrakhan do not simply quote theories; instead, they explain their actions and demonstrate how their actions are congruent with the foretelling of scriptures. Their actions and teachings offer practical evidences of what would otherwise be useless scriptures. This is why Jesus told his critics to study his works because his works would testify of his true divinity (John 5:36-39). Even some of the staunchest critics of Muhammad have admitted that he makes the scriptures most practical and relevant unlike any other leader:

> Elijah Muhammad was a mystic. But his mysticism was applied; it always had a quite earthly purpose. Forerunning transcendental meditation and other modern popular sects, he saw the need for 20th-century religions to declare themselves based on science, not faith. Islam was a science and a "way of life," not a religion, he said.[456]

These men (Muhammad and Farrakhan) do not preach of spiritual issues that cannot be questioned; rather, they teach of spiritual issues in the real world, then they challenge the learned of the world to disprove their claims. The Honorable Elijah Muhammad dared his critics to dispute his position, "Allah raised me up in your midst to do an unbelievable thing that men of science will wonder, 'How did it happen?'"[457] The facts remain that Elijah Muhammad brought a reality to the modern world that has now been labeled the UFO Phenomenon. The first official Government UFO

---

[456] C. Gerald Fraser, "Elijah Muhammad Dead; Black Muslim Leader, 77," *The New York Times*, February 26, 1975.
[457] Elijah Muhammad, "The Theology of Time (Lecture Series)," Vols. August 20, 1972 (Chicago, IL: MUHAMMAD Mosque No. 2, 1972).

investigations began with this little man from Georgia who claimed he was taught by the Supreme Being. Since that time, world governments have collaboratively excluded Elijah Muhammad's name and history from mainstream UFO topics and discussions. Government authorities continue to ensure that reasonable thinkers and researchers never make the connection between the inexplicable power of these circular UFOs and the Nation of Islam.

Since Elijah Muhammad left the scene in 1975, Government authorities have now forwarded their efforts against his designated representative, Minister Louis Farrakhan. There is no denying that Farrakhan has continuously made bold and audacious claims about his connection to these circular planes—claims that have been followed by public appearances of these wheels throughout the world. Yet, these claims go virtually unchallenged, likely due to government and media cover-ups.

The UFO cover-up is not simply to hide the fact that such planes exist; instead, the cover-up is to prevent the public from knowing the source of power that guides these crafts. The underlying reason behind the cover-up is because these UFOs are practical proofs that Elijah Muhammad met God and that Louis Farrakhan is directly connected to the Supreme Being!

From cover to cover, the sacred scriptures of the Holy Qur'an and Bible speak of God operating from vessels that travel in the sky. While many religious adherents only preach the scriptural narratives, Elijah Muhammad and Louis Farrakhan are virtually the only ones who claim to have a realistic God who realistically operates from a real vessel in the sky. The scriptures notate that God appears as a human and gives instructions to his servant (face to face) to warn of his judgment and destruction. What other leader even claims to have been taught and commissioned by God who appeared in person to do exactly what was foretold? The leadership of the Nation of Islam is clearly distinguished in these categories.

When answering whether or not these wheel-like planes exist as revealed to Elijah Muhammad, the answer is either yes or no. Either the Nation of Islam is right or wrong on this issue. Unsurprisingly, all the evidence shows that the information Muhammad brought to the world concerning these planes have been exemplified beyond doubt. Statistical data confirms the fact that hundreds of millions of people from around the globe believe in UFOs as National Geographic acknowledged that thirty-six percent of Americans believe in UFOs (36% of 300 million Americans is at least 108 million).[458] Tens

---

[458] Alon Harish, "Over 1/3 of Americans Believe in UFOs, Study Says," *ABC News*, January 28, 2012.

of millions of actual sightings have taken place in the United States alone.[459] Are all of the countless millions of witnesses concocting virtually the same stories about the same crafts with the same basic descriptions from around the globe? Basic logic demands that even if the majority of these sightings were hoaxes or figments of people's imaginations, there still remain millions of UFO sightings that confirm exactly what Muhammad heralded into the modern world.

According to the statistical figures, more people actually have seen UFOs than people who live in sovereign states like Saint Kitts and Nevis.[460] So to deny the existence of such planes would be as absurd as denying that Saint Kitts and Nevis exist. Even for those who have not witnessed a wheel-like UFO for themselves, does that mean they don't exist? Considering that the number of people who have sighted UFOs far outweigh the number of people who reside in certain small countries, how can anyone logically deny the existence of these planes?

Some skeptics may argue and refuse to believe that these crafts exist because they have never seen one for themselves. Hypothetically, one could say that Michael Jackson never existed just because he or she never personally met him, but that still could not justify that he did not exist. In actuality, just as many people have seen UFOs than have met Michael Jackson in person.

How is it that with millions of authentic UFO photos, video footage, and daily witness reports from around the globe, many Americans remain totally oblivious to this manifest reality? Unfortunately this is not that shocking considering that America is the world's superpower whose education is ranked among the lowest of industrialized nations.[461] This kind of ignorance in the midst of available information is purposely arranged through propaganda and deliberate manipulation of information.

It is a known fact that the U.S. Government has spent decades and countless billions of taxpayer dollars attempting to investigate, conceal, and even battle these anomalous flying objects. From America's early projects such as *Project Blue Book* and *Project Grudge* to President Ronald Reagan's *Strategic*

---

[459] AP/Ipsos Poll, "Majority of Americans Believe in Ghosts (57%) and UFOs (52%)," *Associated Press/Ipsos* (Washington, DC, October 31, 2008). 14 percent of Americans have sighted a UFO (14% of 300 million Americans is over 40 million).

[460] **Saint Kitts and Nevis** is a federal two-island state in the West Indies and the smallest sovereign state in the Americas, both in area and population, having an estimated population of only 52,000 according to 2010 United Nations' Calculations. Saint Kitts also happens to be the birth place of the Honorable Minister Louis Farrakhan's mother.

[461] Harvard University, "Harvard's Program on Education Policy and Governance 2011 Report," Educational, Program on Education Policy and Governance , Harvard University (Cambridge, MA, 2011). 7 "No state within the United States did as well as the top 15 countries in the world."

THE CLEAR EVIDENCE, THE SURE TRUTH

Defense Initiative, there is no denying that the circular planes, heralded by Elijah Muhammad's Nation of Islam, have caused tremendous concern to the world's super power.

Other Governments have finally admitted that this phenomenon is real and have even declassified some of their official files on UFOs.[462] Unsurprisingly, America has yet to fully declassify her investigative studies on UFOs. However the little that has been disclosed about U.S. surveillance on the NOI and UFOs should be enough to convince the most cynical skeptic. Rejecting Elijah Muhammad's teachings about these wheel-shaped planes is akin to rejecting the fact that two plus five equals seven. Once the facts are known, it takes more energy to deny this truth than to accept it.

To deny the reality of the wheels is to deny that human beings can make objects that fly in the sky and into space. Today thousands of airplanes (weighing several tons) travel through the skies every day. NASA's International Space Station (ISS), a habitable satellite, orbits earth every day. Its "length and width is about the size of a football field."[463] If such huge man-made objects can navigate the heavens, is it unreasonable to believe that more advanced humans can do the same? Even if skeptics discard the prophetic and spiritual association with these planes, it would still be absurd to negate the manifest proof of the Mother Wheel and the smaller baby planes that have been seen throughout the world. There is no discipline that can escape dealing with this concept, whether science, religion, education, or basic logic.

Knowing that certain people will refuse to accept basic truths despite clear evidence, Allah (God) makes this admonition in the Holy Qur'an:

> *So let them talk and sport until they meet their day which they are promised.* – Az-Zukhruf 43:83

The evidence is overwhelming. The American leadership and the American people will have to make a decision regarding how to deal with those who represent the sovereignty associated with these wheel-shaped objects. Both history and prophecy connote that very few will accept based on the merit of the evidence. This grim reality becomes easier to believe when considering that the American public has not been trained to think outside of the mainstream paradigm.

---

[462] Steven Greer and Steve Alten, "UFO FILES - COUNTRIES RELEASING," *The Disclosure Project* (2010).
[463] NASA, "International Space Station: Facts and Figures" (NASA, June 3, 2013).

If Elijah Muhammad and Louis Farrakhan are proven representatives of those prophetic objects, wouldn't it be wise to unite with those who are backed by the power of the Supreme Being and his host of angelic scientists? Despite the clear evidence and the certainty of this reality, the prophecies estimate that only a miniscule percentage of the population would accept the unpopular task of standing with those whom the Supreme Being has designated for the people's salvation. Unfortunately, many will side with the more popular deceit of the U.S. Intelligence objectives, which are aimed to keep the masses in the dark. Only a special brand of individuals are capable of recognizing this divine truth and bold enough to stand with the divine messenger connected with these wheel-like crafts. These are the few who are willing to accept and stand on the truth without fear of consequences. These are the few who will accept sound reason and clear evidence despite its unpopularity in a world characterized by ignorance and frivolity. These are the few who ask to be officially registered as witness bearers to the Messenger-Messiah (Holy Qur'an, Al-Imran 3:53).

May Allah (God), the Supreme Being, grant the reader of this book with the light of understanding and clarity of thought so that he or she may stand and act according to the truth herein.

BIBLIOGRAPHY

1. Ṣaḥīḥ al-Bukhārī. "Al-Hadith." *Al-Hadith*.
2. *The Holy Qur'an*.
3. Alberta UFO Study Group. "Summaries of Some Recent Opinion Polls on UFOs." *UFO Evidence*. ufoevidence.org, 2011.
4. Andreasson-Luca, Betty. "B J's Interview with Abductee Betty Andreasson Luca." *UFO Casebook*.
5. Andrews, William, Francis Smith Foster, and Trudier Harris. *The Oxford Companion to African American Literature*. Edited by William Andrews, Francis Smith Foster and Trudier Harris. New York, New York: Oxford University Press, 03/27/1997.
6. Answers. "How many people have seen a UFO?" *Answers.com*. Answers Corporation, 2010.
7. AP/Ipsos Poll. "Majority of Americans Believe in Ghosts (57%) and UFOs (52%)." *Associated Press/Ipsos*. Washington, DC, 2008 йил 31-October.
8. Arizona Daily Star. *Arizona Daily Star*, October 09, 1985.
9. Barkley, Brian. *UFO Conspiracy*. Directed by Brian Barkley. Performed by Joe Leahy. 2004.
10. BBC News. "Longest frozen embryo baby born." *BBC*, July 6, 2005.
11. Beckley, Timothy Green. *The Authentic Book Of Ultra-Terrestrial Contacts: From The Secret Alien Files of UFO Researcher Timothy Green Beckley*. Translated by Jorge J. Martin (Contributor). Inner Light - Global Communications, 2012.
12. Berliner, Don, Marie Galbraith, and Antonio Huneeus. *UFO Briefing Document: The Best Available Evidence* . Research, Presented by CUFONS, FUFOR, MUFON , UFO Research Coalition , UFO Research Coalition , 1995.
13. Berlitz, Charles. *The Dragon's Triangle*. 03/02/1991. Fawcett, 1991.
14. Beynon, Erdmann Doane. "The Voodoo Cult Among Negro Migrants in Detroit." *The American Journal of Sociology* (The University of Chicago Press) 43, no. 6 (May 1938): 894-907.
15. Bloxham, Andy. "Aliens have deactivated British and US nuclear missiles, say US military pilots." *The Telegraph*. Telegraph Media Group Limited, September 27, 2010.
16. Booth, B.J. *1986-UFO Seen from Bridge of USS Edenton*. UFO Case Reports, CMS (Case Management System) , MUFON, MUFON, 2006.
17. —. "Before the Wright Brothers... There Were UFOs." *American Chronicle*, December 8, 2006.

18. Brackman, Harold. "Louis Farrakhan at 80: A Needless Legacy of Hate." *Brandeis Center Blog*, May 3, 2013.
19. Brad Meltzer's Decoded. "UFO." *Brad Meltzer's Decoded.* Vol. Season 2. History Channel, 11 30, 2011.
20. Brookesmith, Peter. *UFO the Government Files.* Barnes Noble Books, 1996.
21. California State Military Department Office of Air Force History. "California and the Second World War: The Battle of Los Angeles." *The Army Air Forces in World War II.* Edited by Wesley Frank Craven and James Lea Cate. Washington, DC: The California State Military Museum, 1983. 277-286.
22. Cameron, Grant, and T. Crain. *UFOs, Area 51, and Government Informants.* Kindle. Keyhole Publishing Company, 2013.
23. Canadia Gallup Poll. Statistical Report, The Toronto Star - 1978, 1974.
24. CENTER FOR MULTICULTURAL HEALTH. "African Americans and Tobacco: The Historical Journey." *Serarching For Answers* (CENTER FOR MULTICULTURAL HEALTH) 1, no. 1 (2006): 1-4.
25. Central Intelligence Agency History Staff. "The Central Intelligence Agency and Overhead Reconnaissance. The U-2 and OXCART Programs, 1954-1974." Declassified CIA Documents, History Staff: Pedlow, Gregory W.; Welzenbach, Donald E., Central Intelligence Agency, Washington, DC, 1992, 407.
26. Christiansen, Scott. "They really do want to believe: Alaska's enduring place in the literature of UFO sightings." *Anchorage Press*, October 25, 2012.
27. Churchill, Ward, and Jim Vander Wall. *The COINTELPRO Papers: Documents from the FBI's Secret Wars Against Dissent in the United States.* South End Press, 1990.
28. CIA. "About CIA." Central Intelligence Agency (CIA), 2006 йил 19-December.
29. Clark, Jerome. *The UFO Book: Encyclopedia of the Extraterrestrial.* Visible Ink Press, 1997.
30. Clarke, Adam. *Clarke's Commentary on the Bible 1 Kings 17:1.* Translated by Text Courtesy of Internet Sacred Texts Archive. Biblos.com, 1831.
31. Clegg, Claude Andrew. *An Original Man: The Life and Times of Elijah Muhammad.* Macmillan, 1998.
32. Connors, Michael D., and Wendy Hall. *Alfred Loedding & the Great Flying Saucer Wave of 1947.* 1st. Rose Press, 1998.
33. Cox, Billy. "The limits of libertarianism?" *Herald-Tribune*, 2008 йил 11-January.

34. Crystal Links. *Ancient Aircraft.* 2000 йил December. http://crystalinks.com/ancientaircraft.html (accessed 2010 йил 28-April).
35. Daniels, Sara, and Pat Schneidman. *Mysteries Of The Unknown: The UFO Phenomenon.* Time-Life, 1987.
36. David, Gary A. "Along the 33rd Parallel: A Global Mystery Circle." In *Underground! The Disinformation Guide to Ancient Civilizations, Astonishing Archaeology and Hidden History*, by Preston Peet. New York, NY: Disinformation Books, 2005.
37. DiBlasio, Natalie. "A third of Earthlings believe in UFOs, would befriend aliens." *USA Today*, 2012 йил 06-June.
38. Dimmick, Ada. "The Dragon's Triangle." Mystery Mag-Earth Energies , April 18, 2005.
39. Dolan, Richard M. *UFOs and the National Security State: Chronology of a Coverup, 1941-1973.* Kindel Edition. Charlottesville, VA: Keyhole Publishing Company, 2000.
40. Eisenman, Robert H., and Michael Wise. *The Dead Sea Scrolls Uncovered: The First Complete Translation and Interpretation of 50 Key Documents withheld for Over 35 Years.* Penguin Books, 1993.
41. Engleberg, Stephen. "Egypt-U.S. Plan to Raid Libya Reported." *The New York Times*, February 21, 1987: 3.
42. Escamilla, Jose, interview by Dara Brown. "The 65th Anniversary of The Battle of Los Angeles." *MSNBC News.* MSNBC, (2007).
43. Farrakhan, Louis. "#AskFarrakhan Tweets." *Minister Louis Farrakhan responds to tweet from Ilia Rashad Muhammad @iliarashad.* Compiled by Ilia Rashad Muhammad. #AskFarrakhan via Twitter, January 13, 2013.
44. —. "#AskFarrakhan Tweets." *Twitter Response to Minister Derrick Reese @HolyTabernacleU regarding Ancient Aliens on History Channel.* #AskFarrakhan via Twitter, January 26, 2013.
45. —. *5th Annual Educational Challenge Conference.* Chicago/Bloomingdale, IL: The Final Call, August 2, 2012.
46. —. "A Saviour Is Born For The Blackman & Woman In America: Saviours' Day Address." Chicago, IL: FCN Inc., February 22, 1981.
47. Farrakhan, Louis, interview by Ashahed Muhammad, Starla Muhammad Richard Muhammad. "Farrakhan Speaks On The Year 2012 & The New Year 2013." *Farrakhan Speaks.* FCN. Chicago. 2013 йил January.
48. —. "God's Judgment on America." Los Angeles, CA: The Final Call, 09 09, 1981.
49. —. "Guidance For Our President & Our Nation." Chicago, IL: The Final Call, 2012 йил 21-October.

50. —. "On The Year 2012 & The New Year 2013." *A Special Roundtable edition of Farrakhan Speaks.* The Final Call, January 7, 2013.
51. —. "Public Lecture Delivered at Christ Universal Temple." Chicago, IL: The Final Call, February 24, 1989.
52. —. "The Announcement: International Press Conference ." Washington, DC, October 24, 1989.
53. Farrakhan, Louis, interview by Jaimie Maussan. "The Islamic Minister Louis Farrakhan speaks openly about UFO disclosure." *FULL ALIEN DISCLOSURE.* Chicago, IL, (April 13, 2011).
54. —. "The Reality Of The Mother Plane." Chicago, IL: The Final Call Inc., January 4, 1987.
55. —. "The Shock of The Hour." Chicago, IL: The Final Call, April 26, 1992.
56. —. "The Time And What Must Be Done." *Saviours' Day 2010 Keynote Address by The Honorable Minister Louis Farrakhan.* Chicago, IL: The Final Call, February 28, 2010.
57. —. "The Time And What Must Be Done: The Great War." *Part 2 of the 2010 Saviours' Day Lecture delivered by The Honorable Louis Farrakhan.* Chicago, IL: The Final Call, March 14, 2010.
58. —. "The Wheel." *The Time And What Must Be Done Lecture Series.* Chicago, IL: Mosque Maryam, March 7, 2010.
59. —. "Who Are The Real Children Of Israel?" Atlanta, GA: The Final Call, 2010 йил 26-June.
60. —. "Who Is God?" *Saviours' Day Keynote Address.* Chicago, IL, February 24, 1991.
61. Fatir, Amir. "Nation of Islam: Mothership Connection." Amir Fatir - Astrologer, Healer and Author, 2002 йил April.
62. FBI COUNTERINTELLIGENCE PROGRAM. "RACIAL INTELLIGENCE (NATION OF ISLAM)." *BLACK NATIONALIST - HATE GROUPS.* FBI Counter Intelligence Program, 1969 йил 7-January.
63. Flynn, David. "Satan's Counterfeits: Judgment Day - UFOs, Angels & End Time Prophecy." Watcher Website, 2012.
64. Fox, James, Tim Coleman, Boris Zubov, and Charles Fox. *Out Of The Blue - The Definitive Investigation of the UFO Phenomenon.* Directed by James Fox, Tim Coleman and Boris Zubov. Produced by James Fox. Performed by Peter Coyote. Hannover House, 2002.
65. Fraser, C. Gerald. "Elijah Muhammad Dead; Black Muslim Leader, 77." *The New York Times*, February 26, 1975.
66. Freedman, Russell. *The Wright Brothers: How They Invented the Airplane.* Holiday House, 1994.

67. Friedman, Stanton. *Flying Saucers and Science: A Scientist Investigates the Mysteries of UFOs: Interstellar Travel, Crashes, and Government Cover-Ups.* New Page Books, 2008.
68. Friedman, Stanton, interview by Larry King. "UFOS: Questions & Controversy." *CNN LARRY KING LIVE.* CNN. 2008 йил 18-January.
69. Friedman, Stanton, and Kathleen Marden. *Captured! The Betty and Barney Hill UFO Experience.* Franklin Lakes, NJ: New Page Books, 2007.
70. GALLUP POLL. Des Moines, IA: Des Moines, 1966.
71. George Knapp in for George Noory. *Coast To Coast AM with George Noory.* Premiere Networks Inc., May 24, 2013.
72. Gildenberg, B.D. "A Roswell Requiem." *Skeptic*, 2003 йил 22-March.
73. Gillispie, Charles Coulston. *The Montgolfier Brothers and the Invention of Aviation, 1783-1784.* First Edition. Princeton University Press, 1983.
74. Goldberg, Jonah. "Treatment of Farrakhan glosses over odd issues." *Jewish World Review*, October 20, 2000.
75. Goldman, Peter. *The Death and Life of Malcolm X.* IL: Univ. of Illinois Press, 10/01/1972.
76. Good, Timothy. *Above Top Secret: The Worldwide U.F.O. Cover-Up.* New York, NY: Quill William Morrow, 1988.
77. —. *Earth: An Alien Enterprise: The Shocking Truth Behind the Greatest Cover-Up in Human History.* Pegasus, 2013.
78. —. *Need to Know: UFOs, the Military, and Intelligence.* First Pegasus Edition. New York, NY: Pegasus Books, 2007.
79. Good, Timothy, interview by Henrik Palmgren. *Secret Space Program, UFOs, ET & Coverup* Red Ice Radio. 2011 йил 24-February.
80. Greer, Steven M. "Project Background." Crozet, VA: The Disclosure Project, 2001 йил April.
81. Greer, Steven. "Steven Greer - Sirius Film, Free Energy, ET's and Freeing Humanity from the NWO." Red Ice Radio, June 13, 2013.
82. Greer, Steven, and Steve Alten. "UFO FILES - COUNTRIES RELEASING." *The Disclosure Project.* 2010.
83. Hamrick, Bob, and Suzanne Hamrick. "Exposin Satan's 'Left Behind' Chapter 16." *UFOs - Demonic Deception? Crop Circles, UFOs & Animal Mutilations Signs Of The Beginning Of The End?* 2011 йил 21-02.
84. Harding, Thomas. "Roswell 'was Soviet plot to create US panic." *The Telegraph*, 2011 йил 13-May.
85. Harish, Alon. "Over 1/3 of Americans Believe in UFOs, Study Says." *ABC News*, 2012 йил 28-January.
86. Harrison, Jeffrey J. "The Chariot." *To The Ends Of The Earth.* 2008.
87. Harvard University. "Harvard's Program on Education Policy and Governance 2011 Report." Educational, Program on Education Policy and Governance , Harvard University, Cambridge, MA, 2011.

88. Hastings, Robert. "UFO-Nukes Press Conference Line-Up." *The Upcoming UFO-Nukes Connection Press Conference.* Toronto: UFO UpDates, 2010 йил 17-Septmber.

89. Hastings, Robert, et al. "UFO Press Conference from The National Press Club." *Robert Hastings Presents.* Washiington, DC: CNN, September 27, 2010.

90. Hilliam, Rachel. *Galileo: Father Of Modern Science (Rulers, Scholars, and Artists of Renaissance Europe).* Rosen Pub Group, 2004.

91. Hind, Cynthia. "The Children of Ariel School - Case No. #96. Ruwa, Zimbabwe." *UFO AFRINEWS*, 1994.

92. History - UFO Hunters. *Aliens in the Movies: UFOs and Alien Invasions in Film.* History.com, 2012.

93. History. "Mysterious Places." *Ancient Aliens.* History.com, 2010 йил 28-October.

94. Holman Bible Dictionary. "Ezekiel." *Holman Bible Dictionary.* Edited by Trent C. Butler. Study Light, 1991.

95. Howe, Stephen. "Malcolm X: A Life of Reinvention, By Manning Marable - Book Review." *The Independent*, 2011 йил 13-May.

96. Hsu, Spencer S., and Carrie Johnson. "Documents show DHS improperly spied on Nation of Islam in 2007." *The Washington Post*, 2009 йил 17-December.

97. Huneeus, Antonio. "Russian style Exopolitics – Kirsan Ilyumzhinov's alien abduction." *Open Minds TV*, June 16, 2010.

98. Huneeus, J. Antonio. "The Laurance Rockefeller UFO Initiative." *Open Minds TV*, September 3, 2010: 54-61.

99. Hynek, J. Allen, interview by Dennis Stacy. *CLOSE ENCOUNTER WITH DR. J. ALLEN HYNEK* Edited by Dale Goudie. The Dean 1985, CUFON 1991, (1985).

100. Ilyumzhinov, Kirsan, interview by British TV. "Meet The President Kirsan Ilyumzhinov." *Meet The President Kirsan Ilyumzhinov.* YouTube. UFO Database. 2007.

101. Islam, True. "The Wheel And The War Of God." In *The Book of God: An Encyclopedia of Proof that the Black Man is God*, by True Islam. Atlanta, GA: A-Team Publishing, 1999.

102. Jacobsen, Annie. *Area 51: An Uncensored History of America's Top Secret Military Base.* Back Bay Books, 2012.

103. Jewish Encyclopedia. "ANGELOLOGY." *The unedited full-text of the 1906 Jewish Encyclopedia.* JewishEncyclopedia.com, 1906.

104. Kane, Jim. "UFO Bases Concealed Under Japanese Mountains? ." *Gather.* Gather.com, October 9, 2012.

105. Kathir, Ibn. "Allah Has No Partner In Anything Whatsoever." *The Holy Book.* theholybook.org, 2006.

106. Keyhoe, Donald. *The Flying Saucers Are Real.* Reprinted 2004. Cosimo Classics, 1950.
107. Keyhoe, Donald, interview by Mike Wallace. *The Mike Wallace Interview* ABC. 1958 йил 8-March.
108. *The UFO Conspiracy.* Video Documentary. Directed by Brian Barkley. Performed by Joe Leahy. New Liberty Videos, 2004.
109. Lendering, Jona. "Messiah (14) Qumran's two Messiahs." *LIVIUS.* 2013.
110. Life Magazine. "UFO's: Why do we believe?" *Life Magazine*, 2000 йил March.
111. Long Beach Independent. "MYSTERY RAID! TWO WAVES OF PLANES SWEEP OVER CITY AS ANTI-AIRCRAFT GUNS ROAR." *Long Beach Independent* , 1942 йил February.
112. Maccabee, Bruce. *UFO/FBI Connection: The Secret History of the Government's Cover-Up.* First. St. Paul, MN: Llewellyn Publications, 2000.
113. Major UFO Press Conference. "Major UFO Press Conference - National Press Club." *Nuclear Weapons Have Been Compromised by Unidentified Aerial Objects.* Washington D.C.: Robert Hastings, 2010 йил 27-September.
114. Mauso, Pablo Villarrubia. *Antonio Villas Boas: "Total Abduction".* Pablo Villarrubia Mauso, 2007.
115. Melanson, Terry. "Antonio Villas Boas: Abduction Episode Ground Zero." *Conspiracy Archive.* 2001.
116. Mitchell, Betty, and Helen Mitchell. *We Met The Space People* . Kindle. Clarksburg, WV: Saucerian Books, 1959.
117. Moskowitz, Clara. "What Makes Earth Special Compared to Other Planets." *Space.com.* Space, July 8, 2008.
118. Mother Earth Travel. "History of Japan Between the Wars, 1920-36." *From Area Handbook of the US Library of Congress.* Mother Earth Travel © 2000-2011, 2000.
119. Muhammad, Abdul-Sharrieff. "Is The Honorable Louis Farrakhan Divinely Guided And Is He Connected To The Wheel?" Nashville, TN: Muhammad Mosque 60, August 12, 2012.
120. Muhammad, Cedric. "Scripture, The Mother Plane, And Minister Farrakhan's Vision From Tepoztlan, Mexico." *Black Electorate.* BlackElectorate.com, July 23, 2002.
121. Muhammad, Elijah. "From Muhammad Speaks Newspaper article dated September 21, 1973." *The Mother Plane.* Compiled by Nasir Makr Hakim. Secretarius MEMPS, 1992.
122. —. *MESSAGE TO THE BLACKMAN In America.* Original Published by MUHAMMAD'S Temple No 2 in Chicago 1965. Chicago, IL: The Final Call Inc., 1965.

123. —. *Our Saviour Has Arrived*. Chicago, IL: MUHAMMAD'S TEMPLE No. 2, 1974.
124. Muhammad, Elijah, interview by Buzz Anderson. *The Buzz Anderson Interview* National Educational Television Network. KQED, San Francisco, Phoenix. December 1964.
125. —. *The Fall Of America*. Chicago, IL: Elijah Muhammad, 1973.
126. —. "The Theology of Time (Lecture Series)." Vols. July 2, 1972. Chicago, IL: MUHAMMAD Mosque No. 2, 1972.
127. —. *The True History Of Jesus*. Secretarius MEMPS Publications, 2008.
128. Muhammad, Jabril. *Closing The Gap: Inner Views of the Heart, Mind & Sprit of the Honorable Minister Louis Farrakhan*. Chicago, IL: FCN Publishing Company, 2006.
129. —. *Is It Possible That The Honorable Elijah Muhammad Is Still Physically Alive???* Fourth. Phoenix, AZ: Nuevo Books LLC, 2007.
130. —. "Motives." Phoenix, AZ, 2000.
131. —. "How well do we understand the Minister and his work?" *The Final Call*, 2010 йил 15-November.
132. —. "The Messenger, Minister Farrakhan and how Allah controls circumstances." *The Final Call*, 2010 йил 26-October.
133. —. "The Wheel: Is It Real or Reel?" *The Final Call*, March 31, 2010.
134. —. "The Wheel." Los Angeles, CA, September 18, 1985.
135. Muhammad, Sultan R. *Table Talks of the Honorable Elijah Muhammad - The Transcripts: Volume One*. Second. Edited by Table Talks Project Editorial Board. Chicago, IL: MUI Press, 2013.
136. Muhammad, Tynnetta. "Minister Farrakhan's Vision-like Experience on the Wheel is Real." *The Final Call*. July 11, 2011.
137. —. ""Woe to the Inhabitants of the Earth and of the Sea For the Devil is Come Down Unto You, Having Great Wrath Because He Knoweth that he Hath But a Short Time!" -Revelations 12:12." *The Final Call*, July 30, 2010.
138. —. "A visit with Study Group 19, Dayton, Ohio and the National Museum of the United States Air Force." *The Final Call*, June 11, 2007.
139. —. "The Mystical Link between The Whirling Dervishes and the Mongolian People of Central Asia." *The Final Call*, January 08, 2008.
140. —. "Thought Never Dies—The Science of God's True Religion." *The Final Call*, November 16, 2004.
141. Muhammad, Wallace D. *The Teachings of W.D. Muhammad Book I Elementary Level*. Chicago, IL: Mosque No. 2, 1976.
142. Muhammad, Wesley. "The Wise of this World Awaited Elijah." *The Final Call*, December 10, 2012.

143. Murphy, Terry. "Unidentified Flying Objects." *Hard Copy*. Edited by Janelle Balnicke. Santa Monica, CA, December 1989.
144. Naor, Mordecai. *Zionism: The First 120 Years, 1882-2002*. Jerusalem: The Zionist Library, 2002.
145. NASA. "International Space Station: Facts and Figures." NASA, June 3, 2013.
146. National Museum of Nature and Science. "Center of the History of Japanese Industrial Technology." 2008.
147. Nelson, Craig. "Ten Things You Didn't Know About the Apollo 11 Moon Landing." *Popular Science*, July 7, 2009.
148. Newsweek Magazine. "Alien Invasion!" *Newsweek*, 1996 йил 7-July.
149. Ogawa, Takanori. *ON LAVA CAVES IN JAPAN AND VICINITY*. Speleological Society of Japan: Association of Japanese Cavers, The Commission On Volcanic Caves, Vulcanospeleology, 2012, 73.
150. Oxford English Dictionary. "UFO." *OED Online*. Oxford University Press, 2012.
151. Parfitt, Tom. "King of Kalmykia." *The Guardian*, September 20, 2006.
152. Partridge, Christopher. *UFO Religions*. Routledge, 2003.
153. People's Daily Online. "Ten Countries Most Often Visited by Extraterrestrials." *People's Daily Online*. People's Daily Online, May 18, 2012.
154. Pipes, Daniel. "How Elijah Muhammad Won." *Daniel Pipes Middle East Forum*. Daniel Pipes, June 2000.
155. Psychology Today. "Do you believe in UFOs?" *Psychology Today Magazine*, 1984 йил June.
156. Ramadan, Tariq. *In The Footsteps of The Prophet: Lessons from the Life of Muhammad*. Oxford University Press, 2009.
157. Randle, Kevin D, and Russ Estes. *The Spaceships of the Visitors: An Illustrated Guide to Alien Spacecraft*. Touchstone, 2000.
158. Randles, Jenny. *The UFO Conspiracy*. New York, NY: Barnes & Noble Inc, 1987.
159. Reagan, Ronald. "Address to the 42nd Session of the United Nations General Assembly." *The United Nations General Assembly*. New York, NY, September 21, 1987.
160. —. "Remarks of the President to Fallston High School Students and Faculty." *The White House Transcripts*. Fallston, MD, December 4, 1985.
161. —. "Speech to the United Nations General Assembly." 42nd General Assembly, 1987 йил 21-September.
162. Reuters. "Reuters Ipsos Poll." Reuters, 2010 йил April.

163. Rieber, Ney. "The Nation of Islam - Islam: Truth or Myth?" *Bible.Ca*. Bible.ca, 2002 йил September.
164. Robinson PhD, Robert G, Charyn D Sutton, Denise A James, and Carole Tracy Orleans Ph.D. *Winning The Fight Against Tobacco*. Educational, Department of Health and Human Services, Center For Disease Control And Prevention, Pathways To Freedom, 2003.
165. Roswell Daily Record. "RAAF Captures Flying Saucer On Ranch in Roswell Region." *Roswell Daily Record*, 1947 йил 08-July.
166. Ruppelt, Edward J. *THE REPORT ON UNIDENTIFIED FLYING OBJECTS*. public domain, Former Head of the Air Force Project Blue Book, Garden City, NY: DOUBLEDAY & COMPANY, INC., 1956.
167. Rux, Bruce. *Architects of the Underworld: Unriddling Atlantis, Anomalies of Mars, and the Mystery of the Sphinx*. Frog Books, 1996.
168. Saucers Incorporated. *Kenneth A. Arnold*. 2011. http://www.kennetharnoldufo.com/kenneth-arnold.html (accessed 2012 йил 29-December).
169. Schiffman, Lawrence H. *Reclaiming the Dead Sea Scrolls: The History of Judaism, the Background of Christianity, the Lost Library of Qumran*. Yale University Press, 1995.
170. Scholem, Gershom. *Major Trends in Jewish Mysticism*. New York, New York: Shocken Books Inc., 1995.
171. Schuessler, John F. *Public Opinion Surveys and Unidentified Flying Objects 50+ years of Sampling Public Opinions*. UFO Statistics, International Director's Office, Mutual UFO Network, Inc. (MUFON), Morrison, CO: MUFON, 2000.
172. Scott, Jefferson. "UFOs and the Christian Worldview." *Jefferson Scott Intelligent Christian Thrillers*. Jefferson Scott, 2007.
173. Seaman, Barrett. "Good Heavens! An astrologer dictating the President's schedule?" *Time Magazine*, May 16, 1988.
174. Sharda. "Unexplained Mystery: The Devil's Sea (The Dragon's Triangle)." Marine Insight, November 30, 2011.
175. Shaw, Dan. "12 Devil's Triangles-10 Vile Vortices Around the World." *12 Devil's Triangles-10 Vile Vortices Around the World*. Vortex Maps, April 27, 2008.
176. Shulze, Glen, and Robert Powell. *Stephenville Lights: A Comprehensive Radar and Witness Report Study*. UFO Sighting, Research, MUFON, MUFON, 2010, 76.
177. Sitchin, Zecharia. *Twelfth Planet: Book I of the Earth Chronicles (The Earth Chronicles)*. 0030. Harper, 2007.
178. Spignes, Stephen J. *The UFO Book of Lists*. Citadel Press, 2000.
179. Symington, Fife. "Symington: I saw a UFO in the Arizona sky." *CNN.com*, 2007 йил 9-November.

180. Tacoma Ledger. "AN ELECTRIC MONSTER Flashes of light and Terrible Sounds Emitted by One in the Bay." *Tacoma Ledger*, July 3, 1893.
181. Taylor, Jeffrey G. *Origin of the Earth and Moon*. Article, Hawaii Institute of Geophysics and Planetology, NASA, Hawaii Institute of Geophysics and Planetology, 09/20/2012.
182. The Atlanta Journal. "U.S. planned to invade Libya in '85." *The Washington Post*, February 20, 1987, The Atlanta Journal ed.: A/1.
183. The Bible Wheel. "Golgotha - The Axis of the Wheel." *The Bible Wheel*. Richard Amiel McGough, 2012.
184. The Disclosure Project. *UFO FILES - COUNTRIES RELEASING*. 2010. http://www.disclosureproject.org/ (accessed 2013 йил 11-March).
185. The Final Call Newspaper. *The Nation of Islam: What has been said.*. Special 70 Year Commemorative Edition. Vol. February. Chicago, IL: Final Call Newspaper, 2000.
186. The New York Times. "NAVY OFFICER SEES METEORS They Were Red Ones, the Largest About Six Suns Big. ." *New York Times*, March 19, 1904.
187. The Official Scriptures of The Church of Jesus Christ of Latter-day Saints. "GOLGOTHA." *Bible Dictionary*. Intellectual Reserve Inc., 2010.
188. The Supreme Wisdom. "Instructions Given To The Laborers By Master Fard Muhammad." *THE SUPREME WISDOM*. Detroit, MI: The Nation Of Islam, 1930-1934.
189. Time Magazine. "Foo-Fighter." *Time*, 1945 йил 15-January.
190. TRENDEX POLL. *Do you believe there is some possibility that they (saucers) may be objects from outer space?* TRENDEX POLL, St. Louis Globe Democrat, 1957.
191. UFO Casebook. "1952 Washington D.C. Sightings." UFOCasesbook.com.
192. UFO Evidence. "Carlos Diaz - UFO Abductee." *UFO Evidence: Scientific Study of the UFO Phenomenon and the Search for Extraterrestrial Life*. The X Factor, Issue 89 (reprinted on Cosmic Conspiracies), 2011.
193. —. "Reverse-Engineering Roswell UFO Technology. A summary of Jack Shulman's speech at the Global Sciences Congress in 1999." *Nexus Magazine*, 1999 йил June-July.
194. Uittenbogaard, Arie. "Meaning and etymology of the Hebrew name Gilgal." Abarim Publications, 2011.
195. United States Senate. "To express the sense of the Senate relating to Louis Farrakhan." *S.AMDT.3363 to H.R.5712*. Compiled by Sponsor: Sen. Don Nickles [OK]. Washington, D.C., 1984 йил 28-June.

196. Vallee, Jacques. *Forbidden Science: Journals 1957-1969*. Marlowe & Co, 1993.
197. Villard, Ray. *Celestial Paternity Test: Moon is Earth's Child*. News, Discovery , Discovery Channel, 04/11/2012.
198. Von Däniken, Erich. *Chariots Of The Gods?* . English translation 1984. Berkley, 1968.
199. Walton, Travis. "Human?" *Fire In The Sky*. 1997 August.
200. WDVM Eyewitness News 9 with Mike Buchanan & Andrea Roan . Washington, DC, October 25-26, 1989.
201. Weaver, Richard L. *Report of Air Force Research Regarding the 'Roswell Incident'*. Research, Security And Special Program Oversight, UNITED STATES AIR FORCE, USAF, 1994.
202. Weaver, Richard L., and James McAndrew. *The Roswell Report Fact vs. Fiction in the New Mexico Desert*. Executive Summary, Headquarters, United States Air Force, United States Air Force, 1995.
203. Wells, H.G. *The First Men in the Moon*. Dover Thrift Editions. Dover Publications, 2000.
204. Wells, H.G., Alexei Panshin, Cory Panshin, and Paul Cook. *The Time Machine - Phoenix Science Fiction Classics*. Phoenix Pick, 2009.
205. Welsh, Patty. "Space Fence program moves forward." *The Official Web site of the United States Air Force*. United States Air Force, December 21, 2012.
206. Wessels, Larry. *Nation of Islam Revisited #2A: Farrakhan Says UFOs Follow HIm Wherever He Goes*. YouTube. Produced by Christian Answers. Performed by Larry Wessels and Wilford Darden. Christian Answers, 09/21/2010.
207. Yenne, William. *Weapons of World War II: The Techno-Military Breakthroughs That Changed History*. New York, NY: Berkley Books, 2003.

INDEX

A

Abdul Sharrieff Muhammad, 241, 242
Aetherius Society, 6
Ancient Aliens, 124, 125
Andreasson
    Betty, 265
Araboth, 224
Area 51, 142, 155, 165
Ariel School
    Sighting, 189
Arnold
    Kenneth, 113, 114, 147, 159
Ascended Master Teachings
    "I AM" Activity, 7

B

Ballard
    Guy, 7
Bara
    Michael, 124
Battle of Los Angeles, 132, 133, 134, 136, 137, 140, 141, 149, 166, 171, 173, 258
Beasley
    Laina, 264
Betty and Barney Hill, 53, 56, 60, 181, 182, 265
Beynon
    Erdmann D., 130, 131
Boas
    Antonio Villas, 52, 53, 60, 180, 181, 182, 265
Brackman
    Harold, 95, 96, 97
Buraq
    Al-Buraq, 16, 233

C

Carter
    Jimmy, 194, 195
Cedric Muhammad, 69, 70, 71, 244
cherub
    cherubim, 16, 101
Chosen people, 94
CIA, 164, 179, 199, 236
Clegg
    Claude, 137, 154

D

Daniken
    Erich von, 67
Däniken. *See* Daniken
Darden
    Wilford, 14
Diaz
    Carlos, 246, 247
Dragon's Triangle, 28, 29

E

Exalted Assembly, 86, 119, 153, 164

F

Fatir
    Amir, 153
FBI, 112, 129, 136, 137, 138, 139, 143, 158, 165, 173, 193, 200, 219, 220, 221, 258
firdaus, 91
foo-fighters, 112, 138, 139, 158, 159
Friedman
    Stanton, 112, 151, 152, 182

G

Gadhafi
    Muammar, 242
galgal, 98, 261
Galileo
    Galilei, 6, 14, 31
Garvey
    Marcus, 11
Gilgal. See galgal, See galgal, See galgal, See galgal, See galgal, See galgal
Goldberg
    Jonah, 244, 245
Greer
    Steven, 59, 166, 269

H

Hastings
    Robert, 59, 60, 154, 197, 198
Huneeus
    Antonio, 250, 251, 252

I

Icke

David, 126
Iliyumzhinov
   Kirsan, 53
Industrial Church of the New World Comforter, 7

J

Jabril Muhammad, xiii, 36, 70, 71, 168, 192, 193, 214, 221, 222, 224, 225, 226, 228, 235, 241, 256, 265
Jacobs
   Robert, 199
Jacobsen
   Annie, 165
Japan
   Nippon, 27, 28, 29, 30, 31, 32, 33, 34, 36, 108, 132, 134, 135, 137, 138, 153, 257
Joshua Farrakhan, 225

K

Keyhoe
   Donald, 115, 128, 167, 168, 169, 170
khayyot
   chayot, 102
Knapp
   George, 191
Knox
   Frank, 134
Koppel
   Ted, 245

L

Lear
   John, 75, 137, 161
Lieb
   Michael, xiii, 67
Lier
   Roger, 112

M

Maccabee
   Bruce, 112, 173
made to appear dead
   shubbiha, 217, 264
Malcolm X, 17, 35, 174, 175
Marcel
   Jesse A., 159, 160
Marshall
   George, 134, 135
Master Fard Muhammad, xii, 3, 4, 11, 13, 20, 28, 30, 33, 34, 36, 37, 40, 45, 46, 47, 48, 50, 60, 66, 75, 84, 86, 106, 108, 109, 117, 123, 124, 129, 159, 160, 162, 163, 164, 166, 168, 177, 178, 183, 186, 187, 192, 193, 195, 200, 201, 210, 211, 213, 220, 224, 239, 254, 258, 260, 261, 263
Maussan
   Jaime, xiii, 174, 247
Melton
   J. Gordon, 7
Merkabah, 65, 93, 94, 100
Million Man March, 149, 244
Mitchell
   Betty and Helen, 188
Montgolfier
   Joseph-Michel, 116
MUFON, 113, 131, 155, 257, 258

N

National Aeronautical and Space Administration
   NASA, 13
New Jerusalem, 22, 104, 105, 106, 107, 153, 186, 214, 248, 255
Noble Drew Ali, 11

O

ofanim
   ophanim, 224
ophanim. See ofanim

P

Padrick
   Sid, 53, 54, 56, 85, 106, 185, 186, 187
parapsychology, 252
Pell
   Claiborne, 252
Phoenix Lights, 199, 257
pre-emptive propaganda, 143, 145, 146, 147, 148
Project Blue Book, 115, 116, 128, 129, 136, 169, 173, 268
Project Mogul, 162
Prophet Muhammad, 16, 46, 79, 81, 86, 88, 90, 91, 202, 203, 232, 233, 239

R

Raëlian Church, 7
Reagan
   Ronald, 102, 195, 196, 230, 232, 233, 234, 235, 242, 243, 268
rekeb
   rakab, 100, 205
Rieber
   Ney, 7, 152
Rockefeller
   Laurance S., 251, 252
Roosevelt

Franklin D., 134, 135, 136, 137
Roswell, 115, 147, 159, 160, 162, 164, 165, 166, 179, 257
Ruppelt
    Edward J., 115, 116, 128
Russert
    Tim, 245

S

Salim Muhammad, 242
Samford
    John, 172, 173
Scholem
    Gershom, 95
Scientology, 6
Scott Jones
    Cecil B., 251
Selective Servic Act, 137
September 17, 2, 54, 232, 246, 247, 248, 250, 262
shihab, 164
Sitchin
    Zecharia, 67, 122, 123
Space Fence, 87
Speilberg
    Steven, 148
Star Wars, 196, 234
Stephenville
    Stephenville, TX UFO Sightings, 257, 258
suspended animation, 264, 265
Symington
    Fife, 198, 199

T

Tepotzlan, 229, 230, 247

Terauchi
    Kenju, 84, 236, 237
Thanatosis, 263
thaqib, 164
Throne of Power
    'arsh, 16, 31, 80, 81, 153, 240, 255
Timothy Good, 53, 54, 84, 85, 106, 111, 124, 132, 181, 184, 185, 186, 195
Tynnetta Muhammad, 179, 226, 263, 264

U

ultra-terrestrials, 189

V

vision-like experience, 2, 99, 229, 232, 233, 236, 237, 247, 256

W

Walton
    Travis, 53, 54, 257, 265
Warith
    Warith D. Mohammed, 17, 220
Washington D.C. UFO Incident, 170, 171
Welles
    Orson, 178
Wells
    H.G., 55, 148
Wesley Muhammad, 207
Wessels
    Larry, 14
Wright Brothers
    Orville, 110, 116

ABOUT THE AUTHOR

Ilia Rashad Muhammad serves as Assistant Student Minister at Muhammad Mosque 55 in Memphis, TN where he facilitates the Study Courses and the FOI Orientation and Processing Class. He is a respected educator in the public school system where he chairs the English and Language Arts Professional Learning Community at a local high school. He has co-authored two acclaimed books, *A Complete Dictionary Of The Supreme Wisdom Lessons* and *In The Light Of Scriptures* with Demetric Muhammad. With an accomplished academic background in research and linguistics, Brother Rashad (as he is often called) holds a Bachelor's degree in English: Technical & Professional Writing from the University of Memphis. He completed his Graduate studies in Education at Union University where his Master Thesis project unveiled "Racism in Education." Brother Rashad is a respected pillar in his community as a God-fearing, family-oriented man who is also proactive in urban agriculture and apiculture. In both theological and academic arenas he is lauded for tackling controversial subject matters that highlight the profundity of the Nation of Islam's teachings. There is much more to come from this individual and the burgeoning intellectual renaissance stemming from the students of the Honorable Louis Farrakhan.

For questions, comments, speaking, engagements, resources, products and services, contact NATION BROTHERS:

Website: www.nationbrothers.com
Email: nationbrothers@nationbrothers.com
Twitter: @iliarashad
Facebook: Ilia Rashad Muhammad

www.ingramcontent.com/pod-product-compliance
Lightning Source LLC
Chambersburg PA
CBHW070947180426
43194CB00041B/1465